Think Biblically!

THINK BIBLICALLY!

RECOVERING A CHRISTIAN WORLDVIEW

GENERAL EDITOR

JOHN MACARTHUR

WITH

THE MASTER'S UNIVERSITY FACULTY

RICHARD L. MAYHUE, ASSOCIATE EDITOR

JOHN A. HUGHES, ASSOCIATE EDITOR

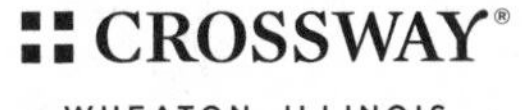

WHEATON, ILLINOIS

Think Biblically!

Published by Crossway
1300 Crescent Street
Wheaton, Illinois 60187

Cover design: Kirk DouPonce, The DesignWorks Group,
www.thedesignworksgroup.com

First printing, new cover 2009

Printed in the United States of America

Trade paperback ISBN: 978-1-4335-0398-6
ISBN-10: 1-4335-0398-0
PDF ISBN: 978-1-4335-0950-6
Mobipocket ISBN: 978-1-4335-0951-3
ePub ISBN: 978-1-4335-1624-5

Library of Congress Cataloging-in-Publication Data

MacArthur, John, 1939-
Think biblically! : recovering a Christian worldview / John MacArthur and the Master's College faculty ; John MacArthur, general editor; Richard L.Mayhue, John A. Hughes, associate editors.
p. cm.
Includes bibliographical references.
ISBN 13: 978-1-58134-412-7 (HC : alk. paper)
ISBN 10: 1-58134-412-0
1. Christian life—Biblical teaching. I. Mayhue, Richard, 1944- . II. Hughes, J. A., 1941- . III. Master's College. IV. Title.
BS680.C47 M335 2003
230—dc21 2002151364

Crossway is a publishing ministry of Good News Publishers.

CH 29 28 27 26 25 24 23 22 21 20 19
20 19 18 17 16 15 14 13 12 11 10 9 8

DEDICATED TO

the Board of Directors, friends of The Master's University,
faculty, staff, alumni, and present/future students at
The Master's University who are committed to
living for God's glory and pleasure according to the
Christian worldview shaped by Scripture

Contents

THE MASTER'S UNIVERSITY CONTRIBUTORS

Patricia E. Ennis, Ed.D, Northern Arizona University
Chairperson, Department of Home Economics
Professor of Home Economics

Clyde P. Greer, Jr., D.A., Carnegie-Mellon University
Chairperson, Department of History and Political Studies
Professor of History

Grant Horner, Ph.D. (A.B.D.), University of North Carolina
Assistant Professor of English

John A. Hughes, Ph.D., Brigham Young University
Vice President for Academic Affairs
Professor of Education

Taylor B. Jones, Ph.D., University of Texas
Chairperson, Department of Biological and Physical Sciences
Chairperson, Department of Mathematics
Professor of Chemistry

John MacArthur, Litt.D, D.D., Talbot Theological Seminary
President
Professor of Bible

R. W. Mackey, II, Ed.D., Pepperdine University
Chairperson, Department of Business Administration
Professor of Business Administration

Richard L. Mayhue, Th.D., Grace Theological Seminary
Senior Vice President and Provost
Professor of Bible

Brian K. Morley, Ph.D., Claremont School of Theology
Professor of Philosophy and Apologetics

Paul T. Plew, Ed.D., Nova Southeastern University
Chairperson, Department of Music
Professor of Music

Stuart W. Scott, D.Min., Covenant Theological Seminary
Associate Professor of Biblical Counseling

John P. Stead, Ph.D., University of Southern California
Professor of History and Political Studies

John D. Street, D.Min., Westminster Theological Seminary
Chairperson, Department of Biblical Counseling
Associate Professor of Biblical Counseling

Mark A. Tatlock, Ed.D., Nova Southeastern University
Vice President for Student Life

PREFACE

In keeping with the mission of The Master's University to empower students for a life of enduring commitment to Christ, biblical fidelity, moral integrity, intellectual growth, and lasting contribution to the kingdom of God, this volume has been written to instruct and exhort all those who will eventually read this material to embrace a Christian worldview. Without apology or reservation, The Master's University is committed to the absolute authority, centrality, inerrancy, infallibility, primacy, and sufficiency of God's Word. Thus Scripture is by far the single most important source that informs and shapes our view of God and His created world.

Think Biblically! targets students and nonstudents alike. In an era of postmodern influence that advocates that there are no absolutes and that everyone's opinion is of equal value, this volume issues a serious call to recover a Christian worldview that is absolute and exclusive. As many individual believers, conservative evangelical churches, and Christian schools drift away from a high view of God and His Word, their worldview will be compromised by error. These essays are intended to reaffirm and restore a biblically-based view of life's reality from God's perspective; some of the content is intended to be prescriptive and some proscriptive. Whether the reader is a student in high school or college, a pastor or professor, a missionary or biblical counselor, a layperson or Christian worker, this book will help refocus proper attention on God's understanding of the world in which one lives.

This volume is not intended to be an unabridged treatment of the subject. For instance, the explanations of and defenses against other worldviews have not been included.[1] Further, no single chapter exhausts its subject but rather furnishes a suggestive, general treatment. Each chapter could have been expanded into a full-length book. Also, additional disciplines could have been treated had space permitted. However, the broad sweep of this presentation is its intended strength.

This work is divided into two major sections. Part One presents "The Biblical Foundation," which deals with six major ideas that frame the basics of a Christian worldview, including a special emphasis on the Gospel of Jesus

Christ. Part Two illustrates "The Biblical Formulation," in which many, but not all, of the more important contemporary outworkings of a Christian worldview are representatively and briefly treated.[2]

The reader will also note a diversity in the levels of style in treating the different topics. At one end are chapters whose documentation is extensive, and at the other are those in which documentation is minimal. To some extent, this diversity results from the nature of individual subjects, and to a lesser degree, the choice of each contributor. Even though the reader might perceive a minor difference of opinion, The Master's University Faculty is unanimously and wholeheartedly committed to a biblical worldview as presented in Scripture.

Each chapter concludes with a Further Reading section. These resources are listed as representative of the best volumes to pursue should the reader wish to further explore the subject matter of any given chapter. The inclusion of a work does not constitute an endorsement of everything in that work but reflects a favorable impression of its general thrust.

The endnotes provide additional information and cited documentation for the worldview literature in each chapter. An Index of Scriptures, an Index of Persons, and an Index of Subjects provide a ready reference. Scripture quotations are taken from the English Standard Version (ESV) unless otherwise noted.

The editors wish to thank many individuals who have assisted in the production of *Think Biblically!* Librarians John Stone and Dennis Swanson helped locate valuable resource material and references; administrative assistants Marjorie Ackerman, Sharon Staats, Tanya ten Pas, and the faculty secretaries workeed on various portions of the project; Dr. W. Gary Phillips and Bob White read the manuscript and offered helpful improvements; Phil Johnson and Gary Knussman helped with several chapters; and various TMC colleagues made valuable suggestions while reading preliminary chapter drafts.

The Master's University faculty offer *Think Biblically!* with the simple prayer that the Lord Jesus Christ will be pleased to encourage this generation of Christians and the next to interpret the world around them with a Christian worldview because they possess "the mind of Christ" (1 Cor 2:16).

John MacArthur
Richard L. Mayhue
John A. Hughes

INTRODUCTION

Weltanschauung.[1] What is it? Everyone has one. It colors the way all people interpret life. It triggers the decisions one makes, not to mention driving one's responses. It comes in many varieties. Philosophy, science, culture, and/or religion generally make the dominant contributions to it. What is it? It is the personal *worldview* of each living individual.

What is a worldview? A worldview comprises one's collection of presuppositions, convictions, and values from which a person tries to understand and make sense out of the world and life. "A world-view is a conceptual scheme by which we consciously or unconsciously place or fit everything we believe and by which we interpret and judge reality."[2] "A worldview is, first of all, *an explanation and interpretation of the world* and second, *an application of this view to life.*"[3]

How does one form a worldview? Where does one begin? Every worldview starts with *presuppositions*—i.e., beliefs that one presumes to be true without supporting independent evidence from other sources or systems. Interpreting reality, in part or in whole, requires that one adopt an interpretive stance since there is no "neutral" thought in the universe. This becomes the foundation upon which one builds.

What are the presuppositions of a Christian worldview that is solidly rooted and grounded in Scripture? Carl F. H. Henry, an important Christian thinker in the last half of the twentieth century, answers the question very simply: ". . . evangelical theology dares harbor one and only one presupposition: the living and personal God intelligibly known in his revelation."[4] Without equivocation, Dr. Henry forthrightly and clearly believes that "Our theological systems are not infallible, but God's propositional revelation is."[5] Henry earlier had elaborated on this theme: "In its ontological and epistemological predictions Christianity begins with the biblically attested self-disclosing God, and not with creative speculation free to modify theism as an interpreter wishes."[6] Ronald Nash approaches the question in a similar manner: "Human beings and the universe in which they reside are the creation of God who has revealed himself in Scripture."[7]

For the sake of this volume, let it be stated that two major presuppositions underlie the chapters that follow. The first will be the eternal existence of the personal, transcendent, triune, Creator God. Second, the God of Scripture has revealed His character, purposes, and will in the infallible and inerrant pages of His special revelation, the Bible, which is superior to any other source of revelation or human reason alone.

What is the Christian worldview?[8] The following definition is offered as a working model:

> The Christian worldview sees and understands God the Creator and His creation—i.e., man and the world—primarily through the lens of God's special revelation, the Holy Scriptures, and secondarily through God's natural revelation in creation as interpreted by human reason and reconciled by and with Scripture, for the purpose of believing and behaving in accord with God's will and, thereby, glorifying God with one's mind and life, both now and in eternity.

What will be some of the benefits of embracing the Christian worldview? Let the following serve as a small sample representing the kinds of crucial life-questions that can be answered with ultimate truth and can be embraced with confident faith.[9]

1. How did the world and all that is in it come into being?
2. What is reality in terms of knowledge and truth?
3. How does/should the world function?
4. What is the nature of a human being?
5. What is one's personal purpose of existence?
6. How should one live?
7. Is there any personal hope for the future?
8. What happens to a person at and after death?
9. Why is it possible to know anything at all?
10. How does one know what is right and what is wrong?
11. What is the meaning of human history?
12. What does the future hold?

Christians of the twenty-first century face the same basic questions about this world and life that confronted the earliest humans in Genesis. They also had to sift through various worldviews to answer the above questions. This has been true throughout history. Consider what faced Joseph (Gen 37—50) and Moses (Ex 2—14) in Egypt, or Elijah when he encountered Jezebel and her pagan prophets (1 Kgs 17—19), or Nehemiah in Persia (Neh 1—2), or Daniel in Babylon (Dan 1—6), or Paul in Athens (Acts 17). They sorted out the difference between truth and error, right and wrong because they placed their faith in the living God and His revealed Word.[10]

What essentially distinguishes the Christian worldview from other worldviews? At the heart of the matter, a Christian worldview contrasts with competing worldviews in that it: 1) recognizes that God is the unique source of all truth, and 2) relates all truth back to an understanding of God and His purposes for this life and the next. Arthur Holmes superbly summarizes the unique implications of a Christian worldview when relating absolute truth to God.

> 1. To say that truth is absolute rather than relative means that it is unchanging and universally the same.
>
> 2. Truth is absolute not in or of itself but because it derives ultimately from the one, eternal God. It is grounded in his "metaphysical objectivity," and that of his creation.
>
> 3. Absolute propositional truth, therefore, depends on the absolute personal truth (or fidelity) of God, who can be trusted in all he does and says.[11]

Are there any common misperceptions about the Christian worldview, especially by Christians? There are at least two mistaken notions. The first is that a Christian view of the world and life will differ on all points from other worldviews. While this is not always true (e.g., all worldviews accept the law of gravity), the Christian worldview will differ and will be unique on the most important points, especially as they relate to the character of God, the nature and value of Scripture, and the exclusivity of Jesus Christ as Savior and Lord. The second is that the Bible contains all that we need to know. Common sense should put this misdirected thought out of business. However, it is true that the Bible alone contains all that Christians need to know about their spiritual life and godliness through a knowledge of the one true God, which is the highest and most important level of knowledge (2 Pet 1:2-4). Also, while it does not exhaustively address every field, when Scripture speaks in any subject area, it speaks authoritatively.

How can a Christian worldview be spiritually profitable and in what life-contexts? First, in the world of *scholarship* the Christian worldview is offered, not as one of many equals or possibilities, but as the one true view of life whose single source of truth and reality is the Creator God. Thus it serves as a bright light reflecting the glory of God in the midst of intellectual darkness.

Second, a Christian worldview can be used as an effective tool in *evangelism* to answer the questions and objections of the unbeliever. However, it must be clearly understood that in the final analysis, it is the Gospel that has the power to bring an individual to salvation (Rom 1:16-17). Carl F. H. Henry clearly makes the point that

> No person can be "argued into becoming a Christian." Yet without meeting rational criteria one's religious experience is less than biblical and evangelical. One can and ought to be persuaded intellectually of the logical consistency and truth of evangelical postulates concerning God and the world. One need not be a believer, however, to understand the truths affirmed by divine revelation. A person persuaded intellectually of the truth of the gospel but seeking to escape or seeking to postpone personal salvific trust invites divine condemnation. But personal faith is a gift of the Spirit. The Holy Spirit uses the truth as a means of conviction and persuasion.[12]

Finally, a Christian worldview is extraordinarily helpful in the realm of *discipleship* to inform and mature a true believer in Christ with regard to the implications and ramifications of one's Christian faith. It provides a framework by which 1) to understand the world and all of its reality from God's perspective and 2) to order one's life according to God's will.

What should be the ultimate goal of embracing the Christian worldview? Why is the Christian worldview worth recovering? Listen to Jeremiah who passes along God's direct answer.

> *Thus says the* LORD*: "Let not the wise man boast in his wisdom, let not the mighty man boast in his might, let not the rich man boast in his riches, but let him who boasts boast in this, that he understands and knows me, that I am the* LORD *who practices steadfast love, justice, and righteousness in the earth. For in these things I delight, declares the* LORD*."*
>
> —JEREMIAH 9:23-24

FURTHER READING[13]

Geisler, Norman L. and William D. Watkins. *Worlds Apart: A Handbook on World Views*. 2nd ed. Grand Rapids, MI: Baker, 1989.

Hoffecker, W. Andrew and Gary Scott Smith, eds. *Building a Christian World View*. 2 vols. Phillipsburg, NJ: Presbyterian and Reformed, 1986, 1988.

Holmes, Arthur F. *Contours of a World View*. Grand Rapids, MI: William B. Eerdmans. 1983.

MacArthur, John. *Why One Way? Defending an Exclusive Claim in an Inclusive World*. Nashville: W Publishing Group, 2002.

Nash, Ronald H. *Worldviews in Conflict: Choosing Christianity in a World of Ideas*. Grand Rapids, MI: Zondervan, 1992.

Noebel, David A. *Understanding the Times*. Manitou Springs, CO: Summit Press, 1991. Reprint, Eugene, OR: Harvest House, 1994.

North, Gary, ed. *Foundations of Christian Scholarship*. Vallecito, CA: Ross House Books, 1979.

Orr, James. *The Christian View of God and the World*. Edinburgh: A. Elliot, 1893. Reprint, Grand Rapids, MI: William B. Eerdmans, 1948.

Phillips, W. Gary and William E. Brown. *Making Sense of Your World from a Biblical Viewpoint*. Chicago: Moody Press, 1991. Reprint, Salem, WI: Sheffield Publishing, 1996.

Wells, David F. *God in the Wasteland: The Reality of Truth in a World of Fading Dreams*. Grand Rapids, MI: William B. Eerdmans, 1994.

PART ONE
THE BIBLICAL FOUNDATION

1

EMBRACING THE AUTHORITY AND SUFFICIENCY OF SCRIPTURE

JOHN MACARTHUR

A truly *Christian* worldview begins with the conviction that God Himself has spoken in Scripture. As Christians, we are committed to the Bible as the inerrant and authoritative Word of God. We believe it is reliable and true from cover to cover, in every jot and tittle (cf. Matt 5:18). Scripture, therefore, is the standard by which we must test all other truth-claims. Unless that axiom dominates our perspective on all of life, we cannot legitimately claim to have embraced a Christian worldview.

"Judeo-Christian ethics" per se are not what make a worldview Christian. Admiration for the Person and moral teachings of Christ does not necessarily make one's point of view Christian either. A truly *Christian* worldview, simply put, is one in which the Word of God, rightly understood, is firmly established as both the foundation and the final authority for everything we hold true.

When we begin with a right view of Scripture, the Bible itself ought to shape what we believe from start to finish. It should govern how we behave. It should frame our entire perspective on life. In other words, if we simply start by affirming what the Bible says about itself, the rest of our worldview should fall into place, with the Bible as the source and touchstone of all we believe. So this is the crucial, foundational starting point in developing a Christian worldview.

But is the Bible, in and of itself, sufficient to furnish us with a *complete* worldview? Many Christians these days seem to imagine that the Bible is neither modern enough nor sophisticated enough to equip people to live in the twenty-first century. Church growth experts tell pastors they must look beyond the Bible for principles of leadership and success gleaned from the modern business world. Psychologists claim the Bible is too simplistic to help people with complex emotional and psychological issues. In every quarter of the evangelical movement today the Scriptures are being set aside in favor of novel philosophies, scientific theories, experimental behavioral and counseling techniques, political correctness, and other similar fads of modern opinion. People who claim to be evangelicals have jumped on almost every novel bandwagon of secular opinion since the middle of the nineteenth century.

Observing the current trends in the church, one would think opinion polls, rather than Scripture, determines truth for Christians. (One Christian pollster recently issued a series of shrill warnings in the form of a book and a series of press releases, saying that the church would soon cease to exist completely if church leaders do not heed modern opinion polls and change the very nature of the church in order to get in step with the times. That point of view is flatly contrary to the principle of Matthew 16:18, where we are told that the gates of hell shall not prevail against the true church.) Obviously, many who call themselves evangelicals operate with something other than a biblical worldview.

The Attack on Biblical Sufficiency

Perhaps the one doctrine most under attack in the church of our generation is the sufficiency of Scripture. Even people who give lip service to the authority, inspiration, and inerrancy of Scripture sometimes balk at affirming its *sufficiency*. The result is virtually the same as a denial of biblical authority, because it directs people away from the Bible in search of other "truth."

What do we mean when we say Scripture is sufficient? We mean that the Bible is an adequate guide for all matters of faith and conduct. Scripture gives us every truth we need for life and godliness. Or to borrow words from the A.D. 1647 Westminster Confession of Faith, "The whole counsel of God, concerning all things necessary for his own glory, man's salvation, faith, and life, is either expressly set down in Scripture, or by good and necessary consequence may be deduced from Scripture: unto which nothing at any time is to be added, whether by new revelations of the Spirit, or traditions of men."[1]

The church, by and large, simply does not believe that anymore. The average Christian seems to assume that something more than Scripture is needed to help us cope in a modern world. Christian bookstores are full of books offering advice drawn from sources other than the Bible on almost every conceivable subject—parenting, Christian manhood and womanhood, success and self-esteem, relationships, church growth, church leadership, ministry, philosophy, and so on. Various self-appointed experts who claim to have discovered some deep truth not revealed in Scripture have now become familiar fixtures on the evangelical landscape. The sufficiency of Scripture is under attack, and the effect on the collective worldview of the evangelical movement has been disastrous.

We see evidence of this in the fact that so many pastors and church leaders now doubt that Scripture is a sufficient diet for the saints. They want to supplement biblical teaching with entertainment and ideas drawn from secular sources. They apparently do not believe that studying, teaching, and applying the Word of God alone is sufficient for meeting people's spiritual needs. And they apparently do not believe that preaching the Bible is sufficiently appealing to unbelievers. They insist instead that in today's media-driven, visually-oriented culture, the message must be augmented by music, drama, comedy, and extrabiblical motivational talks. Biblical principles aren't deemed sufficiently "relevant" by themselves. Numerous churches are replacing preaching with carnal amusements. Pastors who are Bible teachers who carefully and thoroughly feed their people an unbroken pattern of accurate, deep, clear, and convicting understanding of God's Word are more rare as time passes.

Do you want more evidence that evangelicals are losing confidence in the sufficiency of Scripture? You will see it in the rise of evangelical mysticism—the belief that Christians need to listen to God speaking directly to them through strong impressions in their mind, a voice in their head, or other mystical means. Some evangelicals have become obsessed with Satan and demonic powers. They imagine that they can command demons merely by speaking to them. All such mysticism is in reality nothing more than dabbling with the occult. It stems from a loss of confidence in the sufficiency of Scripture. Those who aren't convinced the Bible is a sufficient revelation of truth will be continually looking elsewhere for more "revelation" and new mystical experiences. In doing so, they open the door wide to the worst kinds of demonic deception.

During the past quarter century we have witnessed the abandonment of belief in Scripture's sufficiency in another category: marriage and the family. Christians once believed that if they studied the Word of God and obeyed its principles, they would have a God-honoring family life and a fulfilling marriage that would please the Lord. But now there is a proliferation of new techniques and a plethora of concepts, gimmicks, and opinions apart from the Word being offered as the real keys in dealing with family problems. All of that suggests that Christians no longer believe the Bible is a sufficient source of instruction concerning these matters.

I recently read an article in a respected magazine once known for its defense of Reformation principles—including the sufficiency of Scripture. Unfortunately, in this article the author was explaining why he had abandoned his confidence that the Bible is sufficient. He said he had read data from a poll indicating that the divorce rate among "born-again Christians" is as high as or higher than the divorce rate among non-Christian couples. He said those survey results made him conclude that the Bible simply does not have all the answers when it comes to keeping Christian marriages together. This man, who is a Professor of New Testament in a leading evangelical seminary, decided that the biblical guidelines on marriage are simply too superficial to work in the modern world. In short, he said he had abandoned his confidence in biblical sufficiency because of data from an opinion poll.

But generations of Christians can testify that the Bible's teaching about marriage *is* sufficient, if obeyed, to keep truly Christ-centered marriages healthy and vibrant. We certainly should not be willing to accept uncritically the data of any poll purporting to prove that the marriages of born-again people are more likely to fail than the marriages of unbelievers. In the first place, no pollster could ever accurately determine who is "born again" and who is not. The poll categorized people as "born again" if they claimed any kind of belief in Christ, even if other survey questions revealed they did not understand the essentials of the Gospel. Furthermore, the poll did not distinguish whether the divorce occurred before or after the person's conversion, thereby invalidating the point.

In the second place, no marriage *ever* fails unless one or both of the partners is disobedient to the clear biblical teaching about how to live with one's partner in love and understanding (cf. 1 Pet 3:1-7). The failure of supposedly Christian marriages today is not proof of the insufficiency of Scripture; it is proof of the weakness and biblical illiteracy of those who say they believe Scripture is the Word of God.

Does Scripture Claim to Be Sufficient?

Is there a biblical response to this sinful abandonment of the sufficiency of Scripture? Of course there is. Many passages in the Bible teach that the Scriptures are a perfectly sufficient revelation of "all things that pertain to life and godliness" (2 Pet 1:3).

Second Corinthians 9:8, for example, is filled with superlatives regarding the all-sufficient resources God provides: "And God is able to make *all* grace *abound* to you, so that having *all* sufficiency in *all* things at *all* times, you may *abound* in *every* good work" (emphasis added). That is an amazingly comprehensive statement. For anyone to claim that human philosophy must augment the simple truth of Scripture, or that Scripture cannot deal with certain societal issues and individual problems, is to contradict Paul's divinely inspired testimony in that verse.

When Jesus prayed to the Father for believers' sanctification, He said, "Sanctify them in the truth; your word is truth" (John 17:17). "Sanctify" means "set apart from sin, to be holy and separated to God." Sanctification encompasses the whole concept of spiritual maturity. Jesus was teaching that every aspect of the believer's holiness is the work of the Word of God (not the Word of God plus something else).

In fact, to suggest that the Word of God alone is insufficient is to espouse the very opinion that lies at the heart of virtually every cult that pretends to be Christian. The one thing nearly all of them have in common is the belief that people need the Bible plus something else—the writings of some "enlightened" prophet or seer, the edicts of church tradition, or the conclusions of science and secular philosophy. So, to deny the sufficiency of Scripture is to espouse an age-old heresy. But Scripture consistently teaches that the complete holiness of the believer is the work of the all-sufficient Word of God (cf. John 17:17).

In his first letter to the Corinthians, Paul described how God instructed him and the believers at Corinth: "And we impart this in words not taught by human wisdom but taught by the Spirit, interpreting spiritual truths to those who are spiritual" (2:13). Through the Holy Spirit, God dispenses His wisdom to believers. His Word is so comprehensive, so effective, and so complete that verse 15 says believers can judge (appraise and evaluate) "all things." Christians who know Scripture can have such a comprehensive ability to discern things because, according to verse 16, they have "the mind of Christ."

The mind of Christ is the consummate mind of God—omniscient, supreme, and without any insufficiency. All the church needs to understand any problem, meet any need, or unravel any issue is the mind of God. And the mind of God is revealed to us in Scripture in a way that is adequate for all our spiritual needs.

In Mark 12:24 Jesus challenged the Pharisees, "Is this not the reason you are wrong, because you know neither the Scriptures nor the power of God?" All their errors—like every spiritual error in any context—stemmed from a lack of knowledge and understanding of the Word of God. Notice also that Jesus equated knowing the Scriptures with experiencing "the power of God."

Some modern evangelicals seem to think that if the church wants real power we cannot merely proclaim the Bible. That is the view of many charismatics, who insist that signs and wonders are a necessary supplement to merely proclaiming the truth of God's Word. Others, including some of the most influential pundits of the church growth movement, likewise insist that unless biblical preaching is supplemented with other programs, the church can never successfully save the lost. They err severely, not knowing that the gospel message itself "*is* the power of God for salvation" (Rom 1:16, emphasis added).

How did Jesus handle Satan when the devil tempted Him (Matt 4:1-11)? Did He use some complicated exorcism formula to bind him or banish him to the abyss? No; He simply addressed the devil on three occasions with the words "It is written" and thus refuted the enemy's evil tactics by citing the words of Scripture. So even Christ exercised the power of God through the Word of God, and that is what thwarted Satan's temptation.

The power of God is not found in some mystical, extra-biblical source of knowledge, the use of signs and wonders and ecstatic utterances, the insights of secular psychology and philosophy, or clever insights into people's felt needs. But rather the power of God resides only in the inspired, infallible, and inerrant Word of God. When believers read, study, obey, and apply Scripture, they will realize it has sufficient power to deal with any situation in life.

Jesus also said, "Blessed rather are those who hear the word of God and keep it!" (Luke 11:28). By that He meant that all spiritual sufficiency is bound up in hearing and obeying the Word of God. Normally we equate "blessed" with an emotional tingle or a momentary sense of excitement. But here Jesus used the term to speak of a blissful state of life—a life accompanied by peace and joy, meaning and value, hope and fulfillment—a life that is fundamentally happy and content. Obedience to God's sufficient Word opens the door to that kind of life. Again, Scripture is the answer to all of life's challenges.

In Luke 16 Jesus relates the parable of Lazarus (the beggar full of sores) and the rich man. Lazarus died and went to Abraham's bosom, the place of blessing. The rich man died and went to the place of torment. From his position of suffering, the rich man pleaded with Abraham:

> *"Then I beg you, father, to send him [Lazarus] to my father's house—for I have five brothers—so that he may warn them, lest they also come into this place of torment." But Abraham said, "They have Moses and the Prophets; let them hear them." And he said, "No, father Abraham, but if someone goes to them from the dead, they will repent." He said to him,*

> *"If they do not hear Moses and the Prophets, neither will they be convinced if someone should rise from the dead."*
>
> —LUKE 16:27-31

The rich man's perspective is the same view of many today who always seem to demand some kind of supernatural affirmation of spiritual truth. They imagine that the straightforward statements of Scripture and the power of the Gospel alone are not sufficient. But the Lord, through the words of the parable, argued otherwise and said that even though He Himself would rise from the dead, miracles are not necessary for the Gospel to do its work in changing lives. Why? Because the Word of God through the inspiration and illumination of the Holy Spirit is powerful enough—it is all-sufficient in what it teaches about redemption and sanctification.

Hebrews 4:12 is another significant verse that declares the inherent sufficiency of Scripture: "For the word of God is living and active, sharper than any two-edged sword, piercing to the division of soul and of spirit, of joints and of marrow, and discerning the thoughts and intentions of the heart." The writer is essentially saying Scripture is unique and there is no spiritual weapon for the believer that is superior to it. The Word of God penetrates the inner being and nature of a person. How? Because it is living and powerful, sharper than any other spiritual tool and able to go deeper and cut cleaner and truer than any other resource to which someone might turn. When utilized effectively and properly, Scripture reveals the deepest thoughts and intentions of the human heart, so that "all are naked and exposed to the eyes of him to whom we must give account" (v. 13). Thus, the Bible can do what psychoanalysis can never do. It is sufficient to penetrate and lay bare the deepest part of a person's soul.

James 1:25 also gives testimony to the sufficiency of Scripture: "The one who looks into the perfect law, the law of liberty, and perseveres, being no hearer who forgets but a doer who acts, he will be blessed in his doing." The expression "the perfect law of liberty" is synonymous with the complete—and sufficient—Word of God. Again, bliss, satisfaction, fulfillment, and everything else that pertains to life and conduct for a believer are bound up in obedience to the Word of God.

The apostle Peter wrote: "Like newborn infants, long for the pure spiritual milk, that by it you may grow up" (1 Pet 2:2). Spiritual growth and maturity, the sanctifying process of moving toward Christlikeness, is tied to the believer's desire for "pure spiritual milk"—the Word of God. Of course, newborns do not want anything besides milk and cannot even digest other foods. Peter is saying that as a baby strongly desires milk for nourishment and growth, believers with the same singular desire and devotion should long for the Word of God. The Word provides all the resources they need for spiritual maturity (cf. 2 Pet 1:3).

Even more direct and comprehensive statements on the power and sufficiency of Scripture are those given by Paul in his farewell message to the Ephesian elders: "I did not shrink from declaring to you anything that was profitable . . . for I did not shrink from declaring to you the whole counsel of God. . . . And now I commend you to God and to the word of his grace, which is able to build you up and to give you the inheritance among all those who are sanctified" (Acts 20:20, 27, 32). Paul did not view any portion of God's revelation as unimportant or insufficient to spiritual growth. Nor did he view any of it as incapable of dealing with life's problems.

The Old Testament is equally clear about the sufficiency of Scripture. Deuteronomy 6:4-9 is the basic summary of doctrine for the people of Israel:

> *Hear, O Israel: The* LORD *our God, the* LORD *is one. You shall love the* LORD *your God with all your heart and with all your soul and with all your might. And these words that I command you today shall be on your heart. You shall teach them diligently to your children, and shall talk of them when you sit in your house, and when you walk by the way, and when you lie down, and when you rise. You shall bind them as a sign on your hand, and they shall be as frontlets between your eyes. You shall write them on the doorposts of your house and on your gates.*

That was a simple way to summarize the myriad commands God had given Moses. But the law of God—His revealed Word—was and is the one resource for life and godliness. Everywhere they went, the children of God were always to meditate on and apply the words of the living God. Those words were to occupy their attention as the source and centerpiece of everything. For His people, that is still God's design for life.

A Psalm About the Sufficiency of Scripture

Psalm 19 is, I believe, the most concise and direct treatment of the sufficiency of Scripture in all the Bible. This psalm conveys to us the significance of divine revelation. The first half (vv. 1-6) describes God's revelation in nature, what theologians for years have called *general revelation*. God is revealed in His creation. As Romans 1:20 says, "For his invisible attributes, namely, his eternal power and divine nature, have been clearly perceived, ever since the creation of the world, in the things that have been made."

But while general revelation is sufficient to reveal the fact that God exists, and to teach us something about His attributes, nature alone does not reveal saving truth. The point of the psalm is the superiority—the utter spiritual perfection and all-sufficiency—of *special revelation*, the written Word of God.

And so the second half of the psalm (vv. 7-14) focuses on the absolute and utter sufficiency of Scripture as our one true and infallible guide in life. The psalmist begins this section on the Word of God by writing:

> *The law of the* LORD *is perfect,*
> *reviving the soul;*
> *the testimony of the* LORD *is sure,*
> *making wise the simple;*
> *the precepts of the* LORD *are right,*
> *rejoicing the heart;*
> *the commandment of the* LORD *is pure,*
> *enlightening the eyes;*
> *the fear of the* LORD *is clean,*
> *enduring forever;*
> *the rules of the* LORD *are true,*
> *and righteous altogether.*
>
> —vv. 7-9

Those three verses, consistent with the infinite intelligence of God's mind, contain an absolutely surpassing and comprehensive, yet concise, statement on the sufficiency of Scripture. They contain six basic lines of thought, each with three basic elements: a title for the Word of God, a characteristic of the Word of God, and a benefit of the Word of God. Each of those lines of thought uses the key phrase "of the LORD." Six times the covenant name of God, Yahweh, is used to identify the source of the sufficient Word.

The first title for Scripture is "the law," the Hebrew word *tôrā(h)*, which basically means divine teaching. It points to the didactic or teaching nature of Scripture. In the Scriptures, God dispenses true doctrine to humanity, concerning what we should believe, what kind of character we should cultivate, and how we ought to live. The torah is God's teaching for every area of life.

The first characteristic of God's Word, according to verse 7, is that it is "perfect" (cf. Jas 1:25), in contrast to the imperfect, flawed reasonings of humanity. The Hebrew term translated "perfect" is a common word that also can mean "whole," "complete," or "sufficient." One Old Testament scholar, endeavoring to capture the fullness of the word's meaning, said it means ". . . all-sided so as to cover completely all aspects of life."[2] It is an expression of comprehensiveness, declaring that the Scripture covers everything and lacks nothing.

The first part of verse 7 also lists the first of Scripture's six benefits: it revives the soul. The Hebrew term translated "reviving" speaks of converting, transforming, restoring, and refreshing. It indicates that Scripture is so comprehensive that if carefully obeyed, it can transform a person's whole life in every regard. The truth of Scripture gives full life to all aspects of the soul. "Soul" is translated from a Hebrew word (*nep̄eš*) that means the inner person, the whole self—the heart. In other words, Scripture is so comprehensive that it can transform the entire person by giving him salvation and providing all the means necessary for his sanctification, making the very soul of the individual new (cf. Rom 1:16; 2 Tim 3:15-17; 1 Pet 1:23-25).

Psalm 119, a wonderful parallel to Psalm 19, certainly affirms this. "Let your steadfast love come to me, O LORD, your salvation according to your promise" (v. 41). Salvation is connected to God's promise, or His Word. "This is my comfort in my affliction, that your promise gives me life" (v. 50). "My soul longs for your salvation; I hope in your word" (v. 81; cf. vv. 146 and 174). It is no wonder the apostle Paul commanded Timothy to "preach the word" (2 Tim 4:2). God's Word is sufficient to convert the soul.

Psalm 19:7 also declares a second title and characteristic of Scripture: "the testimony of the LORD is sure." The psalmist uses "testimony" as a poetic parallel to "the law." He is not making a contrast between "law" and "testimony"; he is using the words as synonyms, both referring to Scripture. Furthermore, "testimony" defines God's written Word as a witness to the truth. In the Bible God gives testimony to who He is and what He requires. His testimony is "sure," in sharp contrast to the unsure, insecure, wavering, shifting, and unreliable notions of men. "Sure" means unwavering, immovable, unmistakable, and worthy to be trusted. The truth of God's Word thus provides a solid foundation on which people, without hesitation, can build their lives and eternal destinies (cf. 2 Pet 1:19-21).

The benefit of this sure testimony is that of "making wise the simple." The root of the Hebrew word for "simple" conveys the idea of an open door. A simple person is one who is like an open door—he does not know what to screen out. Everything comes in because he is unlearned, inexperienced, naive, and undiscerning. He may be proud to be "open-minded," though he is really a fool. But the Word of God makes such a person "wise." The word translated "wise" basically means to be skilled in the matters of practical godly living. To be wise is to master the art of daily living by knowing the Word of God and applying it in every situation.

Psalm 119 provides additional testimony to the value of the wisdom only God's Word can supply, demonstrated by the psalmist's request for such wisdom in verse 27: "Make me understand the way of your precepts." In other words, the psalmist is calling on God to teach him, for God knows the right way to live. Wisdom and Scripture are inextricably linked: "Give me understanding, that I may keep your law and observe it with my whole heart" (v. 34; cf. vv. 66, 104, 125, 169). We have more understanding than all the combined "wisdom" of those who propagate human knowledge (see vv. 98-100).

The first half of Psalm 19:8 begins with a third title and characteristic of God's Word: "The precepts of the LORD are right." Here the title David gives to Scripture is "precepts," meaning divine principles, statutes, and guidelines. He characterizes those many precepts simply as "right." That is to say, they show believers the right spiritual path and guide them into the way of true understanding. People who follow the Word of God are not left to wander around in the fog of human opinion.

The result of applying Scripture's principles, obeying its precepts, and walking in its pathways is true joy—"rejoicing the heart." The prophet Jeremiah, in the midst of tremendous human stress—rejection of his person and message, and the disaster befalling his entire nation—gave great testimony to the joy that comes through God's Word: "Your words were found, and I ate them, and your words became to me a joy and the delight of my heart" (Jer 15:16; cf. 1 John 1:4). Psalm 119 provides further confirmation of this truth. In verse 14 the psalmist writes, "In the way of your testimonies I delight as much as in all riches" (cf. v. 111). If those who claim to follow Christ today were as excited about scriptural precepts as they are about the materialism of this world, the character of the church would be wholly different, and our testimony to the world would be consistent and potent.

The second part of Psalm 19:8 lists a fourth title and characteristic to identify the Word of God: "the commandment of the LORD is pure." The word "commandment" emphasizes the authoritative, binding character of Scripture. God requires certain things from people, and He blesses those who comply but judges those who do not. His requirements are "pure," a word actually better translated as "clear" or "lucid." Some elements of Scripture are more obscure and harder to understand than others, but generally the Bible is clear, not obscure.

Scripture's purity and clarity produces the benefit of "enlightening the eyes." It provides illumination in the midst of moral, ethical, and spiritual darkness. It reveals the knowledge of everything not otherwise readily seen (cf. Prov 6:23). One of the main reasons the Word of God is sufficient for all of humanity's spiritual needs is because it leaves no doubt regarding essential truth. Life itself is confusing and chaotic. Seeking truth apart from Scripture only adds to the confusion. Scripture, by contrast, is remarkably clear.

Familiar verses from Psalm 119 contain powerful testimony to the purity and clarity of the Word. "Your word is a lamp to my feet and a light to my path" (v. 105); "The unfolding of your words gives light; it imparts understanding to the simple" (v. 130).

Fifth in the list of Scripture's titles and characteristics is the opening phrase of Psalm 19:9, "the fear of the LORD is clean." Here the psalmist uses the term "fear" as a synonym for the Word of God. Why does he do that? Because the Word intends to convey and provoke in its hearers the fear of God, which will in turn bring about a reverential, worshipful awe in those who believe it (cf. Ps 119:38). And this Scripture that seeks to produce the fear of God in its readers is "clean." That speaks of the utter absence of impurity, filthiness, defilement, or imperfection. God's Word, and God's Word alone, is unsullied by sin, untainted by evil, devoid of corruption, and without error of any kind (cf. 119:9). Psalm 12:6 affirms that "The words of the LORD are pure words, like silver refined in a furnace on the ground, purified seven times" (cf. Ps 119:172).

Consequently, the Bible has the remarkable benefit of "enduring forever" (Ps 19:9). It is "the living and abiding word of God" (1 Pet 1:23) that never changes and never needs to be altered, no matter what the generation.

Sixth and last in David's Psalm 19 litany of praise to the titles and characteristics of Scripture is the second half of verse 9: "The rules of the LORD are true." These "rules" are the judgments and ordinances of God—in essence, divine verdicts. The commandments of the Bible are the eternally supreme Judge's legal decrees for the life and eternal destiny of mankind. And those rules are "true." Even though from an earthly standpoint the truth is very hard for people to discover, the Word of the Lord is always true. Therefore it is always dependable, relevant, and applicable—in contrast to the lies of unregenerate men who are mere pawns and victims of Satan, the father of lies.

The result of the truthfulness of Scripture in verse 9 is that it is "righteous altogether." That phrase conveys the idea of comprehensiveness. Scripture is the complete, sufficient, error-free source of all truth. That is why God issued such commands as "You shall not add to the word that I command you, nor take from it" (Deut 4:2; cf. Rev 22:18-19). Psalm 119:160 is another wonderful statement on the comprehensive, settled nature of Scripture: "The sum of your word is truth, and every one of your righteous rules endures forever" (cf. vv. 89, 142, 151). God's Word contains all the truth necessary for genuine spiritual life, and it perfectly meets all the spiritual needs of mankind.

The second half of Psalm 19 goes on to affirm the supreme value of Scripture:

> *More to be desired are they than gold,*
> *even much fine gold;*
> *sweeter also than honey*
> *and drippings of the honeycomb.*
> *Moreover, by them is your servant warned;*
> *in keeping them there is great reward.*
> *Who can discern his errors?*
> *Declare me innocent from hidden faults.*
> *Keep back your servant also from presumptuous sins;*
> *let them not have dominion over me!*
> *Then I shall be blameless,*
> *and innocent of great transgression.*
>
> —vv. 10-13

First, David says God's Word is more valuable than "much fine gold." To have the incomparable Word of God is far better than possessing earthly wealth. Material blessings are valueless compared to the truth of God's Word.

Second, Scripture is so infinitely precious because it is the source of life's greatest pleasure, described in verse 10 as being "sweeter also than honey and drippings of the honeycomb." Nothing is as enriching, as personally meaningful, as much a source of lasting pleasure as joyful hours spent reading, studying, and meditating on the contents of God's Word (cf. Jer 15:16). The lack of resolution for the difficult problems of life is not a result of Scripture's inadequacy; it's a result of people's inadequate study and application of Scripture. If people loved God's Word the way they should, no one would ever question the Bible's sufficiency.

Third, the Bible is valuable as the greatest source of spiritual protection: "By them is your servant warned" (v. 11). Scripture protects believers in the face of temptation, sin, and ignorance (cf. Ps 119:9-11).

Fourth, Scripture is the source of our greatest profit, for in keeping its truths there is "great reward." True reward does not derive from fleeting materialism or man-centered theories and techniques that fade away, but from obedience to Scripture, which results in eternal glory. In fact, the word "reward" here in Hebrew is literally "the end." The psalmist is saying that in obeying the Word there is a great end, an eternal reward.

The Scripture is also valuable as the supplier of the greatest purification. Even as David is extolling the virtues of Scripture, he asks, "Who can discern his errors?" (v. 12). In light of all the positive characteristics and life-transforming benefits attendant to God's Word, David could not understand why anyone would ever disobey God's precepts. That prompted him to cry out, "Declare me innocent from hidden faults. Keep back your servant also from presumptuous sins; let them not have dominion over me!" (vv. 12-13). "Hidden faults" are the sins we do not plan to commit and often don't remember to confess. "Presumptuous sins" are those arrogant, premeditated ones we commit even though we know better.

David sincerely desired not to have such sins dominate him, so that he could be "blameless, and innocent of great transgression." He employs a Hebrew term for "transgression" that has the idea of willfully breaking free from a restraint or charging past a barrier to escape the dominion of God and the realm of grace. It simply means apostasy. The psalmist was appealing to God for purity of heart, that he might never apostatize, because he realized the Word of God was the only sufficient safeguard against spiritual disaster.

Psalm 19 concludes by expressing the psalmist's commitment to Scripture: "Let the words of my mouth and the meditation of my heart be acceptable in your sight, O LORD, my rock and my redeemer" (v. 14). David wanted the Lord to make his words and thoughts biblical. He wanted to be a man of the Word. A true and consistent commitment to divine revelation is the only commitment that really matters in this life.

Many of the trends in the evangelical church today stem from a willful abandonment of the perspective reflected in this psalm. Because Christians have lost their commitment to the sufficiency of Scripture, they have embraced worldviews that are not truly biblical. That is why Christians are leaving the Word of God (the mind of Christ) in order to chase after all kinds of worldly ideas. Even though they claim to believe in the truthfulness of Scripture, they apparently do not believe the Word is *sufficient* to meet all their needs and those of the people they target. They demonstrate such a lack of faith because they have never really been noble like the Bereans, who daily searched the Scriptures (Acts 17:11). They have treated the Bible in a cursory way and have never enjoyed the power of its rich and profound truths. The church's message must not be the Bible *plus* the world, but the message that the Bible *alone* is sufficient.

Too many people in evangelical churches and schools today simply assume that certain difficult problems they encounter are beyond the purview of Scripture. The real problem is that they are not really devoted to Scripture. They haven't committed themselves to the daily reading and application of the Word of God. Thus they lack genuine discernment and biblical understanding. If they truly studied Scripture, they would know that it is the Christian's one true source of spiritual strength and wisdom. It is the all-comprehensive resource God has given us for dealing with the issues of life. When Christians abandon that resource, it is no wonder that they struggle spiritually.

Is the Bible really sufficient to meet every problem of human life? Of course it is. And anyone who says it is not, whether by explicit statement or by implicit action, calls God a liar and ignores or seriously undermines Paul's clear, self-explanatory instruction to Timothy:

> *But as for you, continue in what you have learned and have firmly believed, knowing from whom you learned it and how from childhood you have been acquainted with the sacred writings, which are able to make you wise for salvation through faith in Christ Jesus. All Scripture is breathed out by God and profitable for teaching, for reproof, for correction, and for training in righteousness, that the man of God may be competent, equipped for every good work.*
>
> —2 TIM 3:14-17

That is the starting point for a true Christian worldview—and it is the point to which Christians must inevitably return in order to evaluate and discern every competing opinion and philosophy. Scripture is true. It is reliable. And above all, it is sufficient to guide us in every aspect of developing a worldview that honors God.

FURTHER READING

Geisler, Norman L. ed. *Inerrancy*. Grand Rapids, MI: Zondervan, 1980.

Kistler, Don. ed. *Sola Scriptura!* Morgan, PA: Soli Deo Gloria, 1995.

MacArthur, John. *Ashamed of the Gospel*. Wheaton, IL: Crossway Books, 1993.

__________. *Our Sufficiency in Christ*. Dallas: Word, 1991; reprint, Wheaton, IL: Crossway Books, 1998.

__________. *Reckless Faith*. Wheaton, IL: Crossway Books, 1994.

Radmacher, Earl and Robert Preus, eds. *Hermeneutics, Inerrancy, and the Bible*. Grand Rapids, MI: Zondervan, 1984.

Warfield, Benjamin Breckinridge. *The Inspiration and Authority of the Bible*. Philadelphia: Presbyterian and Reformed, 1948.

2

Cultivating a Biblical Mind-set

Richard L. Mayhue

"A mind is a terrible thing to waste." This signature sound bite effectively calls to mind a prominent college-level scholarship foundation.[1] Most, if not all, worldviews would embrace this generally accepted aphorism. However, a great divergence of opinion exists in describing what this waste might involve, how extensive it is or can be, how best to prevent this kind of mental resource loss, and what might be the best methods of renewing a damaged or neglected mind.

This chapter builds upon the fundamental idea that a human mind that 1) is redemptively focused on Jesus Christ as Savior and Lord (Rom 8:5-8) plus being renewed regularly by Scripture (Rom 12:2) and 2) is then receiving a quality education (formal or informal) from the perspective of a Christian worldview will be the mind that achieves the greatest gains and experiences the least waste (Ps 119:97-104). While the foundation's classic slogan, mentioned above, embraces the intellectual side of life only, a Christian worldview considers both the intellectual and spiritual aspects of humanity as inseparably and integrally connected from the beginning.

When God created Adam and Eve (Gen 1—2), He brought them into existence in His own image (Gen 1:27) with a mind that immediately allowed them to think, communicate, and act (Gen 2:19-20; 3:1-6).[2] The Creator desired that His creation love Him intensely with the mind (Matt 22:37; 2 John 6). Thus, the intellectual and spiritual dimensions were linked in the creation of humanity and in God's will for them.

Proverbs 27:19 establishes a basic axiom relating to the individual character and mind of a human being.

As in water face reflects face,
so the heart[3] of man reflects the man.

Thus, who Adam and Eve were to become would depend in some measure on how they thought. This basic idea also appears in Proverbs 23:7, "For as he thinks within himself, so he is" (NASB). Jesus used this truism in Matthew 15:18-19 to illustrate that man sins, not because of what he eats physically, but because of what he digests intellectually. A person who thinks righteously will tend to act righteously, and conversely a person who thinks sinfully will act sinfully as a habit. Both the factual and ethical dimensions of one's thought life greatly determine one's behavior. This same principle is generally recognized in the cultural proverb:

Sow a thought, reap an act.
Sow an act, reap a habit.
Sow a habit, reap a character.

One becomes intellectually and spiritually what he/she thinks. So, unquestionably, the mind is a terrible thing to waste because to waste a mind is to waste a person.

Physiologically speaking, the brain is central to human existence and identity. The human race is uniquely set apart from all other aspects of creation by being created in the image of God and by the capacity to think profoundly and then live wisely. Who could imagine that the three-pound human brain—comprising one hundred billion neurons and that handles ten thousand thoughts daily, regulates over 103,000 heartbeats every twenty-four hours, coordinates over 23,000 breaths a day, and controls over six hundred muscles—would also play such a central role in determining the nature and value of our lives? Yet this is exactly what Scripture teaches in Romans 8:5: "For those who live according to the flesh set their minds on the things of the flesh, but those who live according to the Spirit set their minds on the things of the Spirit."

The Mind Has Already Been Wasted

Long before the twentieth century statement, "A mind is a terrible thing to waste" had been penned, the human mind had been seriously ravaged. A focused reading of the Pauline epistles locates numerous references to the human mind that indicate it had been severely damaged shortly after God's creation in Genesis 1—2.

This shocking discovery can best be grasped in the following list of twelve different negative New Testament words that describe the ruin of man's intellectual capacity.

1. Rom 1:28 "debased"
2. 2 Cor 3:14 "hardened"
3. 2 Cor 4:4 "blinded"
4. Eph 4:17 "futility"
5. Eph 4:18 "darkened"
6. Col 1:21 "hostile"
7. Col 2:4 "deluded"
8. Col 2:8 "deceived"
9. Col 2:18 "sensuous"
10. 1 Tim 6:5 "depraved"
11. 2 Tim 3:8 "corrupted"
12. Titus 1:15 "defiled"

As a result of this mental mayhem, people are "always learning and never able to arrive at a knowledge of the truth" (2 Tim 3:7), and some even "have a zeal for God, but not according to knowledge" (Rom 10:2). This represents the most tragic expression of a wasted mind.

Now, this does not mean that humans have been intellectually reduced to the mental ability of animals. It does not suggest that humans cannot achieve at an extraordinary level—for example, a Nobel or Pulitzer honoree. It does not preclude brilliant works of art or spectacular scientific discoveries or even an unprecedented acceleration of societal sophistication such as in the past two centuries. It does not mean that there cannot be a Mensa-level (top 2 percent) of intelligence. It does not mean that individuals cannot perform any good deeds at all or live according to some set of moral values.

But what then does it mean? Before giving a response to this vital question, it would be best to inquire: What happened, and why was the human mind wasted?

How Was the Mind Wasted?

At the completion of creation, "God saw everything that he had made, and behold, it was very good" (Gen 1:31). Adam and Eve were in righteous fellowship with God and had been given dominion over all of God's creation (Gen 1:26-30). A life of earthly bliss described their potential future and that of their offspring before sin entered the picture.

Genesis 3:1-7 describes the far-reaching and devastating blow to the human mind that would affect every human being who lived thereafter. Without question, Satan waged war against God and the human race in this monumental passage where the battlefield turns out to be Eve's mind. In the end, Eve exchanged the truth of God (Gen 2:17) for the lie of Satan (Gen 3:4-5), and the human mind has never been the same since.

The empirical method in primitive form actually originated in Genesis 3 when Eve concluded that the only way she could decide whether God was right or wrong (after Satan had planted seeds of doubt about God's truthfulness in her mind—Gen 3:4) involved testing Him with her own mind and senses. Paul explained it this way in Romans 1:25, speaking of those who would follow on the spiritually perilous path of Eve and then Adam: "they exchanged the truth about God for a lie and worshiped and served the creature rather than the Creator."

In short order, Eve basically bought into the lie of Satan and believed that she had a choice. Either she could disobediently choose to eat or she could obediently choose to refrain. Eve believed that she alone could determine the best choice with her own mind; God's command was no longer authoritative. God's verbal revelation no longer dictated what was right and what was wrong in her life. God's authoritative instruction became optional because all of a sudden, thanks to Satan, there now were other alternatives.

"So when the woman saw that the tree was good for food, and that it was a delight to the eyes, and that the tree was to be desired to make one wise, she took of its fruit and ate, and she also gave some to her husband who was with her, and he ate" (3:6). Here one finds the first historical practice of empirical research and inductive reasoning in its infancy. In the first act of human rebellion, Eve decided to conduct three tests on the tree in order to see whether God or Satan was right.

So she subjected the tree to these tests, the first being that of physical value. She observed the tree, and in examining it she saw that its fruit was "good for food." It had nutritional value. These might have been Eve's thoughts: *Maybe Satan is right. Maybe God was over-restrictive in preventing me from having all of the joy of life and all of the fruit in the garden.*

Based on this positive response, she ran a second test. Eve realized that the fruit was "a delight to the eyes." Not only would it benefit her body nutritionally, but she also discovered that it had emotional or aesthetic value. She gazed upon it and found that it was "a delight to the eyes." Putting this into postmodern language, she felt good about looking at the tree.

Eve wasn't satisfied yet. She wanted to be thorough. Perhaps she thought, *I'll take it one step further*. Then came a final test. She looked and saw that the tree was desirable "to make one wise." It had intellectual value that would make her wise like God.

In the midst of Eve's deliberation, she saw and thought that the tree really was good. It met her needs physically, aesthetically, and intellectually. Her mind drew the inference that God was wrong or that God had lied; Satan's deceit had successfully lured her away from God's absolute and unfailing truth. The human mind was about to be wasted forever. Being deceived led to disobedience, for Eve rejected God's instructions, took from the tree's fruit, and ate. Adam quickly did the same (3:6).

Paul summarizes Eve's disastrous act this way: "But I am afraid that as the serpent deceived Eve by his cunning, your thoughts will be led astray from a sincere and pure devotion to Christ" (2 Cor 11:3; cf. 1 Tim 2:14). The seduction of Eve's mind by Satan's deceit and Adam's blatant disobedience resulted in the corruption of their souls and, as a result, the souls of all humans who would follow (Rom 5:12).

Thus the human mind was wasted by sin. Man's mind was so debilitated that fellowship with God proved no longer humanly possible, and the ability to see and understand life from God's perspective vanished. The human race was now estranged from its God and Creator.

As a result, God's original two created human beings, and every one of their offspring, experienced a brutal reversal in their relationship with God and His world.

1. They no longer would concern themselves with thoughts of God, but with the thinking of men (Ps 53:1; Rom 1:25).
2. They no longer would have spiritual sight, but were blinded by Satan to the glory of God (2 Cor 4:4).
3. They would no longer be wise but foolish (Ps 14:1; Titus 3:3).
4. They would no longer be alive to God, but rather were dead in their sins (Rom 8:5-11).
5. They no longer would set their affections on the things above, but on the things of earth (Col 3:2).
6. They would no longer walk in light, but rather in darkness (John 12:35-36, 46).
7. They no longer would possess eternal life, but rather faced spiritual death—i.e., eternal separation from God (2 Thess 1:9).
8. They would no longer live in the realm of the Spirit, but rather in the flesh (Rom 8:1-5).

Can the Mind Be Reclaimed?

After the fall of Adam and Eve, followed by God's curse on them (Gen 3:16-19), their minds still functioned, but not at the same superior level as before.[4] Before the Fall, Adam and Eve held the mere potential to sin; they possessed a full-blown inclination to sin after the Fall. Their lives were now cursed rather than blessed. Because they rejected the truth of God's revelation to them, they now would have to think and live apart from Him. The human race seemed doomed without hope beyond death.

However, God in His mercy and grace provided a Savior who could reestablish a right relationship between God and the alienated human race on an individual basis (Titus 3:4-7):

> *But when the goodness and loving kindness of God our Savior appeared, he saved us, not because of works done by us in righteousness, but according to his own mercy, by the washing of regeneration and renewal of the Holy Spirit, whom he poured out on us richly through Jesus Christ our Savior, so that being justified by his grace we might become heirs according to the hope of eternal life.*

This personal salvation can be appropriated by faith in God's grace, which provided Jesus Christ as the only Savior who substitutionally bore the sin of those who would believe that Jesus died and was resurrected on the third day, saving them from the wrath of God (Rom 10:9-13; 1 Cor 15:1-4; Eph 2:8-9; 1 Pet 2:24).

The Redeemed Mind

As a result of salvation, the mind of a newly redeemed person knows and comprehends the glory of God (2 Cor 4:6), whereas before it was blinded by Satan (2 Cor 4:4). This person now possesses "the helmet of salvation" to protect the mind against the "schemes" (Eph 6:11; a mind-related word in the Greek New Testament)[5] of Satan rather than being left vulnerable against him as before salvation (Eph 6:17). This new person (2 Cor 5:17-21) now has a knowledge of God and His will that previously he/she did not possess (1 John 5:18-20).[6]

The Renewed Mind[7]

When a person enters into a personal relationship with Jesus Christ, he/she becomes "a new creation" (2 Cor 5:17) who sings "a new song" (Ps 98:1). But that does not mean that everything becomes new in the sense of perfection in one's current walk. The mind acquires a new way to think and a new capacity to clean up old ways of thinking. Unquestionably, God is in the business of mind renewal for Christians.

- "Do not be conformed to this world, but be transformed by the *renewal* of your mind . . ." (Rom 12:2).
- ". . . and to be *renewed* in the spirit of your minds" (Eph 4:23).

• ". . . and have put on the new self, which is being *renewed* in knowledge after the image of its creator" (Col 3:10).

The Bible says to "Set your minds on things that are above, not on things that are on earth" (Col 3:2). Paul put this concept in military terms: "We destroy arguments and every lofty opinion raised against the knowledge of God, and take every thought captive to obey Christ" (2 Cor 10:5).

How does one do this? Scripture is the mind of God. Not all of His mind, to be sure, but all that God cared to give believers. To think like God, one must think like Scripture. That's why Paul encouraged the Colossians to let the word of Christ richly dwell within them (Col 3:16).

Harry Blamires, an Englishman with extraordinary understanding about the Christian mind, puts this quite well:

> To think christianly is to think in terms of Revelation. For the secularist, God and theology are the playthings of the mind. For the Christian, God is real, and Christian theology describes His truth revealed to us. For the secular mind, religion is essentially a matter of theory:[8] for the Christian mind, Christianity is a matter of acts and facts. The acts and facts which are the basis of our faith are recorded in the Bible.[9]

At salvation, Christians are provided with a regenerated mental ability to comprehend spiritual truth. After salvation, Christians need to readjust their thinking chiefly by mind renewal, using the Bible as the means to do so. While the ultimate goal is to have a full knowledge of God and His will (Eph 1:18; Col 1:9-10), the believer must always be on guard lest he/she return to foolish and unbliblical thought patterns due to the lingering effects of sin.

The Illuminated Mind

The Bible says that believers need God's help to understand God's Word.

> *Now we have received not the spirit of the world, but the Spirit who is from God, that we might understand the things freely given us by God. And we impart this in words not taught by human wisdom but taught by the Spirit, interpreting spiritual truths to those who are spiritual.*
>
> —1 COR 2:12-13

Theologians call this *illumination*. People commonly use the expressions "It just dawned on me" or "The light just came on" to describe dim thoughts that later take on new understanding. God's Spirit does that for believers with Scripture.

A great prayer to offer as one studies Scripture is, "Open my eyes, that I may behold wondrous things out of your law" (Ps 119:18). It acknowledges a colossal need for God's light in Scripture. So do verses like, "Teach me, O LORD, the way of your statutes; and I will keep it to the end. Give me understanding, that I may keep your law and observe it with my whole heart" (vv. 33-34; see also v. 102).

God wants Christians to know and understand and obey. So He gives them the help they need through His Holy Spirit. Believers, like the two to whom Jesus spoke on the road to Emmaus, require God's assistance: "Then he opened their minds to understand the Scriptures" (Luke 24:45). God's ministry of illumination by which He gives light to the meaning of Scripture is affirmed by the psalmist (Ps 119:130).

Paul and John also comment on this in the New Testament:

> *. . . having the eyes of your hearts enlightened, that you may know what is the hope to which he has called you, what are the riches of his glorious inheritance in the saints, and what is the immeasurable greatness of his power toward us who believe, according to the working of his great might . . .*
>
> —EPH 1:18-19

> *But the anointing that you received from him abides in you, and you have no need that anyone should teach you. But as his anointing teaches you about everything—and is true and is no lie, just as it has taught you—abide in him.*
>
> —1 JOHN 2:27

The truth about God's illuminating Scripture for Christians should greatly encourage the believer. While it does not eliminate the need for gifted men to teach (Eph 4:11-12; 2 Tim 4:2) or the hard labor of serious Bible study (2 Tim 2:15), it does promise that there is no need to be enslaved to church dogma or to be led astray by false teachers. Primary dependence for learning Scripture needs to be upon the Author of Scripture—God Himself.

The Christlike Mind

When one thinks like God wants him/her to think and acts like God wants him/her to act, then one will receive God's blessing for obedience (Rev 1:3). Spiritually, the Christian will be that obedient child, that pure bride, and that healthy sheep in Christ's flock who experiences the greatest intimacy with God.

It is amazing how scholars and philosophers over the centuries have recognized the importance of the mind, but have all too often rejected the Creator of the mind and the Savior of the soul. Charles Colson recounts one such classic case:

> It was cold and raw that day in 1610 when a French mathematician named René Descartes pulled his cloak around him and climbed into the side compartment of a large stove. Descartes had been wrestling for weeks with questions of doubt and reason in his search for some certainty of a philosophical system. As he warmed himself in his stove, his imagination began glowing with the light of reason, and he resolved to doubt everything that could possibly be doubted.
>
> Hours later Descartes emerged, having determined that there was only one thing he could not doubt, and that was the fact that he doubted. A good day's work. Descartes drew the conclusion, *Cogito, ergo sum*: "I think, therefore I am." Then he went out for a cognac.
>
> Descartes' now-famous postulate led to a whole new promise for philosophic thought: man, rather than God, became the fixed point around which everything else revolved; human reason became the foundation upon which a structure of knowledge could be built; and doubt became the highest intellectual value.[10]

The ultimate form of idolatry would be, like Descartes, to reject the mind of God in Scripture and worship at the altar of one's own independent thinking. A believer's greatest intimacy with the Lord will be those times when our Lord's thoughts supersede ours and one's behavior then models that of Christ.

Unlike Descartes, Christians should be altogether glad to embrace the certain and true mind of God the Father (Rom 11:34), God the Son (1 Cor 2:16), and God the Spirit (Rom 8:27). In contrast to Peter, who was tempted by Satan to set his mind on the things of man, believers are to set their minds on the things of God (Matt 16:23). This has not so much to do with different categories or disciplines of thought but rather with the way things are viewed from a divine perspective.

Christians should stand in awe of God's mind as did the apostle Paul (Rom 11:33-36):

> *Oh, the depth of the riches and wisdom and knowledge of God! How unsearchable are his judgments and how inscrutable his ways! "For who has known the mind of the Lord, or who has been his counselor?" "Or who has given a gift to him that he might be repaid?" For from him and through him and to him are all things. To him be glory forever. Amen.*

God's view is the only true perspective that accurately corresponds to all of reality. God's mind sets the standard for which believers are to strive but that they will never fully achieve. Put another way, man's thoughts will never exceed, equal, or even come close to God's. Over 2,500 years ago the prophet Isaiah said this very thing (Isa 55:8-9):

> *For my thoughts are not your thoughts,*
> *neither are your ways my ways, declares the Lord.*
> *For as the heavens are higher than the earth,*
> *so are my ways higher than your ways*
> *and my thoughts than your thoughts.*

The ultimate pattern of maintaining the Christian mind is the Lord Jesus Christ. Paul declares, "But we have the mind of Christ" (1 Cor. 2:16). How? We have it with the Bible, which is God's sufficient, special revelation (2 Tim 3:16-17; cf. 2 Pet 1:3). In Philippians 2:5 Paul instructs, "Have this mind among yourselves, which is yours in Christ Jesus. . . ." The apostle specifically is pointing to Christ's mind-set of *sacrifice* for God's glory (2:7) and *submission* to God's will (2:8).

How does one having the mind of Christ and being Christianly minded think? The Puritan writer John Owen (A.D. 1616-1683) expressed it this way:

> We can test ourselves by asking whether our spiritual thoughts are like guests visiting a hotel, or like children living at home. There is a temporary stir and bustle when guests arrive, yet within a little while they leave and are forgotten. The hotel is then prepared for other guests. So it is with religious thoughts that are only occasional. But children belong to their house. They are missed if they don't come home. Preparation is continually being made for their food and comfort. Spiritual thoughts that arise from true spiritual mindedness are like the children of the house—always expected, and certainly enquired for if missing.[11]

Truth, Satan, and the Christian Mind

God is true (Ex 34:6; Num 23:19; Ps 25:10; Isa 65:16; John 14:6; 17:3; Titus 1:2; Heb 6:18; 1 John 5:20) and communicates only the truth (Ps 31:5, KJV; 119:43, 142, 151, 160; Prov 30:5; Jas 1:18). Therefore, God's Word is truth (John 17:17), and it sets the disciples of Christ free from sin and spiritual ignorance (John 8:32). That is not surprising since God is perfect in knowledge (Job 36:4) and knows all (1 John 3:20). God defines the standard of rational thought.

But can an earthbound human know the mind of a heavenly God? Ronald Nash eloquently answers this important question.

> There is nothing in the nature of the divine transcendence that precludes the possibility of our knowing the mind of God. There is nothing irrational or illogical about the content of divine revelation. The Christian God is not the Unknown God of ancient Athens or modern Marburg. He is a God who created men and women as creatures capable of knowing His mind and will and who has made information about His mind and will available in revealed truths.[12]

The Christian mind should be a repository of God's revealed truth. It should not fear, quake, waver, compromise, or bend in the face of opposing ideas or seemingly superior arguments (2 Tim 1:7). Truth does not originate from humans but from God. Therefore, Christians should be the champions of truth in a world filled with lies that are deceivingly disguised and falsely declared as the truth.

It was God who invited national Israel, "Come now, let us reason together, says the LORD . . ." (Isa 1:18). The subject matter to be considered was repentance from sin and salvation (vv. 16-20). By application, the same invitation is extended to every person alive. But it will not be without Satan's roadblocks.

To be forewarned is to be forearmed. While a commitment to think Christianly honors Christ, it is not without opposition. Satan would have believers think contrary to God's Word and then act disobediently to God's will.[13]

Remember that before one became a Christian, his/her mind was blinded by the devil: "The god of this world has blinded the minds of the unbelievers, to keep them from seeing the light of the gospel of the glory of Christ, who is the image of God" (2 Cor 4:4).

Even after salvation, Satan continues his intellectual rampage. Paul had a great concern for the Corinthian church, for he writes, "But I am afraid that as the serpent deceived Eve by his cunning, your thoughts will be led astray from a sincere and pure devotion to Christ" (2 Cor 11:3). Eve had allowed Satan to do some thinking for her. Then she did some of her own thinking independent of God. When her conclusions differed from God's, she chose to act on her conclusions, not God's commands, which is sin (Gen 3:1-7).

Satan aims his fiery darts (Eph 6:16) at the minds of believers (2 Cor 11:3), making their thought life the battlefield for spiritual conquest. Scriptural accounts abound of those who succumbed, like Eve (Gen 3) and Peter (Matt 16). Others walked away from the fray as victors, like Job (Job 1—2) and Christ (Matt 4). When Christians fall, they most likely forgot to wear the helmet of salvation and/or to wield the sword of truth (Eph 6:17).

In warning believers about life's ongoing, never-ending battle with Satan, Paul on two occasions tells about the schemes or designs of the devil. Two different Greek words are used,[14] but they both relate to the mind:

> *Put on the whole armor of God, that you may be able to stand against the* schemes *of the devil.*
>
> —EPH 6:11

> *. . . so that we would not be outwitted by Satan, for we are not ignorant of his* designs.
>
> —2 COR 2:11

Since no one is immune from this attack, one really must heed Peter's strong encouragement: "Therefore, preparing your minds for action, and being sober-minded, set your hope fully on the grace that will be brought to you at the revelation of Jesus Christ" (1 Pet 1:13; cf. 3:15).

So far the discussion has been focused on a preventative or defensive military posture in regard to the mind because the majority of Scripture deals with personal protection. However, Paul also addresses how to go on the intellectual offensive in 2 Corinthians 10:4-5.

> *For the weapons of our warfare are not of the flesh but have divine power to destroy strongholds. We destroy arguments and every lofty opinion raised against the knowledge of God, and take every thought captive to obey Christ.*

These "weapons" (v. 4) certainly feature the Word of God wielded by a Christian's mind on the battlefield of worldview warfare. In this context of a mind/idea battle, the targeted "strongholds" (v. 4) are "arguments" (v. 5) and "every lofty opinion" (v. 5) that are "raised against the knowledge of God" (v. 5). In other words, any philosophy, worldview, apologetic, or other kind of teaching that undermines, minimizes, contradicts, or tries to eliminate the Christian worldview or any part of it is to be met head-on with an aggressive, offensive battle plan. God's intended end is the destruction ("destroy" is used twice in vv. 4-5) of that which does not correspond to Scripture's clear teaching about God and His created world.

In the context of 2 Corinthians, Paul would have in view any teaching on any subject that did not correspond to his apostolic instruction that had come into the church. Whether an unbeliever or a believer was responsible, whether the idea(s) came from scholars or the uneducated, whether the teaching found wide acceptance or not, all thoughts/opinions that were not *for* the knowledge of God were to be considered *against* the knowledge of God. Therefore, they were to be targeted for intellectual combat and ultimate elimination. All intellectual activities (e.g., reading, listening to the radio, viewing television and movies, formal academic studies, casual conversations) must always be pursued using the filtering lens of a Christian worldview to determine whether they are allied with the truth of Scripture or are enemies of which to be wary.

Using the Christian Mind

Psalm 119 provides detailed insight into a Christian's new relation to the Bible, which contains the mind of Christ. First, there will be a great love for and tremendous delight in the Scriptures (vv. 47-48).[15] Second, a believer in Christ will have a strong desire to know God's Word as the best way to know God (vv. 16, 93, 176).[16] Third, when one knows God, it then leads to obeying Him (vv. 44-45).[17]

Meditation

To hear something once for most people is not enough. To briefly ponder something profound does not allow enough time to grasp and fully understand its significance. This proves to be most true with God's mind in Scripture. Psalm 119 testifies to the importance and blessing of lingering long over God's Word.

The idea of meditating sometimes lends itself to misunderstanding. Meditation involves prolonged thought or pondering. The American figure of speech for meditating is "to chew" on a thought. Some have likened it to the rumination process of the cow's four-stomach digestive system.

The most vivid picture comes from a coffee percolator. The water goes up a small tube and drains down through the coffee grounds. After enough cycles, the flavor of the coffee beans has been transferred to the water, which is then called coffee. So it is that Christians need to cycle their thoughts through the grounds of God's Word until they start to think like God and then act godly.

Scripture commands that believers meditate in three areas:

1. God Ps 27:4; 63:6.
2. God's Word Josh 1:8; Ps 1:2.
3. God's works Ps 143:5; 145:5.

All 176 verses of Psalm 119 extol the virtue of knowing and living out the mind of God. Meditation is mentioned at least seven times as the habit of one who loves God and desires a closer intimacy with Him: "Oh how I love your law! It is my meditation all the day. . . . My eyes are awake before the watches of the night, that I may meditate on your promise" (vv. 97, 148; see also vv. 15, 23, 27, 48, 78, 99).

Meditating on God's Word will cleanse away the old thoughts that are not of God because meditation places and reinforces new thoughts from Scripture. Also, it puts a protective shield around the mind to block and reject incoming thoughts that contradict God. That is the scriptural process of renewing the mind. A part of Eve's fall can be attributed to her failure to adequately meditate upon God's clear and sufficient Word (Gen 2:16-17).

Think on These Things

Someone has suggested that the mind is the taproot of the soul. That being so, one needs to carefully and nutritionally feed his/her soul by sinking one's taproot deep into God's mind in Scripture. A logical question to ask is, "What's the recommended soul food?" Paul's gourmet menu for the mind includes those thought entrees that are 1) "true," 2) "honorable," 3) "just," 4) "pure," 5) "lovely," 6) "commendable," 7) excellent, and 8) praiseworthy (Phil. 4:8). In meditating on God's Word and thinking on these things, Christians will avoid setting their minds on "earthly things" (Phil 3:19) and will keep from being double-minded (Jas 1:6-8).

Balancing Revelation and Reason

Are divine revelation and human reason like oil and water—do they never mix? Christians have sometimes reached two erroneous extremes in dealing with divine revelation and human reason. First, there is *anti-intellectualism*, which basically concludes that if a subject matter is not discussed in the Bible, it is not worthy of serious study/thought. Or, only what the Bible teaches on a topic should be examined. This unbiblical approach to learning and thinking leads to cultural and intellectual withdrawal. At the opposite extreme is *hyper-intellectualism*, which embraces natural revelation at the same or at a higher level of value and credibility as God's special revelation in Scripture; when the two are in conflict, natural revelation is the preferred source of truth. This unbiblical approach results in scriptural withdrawal.[18]

This matter is not resolved with an either/or approach but rather with a both/and process. The proper balance comes by beginning with Scripture, which is inerrant.[19] Where the Bible speaks to a discipline, its truth is superior. When the Bible does not speak, there is a whole world of God's creation to explore for knowledge, but with the caveat that man's ability to draw conclusions is fallible, unlike God's Word. This is especially true of thinkers who continually reject their need of Christ's salvation. This does not necessarily mean that their facts are wrong or even that their basic ideas are in error. But it does guarantee that their worldview is not in accord with God's perspective.

A recent example of perceived hyper-intellectualism appears in *The Scandal of the Evangelical Mind*, where the author writes, "By 'the mind' or 'the life of the mind,' I am not thinking primarily of theology as such."[20] He goes on, "By an evangelical 'life of the mind' I mean more the effort to think like a Christian—to think within a specifically Christian framework—across the whole spectrum of modern learning."[21] The author's comments raise a most significant question: How can one think Christianly without thinking theologically, and how can one think theologically without thinking biblically? It is not surprising that the writer confesses that he has thought at times that it is impossible to be, with integrity, both evangelical and intellectual.[22] In this writer's opinion, this illustrates unbalanced hyper-intellectualism at its worst, giving too much attention to the fallen mind of man and too little attention to the perfect mind of God and His infallible revelation in Scripture.

A more commendable approach is that of J. Gresham Machen, one of conservative Christianity's finest minds in his day (1881-1937): "Every Christian must think about God; every Christian to some degree must be a theologian."[23] Whatever the subject, one must begin with God's perspective from Scripture rather than with man's opinion from observation, research, and logic. Harry Blamires sums the matter up succinctly: "To think christianly is to think in terms of Revelation."[24] It is clearly a contradiction to declare oneself to be a Christian thinker and then relegate God's mind in Scripture to a place of equal or inferior value to man's thinking.

Arthur F. Holmes, former Chairman of the Department of Philosophy at a well-known Christian college, convincingly states the centrality of God and His special revelation to a Christian worldview:

> The crucial question for the recovery of truth, however, is how a Christian world-view can be introduced into education. My point is not that it ought not be excluded but that in practice, when we think Christianly, it cannot possibly be left out. Our world-view shows itself in the way we shape and relate our ideas and see everything in relation to God.[25]

Unmistakably, from the perspective of and with a Christian worldview, believers are to engage their own minds and the minds of others to the best of their ability and opportunity. However, several wise cautions are in order.

1. To become a scholar and try to change the way one's own generation thinks generally is secondary to becoming a Christian and changing the way one personally thinks about Christ.

2. Formal education in a range of disciplines is a necessary but secondary priority compared to gospel education—i.e., obeying the Great Commission (Matt 28:18-20) and taking the Gospel to the ends of the earth, to every creature.

3. General revelation at best points to a higher power, while special revelation introduces this higher power personally as the triune Godhead of Scripture who created the world and all that is in it (see Isa 40—48 where Jehovah reminds Israel of this critical truth) and provided the only redeemer in the Lord Jesus Christ.

4. To know about the truth is not nearly as important as personally and redemptively being in fellowship with the Truth, Jesus Christ (John 14:6), who is the only source of eternal life.

5. The ultimate accountability in life will not be how much one knows factually, but rather how well one obeys the commandments of God (Eccl 12:13-14).

6. The New Testament church did not have a mandate to nor did they intellectualize their world; rather, they gospelized it by proclaiming the saving grace of Jesus Christ to a broad range of society members, from key political leaders like King Agrippa (Acts 25:23—26:32) to lowly imprisoned slaves like Onesimus (Philem 10).

7. To moralize, politicize, or intellectualize society without first seeing spiritual conversion is to guarantee only a brief and generally inconsistent change that is shallow, not deep, temporary, not lasting, and ultimately damning, not saving.

What then is the key to embracing a Christian worldview and cultivating a biblical mind-set? Holmes provides this wise, contemporary counsel:

> Since Christ the Truth is the unifying focus of the Biblical world-view, to think "Christianly" is to think "world-viewishly." This means we locate each field of inquiry within a Christian understanding of life as a whole, and that we interpret what we know in that larger context. The key ingredients of such a world-view will include the Biblical conceptions of nature, of man, and of history, in relation to the God we know in Christ. To think "Christianly" is to bring these concepts into our thinking about everything else.[26]

Let it be repeated that this is a both/and approach to cultivating a biblical mind-set, not an either/or response. However, the study of special revelation is the first priority followed in the second place by learning from natural revelation. Solomon, the wisest man who ever lived (1 Kgs 3:12; 4:29-34), wrote the same advice almost three thousand years earlier. Here is the most authoritative statement on the subject of the mind and knowledge, since it is Scripture.

> *The fear of the* LORD *is the beginning of knowledge.*
>
> —PROV 1:7

> *The fear of the* LORD *is the beginning of wisdom, and the knowledge of the Holy One is insight.*
>
> —PROV 9:10; CF. 1 COR 1:20-21

The Alpha and the Omega of the Christian worldview is a *knowledge of God* (2 Cor 2:14; 4:6; Eph 1:17; Col 1:10; 2 Pet 1:2-3, 8; 3:18) and a *knowledge of the truth* (1 Tim 2:4; 2 Tim 2:25; Titus 1:1). Above all, at the very center of a Christian worldview is the Lord Jesus Christ, "in whom are hidden all the treasures of wisdom and knowledge" (Col 2:3). Nothing can be fully understood if God is not known first.

THE CHRISTIAN MIND—WASTED OR INVESTED?

These beautiful words from the pen of Kate B. Wilkinson (1859-1928) should be reflected in every Christian's daily prayer regarding the use of his/her mind.

May the mind of Christ my Savior
Live in me from day to day,
By His love and pow'r controlling
All I do and say.[27]

By praying and then living this way, the Christian's mind will never be wasted but, rather, invested in glorifying God by bringing one's worldview into line with the worldview of God's Scripture. That is why all Christians are enjoined to "think biblically!" and thus recover a Christian worldview.

FURTHER READING

Blamires, Harry. *The Christian Mind*. London: SPCK, 1963. Reprint, Ann Arbor, MI: Servant Books, 1978.

__________. *Recovering the Christian Mind*. Ann Arbor, MI: Servant Books, 1988.

__________. *The Post-Christian Mind*. Ann Arbor, MI: Servant Books, 1999.

Holmes, Arthur F. *All Truth Is God's Truth*. Downers Grove, IL: IVP, 1977.

LaHaye, Tim and David Noebel. *Mind Siege*. Nashville: Word, 2000.

Nash, Ronald H. *The Word of God and the Mind of Man*. Grand Rapids, MI: Zondervan, 1982.

Wells, David F. *No Place for Truth*. Grand Rapids, MI: William B. Eerdmans, 1993.

3

Comprehending Creation[1]

John MacArthur

Thanks to the theory of evolution, naturalism is now the dominant religion of modern society. Less than a century and a half ago, Charles Darwin popularized the credo for this secular religion with his book *The Origin of Species*. Although most of Darwin's theories about the mechanisms of evolution were discarded long ago, the doctrine of evolution itself has managed to achieve the status of a fundamental article of faith in the popular modern mind. Naturalism has now replaced Christianity as the main religion of the western world, and evolution has become naturalism's principal dogma.

Naturalism is the view that every law and every force operating in the universe is natural rather than moral, spiritual, or supernatural. Naturalism is inherently anti-theistic, rejecting the very concept of a personal God. Many assume naturalism therefore has nothing to do with religion. In fact, it is a common misconception that naturalism embodies the very essence of scientific objectivity. Naturalists themselves like to portray their system as a philosophy that stands in opposition to all faith-based worldviews, pretending that it is scientifically and intellectually superior precisely because of its supposed non-religious character.

Not so. *Religion* is exactly the right word to describe naturalism. The entire philosophy is built on a faith-based premise. Its basic presupposition—an a priori rejection of everything supernatural—requires a giant leap of faith. And nearly all its supporting theories must be taken by faith as well.[2]

Consider the dogma of evolution, for example. The notion that natural evolutionary processes can account for the origin of all living species has never been and never will be established as *fact*. Nor is it "scientific" in any true sense of the word. Science deals with what can be observed and reproduced by experimentation. The origin of life can be neither observed nor reproduced in any laboratory. By definition, then, true science can give us no knowledge whatsoever about where we came from or how we got here. Belief in evolutionary theory is a matter of sheer faith. And *dogmatic* belief in any naturalistic theory is no more "scientific" than any other kind of religious faith.

Modern naturalism is often promulgated with a missionary zeal that has powerful religious overtones. The popular fish symbol many Christians put on their cars now has a naturalist counterpart: a fish with feet and the word "Darwin" embossed into its side. The Internet has become naturalism's busiest mission field, where evangelists for the cause aggressively try to deliver benighted souls who still cling to their theistic presuppositions. Judging from the tenor of some of the material I have read seeking to win converts to naturalism, naturalists are often dedicated to their faith with a devout passion that rivals or easily exceeds the fanaticism of any radical religious zealot. Naturalism is clearly as much a religion as any theistic worldview.

The point is further proved by examining the beliefs of those naturalists who claim to be *most* unfettered by religious beliefs. Take, for example, the case of Carl Sagan, perhaps the best-known scientific celebrity of the past couple of decades. A renowned astronomer and media figure, Sagan was overtly antagonistic to biblical theism. But he became the chief televangelist for the religion of naturalism. He preached a worldview that was based entirely on naturalistic assumptions. Underlying all he taught was the firm conviction that everything in the universe has a natural cause and a natural explanation. That belief—a matter of faith, not a truly scientific observation—governed and shaped every one of his theories about the universe.

Sagan examined the vastness and complexity of the universe and concluded—as he was bound to do, given his starting point—that there is nothing greater than the universe itself. So he borrowed divine attributes such as infinitude, eternality, and omnipotence, and he made them properties of the universe itself.

"The cosmos is all that is, or ever was, or ever will be," was Sagan's trademark aphorism, repeated on each episode of his highly-rated television series, *Cosmos*. The statement itself is clearly a tenet of faith, not a scientific conclusion. (Neither Sagan himself nor all the scientists in the world combined could ever examine "all that is, or ever was, or ever will be" by any scientific method.) Sagan's slogan is perfectly illustrative of how modern naturalism mistakes religious dogma for true science.

Sagan's religion was actually a kind of naturalistic pantheism, and his motto sums it up perfectly. He deified the universe and everything in it—insisting that the cosmos itself is that which was, and is, and is to come (cf. Rev 4:8).

Having examined enough of the cosmos to see evidence of the Creator's infinite power and majesty, he imputed that omnipotence and glory to creation itself—precisely the error the apostle Paul describes in Romans 1:20-22:

> *For his invisible attributes, namely, his eternal power and divine nature, have been clearly perceived, ever since the creation of the world, in the things that have been made. So they are without excuse. For although they knew God, they did not honor him as God or give thanks to him, but they became futile in their thinking, and their foolish hearts were darkened. Claiming to be wise, they became fools, and exchanged the glory of the immortal God for images resembling mortal man and birds and animals and reptiles.*

Exactly like the idolaters Paul was describing, Sagan put creation in the Creator's rightful place.

Carl Sagan looked at the universe and saw its greatness and concluded nothing could possibly be greater. His religious presuppositions forced him to deny that the universe was the result of intelligent design. In fact, as a devoted naturalist, he *had* to deny that it was created at all. Therefore he saw it as eternal and infinite—so it naturally took the place of God in his thinking.

The religious character of the philosophy that shaped Sagan's worldview is evident in much of what he wrote and said. His novel *Contact* (made into a major motion picture in 1997) is loaded with religious metaphors and imagery. It's about the discovery of extraterrestrial life, which occurs in December 1999, at the dawn of a new millennium, when the world is rife with messianic expectations and apocalyptic fears. In Sagan's imagination, the discovery of intelligent life elsewhere in the universe becomes the "revelation" that affords a basis for the fusing of science and religion into a worldview that perfectly mirrors Sagan's own belief system—with the cosmos as God and scientists as the new priesthood.

Sagan's religion included the belief that the human race is nothing special. Given the incomprehensible vastness of the universe and the impersonality of it all, how could humanity possibly be important? Sagan concluded that our race is not significant at all. In December 1996, less than three weeks before Sagan died, he was interviewed by Ted Koppel on *Nightline*. Sagan knew he was dying, and Koppel asked him, "Dr. Sagan, do you have any pearls of wisdom that you would like to give to the human race?"

Sagan replied,

> We live on a hunk of rock and metal that circles a humdrum star that is one of 400 billion other stars that make up the Milky Way Galaxy, which is one

> of billions of other galaxies, which make up a universe, which may be one of a very large number—perhaps an infinite number—of other universes. That is a perspective on human life and our culture that is well worth pondering.[3]

In a book published posthumously, Sagan wrote, "Our planet is a lonely speck in the great enveloping cosmic dark. In our obscurity, in all this vastness, there is no hint that help will come from elsewhere to save us from ourselves."[4]

Although Sagan resolutely tried to maintain a semblance of optimism to the bitter end, his religion led where all naturalism inevitably leads: to a sense of utter insignificance and despair. According to his worldview, humanity occupies a tiny outpost—a pale blue speck in a vast sea of galaxies. As far as we know, we are unnoticed by the rest of the universe, accountable to no one, and petty and irrelevant in a cosmos so expansive. It is fatuous to talk of outside help or redemption for the human race. No help is forthcoming. It would be nice if we somehow managed to solve some of our problems, but whether we do or not will ultimately be a forgotten bit of cosmic trivia. That, said Sagan, is a perspective well worth pondering.

All of this underscores the spiritual barrenness of naturalism. The naturalist's religion erases all moral and ethical accountability, and it ultimately abandons all hope for humanity. If the impersonal cosmos is all there is, all there ever was, and all there ever will be, then morality is ultimately moot. If there is no personal Creator to whom humanity is accountable and the survival of the fittest is the governing law of the universe, all the moral principles that normally regulate the human conscience are ultimately groundless—and possibly even deleterious to the survival of our species.

Indeed, the rise of naturalism has meant moral catastrophe for modern society. The most damaging ideologies of the nineteenth and twentieth centuries were all rooted in Darwinism. One of Darwin's earliest champions, Thomas Huxley, gave a lecture in 1893 in which he argued that evolution and ethics are incompatible. He wrote that "the practice of that which is ethically best—what we call goodness or virtue—involves a course of conduct which, in all respects, is opposed to that which leads to success in the cosmic struggle for existence."[5]

Philosophers who incorporated Darwin's ideas were quick to see Huxley's point, conceiving new philosophies that set the stage for the amorality and genocide that characterized so much of the twentieth century.

Karl Marx, for example, self-consciously followed Darwin in the devising of his economic and social theories. He inscribed a copy of his book *Das*

Kapital to Darwin, "from a devoted admirer." He referred to Darwin's *The Origin of Species* as "the book which contains the basis in natural history for our view."[6]

Herbert Spencer's philosophy of "Social Darwinism" applied the doctrines of evolution and the survival of the fittest to human societies. Spencer argued that if nature itself has determined that the strong survive and the weak perish, this rule should govern society as well. Racial and class distinctions simply reflect nature's way. There is therefore no transcendent moral reason to be sympathetic to the struggle of the disadvantaged classes. It is, after all, part of the natural evolutionary process—and society would actually be improved by recognizing the superiority of the dominant classes and encouraging their ascendancy. The racialism of writers such as Ernst Haeckel (who believed that the African races were incapable of culture or higher mental development) was also rooted in Darwinism.

Friedrich Nietzsche's whole philosophy was based on the doctrine of evolution. Nietzsche was bitterly hostile to religion, and particularly Christianity. Christian morality embodied the essence of everything Nietzsche hated; he believed Christ's teaching glorified human weakness and was detrimental to the development of the human race. He scoffed at Christian moral values such as humility, mercy, modesty, meekness, compassion for the powerless, and service to one another. He believed such ideals had bred weakness in society. Nietzsche saw two types of people—the master-class, an enlightened, dominant minority; and the "herd," sheeplike followers who were easily led. And he concluded that the only hope for humanity would be when the master-class evolved into a race of *Ubermenschen* (supermen), unencumbered by religious or social mores, who would take power and bring humanity to the next stage of its evolution.

It's not surprising that Nietzsche's philosophy laid the foundation for the Nazi movement in Germany. What *is* surprising is that at the dawn of the twenty-first century, Nietzsche's reputation has been rehabilitated by philosophical spin-doctors and his writings are once again trendy in the academic world. Indeed, his philosophy—or something very nearly like it—is what naturalism must inevitably return to.

All of these philosophies are based on notions that are diametrically opposed to a biblical view of the nature of man, because they all start by embracing a Darwinian view of the origin of humanity. They are rooted in anti-Christian theories about human origins and the origin of the cosmos, and therefore it is no wonder that they stand in opposition to biblical principles at every level.

The simple fact of the matter is that *all* the philosophical fruits of

Darwinism have been negative, ignoble, and destructive to the very fabric of society. Not one of the major twentieth-century revolutions led by post-Darwinian philosophies ever improved or ennobled any society. Instead, the chief social and political legacy of Darwinian thought is a full spectrum of evil tyranny with Marx-inspired communism at one extreme and Nietzsche-inspired fascism at the other. And the moral catastrophe that has disfigured modern western society is also directly traceable to Darwinism and the rejection of the early chapters of Genesis.

At this moment in history, even though most of modern society is already fully committed to an evolutionary and naturalistic worldview, our society still benefits from the collective memory of a biblical worldview. People in general still believe human life is special. They still hold remnants of biblical morality, such as the notion that love is the greatest virtue (1 Cor 13:13), service to one another is better than fighting for personal dominion (Matt 20:25-27), and humility and submission are superior to arrogance and rebellion (1 Pet 5:5). But to whatever degree secular society still holds those virtues in esteem, it does so entirely without any philosophical foundation. Having already rejected the God revealed in Scripture and embraced instead pure naturalistic materialism, the modern mind has no grounds whatsoever for holding to *any* ethical standard, no reason whatsoever for esteeming "virtue" over "vice," and no justification whatsoever for regarding human life as more valuable than any other form of life. Modern society has already abandoned its moral foundation.

As humanity enters the twenty-first century, an even more frightening prospect looms. Now even the church seems to be losing the will to defend what Scripture teaches about human origins. Many in the church are too intimidated or too embarrassed to affirm the literal truth of the biblical account of creation. They are confused by a chorus of authoritative-sounding voices who insist that it *is* possible—and even pragmatically necessary—to reconcile Scripture with the latest theories of the naturalists.

Of course, theological liberals have long espoused theistic evolution. They have never been reluctant to deny the literal truth of Scripture on any issue. But the new trend is different, comprising evangelicals who contend that it is possible to harmonize Genesis 1—3 with the theories of modern naturalism *without* doing violence to any essential doctrine of Christianity. They affirm evangelical statements of faith. They teach in evangelical institutions. They insist they believe the Bible is inerrant and authoritative. But they are willing to reinterpret Genesis to accommodate evolutionary theory. They express shock and surprise that anyone would question their approach to Scripture. And they sometimes employ the same sort of ridicule and intimidation that religious liberals and atheistic skeptics have always leveled against believers: "You don't *seriously* think the universe is less than a billion years old, do you?"

The result is that over the past couple of decades, large numbers of evangelicals have shown a surprising willingness to take a completely non-evangelical approach to interpreting the early chapters of Genesis. More and more are embracing the view known as "old-earth creationism," which blends some of the principles of biblical creationism with naturalistic and evolutionary theories, seeking to reconcile two opposing worldviews. And in order to accomplish this, old-earth creationists end up explaining away rather than honestly exegeting the biblical creation account.

A handful of scientists who profess Christianity are among those who have led the way in this revisionism—most of them lacking any skill whatsoever in biblical interpretation. But they are setting forth a major reinterpretation of Genesis 1—3 designed specifically to accommodate the current trends of naturalist theory. In their view, the six days of creation in Genesis 1 are long ages, the chronological order of creation is flexible, and most of the details about creation given in Scripture can be written off as poetic or symbolic figures of speech.

Many who should know better—pastors and Christian leaders who defend the faith against false teachings all the time—have been tempted to give up the battle for the opening chapters of Genesis. An evangelical pastor recently approached me after I preached. He was confused and intimidated by several books he had read—all written by ostensibly evangelical authors, yet all arguing that the earth is billions of years old. These authors treat most of the evolutionists' theories as indisputable scientific fact. And in some cases they wield scientific or academic credentials that intimidate readers into thinking their views are the result of superior expertise rather than naturalistic presuppositions they have brought to the biblical text. This pastor asked if I believed it possible that the first three chapters of Genesis might really be just a series of literary devices—a poetic saga giving the "spiritual" meaning of what actually occurred through billions of years of evolution.

I answered unapologetically, "No, I do not." I am convinced that Genesis 1—3 ought to be taken at face value—as the divinely revealed history of creation. Nothing about the Genesis text itself suggests that the biblical creation account is merely symbolic, poetic, allegorical, or mythical. The main thrust of the passage simply cannot be reconciled with the notion that "creation" occurred via natural evolutionary processes over long periods of time. And I don't believe a faithful handling of the biblical text, by any acceptable principles of hermeneutics, can possibly reconcile these chapters with the theory of evolution or any of the other allegedly scientific theories about the origin of the universe.

Furthermore, much like the philosophical and moral chaos that results from naturalism, all sorts of theological mischief ensues when we reject or compromise the literal truth of the biblical account of creation and the fall of Adam.

I realize, of course, that some old-earth creationists *do* hold to the literal creation of Adam and affirm that Adam was a historical figure. But their decision to accept the creation of Adam as literal involves an arbitrary hermeneutical shift at Genesis 1:26-27 and then again at Genesis 2:7. If everything around these verses is handled allegorically or symbolically, it is unjustifiable to take those verses in a literal and historical sense. Therefore, the old-earth creationists' method of interpreting the Genesis text actually undermines the historicity of Adam. Having already decided to treat the creation account itself as myth or allegory, they have no grounds to insist (suddenly and arbitrarily, it seems) that the creation of Adam is literal history. Their belief in a historical Adam is simply inconsistent with their own exegesis of the rest of the text.

But it is a *necessary* inconsistency if one is to affirm an old earth and *remain* evangelical. Because if Adam was not the literal ancestor of the entire human race, then the Bible's explanation of how sin entered the world is impossible to make sense of. Moreover, if we didn't fall in Adam, we cannot be redeemed in Christ, because Christ's position as the Head of the redeemed race exactly parallels Adam's position as the head of the fallen race: "For as in Adam all die, so also in Christ shall all be made alive" (1 Cor 15:22). "Therefore, as one trespass led to condemnation for all men, so one act of righteousness leads to justification and life for all men. For as by the one man's disobedience the many were made sinners, so by the one man's obedience the many will be made righteous" (Rom 5:18-19). "Thus it is written, 'The first man Adam became a living being'; the last Adam became a life-giving spirit" (1 Cor 15:45; cf. 1 Tim 2:13-14; Jude 14).

So in an important sense, everything Scripture says about our salvation through Jesus Christ hinges on the literal truth of what Genesis 1—3 teaches about Adam's creation and fall. There is no more pivotal passage of Scripture.

What "old-earth creationists" (including, to a large degree, even the evangelical ones) are doing with Genesis 1—3 is precisely what religious liberals have always done with *all* of Scripture—spiritualizing and reinterpreting the text allegorically to make it mean what they want it to mean. This is a dangerous way to handle Scripture. And it involves a perilous and unnecessary capitulation to the religious presuppositions of naturalism—not to mention a serious dishonor to God.

Evangelicals who accept an old-earth interpretation of Genesis have embraced a hermeneutic that is hostile to a high view of Scripture. They are bringing to the opening chapters of Scripture a method of biblical interpretation that has built-in anti-evangelical presuppositions. Those who adopt this approach have already embarked on a process that invariably overthrows faith. Churches and colleges that embrace this view will not remain evangelical long.

One popular view held by many old-earth advocates is known as the "framework hypothesis." This is the belief that the "days" of creation are not even distinct eras, but overlapping stages of a long evolutionary process. According to this view, the six days described in Genesis 1 do not set forth a chronology of any kind, but rather a metaphorical "framework" by which the creative process is described for our finite human minds.

This view was apparently first set forth by liberal German theologians in the nineteenth century, but it has been adopted and propagated in recent years by some leading evangelicals, most notably Dr. Meredith G. Kline of Westminster Theological Seminary.[7]

The framework hypothesis starts with the view that the "days" of creation in Genesis 1 are symbolic expressions that have nothing to do with time. Framework advocates note the obvious parallelism between days one and four (the creation of light and the placing of lights in the firmament), days two and five (the separation of air and water and the creation of fish and birds to inhabit air and water), and days three and six (the emergence of the dry land and the creation of land animals)—and they suggest that such parallelism is a clue that the structure of the chapter is merely poetic. Thus, according to this theory, the *sequence* of creation may essentially be disregarded, as if some literary form in the passage nullified its literal meaning.

Naturally, advocates of this view accept the modern scientific theory that the formation of the earth required several billion years. They claim the biblical account is nothing more than a metaphorical framework that should overlay our scientific understanding of creation. The language and details of Genesis 1 are unimportant, they say; the only truth this passage aims to teach us is that the hand of divine Providence guided the evolutionary process. The Genesis creation account is thus reduced to a literary device—an extended metaphor that is not to be accepted at face value.

But if the Lord wanted to teach us that creation took place in six literal days, how could He have stated it more plainly than Genesis does? The length of the days is defined by periods of day and night that are governed after day four by the sun and moon. The week itself defines the pattern of human labor and rest. The days are marked by the passage of morning and evening. How could these *not* signify the chronological progression of God's creative work?

The problem with the framework hypothesis is that it employs a destructive method of interpretation. If the plain meaning of Genesis 1 may be written off and the language treated as nothing more than a literary device, why not do the same with Genesis 3? Indeed, most theological liberals *do* insist that the talking serpent in chapter 3 signals a fable or a metaphor, and therefore they reject that passage as a literal and historical record of how humanity fell into sin. Where does metaphor ultimately end and history begin? After the Flood? After the Tower of Babel? And why there? Why not regard all the biblical miracles as literary devices? Why could not the resurrection itself be dismissed as a mere allegory? In the words of E. J. Young, "If the 'framework' hypothesis were applied to the narratives of the virgin birth or the resurrection or Romans 5:12ff., it could as effectively serve to minimize the importance of the content of those passages as it now does the content of the first chapter of Genesis."[8]

Young points out the fallacy of the "framework" hypothesis:

> The question must be raised, "If a nonchronological view of the days be admitted, what is the purpose of mentioning six days?" For, once we reject the chronological sequence which Genesis gives, we are brought to the point where we can really say very little about the content of Genesis one. It is impossible to hold that there are two trios of days, each paralleling the other. Day four . . . speaks of God's placing the light-bearers in the firmament. The firmament, however, had been made on the second day. If the fourth and the first days are two aspects of the same thing, then the second day also (which speaks of the firmament) must precede days one and four. If this procedure be allowed, with its wholesale disregard of grammar, why may we not be consistent and equate all four of these days with the first verse of Genesis? There is no defense against such a procedure, once we abandon the clear language of the text. In all seriousness it must be asked, Can we believe that the first chapter of Genesis intends to teach that day two preceded days one and four? To ask that question is to answer it.[9]

The simple, rather obvious, fact is that no one would ever think the time-frame for creation was anything other than a normal week of seven days from reading the Bible and allowing it to interpret itself. The Fourth Commandment makes no sense whatsoever apart from an understanding that the days of God's creative work parallel a normal human work week.

The framework hypothesis is the direct result of making modern scientific theory a hermeneutical guideline by which to interpret Scripture. The basic presupposition behind the framework hypothesis is the notion that science speaks with more authority about origins and the age of the earth than Scripture does. Those who embrace such a view have in effect made science an authority *over* Scripture. They are permitting scientific hypotheses—mere human opinions that have no divine authority whatsoever—to be the hermeneutical rule by which Scripture is interpreted.

There is no warrant for that. Modern scientific opinion is not a valid hermeneutic for interpreting Genesis (or any other portion of Scripture, for that matter). Scripture is God-breathed (2 Tim 3:16)—inspired truth from God. "For no prophecy was ever produced by the will of man, but men spoke from God as they were carried along by the Holy Spirit" (2 Pet 1:21). Jesus summed the point up perfectly when He said, "Thy word is truth" (John 17:17, KJV). The Bible is *supreme* truth, and therefore it is the standard by which scientific theory should be evaluated, not vice versa.

And Scripture *always* speaks with absolute authority. It is as authoritative when it instructs us as it is when it commands us. It is as true when it tells the future as it is when it records the past. Although it is not a textbook on science, wherever it intersects with scientific data, it speaks with the same authority as when it gives us moral precepts. Although many have tried to set science against Scripture, science never has disproved one jot or tittle of the Bible—and it never will.

It is therefore a serious mistake to imagine that modern scientists can speak more authoritatively than Scripture on the subject of origins. Scripture is God's own eyewitness account of what happened in the beginning. When it deals with the origin of the universe, all science can offer is conjecture. Science has proven nothing that negates the Genesis record. In fact, the Genesis record answers the mysteries of science.

A clear pattern for interpreting Genesis is given to us in the New Testament. If the language of early Genesis was meant to be interpreted figuratively, we could expect to see Genesis interpreted in the New Testament in a figurative sense. After all, the New Testament is itself inspired Scripture, so it is the Creator's own commentary on the Genesis record.

What do we find in the New Testament? In every New Testament reference to Genesis, the events recorded by Moses are treated as historical events. And in particular, the first three chapters of Genesis are consistently treated as a literal record of historical events. The New Testament affirms, for example, the creation of Adam in the image of God (Jas 3:9).

Paul wrote to Timothy, "For Adam was formed first, then Eve; and Adam was not deceived, but the woman was deceived and became a transgressor"

(1 Tim 2:13-14). In 1 Corinthians 11:8-9, he writes, "For man was not made from woman, but woman from man. Neither was man created for woman, but woman for man."

Paul's presentation of the doctrine of original sin in Romans 5:12-21 depends on a historical Adam and a literal interpretation of the account in Genesis about how he fell. Furthermore, everything Paul has to say about the doctrine of justification by faith depends on *that.* "For as in Adam all die, so also in Christ shall all be made alive" (1 Cor 15:22). Clearly Paul regarded both the creation and fall of Adam as history, not allegory. Jesus Himself referred to the creation of Adam and Eve as a historical event (Mark 10:6). To question the historicity of these events is to undermine the very essence of Christian doctrine.

Moreover, if Scripture itself treats the creation and fall of Adam as historical events, there is no warrant for treating the rest of the creation account as allegory or literary device. Nowhere in all of Scripture are any of these events handled as merely symbolic.

In fact, when the New Testament refers to creation (e.g., Mark 13:19; John 1:3; Acts 4:24; 14:15; 2 Cor 4:6; Col 1:16; Heb 1:2, 10; Rev 4:11; 10:6; 14:7), it always refers to a past, completed event—an immediate work of God, not a still-occurring process of evolution. The promised New Creation, a running theme in both Old and New Testaments, is portrayed as an immediate fiat creation too—not an eons-long process (Isa 65:17). In fact, the model for the New Creation is the original creation (cf. Rom 8:21; Rev 21:1, 5).

Hebrews 11:3 even makes belief in creation by divine fiat the very essence of faith itself: "By faith we understand that the universe was created by the word of God, so that what is seen was not made out of things that are visible." Creation *ex nihilo* is the clear and consistent teaching of the Bible.

Evolution was introduced as an atheistic alternative to the biblical view of creation. According to evolution, man created God rather than vice versa. And as we have seen, the evolutionists' ultimate agenda is to eliminate faith in God altogether and thereby do away with moral accountability.

Intuition suggests a series of questions to the human mind when we contemplate our origin: Who is in control of the universe? Is there Someone who is sovereign—a Lawgiver? Is there a universal Judge? Is there a transcendent moral standard to live by? Is there Someone to whom will we be accountable? Will there be a final assessment of how we live our lives? Will there be any final judgment?

Those are the very questions evolution was invented to avoid.

Evolution was devised to explain away the God of the Bible—not because evolutionists really believed a Creator was unnecessary to explain how things began, but because they did not want the God of Scripture as their Judge. Marvin L. Lubenow writes,

> The real issue in the creation/evolution debate is not the *existence* of God. The real issue is the *nature* of God. To think of evolution as basically atheistic is to misunderstand the uniqueness of evolution. Evolution was not designed as a general attack against theism. It was designed as a specific attack against the God of the Bible, and the God of the Bible is clearly revealed through the doctrine of creation. Obviously, if a person is an atheist, it would be normal for him to also be an evolutionist. But evolution is as comfortable with theism as it is with atheism. An evolutionist is perfectly free to choose any god he wishes, as long as it is not the God of the Bible. The gods allowed by evolution are private, subjective, and artificial. They bother no one and make no absolute ethical demands. However, the God of the Bible is the Creator, Sustainer, Savior, and Judge. All are responsible to him. He has an agenda that conflicts with that of sinful humans. For man to be created in the image of God is very awesome. For God to be created in the image of man is very comfortable.[10]

To put it simply, evolution was invented in order to eliminate the God of Genesis and thereby to oust the Lawgiver and obliterate the inviolability of His law. Evolution is simply the latest means our fallen race has devised in order to suppress our innate knowledge and the biblical testimony that there is a God and that we are accountable to Him (cf. Rom 1:28). By embracing evolution, modern society aims to do away with morality, responsibility, and guilt. Society has embraced evolution with such enthusiasm because people imagine that it eliminates the Judge and leaves them free to do whatever they want without guilt and without consequences.

The evolutionary lie is so pointedly antithetical to Christian truth that it would seem unthinkable for evangelical Christians to compromise with evolutionary science in any degree. But over the past century and a half of evolutionary propaganda, evolutionists have had remarkable success in getting evangelicals to meet them halfway. Remarkably, many modern evangelicals—perhaps it would even be fair to say *most* people who call themselves evangelicals today—have already been convinced that the Genesis account of creation is not a true historical record. Thus they have not only capitulated to evolutionary doctrine at its starting point, but they have also embraced a view that undermines the authority of Scripture at *its* starting point.

So-called theistic evolutionists who try to marry humanistic theories of modern science with biblical theism may claim they are doing so because they love God, but the truth is that they love God a little and their academic reputations a lot. By undermining the historicity of Genesis they are undermining faith itself. Give evolutionary doctrine the throne and make the Bible its servant, and you have laid the foundation for spiritual disaster.

Scripture, not science, is the ultimate test of all truth. And the further evangelicalism gets from that conviction, the less evangelical and more humanistic it becomes.

Scripture cautions against false "knowledge" (1 Tim 6:20)—particularly so-called "scientific" knowledge that opposes the truth of Scripture. When what is being passed off as "science" turns out to be nothing more than a faith-based worldview that is hostile to the truth of Scripture, our duty to be on guard is magnified. And when naturalistic and atheistic presuppositions are being aggressively peddled as if they were established scientific fact, Christians ought to expose such lies for what they are and oppose them all the more vigorously. The abandonment of a biblical view of creation has already borne abundant evil fruit in modern society. Now is no time for the church to retreat or compromise on these issues. To weaken our commitment to the biblical view of creation would start a chain of disastrous moral, spiritual, and theological ramifications in the church that will greatly exacerbate the terrible moral chaos that already has begun the unraveling of secular society.

With that in mind I undertook an earnest study of Genesis a couple of years ago. Although the bulk of my ministry has been devoted to a verse-by-verse exposition of the whole New Testament, I recently turned to the Old Testament and began preaching a series on Genesis in our church. This material is the fruit of my research and teaching in Genesis 1—3. We find there the foundation of every doctrine that is essential to the Christian faith. And the more carefully I have studied those opening chapters of Scripture, the more I have seen that they are the vital foundation for everything we believe as Christians.

Sadly, it is a foundation that is being systematically undermined by the very institutions that should be most vigorously defending it. More and more Christian educational institutions, apologists, and theologians are abandoning faith in the literal truth of Genesis 1—3. I recall reading a survey a few years ago that revealed that in one of America's leading evangelical associations, whose membership boasts scores of evangelical Bible colleges and universities, only five or six college-level schools remain solidly opposed to the old-earth view of creation. The rest are open to a reinterpretation of Genesis 1—3 that accommodates evolutionary theories. Scores of well-known Bible teachers and apologists see the whole question as moot, and some even aggressively argue that a literal approach to Genesis is detrimental to the credibility of Christianity. They have given up the battle—or worse, joined the attack against biblical creationism.

I'm thankful for those who are still faithfully resisting the trend—organizations like Answers in Genesis, the Creation Research Society, and the Institute for Creation Research. These organizations and others like them involve many expert scientists who challenge the presuppositions of evolutionists on technical and scientific grounds. They clearly demonstrate that scientific proficiency is not incompatible with faith in the literal truth of Scripture—and that the battle for the beginning is ultimately a battle between two mutually exclusive faiths—faith in Scripture versus faith in anti-theistic hypotheses. It is not really a battle between *science* and the Bible.

My aim is to examine what Scripture teaches about creation. Although I am convinced that the truth of Scripture has scientific integrity, for the most part I intend to leave the scientific defense of creationism to those who have the most expertise in science. My purpose is chiefly to examine what Scripture teaches about the origin of the universe and humanity's fall into sin, and to show why it is incompatible with the naturalists' beliefs and the evolutionists' theories.

As Christians, we believe the Bible is truth revealed to us by God, who is the true Creator of the universe. That belief is the basic foundation of all genuine Christianity. It is utterly incompatible with the speculative presuppositions of the naturalists.

In Scripture the Creator Himself has revealed to us everything essential for life and godliness. And it starts with an account of creation. If the biblical creation account is in any degree unreliable, the rest of Scripture stands on a shaky foundation.

But the foundation is *not* shaky. The more I understand what God has revealed to us about our origin, the more I see clearly that the foundation stands firm. I agree with those who say it is time for the people of God to take a fresh look at the biblical account of creation. But I disagree with those who think that calls for any degree of capitulation to the transient theories of naturalism. Only an honest look at Scripture, with sound principles of hermeneutics, will yield the right understanding of the creation and fall of our race.

The Bible gives a clear and cogent account of the beginnings of the cosmos and humanity. There is absolutely no reason for an intelligent mind to balk at accepting it as a literal account of the origin of our universe. Although the biblical account clashes at many points with naturalistic and evolutionary *hypotheses*, it is not in conflict with a single scientific *fact*. Indeed, all the geological, astronomical, and scientific data can be easily reconciled with the biblical account. The conflict is not between science and Scripture, but between the biblicist's confident faith and the naturalist's willful skepticism.

To many, having been indoctrinated in schools where the line between hypothesis and fact is systematically and deliberately being blurred, that may sound naive or unsophisticated, but it is nonetheless a fact. Again, science has never disproved one word of Scripture, and it never will. On the other hand, evolutionary theory has always been in conflict with Scripture and always will be. But the notion that the universe evolved through a series of natural processes remains an unproven and untestable hypothesis, and therefore it is not "science." There is no proof whatsoever that the universe evolved naturally. Evolution is a mere theory—and a questionable, constantly-changing one at that. Ultimately, if accepted at all, it must be taken by sheer faith.

How much better to base our faith on the sure foundation of God's Word! There is no ground of knowledge equal to or superior to Scripture. Unlike scientific theory, it is eternally unchanging. Unlike the opinions of man, its truth is revealed by the Creator Himself! It is not, as many suppose, at odds with science. True science has always affirmed the teaching of Scripture. Archaeology, for instance, has demonstrated the truthfulness of the biblical record time and time again. Wherever Scripture's record of history may be examined and sought to be either proved or disproved by archaeological evidence or reliable independent documentary evidence, the biblical record has always been verified. There is no valid reason whatsoever to doubt or distrust the biblical record of creation, and there is certainly no need to adjust the biblical account to try to make it fit the latest fads in evolutionary theory.

Therefore my approach in this essay will be simply to examine what the biblical text teaches about creation. My goal is not to write a polemic against current evolutionary thinking. I don't intend to get into in-depth scientific arguments related to the origin of our universe. Where scientific fact intersects with the biblical record, I will highlight that. But my chief aim is to examine what the Bible teaches about the origin of the universe, and then look at the moral, spiritual, and eternal ramifications of biblical creationism to see what it has to do with people in today's world.

I'm indebted to several authors who have treated this subject before and whose works were very helpful in framing my own thoughts on these matters. Chief among them would be Douglas F. Kelly,[11] John Ankerberg and John Weldon,[12] Phillip E. Johnson,[13] Henry Morris,[14] and Ken Ham.[15]

Again, a biblical understanding of the creation and fall of humanity establishes the necessary foundation for the Christian worldview. Everything Scripture teaches about sin and redemption assumes the literal truth of the first three chapters of Genesis. If we wobble to any degree on the truth of this passage, we undermine the very foundations of our faith.

If Genesis 1—3 doesn't tell us the truth, why should we believe anything else in the Bible? Without a right understanding of our origin, we have no way to understand *anything* about our spiritual existence. We cannot know our purpose, and we cannot be certain of our destiny. After all, if God is not the Creator, then maybe He's not the Redeemer either. If we cannot believe the opening chapters of Scripture, how can we be certain of *anything* the Bible says?

Much depends, therefore, on a right understanding of these early chapters of Genesis. These chapters are too often mishandled by people whose real aim is not to understand what the text actually teaches but who want to adjust it to fit a scientific theory. The approach is all wrong. Since creation cannot be observed or replicated in a laboratory, science is not a trustworthy place to seek answers about the origin and fall of humanity. Ultimately, the only reliable source of truth about our origin is what has been revealed by the Creator Himself. That means the biblical text should be our starting place.

I am convinced the correct interpretation of Genesis 1—3 is the one that comes naturally from a straightforward reading of the text. It teaches us that the universe is relatively young, albeit with an appearance of age and maturity—and that all of creation was accomplished in the span of six literal days.

To those who will inevitably complain that such a view is credulous and unsophisticated, my reply is that it is certainly superior to the irrational notion that an ordered and incomprehensibly complex universe sprung by accident from nothingness and emerged by chance into the marvel that it is.

Scripture offers the only accurate explanations that can be found anywhere about how our race began, where our moral sense originated, why we cannot seem to do what our own consciences tells us is right, and how we can be redeemed from this hopeless situation. Scripture is not merely the best of several possible explanations. It is the Word of God.

Creation: Believe It or Not

It's hard to imagine anything more absurd than the naturalist's formula for the origin of the universe: *Nobody times nothing equals everything.* There is no Creator; there was no design or purpose. Everything we see simply emerged and evolved by pure chance from a total void.

Ask the typical naturalist what he believes about the beginning of all things, and you are likely to hear about the Big Bang theory—the notion that the universe is the product of an immense explosion. As if an utterly violent and chaotic beginning could result in all the synergy and order we observe in the cosmos around us. But what was the catalyst that touched off that Big Bang in the first place? (And what, in turn, was the catalyst for *that*?) Something incredibly large had to fuel the original explosion. Where did that "something" originate? A Big Bang out of nowhere quite simply could *not* have been the beginning of all things.

Is the material universe itself eternal, as some claim? And if it is, why hasn't it wound down? For that matter, what set it in motion to begin with? What is the source of the energy that keeps it going? Why hasn't entropy caused it to devolve into a state of inertia and chaos, rather than (as the evolutionist must hypothesize) apparently developing into a more orderly and increasingly sophisticated system as the Big Bang expands?

The vast array of insurmountable problems for the naturalist begins at the most basic level. What was the First Cause that caused everything else? Where did matter come from? Where did energy come from? What holds everything together, and what keeps everything going? How could life, self-consciousness, and rationality evolve from inanimate, inorganic matter? Who *designed* the many complex and interdependent organisms and sophisticated ecosystems we observe? Where did *intelligence* originate? Are we to think of the universe as a massive perpetual-motion apparatus with some sort of impersonal "intelligence" of its own? Or is there, after all, a personal, intelligent Designer who created everything and set it all in motion?

Those are vital metaphysical questions that *must* be answered if we are to understand the meaning and value of life itself. Philosophical naturalism, because of its materialistic and anti-supernatural presuppositions, is utterly incapable of offering *any* answers to those questions. In fact, the most basic dogma of naturalism is that everything happens by natural processes; nothing is supernatural; and therefore there can be no personal Creator. That means there can be no design and no purpose for anything. Naturalism therefore can provide no philosophical basis for believing that human life is particularly valuable or in any way significant.

On the contrary, the naturalist, if he is true to his principles, must ultimately conclude that humanity is a freak accident without any purpose or real importance. Naturalism is therefore a formula for futility and meaninglessness, erasing the image of God from our race's collective self-image, depreciating the value of human life, undermining human dignity, and subverting morality.

Evolution Is Degrading to Humanity

The drift of modern society proves the point. We are witnessing the abandonment of moral standards and the loss of humanity's sense of destiny.

Rampant crime, drug abuse, sexual perversion, rising suicide rates, and the abortion epidemic are all symptoms that human life is being systematically devalued and an utter sense of futility is sweeping over society. These trends are directly traceable to the ascent of evolutionary theory.

And why not? If evolution is true, humans are just one of many species that evolved from common ancestors. We're no better than animals, and we ought not to think that we are. If we evolved from sheer matter, why should we esteem what is spiritual? In fact, if everything evolved from matter, nothing "spiritual" is real. We ourselves are ultimately no better than or different from any other living species. We are nothing more than protoplasm waiting to become manure.

As a matter of fact, that is precisely the rationale behind the modern animal-rights movement, a movement whose *raison d'être* is the utter degradation of the human race. Naturally, all radical animal-rights advocates are evolutionists. Their belief system is an inevitable byproduct of evolutionary theory.

People for the Ethical Treatment of Animals (PETA) is well known for its stance that animal rights are equal to (or more important than) human rights. They maintain that killing any animal for food is the moral equivalent of murder; eating meat is virtually cannibalism; and man is a tyrant species, detrimental to his environment.

PETA opposes the keeping of pets and "companion animals"—including guide dogs for the blind. A 1988 statement distributed by the organization includes this: "As John Bryant has written in his book *Fettered Kingdoms,* [companion animals] are like slaves, even if well-kept slaves."

Ingrid Newkirk, PETA's controversial founder, says, "There is no rational basis for saying that a human being has special rights. . . . A rat is a pig is a dog is a boy."[16] Newkirk told a *Washington Post* reporter that the atrocities of Nazi Germany pale by comparison to killing animals for food: "Six million Jews died in concentration camps, but six *billion* broiler chickens will die this year in slaughterhouses."[17]

Clearly, Ms. Newkirk is *more* outraged by the killing of chickens for food than she is by the wholesale slaughter of human beings. One gets the impression she would not necessarily consider the extinction of humanity an undesirable thing. In fact, she and other animal-rights advocates often sound downright misanthropic. She told a reporter, "I don't have any reverence for life, only for the entities themselves. I would rather see a blank space where I am. This will sound like fruitcake stuff again but at least I wouldn't be harming anything."[18] And the summer issue of *Wild Earth* magazine, a journal promoting radical environmentalism, included a manifesto for the extinction of the human race, written under the pseudonym "Les U. Knight." The article said, "If you haven't given voluntary human extinction much thought before, the idea of a world with no people in it may seem strange. But, if you give it a chance, I think you might agree that the extinction of Homo sapiens would mean survival for millions, if not billions, of Earth-dwelling species. . . . Phasing out the human race will solve every problem on earth, social and environmental."[19]

That is worse than merely stupid, irrational, immoral, or humiliating; it is *deadly*.

But there's even an organization called The Church of Euthanasia. Their web page advocates suicide, abortion, cannibalism, and sodomy as the main ways to decrease the human population. Although the web page contains elements of parody deliberately designed for shock value,[20] the people behind it are deadly serious in their opposition to the continuance of the human race. They include detailed instructions for committing suicide. The one commandment church members are required to obey is "Thou shalt not procreate." By deliberately making their views sound as outrageous as possible, they have received widespread coverage on talk shows and tabloid-style news programs. They take advantage of such publicity to recruit members for their cause. Despite their shocking message, they have evidently been able to persuade numerous people that the one species on earth that *ought* to be made extinct is humanity. Their web site boasts that people in the thousands have paid the ten dollar membership fee to become "church members."

That sort of lunacy is rooted in the belief that humanity is simply the product of evolution—a mere animal with no purpose, no destiny, and no likeness to the Creator. After all, if we got where we are by a natural evolutionary process, there can be no validity whatsoever to the notion that our race bears the image of God. We ultimately have no more dignity than an amoeba. And we *certainly* have no mandate from the Almighty to subdue the rest of creation.

And if a human being is nothing more than an animal in the process of evolving, who can argue against the animal-rights movement? Even the most radical animal-rights position is justified in a naturalistic and evolutionary worldview. If we really evolved from animals, we are in fact just animals ourselves. And if evolution is correct, it is a sheer accident that man evolved a superior intellect. If random mutations had occurred differently, apes might be running the planet and humanoids would be in the zoo. What right do we have to exercise dominion over other species that have not yet had the opportunity to evolve to a more advanced state?

Indeed, if man is merely a product of natural evolutionary processes, then he is ultimately nothing more than the accidental byproduct of thousands of haphazard genetic mutations. He is just one more animal that evolved from amoeba, and he is probably not even the highest life-form that will eventually evolve. So what is special about him? Where is his meaning? Where is his dignity? Where is his value? What is his purpose? Obviously he has none.[21]

It is only a matter of time before a society steeped in naturalistic belief fully embraces such thinking and casts off all moral and spiritual restraint. In fact, that process has begun already. If you doubt that, consider some of the televised debauchery aimed at the MTV/Jerry Springer generation.

Evolution Is Hostile to Reason

Evolution is as irrational as it is amoral. In place of God as Creator, the evolutionist has substituted chance—sheer fortune, accident, happenstance, serendipity, coincidence, random events, blind luck. Chance is the engine most evolutionists believe drives the evolutionary process. Chance is therefore the ultimate creator.

Naturalism essentially teaches that over time and out of sheer chaos, matter evolved into everything we see today by pure chance. And this all happened without any particular design. Given enough time and enough random events, the evolutionist says, *anything* is possible. And the evolution of our world with all its intricate ecosystems and complex organisms is therefore simply the inadvertent result of a very large number of indiscriminate but extremely fortuitous accidents of nature. Everything is the way it is simply by the luck of the draw. And thus chance itself has been elevated to the role of creator.

John Ankerberg and John Weldon point out that matter, time, and chance constitute the evolutionists' holy trinity. Indeed, these three things are all that is eternal and omnipotent in the evolutionary scheme: matter, time, and chance. Together they have formed the cosmos as we know it. And they have usurped God in the evolutionist's mind. Ankerberg and Weldon quote Jacques Monod, 1965 Nobel Prize-winner for his work in biochemistry. In his book *Chance and Necessity,* Monod wrote, "[Man] is alone in the universe's unfeeling immensity, out of which he emerged by chance. . . . Chance *alone* is at the source of every innovation, of all creation in the biosphere. Pure chance, absolutely free but blind, [is] at the very root of the stupendous edifice of evolution."[22]

Obviously, that is a far cry from being created in the image of God. It is also utterly irrational. The evolutionary idea not only strips man of his dignity and his value, but it also eliminates the ground of his rationality. Because if everything happens by chance, then in the ultimate sense, nothing can possibly have any real purpose or meaning. And it's hard to think of any philosophical starting point that is more irrational than that.

But a moment's reflection will reveal that chance simply *cannot* be the cause of anything (much less the cause of *everything*). Chance is not a force. The only legitimate sense of the word *chance* has to do with mathematical probability. If you flip a coin again and again, quotients of mathematical probability suggest that it will land tails-up about fifty times out of a hundred. Thus we say that when you flip a coin, there's a fifty-fifty "chance" it will come up tails.

But chance is not a force that can actually flip the coin. Chance is not an intellect that designs the pattern of mathematical probabilities. Chance *determines* nothing. Mathematical probability is merely a way of measuring what actually *does* happen.

Yet in naturalistic and evolutionary parlance, chance becomes something that determines what happens in the absence of any other cause or design. Consider Jacques Monod's remark again: "Chance . . . is at the source of every innovation, of all creation." In effect, naturalists have imputed to *chance* the ability to cause and determine what occurs. And that is an irrational concept.

There are no uncaused events. Every effect is determined by some cause. Even the flip of a coin simply cannot occur without a definite cause. And common sense tells us that whether the coin comes up heads or tails is also determined by *something*. A number of factors (including the precise amount of force with which the coin is flipped and the distance it must fall before hitting the ground) determine the number of revolutions and bounces it makes before landing on one side or the other. Although the forces that determine the flip of a coin may be impossible for us to control precisely, it is those forces, not "chance," that determine whether we get heads or tails. What may appear totally random and undetermined to us is nonetheless definitively determined by *something*.[23] It is not caused by mere chance, because chance simply does not exist as a force or a cause. Chance is nothing.

Fortune was a goddess in the Greek pantheon. Evolutionists have enshrined chance in a similar way. They have taken the myth of chance and made it responsible for all that happens. Chance has been transformed into a force of causal power, so that *nothing* is the cause of *everything*. What could be *more* irrational than that? It turns all of reality into sheer chaos. It therefore makes everything irrational and incoherent.

The entire concept is so fraught with problems from a rational and philosophical viewpoint that one hardly knows where to begin. But let's begin at the beginning. Where did matter come from in the first place? The naturalist would have to say either that all matter is eternal, or that everything appeared by chance out of nothing. The latter option is clearly irrational.

But suppose the naturalist opts to believe that matter is eternal. An obvious question arises: What caused the first event that originally set the evolutionary process in motion? The only answer available to the naturalist is that chance made it happen. It literally came out of nowhere. No one and nothing made it happen. That, too, is clearly irrational.

So in order to avoid *that* dilemma, some naturalists assume an eternal chain of random events that operate on the material universe. They end up with an eternal but constantly changing material universe governed by an endless chain of purely random events—all culminating in magnificent design without a designer, and everything happening without any ultimate cause. At the end of the day, it is still irrational. It evacuates purpose, destiny, and meaning from everything in the universe. And it therefore it leaves no ground for anything rational.

In other words, nihilism is the only philosophy that works with naturalism. *Nihilism* is a philosophy that says everything is entirely without meaning, without logic, without reason. The universe itself is incoherent and irrational. Reason has been deposed by pure chance.

And such a view of chance is the polar opposite of reason. Commonsense logic suggests that every watch has a watchmaker. Every building has a builder. Every structure has an architect. Every arrangement has a plan. Every plan has a designer. And every design has a purpose. We see the universe, infinitely more complex than any watch and infinitely greater than any man-made structure, and it is natural to conclude that Someone infinitely powerful and infinitely intelligent made it. "For his invisible attributes, namely, his eternal power and divine nature, have been clearly perceived, ever since the creation of the world, in the things that have been made. So they are without excuse" (Rom 1:20).

But naturalists look at the universe, and despite all the intricate marvels it holds, they conclude that no one made it. Chance brought it about. It happened by accident. That is not logical. It is absurd.

Abandon logic and you are left with pure nonsense. In many ways the naturalists' deification of chance is worse than all the various myths of other false religions, because it obliterates all meaning and sense from everything. But it is, once again, pure religion of the most pagan variety, requiring a spiritually fatal leap of faith into an abyss of utter irrationality. It is the age-old religion of fools (Ps 14:1)—but in modern, "scientific" dress.

What could prompt anyone to embrace such a system? Why would someone opt for a worldview that eliminates all that is rational? It boils down to the sheer love of sin. People want to be comfortable in their sin, and there is no way to do that without eliminating God. Get rid of God, and you erase all fear of the consequences of sin. So even though sheer irrationality is ultimately the only viable alternative to the God of Scripture, multitudes have opted for irrationality just so they could live guilt-free and shamelessly with their own sin. It is as simple as that.

Either there is a God who created the universe and sovereignly rules His creation, or everything was caused by blind chance. The two ideas are mutually exclusive. If chance rules, God cannot. If God rules, there's no room for chance. Make chance the cause of the universe and you have effectively done away with God.

As a matter of fact, if chance as a determinative force or a cause exists even in the frailest form, God has been dethroned. The sovereignty of God and "chance" are inherently incompatible. If chance causes or determines *anything,* God is not truly God.

But again, chance is not a force. Chance cannot make anything happen. Chance is nothing. It simply does not exist. And therefore it has no power to do anything. It cannot be the cause of any effect. It is an imaginary hocus-pocus. It is contrary to every law of science, every principle of logic, and every intuition of sheer common sense. Even the most basic principles of thermodynamics, physics, and biology suggest that chance simply cannot be the determinative force that has brought about the order and interdependence we see in our universe—much less the diversity of life we find on our own planet. Ultimately, chance simply cannot account for the origin of life and intelligence.

One of the oldest principles of rational philosophy is "*Ex nihilo, nihilo fit*" ("out of nothing, nothing comes"). And chance is nothing. Naturalism is rational suicide.

When scientists attribute instrumental power to chance they have left the realm of reason, they have left the domain of science. They have turned to pulling rabbits out of hats. They have turned to fantasy. Insert the idea of chance, and all scientific investigation ultimately becomes chaotic and absurd. That is precisely why evolution does not deserve to be deemed true science; it is nothing more than an irrational religion—the religion of those who want to sin without guilt.

Someone once estimated that the number of random genetic factors involved in the evolution of a tapeworm from an amoeba would be comparable to placing a monkey in a room with a typewriter and allowing him to strike the keys at random until he accidentally produced a perfectly spelled and perfectly punctuated typescript of Hamlet's soliloquy. And the odds of getting all the mutations necessary to evolve a starfish from a one-celled creature are comparable to asking a hundred blind people to make ten random moves each with five Rubik's cubes, and finding all five cubes perfectly solved at the end of the process. The odds against *all* earth's life-forms evolving from a single cell are, in a word, impossible.

Nonetheless, the absurdity of naturalism goes largely unchallenged today in universities and colleges. Turn on the Discovery Channel or pick up an issue of *National Geographic* and you are likely to be exposed to the assumption that chance exists as a force—as if mere chance spontaneously generated everything in the universe.

One Nobel laureate, Harvard professor George Wald, acknowledged the utter absurdity of this. Pondering the vast array of factors both real and hypothetical that would have to arise spontaneously all at once in order for inanimate matter to "evolve" into even the most primitive one-celled form of life, he wrote, "One has only to contemplate the magnitude of this task to concede that the spontaneous generation of a living organism is impossible." Then he added, "Yet here we are—as a result, I believe, of spontaneous generation."[24] How did Wald believe this "impossibility" came about? He answered: "Time is in fact the hero of the plot. The time with which we have to deal is of the order of two billion years. What we regard as impossible on the basis of human experience is meaningless here. Given so much time, the 'impossible' becomes possible, the possible probable, and the probable virtually certain. One has only to wait: time itself performs the miracles."[25] Given enough time, that which is impossible becomes "virtually certain." That is sheer double-talk. And it perfectly illustrates the blind faith that underlies naturalistic religion.

There is no viable explanation of the universe without God. So many immense and intricate wonders could not exist without a designer. There's only one possible explanation for it all, and that is the creative power of an all-wise God. He created and sustains the universe, and He gives meaning to it. And without Him, there is ultimately no meaning in anything. Without Him, we are left with only the absurd notion that everything emerged from nothing without a cause and without any reason. Without Him we are stuck with that absurd formula of the evolutionist: nothing times nobody equals everything.

Evolution Is Antithetical to the Truth God Has Revealed

By contrast, the actual record of creation is found in Genesis 1:1: "In the beginning, God created the heavens and the earth." It would be hard to state an answer to the great cosmic question any more simply or directly than that.

The words of Genesis 1:1 are precise and concise beyond mere human composition. They account for everything evolution *cannot* explain. Evolutionary philosopher Herbert Spencer, one of Darwin's earliest and most enthusiastic advocates, outlined five "ultimate scientific ideas": time, force, action, space, and matter.[26] These are categories that (according to Spencer) comprise everything that is susceptible to scientific examination. That simple taxonomy, Spencer believed, encompasses all that truly exists in the universe. *Everything* that can be known or observed by science fits into one of those categories, Spencer claimed, and nothing can be truly said to "exist" outside of them.

Spencer's materialistic worldview is immediately evident in the fact that his categories leave room for nothing spiritual. But set aside for a moment the rather obvious fact that something as obvious as human intellect and emotion do not quite fit into any of Spencer's categories. A moment's reflection will reveal that evolutionary principles *still* cannot account for the actual origin of *any* of Spencer's categories.[27] The evolutionist must practically assume the eternality of time, force, action, space, and matter (or at least one of these[28])—and then he or she proceeds from there to hypothesize about how things have developed out of an originally chaotic state.

But Genesis 1:1 accounts for all of Spencer's categories. "In the beginning"—that's *time.* "God"—that's *force.*[29] "Created"—that's *action.* "The heavens"—that's *space.* "And the earth"—that's *matter.* In the first verse of the Bible God laid out plainly what no scientist or philosopher ever cataloged until the nineteenth century. Moreover, what evolution still cannot possibly explain—the actual origin of everything that science can observe—the Bible explains in a few succinct words in the very first verse of Genesis.

About the uniqueness of the Bible's approach to creation, Henry Morris writes,

> Genesis 1:1 is unique in all literature, science, and philosophy. Every other system of cosmogony, whether in ancient religious myths or modern scientific models, starts with eternal matter or energy in some form, from which other entities were supposedly gradually derived by some process. Only the Book of Genesis even attempts to account for the ultimate origin of matter, space, and time; and it does so uniquely in terms of special creation.[30]

And thus in that very first verse of Scripture, each reader is faced with a simple choice: Either you believe God *did* create the heavens and the earth, or you believe He *did not.* If He did not, He does not exist at all, nothing has any purpose, and nothing makes any sense. If on the other hand there is a creative intelligence—if there is a God—then creation is understandable. It is possible. It is plausible. It is rational.

Ultimately, those are the options every reader of Genesis is faced with. Either the vast array of complex organisms and intelligence we observe reflect the wisdom and power of a personal Creator (and specifically, the God who has revealed Himself in Scripture), or all these marvels somehow evolved spontaneously from inanimate matter, and no real sense can be made of anything.

Even among the best scientists who have left their mark on the scientific world, those who think honestly and make honest confessions about origins will admit that there must be a creative intelligence. (Einstein himself firmly believed that a "Cosmic Intelligence" *must* have designed the universe, though like many others today who accept the notion of "intelligent design," he avoided the obvious conclusion that if there's a "Cosmic Intelligence" powerful enough to design and create the universe, that "Intelligence" is by definition Lord and God over all.) And although the scientific and academic communities often mercilessly attempt to silence such opinions, there are nonetheless many men of integrity in the scientific community who embrace the God of Scripture and the biblical creation account.[31]

God *did* create the heavens and the earth. And there is only one document that credibly claims to be a divinely revealed record of that creation: the book of Genesis. Unless we have a creator who left us with no information about where we came from or what our purpose is, the text of Genesis 1—2 stands for all practical purposes unchallenged as the only divinely revealed description of creation. In other words, if there is a God who created the heavens and the earth, and if He revealed to humanity any record of that creation, Genesis *is* that record. If the God of Scripture did *not* create the heavens and the earth, then we have no real answers to anything that is truly important. Everything boils down to those two simple options.

So whether we believe the Genesis record or not makes all the difference in the world. Douglas Kelly, professor of systematic theology at Reformed Theological Seminary, has written on this subject with great insight. He says, "Essentially, mankind has only two choices. Either we have evolved out of the slime and can be explained only in a materialistic sense, meaning that we are made of nothing but the material, or we have been made on a heavenly pattern."[32]

He's right. Those are ultimately the only two options. We can either believe what Genesis says, or not. If Genesis 1:1 is true, then the universe and everything in it was created by a loving and personal God, and His purposes are clearly revealed to us in Scripture. Further, if the Genesis account is true, then we bear the stamp of God and are loved by Him—and *because* we are made in His image, human beings have a dignity, value, and obligation that transcends that of all other creatures. Moreover, if Genesis is true, then we not only have God's own answers to the questions of what we are here for and how we got where we are, but we also have the promise of salvation from our sin.

If Genesis is *not* true, however, we have no reliable answer to anything. Throw out Genesis and the authority of *all* Scripture is fatally compromised. That would ultimately mean that the God of the Bible simply doesn't exist. And if some other kind of creator-god *does* exist, he evidently doesn't care enough about his creation to provide any revelation about himself, his plan for creation, or his will for his creatures.

There are, of course, several extrabiblical accounts of creation from pagan sacred writings. But they are all mythical, fanciful, and frivolous accounts, featuring hideously ungodly gods. Those who imagine such deities exist would have to conclude that they have left us without any reason for hope, without any clear principles by which to live, without any accountability, without any answers to our most basic questions, and (most troubling of all) without any explanation or solution for the dilemma of evil.

Therefore if Genesis is untrue, we might as well assume that no God exists at all. That is precisely the assumption behind modern evolutionary theory. If true, it means that impersonal matter is the ultimate reality. Human personality and human intelligence are simply meaningless accidents produced at random by the natural processes of evolution. We have no moral accountability to any higher Being. All morality—indeed, all truth itself—is ultimately relative. In fact, truth, falsehood, goodness, and evil are all merely theoretical notions with no real meaning or significance. Nothing really matters in the vast immensity of an infinite, impersonal universe.

So if Genesis is false, nihilism is the next best option. Utter irrationality becomes the only "rational" choice.

Obviously, the ramifications of our views on these things are immense. Our view of creation is the necessary starting point for our entire worldview. In fact, so vital is the issue that Francis Schaeffer once remarked that if he had only an hour to spend with an unbeliever, he would spend the first fifty-five minutes talking about creation and what it means for humanity to bear the image of God—and then he would use the last five minutes to explain the way of salvation.[33]

The starting point for Christianity is not Matthew 1:1 but Genesis 1:1. Tamper with the book of Genesis and you undermine the very foundation of Christianity. You cannot treat Genesis 1 as a fable or a mere poetic saga without severe implications to the rest of Scripture. The creation account is where

God starts His account of history. It is impossible to alter the beginning without impacting the rest of the story—not to mention the ending. If Genesis 1 is not accurate, then there's no way to be certain that the rest of Scripture tells the truth. If the starting point is wrong, the Bible itself is built on a foundation of falsehood.

In other words, if you reject the creation account in Genesis, you have no basis for believing the Bible at all. If you doubt or explain away the Bible's account of the six days of creation, where do you put the reins on your skepticism? Do you start with Genesis 3, which explains the origin of sin, and believe everything from chapter 3 on? Or maybe you don't sign on until sometime after chapter 6, because the Flood is invariably questioned by scientists too. Or perhaps you find the Tower of Babel too hard to reconcile with the linguists' theories about how languages originated and evolved. So maybe you start taking the Bible as literal history beginning with the life of Abraham. But when you get to Moses' plagues against Egypt, will you deny those too? What about the miracles of the New Testament? Is there any reason to regard *any* of the supernatural elements of biblical history as anything other than poetic symbolism?

After all, the notion that the universe is billions of years old is based on naturalistic presuppositions that (if held consistently) would rule out *all* miracles. If we're worried about appearing "unscientific" in the eyes of naturalists, we're going to have to reject a lot more than Genesis 1—3.

Once rationalism sets in and you start adapting the Word of God to fit scientific theories based on naturalistic beliefs, there is no end to the process. If you have qualms about the historicity of the creation account, you are on the road to utter Sadduceeism—skepticism and outright unbelief about *all* the supernatural elements of Scripture. Why should we doubt the literal sense of Genesis 1—3 unless we are also prepared to deny that Elisha made an axe-head float, or that Peter walked on water, or that Jesus raised Lazarus from the dead? And what about the greatest miracle of all—the resurrection of Christ? If we're going to shape Scripture to fit the beliefs of naturalistic scientists, why stop at all? Why is one miracle any more difficult to accept than another?

And what are we going to believe about the *end* of history as it is foretold in Scripture? All of redemptive history ends, according to 2 Peter 3:10-12, when the Lord uncreates the universe. The elements melt with fervent heat, and everything that exists in the material realm will be dissolved at the atomic level, in some sort of unprecedented and unimaginable nuclear meltdown. Moreover, according to Revelation 21:1-5, God will immediately create a new heaven and a new earth (cf. Isa 65:17). Do we really believe He can do that, or will it take another umpteen billion years of evolutionary processes to get the new heaven and the new earth in working order? If we really believe He can destroy *this* universe in a split second and immediately create a whole new one, what's the problem with believing the Genesis account of a six-day creation in the first place? If He can do it at the end of the age, why is it so hard to believe the biblical account of what happened in the beginning?

So the question of whether we interpret the Creation account as fact or fiction has huge implications for every aspect of our faith. Frankly, believing in a supernatural creative God who made everything is the only possible rational explanation for the universe and for life itself. It is also the only basis for believing we have any purpose or destiny. It is the only proper start to a Christian worldview.

Further Reading

Johnson, Phillip E. *Reason in the Balance*. Downers Grove, IL: IVP, 1995.
Kelly, Douglas F. *Creation and Change*. Fearn, Ross-shire, U.K.: Christian Focus, 1997.
MacArthur, John. *The Battle for the Beginning*. Nashville: W Publishing Group, 2001.
Morris, Henry. *The Genesis Record*. Grand Rapids, MI: Baker, 1976.
Whitcomb, John C. *The Early Earth*, rev. ed. Grand Rapids, MI: Baker, 1986.

4

COMING TO GRIPS WITH SIN[1]

JOHN MACARTHUR

Genesis 3 is one of the most vitally important chapters in all the Bible. It is the foundation of everything that comes after it. Without it, little else in Scripture or in life itself would make sense. Genesis 3 explains the condition of the universe and the state of humanity. It explains why the world has so many problems. It explains the human dilemma. It explains why we need a Savior. And it explains what God is doing in history.

In other words, the truth revealed in Genesis 3 is the necessary foundation for a true and accurate worldview. Every worldview that lacks this foundation is utterly and hopelessly wrong.

When God completed His perfect creation, there was no disorder, no chaos, no conflict, no struggle, no pain, no discord, no deterioration, and no death. Yet our lives today are filled with all those things all the time. Frankly, we find it hard to imagine what a perfect world would have been like. Genesis 3 explains how we got from that paradise of unimaginable perfection to where we are today.

Evolution offers no explanation for the human dilemma, much less any solution to it. Why is human existence fraught with so many moral and spiritual problems? Evolution will never be able to answer that question. In fact, pure naturalistic evolution cannot account for *anything* that is moral or spiritual.

Yet we are clearly moral and spiritual creatures, and we all know this. The concepts of good and evil are innate in the human psyche. (Even the most atheistic evolutionists have consciences.) We know from bitter experience that we cannot keep ourselves from evil. We find the pull of sin irresistible. We *cannot* do everything we know we ought to do. Worse, we cannot reform ourselves. Evolution offers no explanation for this dilemma and no hope for a solution.

Instead, the doctrine of evolution (if followed consistently) ends with a denial of the reality of evil. If naturalistic evolution is correct and there is no God, neither can there be any inviolable moral principles that govern the universe. And therefore there is no moral accountability of any kind. In fact, if evolution is true, things are the way they are by sheer chance, for no transcendent reason. Nothing under such a system could ever have any real moral significance. The very notions of good and evil would be meaningless concepts. There would be no reason to condemn a Hitler or applaud a Good Samaritan.

Who designed us to distinguish between good and evil? Where did the human conscience come from? And why is human nature universally drawn to evil? Evolutionists are clueless.

Scripture says we were made in the image of God but are fallen creatures, born with an inclination to sin. We inherited our sinfulness from Adam. When he sinned, he plunged the whole race into a helplessly fallen state of bondage to evil. That, in a nutshell, is the doctrine known as "original sin."

The biblical description of humanity's fall into sin refutes the fundamental idea of evolution. Instead of teaching that man began at the bottom of the moral ladder and slowly rose higher by social and psychological evolution, Genesis 3 teaches us the opposite. Man began at the pinnacle of the created order, but because of Adam's sin, the history of humanity is the story of a disgraceful moral and spiritual decline (cf. Rom 1:21-32). Humanity today is *worse* than ever before (2 Tim 3:13).

Who can deny that evil is pervasive in this world? Evidence of it is all around us. And in particular, the universal moral depravity of human beings is abundantly clear. G. K. Chesterton wryly referred to the doctrine of original sin as "the only part of Christian theology which can really be proved." He goaded modernist theologians who "in their almost too fastidious spirituality, admit divine sinlessness, which they cannot see even in their dreams. But they essentially deny human sin, which they can see in the street."[2]

Evidence of the sinfulness of our race is all around us. It is published in the daily newspapers; it is shown to us on the evening news; and it is writ large in human history. No one in all our acquaintance is sin-free. Most of all, if we're honest with ourselves, some of the most persuasive proofs of our hopeless depravity are presented to us by our own consciences.

How did we get in this state? Genesis 3 answers that question with clarity and simplicity. Our first ancestor, Adam, deliberately disobeyed God. Somehow his sin defiled the whole race, and now every one of his natural offspring has inherited a love for sin and a contempt for true righteousness. And this manifests itself in our behavior.

According to Romans 5:12 and 1 Corinthians 15:22, when Adam sinned he brought death and judgment not only upon himself but upon the whole human race. Every one of us inherits sin and guilt from Adam. And that is what is wrong with us. That is why we have a vile, rebellious, corrupt, destructive nature—a sinful heart that corrupts all our thoughts, emotions, and will. "For the mind that is set on the flesh is hostile to God, for it does not submit to God's law; indeed, it cannot. Those who are in the flesh cannot please God" (Rom 8:7-8). That inability to love, obey, or please God is the very essence of human depravity.

And the only solution to that predicament is the re-creative work of God (2 Cor 5:17). That is why Jesus told Nicodemus, "You must be born again" (John 3:7). "Unless one is born again he cannot see the kingdom of God" (v. 3). This is what salvation is all about: God miraculously changes the nature of those whom He redeems, so that they are drawn to the very same righteousness they formerly hated. This was the central promise of the New Covenant: "I will sprinkle clean water on you, and you shall be clean from all your uncleannesses, and from all your idols I will cleanse you. And I will give you a new heart, and a new spirit I will put within you. And I will remove the heart of stone from your flesh and give you a heart of flesh. And I will put my Spirit within you, and cause you to walk in my statutes and be careful to obey my rules" (Ezek 36:25-27).

In other words, nothing we can do for ourselves will free us from the bondage of sin. Adam's transgression had a catastrophic effect, not only on him and his environment, but also on his progeny, including you and me. And we cannot make sense of our moral plight until we come to grips with where it all began.

All creation was tainted and cursed because of Adam's sin. Romans 8:20-22 says, "For the creation was subjected to futility, not willingly, but because of him who subjected it, in hope that the creation itself will be set free from its bondage to decay and obtain the freedom of the glory of the children of God. For we know that the whole creation has been groaning together in the pains of childbirth until now." In other words, because of sin, no part of creation now exists as God originally made it. It "was subjected to futility," meaning that it was rendered unable to achieve the purpose for which it was originally designed. It was spoiled—defiled by sin, and thus subject to God's curse instead of His blessing. It was enslaved to corruption and placed in bondage to the debasing effects of sin—including decay, degradation, and death. All creation now groans and labors with birth pangs—picturesque language depicting the suffering and pain caused by sin's defilement. All these things, according to Scripture, are the effects of Adam's disobedience.

This clearly argues against evolution. If God used evolutionary processes or "natural selection" to create the world in the first place, then death, decay, mutation, and corruption were part of creation from the beginning. If death and natural selection were part of the means God used to create the world, then nothing was actually created perfect; everything had defects built in. But Scripture plainly attributes all such things to Adam's sin. They are the consequences of the curse that came after that first act of disobedience.

And deliverance from this state will not come from any process of evolution either. In fact, the whole of creation—including the human race—is now subject to a kind of *devolution,* which no amount of education, enlightenment, environmentalism, psychology, civilization, or technology will ever be able to reverse. What is needed is *redemption* (Rom 8:23).

The remainder of Genesis is filled with evidence of humanity's downward spiral into utter moral degradation. Genesis 3 is the turning point. Before that, God looked at creation and pronounced everything "very good" (1:31). But after Genesis 3, all human history has been colored by that which is very *bad.* (And the only exceptions are examples of God's redemptive work; they are *not* examples of human nobility.)

Genesis 4 records the first murder, a case of fratricide. Verse 19 contains the first mention of polygamy. Verse 23 tells of another act of murder. And from there the human race declines so grievously that by Genesis 6:5, "The LORD saw that the wickedness of man was great in the earth, and that every intention of the thoughts of his heart was only evil continually." So God destroyed the entire race, except for one family.

Genesis also records the beginnings of such evils as homosexuality (19:1-5), incest (19:30-38), idolatry (31:30-35), rape (34:1-2), mass murder (34:25-29), harlotry (38:14-19), and numerous other forms of wickedness.

All of this stemmed from Adam's one act of disobedience (Rom 5:19). Adam's sin poisoned not only his offspring, but also the rest of creation. How did this evil come about? Again, Genesis 3 gives a clear answer.

Here is the biblical account of what happened to spoil the paradise of Eden:

> *Now the serpent was more crafty than any other beast of the field that the* LORD *God had made. He said to the woman, "Did God actually say, 'You shall not eat of any tree in the garden'?" And the woman said to the serpent, "We may eat of the fruit of the trees in the garden, but God said, 'You shall not eat of the fruit of the tree that is in the midst of the garden, neither shall you touch it, lest you die.'" But the serpent said to the woman, "You will not surely die. For God knows that when you eat of it your eyes will be opened, and you will be like God, knowing good and evil." So when*

> *the woman saw that the tree was good for food, and that it was a delight to the eyes, and that the tree was to be desired to make one wise, she took of its fruit and ate, and she also gave some to her husband who was with her, and he ate. Then the eyes of both were opened, and they knew that they were naked. And they sewed fig leaves together and made themselves loincloths.*
>
> —GEN 3:1-7

This is not a fable or a myth. It is presented as history, and it is treated as history throughout the remainder of Scripture (cf. Rom 5:12-19; 2 Cor 11:3; 1 Tim 2:13-14; Rev 12:9; 20:2).

THE SOLICITOR

Many would point to the talking serpent as evidence that this account is mythical. Yet Jesus Himself alluded to this account as real and historical when He referred to the devil as a murderer and a liar and the father of lying (John 8:44).

According to Genesis 3:1, "Now the serpent was more crafty than any other beast of the field that the LORD God had made." We are not to think God created reptiles with the ability to talk and reason. The cunning this particular serpent displayed is not a characteristic of serpents in general. What is described here is something more than a mere animal; he is a being who knew God, a personality who spoke with great intelligence and shrewdness. He was a moral being who was opposed to God. He was deceptive, hostile, and bent on destroying the moral innocence of the first couple.

We learn by comparing Scripture with Scripture that this serpent was really Satan, masquerading as an animal (cf. 2 Cor 11:3; Rev 12:9). Satan, master of disguises, who even has the power to transform himself into an angel of light (2 Cor 11:14), had apparently either taken the physical form of a serpent or somehow possessed the body of one of the creatures in the garden.

The name *Satan* is a transliteration of the Hebrew word for "adversary." In its Old Testament occurrences, the word is often used with a definite article, suggesting that it was not originally a proper name but a descriptive expression ("the adversary"). The technical meaning of the Hebrew term conveys a legal nuance that speaks of one's adversary—the one who brings an accusation—in a legal context. And of course this is perfectly descriptive of Satan's role. He is the accuser of the brethren (Rev 12:10). In the Old Testament book of Job we see him working behind the scenes to discredit and ruin Job. And in the New Testament he seeks power over Peter, so that he can sift him like wheat at the hour of Peter's greatest vulnerability (Luke 22:31). So his behavior and his activity are always consistent with what we see in Genesis 3.

Where did Satan himself come from, and how are we to understand his character and work, in light of the fact that God had declared all His creation good?

God did not make Satan evil. As we saw at the end of the previous chapter, everything God made was good, and evil did not exist in His creation. In Genesis 1:31 God emphatically declared everything He had made "very good." Satan appears suddenly and unexpectedly in Genesis 3:1. That means Satan's fall must have occurred sometime between the end of creation (marked by that glorious day of rest on day seven) and the events described in Genesis 3—which appear to have come very soon after Adam's and Eve's creation, before they had conceived any offspring.

Genesis, maintaining an earthly perspective on the creation story, is silent about the fall of Satan, which occurred in heaven. From elsewhere in Scripture, however, we learn that Satan was an angel who fell when he was lifted up with pride. Perhaps the clearest account of Satan's rebellion is given in Ezekiel 28.

> *Moreover, the word of the* LORD *came to me: "Son of man, raise a lamentation over the king of Tyre, and say to him, Thus says the* LORD *God: You were the signet of perfection, full of wisdom and perfect in beauty. You were in Eden, the garden of God; every precious stone was your covering, sardius, topaz, and diamond, beryl, onyx, and jasper, sapphire, emerald, and carbuncle; and crafted in gold were your settings and your engravings. On the day that you were created they were prepared. You were an anointed guardian cherub. I placed you; you were on the holy mountain of God; in the midst of the stones of fire you walked. You were blameless in your ways from the day you were created, till unrighteousness was found in you. In the abundance of your trade you were filled with violence in your midst, and you sinned; so I cast you as a profane thing from the mountain of God, and I destroyed you, O guardian cherub, from the midst of the stones of fire. Your heart was proud because of your beauty; you corrupted your wisdom for the sake of your splendor. I cast you to the ground; I exposed you before kings, to feast their eyes on you. By the multitude of your iniquities, in the unrighteousness of your trade you profaned your sanctuaries; so I brought fire out from your midst; it consumed you, and I turned you to ashes on the earth in the sight of all who saw you. All who know you among the peoples are appalled at you; you have come to a dreadful end and shall be no more forever."*
>
> —vv. 11-19

Although this is addressed as a prophetic word against the king of Tyre, the context makes clear that its message reached beyond that earthly king to the supernatural source of his wickedness, pride, and corrupted authority. This was a prophetic message from God to Satan.

The text clearly identifies the object of those words of condemnation by saying, "You were in Eden, the garden of God" (v. 13). The words were addressed to no mere man, but to an angelic being, "an anointed guardian cherub" (v. 14). He was the very epitome of created perfection, "the signet of perfection, full of wisdom and perfect in beauty" (v. 12). The Lord says to him, "You were blameless in your ways from the day you were created, till unrighteousness was found in you" (v. 15). This can be none other than the fallen creature who masqueraded as a serpent in Eden. It is that fallen angelic creature known to us as Satan.

The passage in Ezekiel clearly states that this creature was once an angel, one of the cherubim whose role was heavenly worship. That explains the reference in verse 13: "crafted in gold were your settings and your engravings. On the day that you were created they were prepared." In fact, he seems to have been the highest-ranking cherub ("an anointed guardian cherub"), a creature whose beauty and majesty were unsurpassed. He may have been the highest of all archangels.

How sin arose in him is not explained, but *where* that sin originated is clear: "unrighteousness was found *in you*" (v. 15, emphasis added). It was not a defect in the way he was made ("You were blameless in your ways from the day you were created"). The evil did not come from his Maker; and yet it did not arise from outside the creature; it was found *in* him. And as a result the Lord says, "you were filled with violence in your midst, and you sinned" (v. 16).

How could this creature have been unsatisfied with his perfection? What could have provoked him to rebel against his Creator? The text offers no explanation, except to underscore the truth that the fault arose within the creature himself and in no sense was the result of any imperfection in the way he was created. Nor was his fallenness a state that was imposed on him against his will. It was a choice he made for himself.

Another text (Isaiah 14) sheds even more light on Satan's fall. Like the passage in Ezekiel, it is a prophetic condemnation addressed to an earthly king, the king of Babylon (v. 4). But like the Ezekiel passage, it contains expressions that seem to look beyond any earthly ruler and to address Satan himself.

> *"How you are fallen from heaven, O Day Star, son of Dawn! How you are cut down to the ground, you who laid the nations low! You said in*

> *your heart, 'I will ascend to heaven; above the stars of God I will set my throne on high; I will sit on the mount of assembly in the far reaches of the north; I will ascend above the heights of the clouds; I will make myself like the Most High.' But you are brought down to Sheol, to the far reaches of the pit."*
>
> —vv. 12-15

"Lucifer" means "shining one," a fitting name for the anointed cherub. And the sin for which he is condemned is a sin that arose from his own heart. It is the sin of pride. He wanted to exalt his throne above all others and "make myself like the Most High" (v. 14). He literally intended to usurp the throne of God. All of that supports the notion that the creature in view here is Satan. We know from 1 Timothy 3:6, for example, that this very attitude of pride was the reason for Satan's downfall and condemnation.

And the moment he was lifted up with pride, he fell. Jesus said, "I saw Satan fall like lightning from heaven" (Luke 10:18). As quickly as Satan sought to go up, he went down. Though his desire was to be like God, he instantly became as much *unlike* God as possible.

He did not fall alone. According to Revelation 12:4, a third of the angels in heaven went with him. They evidently became demons, ministers of Satan, and deceivers like him (2 Cor 11:14-15). According to Matthew 25:41, everlasting fire is prepared for them. Their ultimate doom is as certain as the unchanging faithfulness of God.

Why did God not consign them all to the eternal flames the moment they fell? Scripture does not explicitly answer that question, but it is clear that Satan and the demons have been given opportunity to exploit every avenue of their power until God destroys them at the end of human history. Despite their evil influence and the utter incorrigibility of their wickedness, they somehow fit into God's plan to show grace and mercy and provide salvation for fallen humans. The time for their destruction is set (Matt 8:29). Their doom is absolutely certain, but until God's purposes are fulfilled, they have a measure of freedom to advance their evil agenda—perhaps to prove in the end that there is no conceivable evil over which God cannot triumph.

Remember that salvation for the human race was planned and promised before Satan ever fell—before the foundation of the world (Eph 1:4; 2 Tim 1:9; Titus 1:1-2; Rev 13:8). So even Satan's fall and his deception in Eden fit into the eternal plan of God.

In other words, God *allowed* Satan to confront Eve. This encounter in the garden was not an unexpected event that somehow derailed the plan of God. God had planned for it from the beginning.

The Strategy

Satan's strategy in tempting Eve is the same strategy he always uses. He is a liar and the father of lying (John 8:44). But he comes disguised as one who brings the truth—"an angel of light" (2 Cor 11:14).

Only in lying is Satan consistent. Everything from him is deceptive. ". . . there is no truth in him. When he lies, he speaks out of his own character, for he is a liar and the father of lies" (John 8:44). But here he begins with what sounds like a very innocent question from an interested observer concerned about Eve's well-being: "Did God actually say, 'You shall not eat of any tree in the garden'?" (Gen 3:1).

"Did God actually say . . . ?" That is the first question in Scripture. Before this, there were only answers; no dilemmas. But his question was wickedly designed to start Eve on the path of doubting and distrusting what God had said. That sort of doubt is the very essence of all sin. The gist of *all* temptation is to cast doubt on God's Word and to subject it to human judgment. That is what the serpent was doing here.

In fact, notice how Satan cunningly twisted and misrepresented the Word of God. God had said, "You may surely eat of every tree of the garden, but of the tree of the knowledge of good and evil you shall not eat, for in the day that you eat of it you shall surely die" (Gen 2:16-17). God's emphasis had been on their perfect freedom to eat from *all* the trees except one. Satan's question turned the emphasis around and stressed the negative, implying that God was fencing them in with restrictions. Notice also how starkly the serpent's words contrasted with God's actual command. God had said, "*You may surely eat* of every tree of the garden" (emphasis added). The emphasis was on their freedom to eat. Satan's version negated the whole point: "*You shall not eat* of any tree in the garden" (emphasis added). In this way he focused her attention on the prohibition and set her up for the main assault on God's Word.

Satan's motive was the utter destruction of the first couple, even though he was pretending to have their best interests at heart. That's why Jesus said, "He was a murderer from the beginning" (John 8:44). The serpent had deliberately confronted Eve when she was isolated from Adam and most vulnerable. He aimed his initial attack at her alone ("the weaker vessel," 1 Pet 3:7). Clearly his aim was to deceive her by his craftiness (2 Cor 11:3) while she was unprotected by Adam.

If Eve was surprised to hear a serpent speak, Scripture does not say so. After all, Eden was new and undoubtedly filled with many wonders, and the first couple was still just discovering all the marvels of creation. In that paradise, Eve had never known fear or encountered danger of any kind. So she conversed with the serpent as if this were nothing extraordinary. She had no reason to be suspicious. She herself was innocent, having never before encountered "the schemes of the devil" (Eph 6:11).

Satan's strategy was to portray God as narrow, strict, uncharitable, too restrictive—as if He wanted to limit human freedom and deprive Adam and Eve of enjoyment and pleasure. Satan was implying that evil and untruthfulness were part of God's character. He was hinting to Eve that God might be cruel and uncaring.

Moreover, the reptile Satan slyly insinuated that *he* was more devoted to Eve's well-being than God was. He implied that he was for freedom while God was restrictive. The fact that God gave Adam and Eve *everything* else to eat was set aside as negligible. Thus Satan cast suspicion on God's goodness.

Eve was unaware of Satan's strategies; so she replied naively—defending God to some degree: "We may eat of the fruit of the trees in the garden" (v. 2). Evidently she did not know that this was God's supernatural foe. Scripture says she was "deceived" (2 Cor 11:3; 1 Tim 2:14). Satan beguiled her by taking advantage of her innocence.

But even though she did not know her enemy, she should have been able to thwart this attack. She had sufficient advantage to do so. She knew God. She knew God's character as good—and *only* good. She had experienced nothing but abundant blessing and unrestrained generosity from His hand. She was surrounded by all of creation, which abundantly displayed God's good will. She also had a clear, unambiguous command from God. And even that command not to eat of one tree was a gracious restriction for her own good.

She should have been suspicious of the talking reptile. She should have found out more about her tempter before she yielded to his enticements. Above all, she should have made a strong and emphatic disavowal of the suspicion that God had withheld some goodness from her and her husband.

Instead, her reply was only a partial refutation of the reptile's allegations. She said, "We may eat of the fruit of the trees in the garden, but God said, 'You shall not eat of the fruit of the tree that is in the midst of the garden, neither shall you touch it, lest you die'" (vv. 2-3).

Let's analyze her response. Notice first that she omitted the word "every" when she said, "We may eat of the fruit of the trees in the garden"—suggesting that she was already beginning to lose sight of the vast goodness of God. Then she moved further, recounting the restriction God had imposed on them without defending His goodness. And worst of all, she added something to the words of the command, claiming God had said, "neither shall you touch it, lest you die." Apparently beginning to feel the restriction was harsh, she added to the harshness of it.

Her heart had already set its course. She was not defending God and His goodness. She was not affirming His glorious majesty and holy perfection. She ignored the fact that God's desire was only for her good. She did not take offense at the serpent's insult against God's character. And so she played right into his hands. She was already starting to believe Satan rather than God.

The fall was inevitable from the instant she began to doubt. The course for her subsequent action was set by that wavering in her heart. What followed was merely the evidence that wickedness had entered her heart already.

At this point, Satan knew he had succeeded and pushed for total victory. Immediately he suggested that he knew more than God. His next statement was an assertion that flatly contradicted the Word of God and impugned the motives of God: "You will not surely die. For God knows that when you eat of it your eyes will be opened, and you will be like God, knowing good and evil" (vv. 4-5). This bold denial stated definitely what Satan had merely implied before. Now he openly slandered not only the goodness of God, but also God's truthfulness.

Suspicion had already found root in Eve's mind. God's majesty had been insulted; His goodness had been maligned; His trustworthiness had been defamed. And she had not responded in faith. So Satan moved in for the kill.

"God is a liar," he implied. "He has deceived you, taken your freedom, and restricted your joy." Satan's lie is still the same today: "You can be free. Do whatever you want. It is *your* life. There are no divine laws, no absolute authority, and above all, no judgment. You will not surely die."

At this point, Eve was faced with a clear choice. She could believe God or believe the devil. That is the same choice that has confronted humanity ever since. Who is telling the truth—God or Satan? Does God want to place undue restrictions on you? Does He want to cramp your freedom and minimize your joy? If God is like that, Satan implies, He doesn't love you—He is not to be trusted.

The lie is the same today. God's authority is often portrayed as too restrictive, destructive of human freedom, and detrimental to our well-being. In the words of E. J. Young,

> Modern psychology, we can hear the tempter saying, has brought to light the deep recesses of the human soul. That soul is a very tender thing, and to restrain and bind it by the imposition of categorical law is to harm it. The soul should be free to develop and to express itself, and this it can do only through freedom and love. Narrowness and restriction, such as absolute

> authority impose, must be abandoned, if there is to be any development of the personality. Would you be warped in your personality? If so, then continue submitting to God and His commandments.[3]

Satan was suggesting to Eve that the only reason God could be so restrictive, forbidding them to eat from that tree, was because there was some flaw in His character. His love must be defective. He wanted to keep them from being all they could be, lest they rival His greatness.

And thus what Satan offered them was precisely what he himself tried to obtain but could not: "you will be like God" (v. 5).

Satan knew from personal experience that God tolerates no rivals. God later said through Isaiah, "I am the LORD; that is my name; my glory I give to no other, nor my praise to carved idols" (Isa 42:8). God yields His rightful place to no one. That is what makes Him God. His glory outshines the glory of all others. He has no equals, and therefore all who pretend equality with Him or seek recognition as His equal, He must reject. That is because He is holy, not because He is selfish.

But Satan implied that this was some kind of petty jealousy on God's part, as if God must keep Adam and Eve from becoming all they could be lest they become a threat to the Almighty. The suggestion is absurd, but for Eve it was an intoxicating thought. Perhaps she thought it a noble aspiration to be like God. She may have convinced herself it was an honorable desire.

The reptile's false promise ("you will be like God") is the seed of all false religion. Numerous cults, ranging from Buddhism to Mormonism, are based on the same lie. It is a twisting of the truth. God *wants* us to be like Him, in the sense that we share His communicable attributes—holiness, love, mercy, truthfulness, and other expressions of His righteousness. But what Satan tried to do—and what he tempted Eve to try doing—was to intrude into a realm that belongs to God alone and to usurp His power, His sovereignty, and His right to be worshiped. And those things are forbidden to any creature.

Notice how Satan characterized equality with God: "you will be like God, knowing good and evil" (v. 5). This was a dangerous half-truth. If they ate the fruit, they would indeed know evil, but not as God knows it. They would know it experientially. What Satan held out to them as the doorway to fulfillment and truth was in reality a shortcut to destruction. "There is a way that seems right to a man, But its end is the way to death" (Prov 14:12).

THE SEDUCTION

James 1:13-15 says, "Let no one say when he is tempted, 'I am being tempted by God,' for God cannot be tempted with evil, and he himself tempts no one.

But each person is tempted when he is lured and enticed by his own desire. Then desire when it has conceived gives birth to sin, and sin when it is fully grown brings forth death." That process was already underway in Eve.

Sin in the mind goes to work in the emotions. That incites the will, which yields the act.

Verse 6 says, "So when the woman saw that the tree was good for food, and that it was a delight to the eyes, and that the tree was to be desired to make one wise, she took of its fruit and ate, and she also gave some to her husband who was with her, and he ate." Self-fulfillment had become Eve's goal, and for the first time ever, her own self-interest and self-satisfaction were what drove her. *Sin had already been conceived in her heart.* Now that sin was beginning to work in her to bring about the evil act. But she was guilty already, for she had sinned in her heart. Jesus said, "Everyone who looks at a woman with lustful intent has *already* committed adultery with her in his heart" (Matt 5:28, emphasis added).

Eve saw three features of the forbidden fruit that seduced her. First, "The tree was good for food." We have no idea what kind of fruit it was. It is often portrayed as an apple, but the text does not say it was an apple. The specific variety of fruit is not important. What is important is that Eve was seduced by her *physical appetite*.

This was not a legitimate hunger. There was plenty of food in the garden if Eve was hungry. It was an illicit appetite. It was a fleshly lust provoked by a selfish discontent and a distrust in God—as if He were keeping something good from her.

Second, she saw "that it was a delight to the eyes." This seduction appealed to her *emotional appetite*. The fruit excited her sense of beauty and other passions. Not that there wasn't plenty of other attractive fruit in the garden. There was a rich variety of colors, shapes, and sizes, and it all looked good. But Eve was focused on *this* fruit, because Satan had planted the idea in her mind that it represented something good that God was keeping from her. As covetousness grew in her heart, the forbidden fruit looked better and better.

Third, she saw "the tree was to be desired to make one wise." This was an appeal to her intellectual appetite. Incipient pride caused her to fancy the "wisdom" that would come with knowing good and evil. She desired that knowledge and was tempted by the false promise that it would make her like God.

Thus she was seduced by "the desires of the flesh and the desires of the eyes and pride in possessions"—everything evil in this world (1 John 2:16-17). Temptation always comes in one or more of those three categories.

When Satan tempted Christ, he urged Him to turn stones to bread (Matt 4:3). That was an appeal to the lust of the flesh. The devil also showed Him all the kingdoms of the world and their glory, promising Him authority over them (vv. 8-9). That was an appeal to the lust of the eyes. And he set Him on the pinnacle of the Temple (v. 5), appealing to the pride of life. That's why Hebrews 4:15 says, "[He] in every respect has been tempted as we are, yet without sin."

THE SIN

Ultimately, predictably, the doubt and covetousness in Eve's head gave way to evil behavior. When sin penetrates the mind, emotions, and will, it will *always* be manifest in sinful actions.

Verse 6 says, "she took of its fruit and ate." It was a simple act with a massive impact. Emboldened by her own misdeed—perhaps relieved by the fact that she had not been instantly struck dead—"she also gave some to her husband who was with her, and he ate."

Adam appears, from where we are not told, and, discovering that his wife had already disobeyed the Lord's command, he partook with her. There is no record of how Adam was enticed to do this. We could surmise that Eve related the words of the serpent to him. She may have also enticed him with a recounting of how pleasurable the forbidden fruit was. (Scripture acknowledges that there is pleasure in sin for a season—Heb 11:25.) In any case, Adam doesn't appear to have needed much convincing. It is ironic that the one whom God had given to Adam to be his *helper* became the instrument of disaster and death to him.

But Adam's guilt was greater, not less, than Eve's. And throughout Scripture Adam is the one who is indicted for the Fall (cf. Rom 5:12-19; 1 Cor 15:22). Eve was immensely guilty, of course. But she was deceived; Adam apparently disobeyed deliberately (1 Tim 2:14). He bore the ultimate responsibility for the Fall, and his actions were determinative for all his offspring.

How was Adam's guilt and the corruption caused by his sin passed to his progeny? Scripture does not expressly say. But it is enough for us to know that it happened.

Once Adam ate the fruit, the principle of decay and death began to rule creation. And the whole human race was plunged into evil. God Himself would have to become a man and die in order to undo it.

Adam and Eve could never have known the impact of their sin. Perhaps Satan had some grasp of it, and he reveled in it. Certainly God knew, and yet He allowed it so that He could display His glory in destroying evil.

THE SHAME

Now that Adam and Eve knew evil by personal experience, their minds were open to a whole new way of thinking. They were susceptible to evil thoughts. They were drawn by evil desires. They no longer desired fellowship with God as they had before. And above all, they were conscious of their own guilt.

The serpent had promised them enlightenment—"Your eyes will be opened" (v. 5). What they actually received was a hideously twisted caricature of enlightenment. It was eye-opening only in a negative sense. It opened their eyes to the meaning of guilt, but it made them want to hide their eyes in shame. And in reality, it brought them into a state of spiritual blindness from which they could never recover without a divinely-wrought miracle of regeneration.

Their knowledge of evil was real too—but it was nothing like God's. A healthy oncologist "knows" cancer, and with an expertise that surpasses his patients' experiential knowledge. But the person who is dying of cancer also "knows" cancer in an intimate way—but in a way that is also destructive. Adam and Eve now had a knowledge of evil that was like the terminal cancer patient's knowledge of carcinoma. It was not the kind of enlightenment Satan had led Eve to believe she would obtain. She and Adam did *not* become like God, but the opposite.

Sin instantly destroyed their innocence. They felt it strongly. They suddenly were self-conscious about their guilt. They felt exposed. This manifested itself in shame about their nakedness. Even the holy gift of their physical relationship was polluted with a sense of shame. Gone was the purity of it. Now present were wicked and impure thoughts they had never known before.

And in that state of self-conscious shame, "They sewed fig leaves together and made themselves loincloths" (v. 7). This was a noble effort to cover their sin and mask their shame. Ever since then, clothing has been a universal expression of human modesty. It is fitting and right that fallen man should want to cover his shame. Naturists and anthropologists are wrong when they try to portray public nudity as a return to innocence and nobility. Nudity does not recover fallen man's innocence; it only displays a denial of the shame we ought to feel. It is appropriate that those bearing the guilt of sin should cover themselves. And God Himself demonstrated this when He killed animals to use their skins as a covering for the fallen couple (Gen 3:21).

In fact, this was a graphic object lesson showing that *only* God can provide a suitable covering for sin, and the shedding of blood is a necessary part of the process (Heb 9:22).

Like Lucifer, Adam and Eve fell so far that now there was nothing good in them (cf. Gen 6:5; Job 15:14-16; Rom 7:18; 8:7-8; Eph 2:1-3). Nothing in life or in the world would ever be the same. God Himself cursed the earth, so that thorns now grow naturally, and fruit trees have to be cultivated. A multitude of woes, including increased pain in childbearing, sorrow, toil, distress, disease, and death, would now plague all of creation. An avalanche of sin was loosed and could never stop.

FURTHER READING

Feinberg, John S. *The Many Faces of Evil.* Grand Rapids, MI: Zondervan, reprint 1994.

Luther, Martin. *On the Bondage of the Will* (1525), trans. J. I. Packer and O. R. Johnston. Westwood, NJ: Revell, 1957.

Owen, John. *Sin and Temptation* (1656, 1658, 1667), abr. and ed. James M. Houston. Portland: Multnomah, 1983.

Watson, Thomas. *The Mischief of Sin* (1671). Pittsburgh: Soli Deo Gloria, reprint 1994.

Young, Edward J. *Genesis 3*. Edinburgh: Banner of Truth, 1966.

5

Having an Eternally Right Relationship with God

John MacArthur

Obviously, an authentically Christian worldview hinges on a right knowledge of the Gospel. Therefore, the person whose understanding of the Gospel is inaccurate has no Christian worldview.

What is the Gospel? What is the essential content of the Christian message? We would get no end of answers if we polled everyone who *professes* to be a Christian. As always, then, we must turn to Scripture to answer the question with clarity and with absolute authority.

The very heart of the gospel message is distinctively articulated in 2 Corinthians 5:18-21. That passage sets forth the central meaning of Christ's life and death in no uncertain terms:

> *All this is from God, who through Christ reconciled us to himself and gave us the ministry of reconciliation; that is, in Christ God was reconciling the world to himself, not counting their trespasses against them, and entrusting to us the message of reconciliation. Therefore, we are ambassadors for Christ, God making his appeal through us. We implore you on behalf of Christ, be reconciled to God. For our sake he made him to be sin who knew no sin, so that in him we might become the righteousness of God.*

Notice carefully that Christ's main role in coming to earth was to reconcile a world of fallen humans to God. Christians are blessed and commanded to engage in that ministry, because God has committed to us the ministry and the message of reconciliation.

Consider a few fundamental truths that are either assumed, implied, or explicitly stated in that passage: Every person is fallen and sinful and therefore *needs* to be reconciled with God. God Himself accomplishes that reconciliation (because sinners could never do it for themselves), and He does it through Christ who was perfectly sinless (He "knew no sin"). He made atonement for others' sins by an exchange of His righteousness for their sin. In other words, He was "made . . . sin" (i.e., He took others' sin on Himself and bore the punishment for it), and He makes believers righteous through their union with Him. Although God is the offended Deity, He is the very One who seeks and initiates our reconciliation. He does not take pleasure in the destruction of sinners (cf. Ezek 18:32; 33:11). But He makes an appeal to the whole world through the Christian message, imploring sinners to be reconciled with Him. All of that is the very essence of the gospel message.

To be a Christian, therefore, is to be reconciled with God. As Christians, we are also called to participate in the ministry of reconciliation, by beseeching other men and women on Christ's behalf to be reconciled to God. The term *reconciliation* is therefore practically the theme of true Christianity. It is a reconciliation for sinners who have offended and spurned a righteous Deity and yet are redeemed through no merit of their own. In fact, true reconciliation is accomplished *only* through the work of Christ. The ministry of reconciliation that has been committed to Christians is therefore the greatest work in the world; and the message of reconciliation is the most essential message.

That is why the gospel of reconciliation was always at the heart of Paul's preaching. In 1 Corinthians 1:17 he says, "For Christ did not send me to baptize but to preach the gospel, and not with words of eloquent wisdom, lest the cross of Christ be emptied of its power." His primary concern was always for the purity of the message. To adulterate or alter the simple, straightforward truth about reconciliation in the cross would be to empty the entire Gospel of its power. So Paul was committed to the proclamation of the gospel message—unstintingly, unhesitatingly, and unreservedly (Rom 1:15-16; 1 Cor 2:1-2).

God has likewise called every Christian to be an ambassador carrying that very same message of reconciliation to the world. The word rendered "ambassadors" in 2 Corinthians 5:20 is a noble, multifaceted Greek term (*presbeuō*), which is related to the word usually translated "elder" (*presbuteros*). Thus the term ambassador carries the idea of someone who is mature and stately. (In ancient times, old and experienced men were usually the ones chosen to be ambassadors of emperors and kings, because of the dignity and wisdom they brought to the task.) But this does not mean that only pastors or mature Christians are Christ's ambassadors. On the contrary, Paul is writing to the rank-and-file members of the Corinthian church (some of whom were notoriously immature spiritually). He is teaching that all

Christians are ambassadors, invested with all the honor and dignity one would normally owe an esteemed elder. After all, an ambassador is someone who represents a ruler and delivers a message on that ruler's behalf. The ambassador, therefore, receives honor not because of his own personal worthiness, but because of whom he represents. So it is the importance of the mission, the weight of the message, and the eminence and excellence of the One we represent that gives every Christian the status of an ambassador.

A good ambassador does not make up a message on his own authority. He is commissioned to carry someone else's message and to deliver it faithfully. He is not authorized to alter the message in any way. He cannot adjust it to fit his own personal preferences. He cannot embellish it with his own opinions. He speaks for a higher authority, and he is responsible to deliver the message in unadulterated form.

By the same token, to scorn or mistreat an ambassador is to insult the ruler for whom he speaks. To send him away is to break off relations with the government he represents. An ambassador is essentially his ruler's mouthpiece. He never offers his own promises or demands his own privileges; rather he speaks on behalf of his government. His only authority is derived from his head of state, and to reject the ambassador is to reject the one who sent him.

By definition, an ambassador serves in a foreign land. He spends his life as a stranger and an alien. He has to speak a different language. He has to interact with a different culture and tradition and adapt to a different lifestyle. Those are all relevant analogies that help us understand the calling and task of Christians as ambassadors.

As ambassadors for the kingdom of God, Christians live and serve in an alien world. Paul says the believer comes with authority from his King, representing the kingdom. He comes with a word of reconciliation from the court of heaven to plead with people to be reconciled to God.

This perspective ought to shape our worldview as Christians: Having been reconciled to Christ and redeemed out of the world of sinful humanity, we nonetheless remain here in this world as "sojourners and exiles" (1 Pet 2:11; cf. Heb 11:13). We serve as ambassadors of God, commissioned by Him to proclaim a message of reconciliation to other fallen creatures. That is our central duty, and it should shape our entire perspective on the world.

If we examine 2 Corinthians 5:18-21 a little more closely, some magnificent truths emerge to clarify the ministry of reconciliation for us. Here is the Gospel in outline form. If we want a brief summary of what Christianity is all about, we can hardly find a better text than these few verses in 2 Corinthians. We can glean from them four monumental truths about the reconciliation promised in the Gospel.

Sinners Are Reconciled by the Will of God

First of all, reconciliation was conceived and initiated by God. "All this is from God, who through Christ reconciled us to himself" (v. 18). "All this" refers to the truths Paul had just set forth in verses 14-17. The transformation described there—conversion, salvation, everything connected with the new nature and new life in Christ—is entirely from God. Sinners themselves cannot merely decide to be reconciled to God and therefore make that happen. They have no power to satisfy God's wrath toward sin, His holy justice, or His perfect standard of righteousness. They cannot even change *themselves* on their own (cf. Jer 13:23), much less change God's attitude toward them. Sinners are simply offenders who have broken the law of God and are therefore naturally at spiritual enmity with Him. Any change or reconciliation that is going to come about in that relationship must come from God. This is the very reason why the Gospel is such good news: God loved sinners so much that He made a way to reconcile Himself with them, to make them His children—and yet without violating His justice.

Paul essentially declares that God's own sovereign will is the objective basis of reconciliation, even as he told the Roman believers: "For if while we were enemies we were reconciled to God by the death of his Son, much more, now that we are reconciled, shall we be saved by his life. More than that, we also rejoice in God through our Lord Jesus Christ, through whom we have now received reconciliation" (Rom 5:10-11; cf. Col 1:19-22).

The word "reconcile" (*katallassō*) means "to change" or "to exchange." The exchange involves nothing the sinner accomplishes, but only what he embraces. Stated another way, reconciliation with God is not something sinners accomplish when they decide to stop rejecting God. Instead, it is something God accomplishes when He decides to embrace sinners who repent and believe. *He* had to be willing to remove the guilt of sin, which caused such profound alienation and separation between humanity and Himself. Wherever we find the language of reconciliation in the New Testament, God is always the initiator of the reconciling activity. *He* is the One who removes the guilt. He is by nature a compassionate Savior (1 Tim 2:3-4; 2 Pet 3:9; cf. 1 Tim 4:10; Titus 1:3).

God made reconciliation possible entirely through His Son—"who through Christ reconciled us to himself." Why? Because Jesus Christ is the only mediator who could stand between God and man (John 14:6; Acts 4:12; 1 Tim 2:5-6). He alone could offer the one perfect sacrifice to satisfy the justice of God. "[God] will by no means clear the guilty" (Ex 34:7). Divine wrath against sin—the wages of sin (Rom 6:23)—had to be meted out. Unless that holy requirement was satisfied, no sinner could be reconciled. And, therefore, Christ died as a sacrifice for the sins of all who believe. *He paid the price of their sin.* His death was the most magnanimous expression of selfless love the universe will ever know. An infinitely holy God extended His love toward sinners to such a degree that He gave up His own Son in an ignominious death to bear the punishment sinners deserved. That occurred so that they might become His children and be made righteous instead of guilty. Only then could the reconciliation and transformation described in 2 Corinthians 5:14-17 take place.

The entire New Testament makes it clear that it was God who called, God who sent His Son, and God who saved. All the glory must go to Him as the source of reconciliation (cf. Acts 2:22-23; 1 Cor 8:6; 11:12b; Jas 1:17).

Sinners Are Reconciled by a Decree of Justification

Reconciliation involves a legal decree of forgiveness for sins. God does not admit sinners into the circle of His blessing while leaving them guilty and sin-stained. He absolves them of their guilt and imputes to them a perfect righteousness, so that they stand before God without guilt, robed in a righteousness that is not of their own making (Phil 3:9). Second Corinthians 5:19 makes reference to this truth—the biblical doctrine of justification—when it says, "In Christ God was reconciling the world to himself, *not counting their trespasses against them*" (emphasis added).

The only way sinners could ever be reconciled to God was if the sin that separated them from God were no longer an issue. Therefore, sin had to be dealt with and not counted against them. And God graciously and mercifully did that by the means of justification, which is a divine decree whereby believing sinners are declared righteous by virtue of their being covered with the righteousness of Christ and by having their sins atoned for. That is why God does not count their trespasses against them. Rather, He imputes to them the perfect righteousness of Jesus (Rom 3:21-26; 4:5-8; Col 2:13-14; cf. Matt 18:23-27; Eph 2:1-9).

It is important to understand justification as a legal decree, not a process. It happens instantaneously, the very instant the sinner savingly trusts in the atoning death of Jesus Christ. That person is immediately forgiven of all sin and is counted as fully righteous before God. Of course, experientially we will not achieve complete righteousness and total perfection until we see Christ and are finally glorified (Rom 8:23; 1 Cor 13:12; 2 Cor 3:18; 1 John 3:2). But we who believe are fully justified here and now, not because of our own flawed and feeble works of "righteousness," but because of Christ's perfect, true righteousness, which is imputed or credited to our eternal account.

The phrase in 2 Corinthians 5:19, "reconciling the world to himself," interjects a complicated, difficult, and sometimes debated issue into the matter of divine reconciliation. If Paul had said, "reconciling *believers* to Himself," or "reconciling *sinners* to Himself," the matter would undoubtedly have been easier to understand. But because the apostle wrote, "in Christ God was reconciling the *world* to himself" (emphasis added), the verse is a little more difficult to interpret accurately.

Universalists (people who erroneously believe that everyone eventually will be saved) use verse 19 to argue their case. If God through Christ has reconciled the world to Himself, they claim, then that must mean God has removed the barrier of sin between Himself and *everyone* in the world. Therefore all without exception are automatically going to be saved. But we know that is not true. This very passage is all about imploring unreconciled people to be reconciled. Elsewhere Scripture clearly states that *many* people will be eternally condemned to hell to be punished for their own sins (cf. Matt 7:13, 22-23; Rev 21:8).

So what did Paul mean when he said God was in Christ "reconciling the world to himself"? To answer that, we must understand that when the Bible speaks of Christ's dying for the whole world it speaks of mankind in general, regardless of class and ethnic distinctions, not of every specific individual without exception. "World" indicates the sphere or class of beings for whom God provided reconciliation. It speaks of the broad sweep of humanity—people from every tribe, tongue, and nation. Gentiles as well as Jews. Greeks as well as Hebrews. "The world."

It is in that sense that Christ died to reconcile "the world" to God, not counting their trespasses against them. He does not guarantee or even intend the salvation of *all* people without exception, but He is calling out from among humanity a believing remnant drawn from every nation, every culture, and every ethnic group (cf. Acts 15:14). That is what Paul means when he speaks of "the world." He chose that word deliberately, not to signify that salvation is universal, but to emphasize that it is not limited to one people or nation.

Of course, Christ's sacrifice is of infinite worth and value, abundantly sufficient to atone for the sins of the whole world, if that had been God's design. But we know many will *not* be saved. Therefore, it twists the meaning of verse 19 to suggest, as some have, that no sinner anywhere has any need to fear retribution for sin. Clearly, it is not the world in general whose trespasses are not counted against them, because the trespasses of many *will* be counted against them in the final judgment. So "the world" that is reconciled is the world of those who are justified.

Sinners Are Reconciled Through the Obedience of Faith

Who are the justified ones? They are the ones who believe. Faith is the instrument of justification. Faith does not *merit* justification. It is not the *ground* of our justification or the *reason* for our justification. Faith itself does not constitute the righteousness by which we are justified (as some have erroneously thought). But faith is the *instrument* by which sinners lay hold of justification. Righteousness is imputed to them by faith (Rom 4:5-6, 22-24). Faith is, therefore, what the Gospel demands from hearers.

Second Corinthians 5:20 speaks of the gospel call to faith. The apostle declares, "Therefore, we are ambassadors for Christ, God making his appeal through us. We implore you on behalf of Christ, be reconciled to God." What must people do to be reconciled with God? Scripture answers that question repeatedly, always with the same answer: "Believe in the Lord Jesus, and you will be saved, you and your household" (Acts 16:31; cf. John 3:16; 5:24; Rom 5:1; 10:9-10). So when we plead with people to be reconciled with God, we are calling them to faith in Christ.

The plea to "be reconciled to God" is in no way contradictory to the truth we have already noted—that reconciliation is completely from God and by means of a sovereign, declarative act of justification. But at the same time, reconciliation does not occur apart from the sinner's trusting wholeheartedly in Christ's atoning work.

Faith itself is not the sinner's work; it is a gift of God (Eph 2:8-9; John 6:44, 65; Phil 1:29). He sovereignly draws those whom He chooses (the elect) to faith in Christ (John 6:37; Rom 8:29-30; 2 Thess 2:13-14). And yet *all* are commanded to repent and believe (Acts 17:30). Sinners who reject the Gospel are held responsible for their unbelief (John 3:18; 16:8-9). The Bible teaches that God is sovereign in salvation. But just as plainly, it teaches that sinners are responsible for their own unbelief—because unbelief is willful disobedience (Heb 2:3; 12:25; 1 John 5:10).

Charles Spurgeon said this about the twin truths of divine sovereignty and human responsibility:

> If . . . I find taught in one part of the Bible that everything is fore-ordained, that is true; and if I find, in another Scripture, that man is responsible for all his actions, that is true; and it is only my folly that leads me to imagine that these two truths can ever contradict each other. I do not believe they can ever be welded into one upon any earthly anvil, but they certainly shall be

> one in eternity. They are two lines that are so nearly parallel, that the human mind which pursues them farthest will never discover that they converge, but they do converge, and they will meet somewhere in eternity, close to the throne of God, whence all truth doth spring.[1]

This much is plain: No one is excluded from the plea to be reconciled. Jesus said, "whoever comes to me I will never cast out" (John 6:37). The apostle John wrote, "But to all who did receive him [Jesus], who believed in his name, he gave the right to become children of God, who were born, not of blood nor of the will of the flesh nor of the will of man, but of God" (John 1:12-13; cf. Rom 3:26; 10:9-10). Scripture closes with this invitation: "The Spirit and the Bride say, 'Come.' And let the one who hears say, 'Come.' And let the one who is thirsty come; let the one who desires take the water of life without price" (Rev 22:17).

So every believer has the privilege and the duty to proclaim the Gospel to sinners and to urge them, beg them, and implore them, on Christ's behalf, to be reconciled to God through faith.

Faith has objective content. One must believe that God raised Jesus from the dead and that He now is Lord. But the ultimate object of true faith is not merely a doctrinal statement; it is a *Person*—Christ. The call to faith is a call to embrace Him as He is set forth in the Gospel. Faith, therefore, also has a subjective side—its attitude—that often gets overlooked. James 4:8-10 describes this attitude: "Draw near to God, and he will draw near to you. Cleanse your hands, you sinners, and purify your hearts, you double-minded. Be wretched and mourn and weep. Let your laughter be turned to mourning and your joy to gloom. Humble yourselves before the Lord, and he will exalt you." The sinner must come before God, recognize his fallen condition (that his inner being is spiritually filthy, double-minded, miserable, wretched, and blind), plead for God's mercy, and lay hold of Christ by faith as the only Savior who can redeem people from their sins.

God is making His appeal through us, His ambassadors, and imploring sinners (literally, "begging them")—urging them to seek reconciliation with God through faith in Christ.

Sinners Are Reconciled Because of the Work of Substitution

The real heart of 2 Corinthians 5:18-21 is the glorious truth of *how* our reconciliation was bought and paid for. This passage shows as clearly as any passage in Scripture that *Christ atoned for sins by becoming a substitute for sinners.* Verse 21 sets forth this powerful biblical truth in unmistakable terms: "For our sake he made him to be sin who knew no sin, so that in him we might become the righteousness of God." That one sentence resolves for us the main difficulty of the divine plan to redeem sinners. How can depraved sinners be reconciled to a holy God? Here we learn that the entire basis of the sinner's reconciliation to God is the substitutionary death of Jesus Christ.

The apostle Peter elsewhere writes, "He himself bore our sins in his body on the tree, that we might die to sin and live to righteousness. By his wounds you have been healed" (1 Pet 2:24). Peter is quoting from Isaiah 53, another key passage about substitutionary atonement. Isaiah writes, "Surely he has borne our griefs and carried our sorrows . . . he was wounded for our transgressions; he was crushed for our iniquities; upon him was the chastisement that brought us peace, and with his stripes we are healed. . . . The LORD has laid on him the iniquity of us all" (vv. 4-6).

Second Corinthians 5:21 contains four features that identify and summarize the significance of the work of substitution: the beneficiaries, the Benefactor, the substitute, and the benefit.

The Beneficiaries

First of all, the *beneficiaries of substitution* are believers. The text says, "For our sake"—the "our" referring to Paul's believing audience (along with "we" in v. 20 and "us" in vv. 18-19). He was speaking of those who are transformed and are in Christ (v. 17), those who have been reconciled (v. 18). It was for them in particular that Christ died as a substitute.

The Benefactor

The final word of verse 20 identifies *substitution's Benefactor*. It is none other than God. Remember, God is the One who designed and brought to fruition our reconciliation. He was the One who demanded a Substitute; He was the one who chose our Substitute; He was the one who ordained and executed the entire plan. Mankind had nothing to do with initiating the concept of substitution.

It was for believers' sake, however, that God planned it (cf. Rom 3:10-20). Only God the Father could ask His Son to become incarnate, enter into the world, humble Himself, take on the form of a man, and be obedient unto death, even the death of the cross (see Phil 2:5-8). Only God could decide how His own infinite holiness, intense hatred of sin, and inflexible justice could be perfectly satisfied without destroying the sinner in that satisfaction. In other words, God determined what would propitiate His wrath. And although the price was inconceivably awful, He was willing to make the sacrifice.

God acted as the Benefactor in providing substitution for sinners simply because of His own great love (John 3:16). "God shows his love for us in that while we were still sinners, Christ died for us" (Rom 5:8). While believers were still His enemies, God reconciled them to Himself through the death of His Son (Rom 5:10). Ephesians 2:4-5 says, "But God, being rich in mercy, because of the great love with which he loved us, even when we were dead in our trespasses, made us alive together with Christ" (cf. 1:3-7; Col 1:12-14).

This truth is what makes biblical Christianity different from all the religions of the world. Most of them operate on the premise that God is an angry, hateful, or indifferent deity who could not care less about the prosperity of beings who grub around underneath Him in this world. All of them teach that if God's righteousness is to be satisfied, it is the sinner himself who must provide the satisfaction. Therefore the goal of virtually all religions is somehow to appease God. Either they must placate an otherwise hostile and angry God through self-atonement, or their adherents imagine that they can please a benevolent God merely by being benevolent themselves. If people in those systems are going to be reconciled to their god or gods, they must *do* something—usually by performing religious ceremonies, observing rituals, fulfilling duties, or offering prayers by which they can appease this deity and thereby earn his favor.

But the good news of biblical Christianity is that God Himself has already supplied on our behalf all that is necessary to appease Him. We are not left to work out a plan of reconciliation for ourselves or to obtain our own righteousness. We can lean trustingly on the good news that God is the Benefactor. He has effected the substitutionary atonement to pay the full price of sin, and He now offers forgiveness and reconciliation to all who believe and trust Christ alone. That is the Gospel.

It took death to pay the price of sin because, as it says in Ezekiel 18:4, "The soul who sins shall die" (cf. Rom 6:23). God made that abundantly clear throughout the whole Old Testament economy. The Jews spent most of their lives either coming from or going to a sacrifice. They continually killed and offered animals as sacrifices—tens of millions of them over the centuries—to deal with sin, to show people how wicked they were, and to illustrate the fact that sin requires death. The blood of those animals could never take away sin (Heb 10:11). But the nonstop offering of those animals nonetheless demonstrated that the wages of sin is death. Believing Jews longed for the ultimate Lamb of God who once and for all would take away the sin of the world. Essentially, God's own Son, Jesus Christ, in obedience to the Father's plan, fulfilled that longing (cf. Heb 7:26-27; 9:11-12). And Christ did so under no coercion, but willingly: "I lay down my life that I may take it up again. No one takes it from me, but I lay it down of my own accord. I have authority to lay it down, and I have authority to take it up again. This charge I have received from my Father" (John 10:17-18).

The Substitute

The third feature of the work of substitution contained in 2 Corinthians 5:21 is the *identity of the Substitute*: "He made him to be sin who knew no sin." That is not describing any ordinary human being, because no mere man meets that sinless qualification (cf. Rom 3:23). Still, the substitute had to be a human being, because God required that a human must die for humans. The substitute could not be a sinful human being (or else he would have to die for his own sin and thus be unable to provide atonement for someone else's sin). So the substitute had to be a sinless man.

The only way God could provide a sinless man as a substitute for sin was to provide a Man who was God, because God alone is sinless. He made that provision by sending into the world in the form of a man His own Son, the sinless and perfect Christ—as holy as (and of the same substance as) the Father and the Holy Spirit. Paul told the Galatians, "When the fullness of time had come, God sent forth his Son, born of woman, born under the law, to redeem those who were under the law" (Gal 4:4-5). Jesus Christ, then, is "him . . . who knew no sin." The testimony of the New Testament affirms that. "For we do not have a high priest who is unable to sympathize with our weaknesses, but one who in every respect has been tempted as we are, yet without sin" (Heb 4:15; cf. 7:26; Luke 23:4; John 8:46; 1 Pet 1:18-19; 2:22; 3:18; 1 John 3:5).

What does the phrase "he made him to be sin" mean? In view of the utter sinlessness of Christ, it clearly does not mean that Christ became a sinner and committed sins or broke God's law. Our Lord had no capacity to sin. He remained the sinless, eternal God while becoming fully man. And certainly it is unthinkable that God would turn Him into a sinner.

We return to Isaiah 53 to understand how Christ was "made . . . sin":

> *Surely he has borne our griefs and carried our sorrows; yet we esteemed him stricken, smitten by God, and afflicted. But he was wounded for our transgressions; he was crushed for our iniquities; upon him was the chastisement that brought us peace, and with his stripes we are healed. All we*

> *like sheep have gone astray; we have turned every one to his own way; and the* L*ORD has laid on him the iniquity of us all. (vv. 4-6)*

Christ was "made . . . sin" by being made a substitute for sinners. He bore their guilt. He was punished for it. Simply put, God treated Christ as if He were a sinner, by making Him pay the penalty for sin though He was innocent. More than that, God treated Him as if He were guilty of all the sins of all who would ever believe. Sin, not His but ours, was credited or imputed to Him as if He had committed it, and He then paid the price on the cross.

That imputation is the *only* means by which Christ was "made . . . sin." The Father then poured out the full fury of His wrath against all that sin; because sin was laid on Him, Jesus experienced the full force of divine wrath against sin. He suffered as much of the wrath of God as someone would experience in an eternity of torment in hell. In other words, He paid an infinite price. Is it any wonder that He cried out, "My God, my God, why have you forsaken me?" (Matt 27:46)? He was treated as a sinner and thus, for a time on the cross, felt complete alienation from the Father. Although Christ was in practice and reality perfectly holy, God considered Him forensically guilty.

Anyone trying to achieve reconciliation with God by his own efforts, apart from trust in the Substitute, is cursed. Galatians 3:10 says, "For all who rely on works of the law are under a curse." Anyone who tries to earn his way to heaven by doing good works, performing religious duties, or adhering to some moral or ceremonial law is doomed to failure. "Cursed be anyone who does not confirm the words of this law by doing them" (Deut 27:26). He is accursed because the first time he violates one part of the law, he is deemed guilty of all (cf. Jas 2:10). That is why the law can damn sinners, but it cannot save them (cf. Gal 2:21).

There is a penalty associated with the curse of the law, and someone had to pay it on behalf of those whom God would redeem. Thus Paul declared, "Christ redeemed us from the curse of the law by becoming a curse for us" (Gal 3:13). That perfectly illustrates the principle of imputation. Christ became sin by imputation, just as all who embrace His atoning work become righteous by imputation. Our sin was imputed to Him so He could pay for it, just as His righteousness was imputed to us so we could be justified and reconciled to the Father.

In other words, on the cross God treated Christ as if He sinned all the sins of everyone who would ever believe, so that He could treat them as if they had lived Christ's perfect life. That is precisely what Paul means in

2 Corinthians 5:21: "[God] made him to be sin who knew no sin, so that in him we might become the righteousness of God."

The Benefit

Here is the *benefit or purpose of substitution*: "so that in him we might become the righteousness of God." Basically, that is the wonderful result sinners realize from justification. They receive a righteousness not derived from keeping the law, but laid hold of by faith in Christ. It is a true righteousness that comes from God. As Paul testified to the Philippians, it is "not . . . a righteousness of my own that comes from the law, but that which comes through faith in Christ, the righteousness from God that depends on faith" (Phil 3:9).

So the righteousness God requires from the sinner is the very righteousness He provides for those who believe. When God looks at believers, He sees individuals covered by the righteousness of Jesus Christ. And conversely, all their sins are eternally forgiven because Jesus has already paid the penalty for them.

What about the sins believers commit after their conversion? Christ died for those sins too, because, from the divine perspective, the atonement was conceived and designed while all sins were still in the future. Christ is "the Lamb slain from the foundation of the world" (Rev 13:8, KJV). God's eternal plan was for Christ to die for believers' sins, even while all those sins were yet future (Acts 2:23; 4:27-28).

The efficacious benefit of God's plan of redemption is the righteousness Paul refers to in the book of Romans: "the righteousness of God through faith in Jesus Christ for all who believe" (3:22). Faith is the key to experiencing this benefit, and that faith involves acknowledging certain things. We must confess that we are sinners, desperately alienated from God. We must believe that in ourselves we have no hope of reconciliation with God, and unless we repent, we will be forever separated from God and suffer eternal torment. We must believe that God sent His Son into the world in the form of a man to die as a substitute for sinners and to receive the full fury of God's wrath in their place. We must believe that God's justice was satisfied by Jesus' sacrifice, as demonstrated by the fact that God raised Jesus from the dead. And finally we must believe that God exalted Jesus to His right hand, seated Him on a throne, and gave Him a name "that is above every name, so that at the name of Jesus every knee should bow, in heaven and on earth and under the earth, and every tongue confess that Jesus Christ is Lord, to the glory of God the Father" (Phil 2:9-10).

That is the Gospel. It is the heart of historic, biblical Christianity. It is also the heart and soul of an authentically Christian worldview.

FURTHER READING

MacArthur, John. *Saved Without a Doubt*. Wheaton, IL: Victor, 1992.

__________. *The Gospel According to the Apostles*. Nashville: Word, 2000.

__________. *The Gospel According to Jesus*. Grand Rapids, MI: Zondervan, 1988.

Morris, Leon. *The Apostolic Preaching of the Cross*. Grand Rapids, MI: William B. Eerdmans, 1955.

Packer, J. I. *Evangelism and the Sovereignty of God*. Downers Grove, IL: IVP, 1961.

6

Viewing the Nations from God's Perspective

Mark A. Tatlock

Globalization, internationalism, multiculturalism, diversity, tolerance, and racial reconciliation are common references in today's headlines. What do any of these words have to do with a Christian's view of the world? Do these agendas relate at all to a biblical position on God's sovereignty, creation, redemption, or the church? Do ethnic demographics, geopolitical shifts, or the internationalization of industry have any bearing on the believer's understanding of the kingdom? Does global poverty, the increase of orphans due to AIDS, religious persecution, modern-day slavery, or injustice require a response by the Body of Christ?

> . . . the body of Christ was, from the start, also meant to become a global community . . . long before the present process of technological and economic globalization began, God's message of global Good News went forth and began its work. The idea of globalization therefore, is not foreign to the Bible.[1]

It is critical that Christians possess a theologically informed, biblically principled world vision. The education of today's church member must include a biblical response to peoples of the world. This requires that a theology of cross-cultural ministry be defined and articulated by the church. In doing so, the church can fully find its voice and express itself confidently among those secular opinions heard in today's classrooms, boardrooms, and courtrooms.

From creation to the final consummation of the end times, God extends a message of hope, forgiveness, and reconciliation to those in every tribe, tongue, and nation. Scripture presents a solid case for unity, peace, justice, and love between people of all nations. The blueprint for the formation of the church is specifically sketched as cross-cultural in scope and intent. The implications of this message have a bearing on all contemporary attempts to deal with the effects of the Fall, particularly those of hate, fear, misunderstanding, prejudice, and injustice. When one examines the clear biblical teaching regarding creation, a biblical theology of cross-cultural ministry emerges. The ideas of creation, covenant, cultures, Christ, commission, church, and consummation provide a clear and concise way to discuss the dynamic reality of God's view toward the nations.

Creation

It is critical that any theologically informed worldview begin with the account of creation. Genesis 1:1 states clearly that there is only one Creator. Roger Hedlund explains, "Creation by God means that there is but one human race . . . and that Yahweh is no tribal deity but God and Father of all."[2] Every man, woman, and child owes his or her very existence to this true God. The Fatherhood of God in a physical sense is inclusive by definition and biblical declaration (Mal 2:10). "Ethnic and cultural diversity is part of the creative design of God. . . . Racism is a perversion of creation."[3]

There was no pantheon of gods involved in creation. The universe was not created by committee. In the obvious vacuum of multiple creators, any other false deity's claim to creation rights is invalid. Any attempt by a false religion to ascribe authority or worship to a god other than Yahweh is an attempt to rob God of the glory that He alone deserves.

> *For although they knew God, they did not honor him as God or give thanks to him, but they became futile in their thinking, and their foolish hearts were darkened. Claiming to be wise, they became fools, and exchanged the glory of the immortal God for images resembling mortal man and birds and animals and reptiles . . . they exchanged the truth about God for a lie and worshiped and served the creature rather than the Creator, who is blessed forever! Amen.*
>
> —ROM 1:21-23, 25

Rejecting the Creator results in elevating the creation. Whether it be the idolatry of paganism or the self-deification of humanism, the result is the same. Unregenerate man will always attempt to draw glory away from the Creator and attribute it to something that falls into the creation category. But only the one, true Creator God deserves all worship.

The Rebellion of Satan

This principle is demonstrated in the account of Satan's rebellion. Isaiah 14:14 describes how Satan asserted his independence and made his mission to be "like the Most High." Here one witnesses the very essence of sin—the substitution of the creation as the object of worship. Revelation 12:4 reports that many other angels followed Satan, attributing supreme worth and honor—deserved only by God—to Satan. It is critical to observe that, at the very moment they made this choice, a second kingdom was established, the kingdom of this world. This two-kingdom reality constructed for man an alternative stage on which to play out his life and allowed for his choice to either follow God or embrace idolatry.

Scripture testifies that God Himself refuses to allow His authority to be assumed by any created being (Isa 42:8). History will play out the drama of Satan and man vying for God's glory. The great white throne judgment will be the final event wherein all who have elevated an object of creation, including man, to a position of deity will be held accountable for their choice (Rev 20:11-15).

Scripture tells the beautiful story of a God who so loves His creation that He designed a plan of redemption, calling man into a reconciled relationship with the Creator. Man was created to have perfect fellowship with God (Gen 2:4-25). It was God's intent to see His creation experience an intimate relationship with Him centering on man's willingness to honor the Creator for who He alone is. Redemption is the way to make right what went disastrously wrong in the Fall. The tragedy of Adam and Eve's choice was the exchange of their intimate relationship with the awesome Creator for the lie that they too could possess some of the glory of the Creator. When they asserted their independence (Gen 3:1-7), they adopted the same mission as Satan: to elevate self to the position of ultimate authority and autonomy. This is evident when one examines what occurred in the dialogue between Satan and Eve.

The Fall of Man

Genesis 3:13 states that Eve was deceived by the Tempter (see also 2 Cor 11:3; 1 Tim 2:14). It is critically important to examine what lie Eve heard. For if the Fall hinged on the acceptance of a lie, then a more accurate understanding of the nature of disobedience can be better determined. Placed in dialogue format, the exchange between the Devil and Eve reveals that Eve was not as much a victim as is typically taught.

> *[Serpent:] "Did God actually say, 'You shall not eat of any tree in the garden'?"*
>
> *[Eve:] "We may eat of the fruit of the trees in the garden, but God said, 'You shall not eat of the fruit of the tree that is in the midst of the garden, neither shall you touch it, lest you die.'"*
>
> *[Serpent:] "You will not surely die. For God knows that when you eat of it your eyes will be opened, and you will be like God, knowing good and evil."*
>
> *So when the woman saw that the tree was good for food, and that it was a delight to the eyes, and that the tree was to be desired to make one wise, she took of its fruit and ate, and she also gave some to her husband who was with her, and he ate.*
>
> —GEN 3:1-6

The two statements made by Satan give us the clearest understanding of what occurred at the Fall. The first statement, "You will not surely die," is the lie that Eve chose to believe. This is a deceptive statement because it completely contradicts the warning God gave to Adam in Genesis 2:17, ". . . but of the tree of the knowledge of good and evil you shall not eat, for in the day that you eat of it you shall surely die." The amazing thing to recognize is that Satan told the truth regarding the nature of the tree. It did represent the knowledge that only God possessed, until Eve ate. The real temptation for Eve was the idea that she could be like God.

This desire to rob God of the glory He alone deserves and to redirect it to oneself is the essence of the rebellion as described in Romans 1. This choice, motivated by the same idolatrous desire as that of Satan and the fallen angels, made necessary a God-initiated provision for enabling man to repent from sin. The mission of God, to restore Himself to the rightful place of worship by His creation, required a work of reconciliation that could not be accomplished by man (2 Cor 5:18-21). God acted swiftly to introduce this plan. In Genesis 3:14-15 the curse is pronounced upon Satan and man and includes the promised victory of God's kingdom. Theologians refer to this passage as the "proto-evangel," literally meaning "first Gospel." In God's pronouncement of judgment, He states that the Seed of the woman would wield a final defeating blow to the counterfeit kingdom established by Satan's rebellion. Scripture then embarks on a sixty-six book account of how God has been at work throughout human history, reconciling men and women from every people group back to a pre-Fall relationship with Himself, the Creator. The promise of a coming Redeemer "was given to the entire human race. . . . Its racial scope must not be overlooked, for only as Christ becomes the Saviour of the total human race is Genesis 3:15 fulfilled."[4]

Covenant

> The Old Testament is filled with passages in which people will stream to Mount Zion and seek the God of Israel because of His mighty deeds on behalf of His special people.[5]

When God called Abram to be the father of the Jewish nation, He stated the extent of influence that the Jews would have and what that influence specifically would be. In Genesis 12:1-3 God declares to Abram, "I will make you a great nation, and I will bless you . . . so that you will be a blessing . . . and in you all the families of the earth shall be blessed." Though God was promising to establish a great nation, it is clear that it was to be a means to a larger, wider-reaching work, since "all the families of the earth" refers to God's intent as Creator to be a Father to mankind. "All the families of the earth" must be understood as inclusive of people from every cultural context. This promise of blessing is a direct reference to God's reconciling work of salvation, which is clarified in Galatians 3:8-9.

> *And the Scripture, foreseeing that God would justify the Gentiles by faith, preached the gospel beforehand to Abraham, saying, "In you shall all the nations be blessed." So then, those who are of faith are blessed along with Abraham, the man of faith.*

This covenant explained that all Jews and Gentiles who would place their faith in the one true God are children of Abraham. Therefore, the word "blessed" here means "salvation."

> What we may conclude from the wording of Genesis 12:3 and its use in the New Testament is that God's purpose for the world is that the blessing of Abraham would reach to all the ethnic people groups of the world. This would happen as people in each group put their faith in Christ and thus become "sons of Abraham" and "heirs of the promise." This event of individual salvation as persons trust Christ will happen among "all the nations."[6]

God changed Abram's name to signal the intent of His redemptive strategy, for the new name, Abraham ("father of a multitude"), in Hebrew points to redemption. Based on the Hebrew word usage in the text, Michael Grisanti affirms, "God's program has worldwide implications and is not limited to

Israel. . . . It is God's intention to use Abraham to bless the nations. . . . This passage delineates God's choice of an instrument through whom He will bless the world."[7] This covenant statement is repeated throughout multiple generations of Abraham's descendants (Gen 18:18; 22:18; 26:4; 28:14). We also see it repeated to the children of Israel after they had taken possession of the promised land under the leadership of Joshua (Josh 23—24).

CULTURES

Declare his glory among the nations,
his marvelous works among all peoples!
For great is the LORD, and greatly to be praised;
he is to be feared above all gods.
For all the gods of the peoples are worthless idols,
but the LORD made the heavens. . . .
Ascribe to the LORD, O families of the peoples,
ascribe to the LORD glory and strength! . . .
Say among the nations, "The LORD reigns!"

—PS 96:3-5, 7-10

Israel lived in a multicultural context. From the journeyings of Abraham, Jacob, Joseph, and Moses in Egypt, to the constant engagement of the Philistines, Amorites, and Moabites, to the Babylonian and Assyrian captivities, the Israelites had opportunity to declare the glories of the one true God. Each book of the Bible refers to Israel's responsibility to the nations (e.g., Ps 67; 98:2-3; Isa 49:6; Jer 33:7-9; Jon 4:1-11). In Exodus 19:5-6 God asks Moses to tell the Israelites that they are to serve in a priestly capacity, functioning as mediators between sinful men and a holy God. Two Old Testament accounts illustrate the opportunities that Israel was given to serve as priests: Solomon's reign and Daniel's captivity.

Solomon's Reign

Solomon, gifted by God with unprecedented wisdom, was commissioned to construct the Temple. Solomon understood from the history of his own people that the Temple was to be a place of worship for Jehovah. It would herald the final settlement of the Israelite people in the land that God had promised to them in the Abrahamic Covenant. Solomon's life provides us with a picture of how the Jews were to fulfill their priest-like role among the nations. We capture two glimpses of this priesthood principle—the first, a positive one, and the second, a devastating compromise of this responsibility.

In 1 Kings 8:22-61, Solomon is standing before the newly completed

Temple. As he offers an extensive prayer of dedication, he includes a reference to Israel's priest-like role to the Gentile nations. In verses 41-43 he prays:

> *Likewise, when a foreigner, who is not of your people Israel, comes from a far country for your name's sake (for they shall hear of your great name and your mighty hand, and of your outstretched arm), when he comes and prays toward this house, hear in heaven your dwelling place and do according to all for which the foreigner calls to you, in order that all the peoples of the earth may know your name and fear you, as do your people Israel, and that they may know that this house that I have built is called by your name.*

It is evident that Solomon understood that the blessing was to extend through Israel to all peoples. He knew God allowed the Moabite family of Moses' wife to be joined to Israel by faith. He knew God allowed the Canaanite prostitute Rahab to be joined to Israel by faith. He knew God allowed Ruth to make the God of her mother-in-law Naomi *her* God. Obviously, God had great love and compassion for the Gentiles. And those who by faith embraced Jehovah were children of the covenant as well.

How tragic it is then to see this great and wise king violate God's instructions. First Kings 11:1-13 unfolds the account of Solomon "lov[ing] many foreign women."

> *For when Solomon was old his wives turned away his heart after other gods, and his heart was not wholly true to the* LORD *his God, as was the heart of David his father. For Solomon went after Ashtoreth the goddess of the Sidonians, and after Milcom the abomination of the Ammonites. So Solomon did what was evil in the sight of the* LORD *and did not wholly follow the* LORD*, as David his father had done. Then Solomon built a high place for Chemosh the abomination of Moab, and for Molech the abomination of the Ammonites, on the mountain east of Jerusalem. And so he did for all his foreign wives, who made offerings and sacrificed to their gods.*
>
> —1 KGS 11:4-8

It is a dramatic contrast to watch Solomon compromise the priest-like responsibility of the nation and invite into the nation the very gods Joshua and the children of Israel had purged from the land. He who erected the most magnificent Temple for the world to come and worship Jehovah later erected temples to foreign idols.

Daniel's Captivity

Even when the consequence for the nation's idolatry was exile and captivity, God used the Israelites as an expansive covenant force. Daniel and his friends Shadrach, Meshach, and Abednego faithfully fulfilled their priestly role. As youths taken into Nebuchadnezzar's court, they attempted to demonstrate that Jehovah was the powerful Creator. Their challenge to live not on the king's finest food but on vegetables and water proved they understood the need to witness before idolatrous foreigners. Later when Nebuchadnezzar exposed his ambitions to be worshiped as only God deserved (Dan 3:4-5), the three friends refused to bow down and worship the statue he had placed on the plain of Dura. God protected them and showed Himself to be all-powerful.

The elevation of Daniel to a position of great influence in the court proves to be a most powerful illustration of this principle. Nebuchadnezzar, evidencing his desire to be worshiped as the Most High, was plagued by a dream. Daniel, asked to interpret the dream, warned Nebuchadnezzar of his need to repent and honor Jehovah. Daniel 4:28-37 describes the account of God's changing the heart of this king. "At the end of twelve months he was walking on the roof of the royal palace of Babylon, and the king answered and said, 'Is not this great Babylon, which I have built by my mighty power as a royal residence and for the glory of my majesty?'" (vv. 29-30). God immediately struck Nebuchadnezzar down to crawl on his belly like an animal for seven years, until he would recognize that the Most High is ruler over the realm of all mankind. This is an amazing picture of God's grace, extended even to this foreign, self-deifying king.

> *At the end of the days I, Nebuchadnezzar, lifted my eyes to heaven, and my reason returned to me, and I blessed the Most High, and praised and honored him who lives forever. . . . Now I, Nebuchadnezzar, praise and extol and honor the King of heaven, for all his works are right and his ways are just; and those who walk in pride he is able to humble.*
>
> —DAN 4:34, 37

Whether during the period of the Exodus, the judges, or the prophets, the recurring theme is that of the Creator calling back His chosen people to loyalty and obedience to their covenant responsibility. God consistently demonstrated that the intent of the covenant blessing was global, and not limited to the nation of Israel.

> [Israel] was marked out long ago in the time of Abraham, "to be a covenant to the people" of the earth. Once the word "people" is shown to be equal to the Gentile nations of the earth, then it must mean that all the Gentiles

> and peoples of the world are to be consolidated in the very same covenant that Yahweh had made with Abraham, Isaac, Jacob, and David and that Jeremiah spelled out in the New Covenant. . . . [The covenants] were initially given to Israel so that Israel could share them with the peoples of the earth.[8]

This reality informs every believer's understanding of God's ultimate plan for history: the loving reconciliation of men and women from every tribe and nation back to a pre-Fall garden walk with Him. This is the hope of eternity. It proves to be the mission of Christ, it proves to be the commission of the church, and it proves to be the promise of eternity future.

Christ

In the New Covenant, Christ is the ultimate fulfillment of God's covenant promise to extend the blessing of salvation to all the nations. In Him, the consistency of God's plan to offer salvation to the Jews first, but also to the Gentiles (Rom 1:16-17) is recognized. The nativity narrative includes two bold allusions to the broad scope of God's plan. Luke 2 tells of the angels' appearance to the Jewish shepherds in the fields near Bethlehem. But also included in the narrative is the account of Magi or wise men traveling from the East to find the promised Messiah. These men, most probably from the area of ancient Babylon, were searching the heavens for the promised sign of one who would come and rule. Their eventual arrival at the Child's home, bearing valuable gifts, resulted in their active worship of Christ. The fact that both Jews and Gentiles are included in this narrative account hints that from the very beginning of Christ's earthly life, God's commitment to reconcile all men to Himself was evident.

The second allusion to God's multicultural program comes eight days after Christ's birth. Mary and Joseph, obeying the command to dedicate their child at the Temple, were met by a man named Simeon. Luke 2:25-26 reveals that God had promised Simeon he would not die until he had seen the promised Savior. Simeon, upon seeing Mary and Joseph enter the Temple court, immediately recognizes the Child as the fulfillment of God's promise. He made a critical statement as he took the child into his arms and said, "Lord, now you are letting your servant depart in peace, according to your word; for my eyes have seen your salvation that you have prepared in the presence of all peoples, a light for revelation to the Gentiles, and for glory to your people Israel" (vv. 29-32). Here is an obvious emphasis on the multi-ethnic scope of redemption.

The fact that Christ was born a Jew is consistent with God's covenant plan to work through the Jewish nation to offer salvation. Unfortunately, most of the Jews failed to understand the scope of God's kingdom plan. Particularly during the lifetime of Christ, they were adamant that the blessing of the covenant would be limited, aimed only at benefiting the Jewish people. This blind perspective resulted in Christ's repeated confrontation of the Jews in His earthly ministry and proved to be a source of their hatred for Him. Luke 4:24-27 records Christ's first sermon in the city of Nazareth.

> *And he said, "Truly, I say to you, no prophet is acceptable in his hometown. But in truth, I tell you, there were many widows in Israel in the days of Elijah, when the heavens were shut up three years and six months, and a great famine came over all the land, and Elijah was sent to none of them but only to Zarephath, in the land of Sidon, to a woman who was a widow. And there were many lepers in Israel in the time of the prophet Elisha, and none of them was cleansed, but only Naaman the Syrian."*

Christ specifically chose two Old Testament references to the faith of non-Jewish individuals. Both the widow of Zarephath and Naaman are illustrations of the intended scope of God's covenant plan. To the Jews, looking for an earthly Messiah with nationalistic intentions, these references to Gentile individuals were perceived as inconsistent with their expectation of the Messiah. This failure on the Jews' part to understand God's redemptive plan and their role in it led to continual conflict with Christ during His earthly ministry.

When Christ attempted to explain the concept of loving your brother, using the example of the Good Samaritan (Luke 10:25-37), it was the Jews in the story who neglected to love one of their own who had suffered the injustice of robbery and abuse. The hero in Christ's account is the hated Samaritan. Jews, who despised Samaritans because of their ethnically-mixed heritage, heard Christ elevating him over Jews as an example of kingdom faith. In an even bolder fashion, Christ emphasized the failure of the Jews to embrace God's plan when He was approached by a Roman centurion (Matt 8:5-13). The centurion's faith-based request to have his servant healed by Christ provided our Savior with an opportunity to contrast what saving faith looks like compared to the national and religious pride of the Jews.

> *When Jesus heard this, he marveled and said to those who followed him, "Truly, I tell you, with no one in Israel have I found such faith. I tell you, many will come from east and west and recline at table with Abraham, Isaac, and Jacob in the kingdom of heaven, while the sons of the kingdom*

> *will be thrown into the outer darkness. In that place there will be weeping and gnashing of teeth."*
>
> —MATT 8:10-12

Here another Gentile is elevated as one who will partake in the promised kingdom, and it is revealed that many Jews will be excluded.

On several other occasions, Christ confronted the pride and ethnocentrism of the Jews (e.g., Matt 12:38-42; 15:21-28; John 4:9). One of the most interesting instances is the expulsion of the moneylenders and vendors from the Temple courts. Mark 11:15-17 portrays the anger of Christ directed at those who had compromised the function of the Temple as a place for reconciliation and worship. It is significant that this occurred in the area of the Temple referred to as "the Court of the Gentiles." In the design of the Temple, God had intended for there to be a recognized place of worship for the foreigner. This is consistent with Solomon's prayer of dedication in 1 Kings 8. Not only was Christ cleansing the Temple from those who were violating its consecrated purpose, He was also illustrating that the Jews had come to disregard the rightful place of a foreigner to worship their God. By His expression of anger, He affirmed the significance of this dedicated place of worship for the nations.

COMMISSION

When Christ prepared to ascend to heaven, He revealed to His followers what would be His intended pattern for ministry. The following statements comprise the essence of Christ's commission: "Go therefore and make disciples of all nations" (Matt 28:18-20); "Go into all the world and proclaim the gospel to the whole creation" (Mark 16:15-16); "repentance and forgiveness of sins should be proclaimed in his name to all nations, beginning from Jerusalem" (Luke 24:47); "you will be my witnesses in Jerusalem and in all Judea and Samaria, and to the end of the earth" (Acts 1:8b). In declaring that His followers should make disciples of all men, He uses the explicit phrase "of all nations." This phrase translated "all nations" or "all peoples" (*panta ta ethne*) in Matthew 28:19 relates directly to the "all the families of the earth" phrase in the Abrahamic covenant (Gen 12:3).

> The sweep of all the [linguistic] evidence makes it abundantly clear that God's gift of a blessing through the instrumentality of Abraham was to be experienced by nations, clans, tribes, people groups, and individuals. It would be for every size group, from the smallest people group to the greatest nation.[9]

The interaction with secular nations meant interaction with man-made deities. The goal of missions is a rejection of idolatry, including man himself, and the reconciliation of true worshipers to God. "Worship launches mission outreach, and worship is the outcome of this outreach as new believers join in honoring our Lord. Active witness connects the starting line with the goal."[10]

CHURCH

Acts 1:8 explains how God's redemptive plan for all peoples would be geographically implemented. Beginning in Jerusalem, extending throughout Judea, to Samaria, it would go forth to every other nation—i.e., "the end of the earth." This order honors God's promise to offer salvation first to the Jew and then to the Gentile.

> Mission takes place in a world of cultures. The book of Acts shows the progression of the gospel from the "Jewish" Jews of Jerusalem into the Judean countryside, then to the Samaritans and to the Hellenized Jews, and from the latter to the Gentiles at Antioch, and finally to the multiple cultures of the Roman Empire and the world.[11]

Acts provides a historical narrative of the emerging growth of the early church, demonstrating how first Peter and James, then Philip, and finally Paul and his partners follow the explicit command of Christ to geographically extend His salvific mission. The book of Acts introduces the church as God's primary vehicle for extending His redemptive plan.

Witnesses in Jerusalem

Peter, the apostle to whom Christ personally expressed His vision for the church (Matt 16:18), was entrusted with preaching the first gospel sermon inaugurating the church (Acts 2:14-40). This occurred during the time of Pentecost, just ten days after the ascension of Christ. Pentecost, also known as the Feast of Weeks or Harvest, required that every Jewish male appear at the sanctuary for this feast. Because of the scattering of the Jews due to persecution during the Intertestamental period, Jews had occupied many countries in the Roman Empire. These Jewish men (not native speakers of Aramaic or Hebrew, but speakers of their native country's language) witnessed the coming of the Holy Spirit and the proclamation of the Gospel (Acts 2:1-41). "People from every continent of the then known world were there. Asia, Africa, and Europe were represented. . . . From its inception, the church had a focus as big as the world."[12] In His great wisdom and power, God demonstrated His far-reaching plan for redemption. Men who would return to their home countries following the feast heard the Gospel in their own language. The fact that these men were Jewish again affirms God's covenant plan to extend salvation, beginning first with the Jewish people. Through them, Gentiles of other nations would be confronted in their idolatry.

In his sermon, Peter rehearses God's promise to the nation of Israel, that through them the promised Messiah would come (Acts 2:29-36). Peter would later serve as the lead counsel for the Jerusalem church when they were tempted to exclude any Gentiles from true fellowship as equals in the kingdom. God prepares Peter in Acts 10:1—11:18 by giving him a vision and sending him to the home of the Roman centurion Cornelius. Through the work of the Holy Spirit, Peter recognizes the meaning of the vision to be that all people, Jews and Gentiles, are to be considered equal hearers of the covenant promise of salvation. This incident is critical because Peter, the "apostle to the Jews," now understood that the church was to include people from all ethnic races. He subsequently led the Jewish church to accept Gentile believers as equals at the Jerusalem Council described in Acts 15.

Witnesses in Judea and Samaria

Judea and Samaria represent the second phase of the church's expansion. Philip played a key role in this expansion by preaching the kingdom to the Samaritans (Acts 8:5-25). He was joined by Peter and John (v. 14), who prayed for the Samaritans to receive the Holy Spirit. Here the church was extended through their witness to this previously rejected people. Philip was then called by an angel of the Lord to leave Samaria and journey to the southern part of Judea. On this journey he encountered not a Jew, but an African. This man, referred to most often as the Ethiopian eunuch, was a high-ranking official in the court of Candace, queen of Ethiopia. It is no mistake that this account of an African being led to Christ through the Old Testament writings of Isaiah is included in the book of Acts. It perfectly illustrates God's inclusion of peoples from the full breadth of nations in His redemptive plan. As well, it is prophetic in anticipating the next phase of church expansion—unto the uttermost parts.

Witnesses to the Ends of the Earth

Paul's journeys manifest his understanding of God's prescribed missionary method. By entering a city and proceeding directly to the synagogue, Paul showed God's desire that the Jew be given first opportunity to receive the gospel message. Met with direct hostility and persecution, Paul would then proceed to Gentile forums such as Tyrannus' classroom in Ephesus, the marketplace such as that in Corinth, or the center of philosophical debate such as that in Athens. His authorship of multiple church epistles during these trips helps us to understand these books of the Bible not only as general or pastoral epistles, but as letters to missionary church plants, each one a picture of God's redeeming work among primarily non-Jewish peoples.

Paul's statement in 2 Corinthians 5:20 is useful as an overarching theme for his life: "Therefore, we are ambassadors for Christ, God making his appeal through us. We implore you on behalf of Christ, be reconciled to God." The allusion to an ambassador as a picture of Paul's church-planting ministry provides an effective connotation. It is an ambassador who is tasked primarily with brokering peace between warring kingdoms. Man, representing the fallen kingdom of this world, and God, representing His perfect, righteous heavenly kingdom, find their agents of peace in those who are functioning as spiritual ambassadors. Christ Himself serves as the ultimate ambassador, and the church as His commissioned representatives. For it is in His authority, and His alone, that the followers of Christ proclaim the hope-filled message of reconciliation and peace (Matt 12:18). "Paul says much about missions and evangelism. Supremely an exponent and propagator of the gospel, he expected the early churches to be of like mind (Rom 10:12-18; 1 Cor 9:16-18; Eph 3:1-12; Phil 2:15-16; 1 Tm 2:1-7)."[13]

> In infinite wisdom God designed salvation; in infinite grace and at infinite cost God procured salvation in Christ Jesus, His only begotten Son; in infinite power God sent forth the Holy Spirit to actualize salvation in the individual and in history; in infinite compassion God instituted mission and missions—first through Israel and now through His church—in order that hopeless mankind might hear, know and believe the good news at the infinite salvation of God for mankind.[14]

Today's church finds itself central to this epoch of the mission mandate that continues to look toward the extension of the Gospel around the world, penetrating every people group on the globe.

> The book of Acts demonstrates the progression of the message of Christ to "the end of the earth," which for Luke is Rome, the center of the Roman Empire. The "all nations" of Luke 24:47, however, do not receive the preaching of the Gospel in the book of Acts, and this dimension of the Old Testament promise is still not completely fulfilled today. That the fulfillment of this command is promised in the Old Testament should give the church confidence and urgency as it moves forward to accomplish the task.[15]

The reader of Scripture should recognize the picture of eternity drawn at the consummation of all human eras to be the reestablishment of God's one kingdom. In this kingdom, men and women from every people group will manifest the realization of God's covenant plan and great commission assignment.

Consummation

There is an end to God's redemptive timeline. There will come a day when the opportunity to respond to God's invitation for reconciliation will no longer be available, and He will judge every man's confession. This future day is what inspires Christians to have hope and faith in this lifetime. This same future should be considered with dread by those who reject His loving offer. Regardless of man's acceptance or rejection, every human will affirm the truth of who Christ is. Isaiah 45:23 states, "'To me every knee shall bow, every tongue shall swear allegiance.'" This prediction, made also in Romans 14:11 and Philippians 2:9-11, makes it clear that every knee will bow and every tongue confess that Jesus is Lord.

In the beautiful picture of the eternal state described by John, one views the fulfillment of all God's redemptive plans.

> *And I saw no temple in the city, for its temple is the Lord God the Almighty and the Lamb. And the city has no need of sun or moon to shine on it, for the glory of God gives it light, and its lamp is the Lamb. By its light will the nations walk, and the kings of the earth will bring their glory into it, and its gates will never be shut by day—and there will be no night there. They will bring into it the glory and the honor of the nations.*
>
> —REV 21:22-26

From Genesis 1:1 to Revelation 22:21, this theme of God's eternal plan for His creation to worship Him alone demands His perfect, grace-based provision for the forgiveness of sins. "Thus this theme of a mission to the whole world forms one giant envelope framing the whole Bible, from Genesis to Revelation."[16]

Intercultural Ministry Today

The overwhelmingly consistent and bold theme in Scripture is that all men and women, from either Jewish or non-Jewish descent, are valued in God's sight. His love is not limited to one people; it is exhaustively demonstrated to all peoples. This multi-ethnic emphasis leads the Christian to make the following observations:

• God created men and women of every cultural group.

• God's love is extended to people from every cultural group.

• Because of God's expansive love, every church member should demonstrate a commitment to love people from every cultural group.

• All believers must reject the idolatry represented within any cultural group.

• Every church should reflect a vision to reach the nations as part of its mission.

• All believers should recognize their primary identity as citizens of heaven, even above their own national citizenship.

The missions movement of today no longer thinks in terms of foreign missions alone. A student of global, national, and local demographics will quickly recognize that cross-cultural ministry can occur anywhere today due to modern communication and transportation capabilities. This change in missionary thinking means that every local church must do more than just support missionaries sent overseas to fulfill their role in God's redemptive plan.

Intentional local outreach programs should look at individuals from other ethnic backgrounds as primary emphases in evangelism and discipleship. Groups such as new immigrants, international university students, nonnative English speakers, international businesspeople, and refugees deserve the church's immediate attention. It is often the case that these people groups represent the most impoverished and needy. An effective strategy to reach out to these peoples must include practical expressions of Christ's love. By meeting both physical and spiritual needs, the church manifests the clearest picture of Christ's method of mission.

Confronting issues of racial and economic prejudice is part of missions work, the work of the church. Left without a Christian response, advocates for the poor or minorities must turn to political means for relief. Unfortunately, they must rely on a rights-based approach rather than a biblical love-based approach. Without the church leading the way, secular agendas of multiculturalism, diversity, tolerance, and racial reconciliation provide only a humanistic, man-centered solution. Each of these fall far short of the eternal love and unity promised by God for those from every nation who believe in Christ. Thus today's church must evaluate its priorities.

If God has such affection for His creation, then every contemporary church and church member must understand their role in this master plan of God. They will in turn be forced to look at cross-cultural ministry as the consistently historical and future work of God. Our God has a heart for the nations. He views them as equal to each other and important to His kingdom. Any church or church member who neglects to prioritize a gospel witness to men and women of all ethnic people groups neglects to fully understand the very heart of God Himself and misses His perspective of the nations.

Further Reading

Bolt, Peter and Mark Thompson. *The Gospel to the Nations: Perspectives on Paul's Mission.* Downers Grove, IL: IVP, 2000.

Hedlund, Roger. *The Mission of the Church in the World.* Grand Rapids, MI: Baker, 1985.

Kaiser, Walter C., Jr. *Mission in the Old Testament: Israel as a Light to the Nations.* Grand Rapids, MI: Baker, 2000.

Köstenberger, Andreas J. and P. T. O'Brien. *Salvation to the Ends of the Earth: A Biblical Theology of Mission.* Downers Grove, IL: IVP, 2001.

O'Brien, P. T. *Gospel and Mission in the Writings of Paul: An Exegetical and Theological Analysis.* Grand Rapids, MI: Baker, 1995.

Peters, George W. *A Biblical Theology of Missions.* Chicago: Moody Press, 1972.

Piper, John. *Let the Nations Be Glad: The Supremacy of God in Missions.* Grand Rapids, MI: Baker, 1993.

Zuck, Roy B., ed. *Vital Missions Issues: Examining Challenges and Changes in World Evangelism.* Grand Rapids, MI: Kregel, 1998.

PART TWO

The Biblical Formulation

7

UNDERSTANDING OUR POSTMODERN WORLD

BRIAN K. MORLEY

A western apologist once visited a tribal area of Africa and conducted an elaborate seminar for Christians on how to prove the existence of God. Afterwards a person came up and complimented him on his presentation but added politely that no one in that part of Africa doubted that God exists. What they wanted to know was which God to serve. The visitor meant well but failed to understand the specific spiritual questions being asked by that particular culture.

The more one understands about people's ideas, the better one can communicate the truth of Scripture and the Gospel to them. That is why one learns about cults and religions, and why missionaries try to understand the cultures in which they live. But not enough Christians in the West put much effort into understanding the culture in which they live.

New believers who come into the church bring their worldviews with them. Furthermore, those Christians already in the church who do not understand worldview issues will not realize when they are embracing non-Christian concepts. Paul warned the Colossians not to allow themselves to be taken "captive by philosophy" (Col 2:8). Most Christians assume that the best way to prevent that is to avoid learning anything contrary to what they believe. But like it or not, worldview issues are all around, pressing in from the surrounding culture. Instead of trying to completely shield oneself from culture, Paul would advise a different approach: understanding something about the ideas that intrude and learning to discern between truth and error.

Biblically speaking, it is the Christian who should be doing the capturing, not the other way around. Paul said he destroyed "arguments and every lofty opinion raised against the knowledge of God," and he took "every thought captive to obey Christ" (2 Cor 10:4-5). Christians are to tear down intellectual strongholds in order to free those who are deceived spiritually and are held captive by forces of darkness (2 Tim 2:26).

Paul knew the culture of his day. He could quote philosophers from memory (cf. Acts 17:28; Titus 1:12), use their terminology, and examine their views from a Christian perspective (cf. Acts 17:22-31). Not enough Christians today can do that—including pastors, counselors, or even Christian scholars.

Western culture is undergoing sweeping and profound changes that are transforming the prevailing cultural worldview, especially with regard to the nature of truth. Like other periods of major change in history, the present one is a mixture of the old and new. In order to avoid becoming captives, and instead becoming capable of destroying strongholds so that Christians can do the capturing, one will have to go back and examine some past intellectual battles.

Christianity grew to dominate culture in the Middle Ages, joining faith (what is known by revelation) and reason to form a worldview that encompassed all of knowledge. Modernism rejected the medieval concept that knowledge is based on authority. Modernists based knowledge on the process of objective reasoning from observation, which became their concept of science. By the late eighteenth century, some began to challenge the supremacy of reason, the possibility of objectivity, and the ability to know the world as it is. The twentieth century saw increasing doubts about the objectivity and benefits of science, the self as a foundation for knowing, the connection between language and the world, and the very possibility of a worldview.

Within western-oriented cultures today there is an uneasy coexistence of modernism and what is loosely called postmodernism,[1] the name for the intellectual and cultural movement that reacted to modernism. Postmodernism is especially challenging for Christians, who claim to have the correct interpretation of an inspired text and an objectively true message that applies to all peoples and cultures.

The Road to Modernism

Unlike Judaism, which God established as a separate culture, the church was born into an existing culture. It shared with that culture and other ancient cultures the view that supernatural purposes shape events in nature and history. In spite of unseen forces, the physical world is real and can be known and described adequately in language. Early Christians seemed to have no doubt that words refer to things, and that propositions are true when they correspond to reality (called *the correspondence theory of truth*).

Differences between Christianity and Greco-Roman society brought persecution until the fourth century when Constantine conquered the Empire in the name of Christ. From that time forward, the church lived in an uneasy alliance with government, through which it eventually came to dominate all aspects of culture.

The goal of many medieval scholars was to form a grand synthesis of all knowledge—spiritual, philosophical, and scientific. It was thought that all parts of a worldview could be connected. For example, what we believe about logic and mathematics should fit the nature of God; beliefs about the arts should fit what we know about the spiritual nature of humanity; the role of government fits with a sovereign God and fallen humanity. In keeping with this mentality, Thomas Aquinas (1225-1274) believed that there can be perfect harmony between the Bible, reason, and science because God is both the author of the Bible and the Creator.

The foundations that made this grand synthesis possible were soon challenged. For one, John Scotus (ca. 1274-1308) said that the will, not the intellect, is primary, and that this is true of God as well as humanity. This means that God does whatever He wants, not necessarily what is rational. If God did only what is rational, we could figure out truth with our minds by figuring out what is rational. But without rationality as a guide, we simply have to observe what God chose to do. Supposing that God's will is primary helped shift the intellectual balance from reason to observation, and therefore to science.

Those who followed the Islamic philosopher Averroes (1126-1198) held to a theory of double truth by which reason could lead to one conclusion while faith could lead to another. William of Occam (1285-1347) continued to widen the divide between areas of knowledge by advocating that theology be separated from other fields. He intended to protect theology from attack, but eventually his work had the opposite effect.

For various reasons, the church's spiritual and moral authority and power waned. In the sixteenth century, the Reformation church split from what we now call the Catholic Church. In the wars that ensued, thousands were killed in the name of doctrine. French philosopher René Descartes (1596-1650) sought certainty in the midst of the turbulence. He systematically doubted everything until he found the one thing he could not doubt—that he was doubting. This led to his famous statement, "I think; therefore I am," and he proceeded to build up from there to an entire worldview. He bypassed the authority of the church and tradition to the ground of knowing the self. He thought the self could know reality as it is and was confident that one can accurately know his/her inner states.

It is significant that he thought he could be certain about some beliefs without having to appeal to other beliefs, a view known as *foundationalism*. Foundationalism accepts that some things can be known without having to prove them with other beliefs. Beliefs might be foundational because they are evident to our senses (e.g., "there is a light on in the room"), or because to doubt them would be nonsensical or self-contradictory (e.g., "the whole is greater than the parts"). These sorts of beliefs need not be proved, just as no one would need to prove to you that your toe hurts after you stub it—you just know it hurts. Foundationalists seek to ultimately ground our non-foundational beliefs (beliefs that need to be proved using other beliefs) on our undoubtable, foundational beliefs. Many hold, as well, that these foundational beliefs help connect us to reality and save us from an endless chain of proof in which we believe A because we believe B, and believe B because of C, and so on. It is thought that the proof process has stopping points, because somewhere in all the things we know are some foundational beliefs, which need not be proved.

Because Descartes built his worldview on what he could know apart from presupposing church dogma and classical learning, he is regarded as the father of modern philosophy.[2] The Renaissance in which he lived was a time of searching for new foundations of knowledge. People turned first to classical civilization, then to the study of nature, using observation rather than tradition. Everywhere people were turning aside from the authority of the church and tradition to find answers independently. Increasingly, explanations for things were in terms of natural rather than supernatural causes. Theology, which once regulated knowledge and life, was becoming a separate field, disconnected from everything else. Though its increasing isolation seemed to put it out of reach of attack, it would soon go begging for relevance.

The modern mind-set was further shaped in the Enlightenment of the eighteenth century, sometimes called *the Age of Reason*. It was thought that humanity could solve all its problems if people would sweep away superstition and unfounded beliefs and instead embrace objectivity and reason. Humanity is not hopelessly sinful and utterly dependent on God, but merely ignorant. For them, reason was not the abstract deduction of one truth from another, used by medievals, Descartes, and Spinoza (1632-1677). Rather, it was the objective drawing of conclusions from observation, the method of Francis Bacon (1561-1626) and John Locke (1632-1704). Reason seemed to be the answer to everything. Even nature itself seemed to be reasonable in that it showed design and obeyed natural laws. Some concluded, therefore, that it would be far better to get back to nature and be free of the artificial influences of society and church. Doctrine, which had been so important in the Middle Ages, was rejected as dangerous because people fought disastrous wars over it. Tolerance—not conviction—was the chief virtue; and science, not religion, would show us the way, they thought.

So the modern worldview replaced the medieval synthesis of faith and reason. Where the medievals had based knowledge on deductions from a supernatural tradition, modernism attempted to start on ground that was as neutral as possible. They believed it was possible to investigate an issue from a viewpoint that is free from all perspectives and requires only minimal assumptions, those that people could agree upon even if they hold different views on an issue. Investigations then could begin on intellectually neutral ground that is common to all perspectives on a matter. Modernists thought that the ideal way to reach a conclusion is to reason objectively from observation; in other words, scientifically. Working in this way, a person could discover objective truth that is universal, eternal, and independent of all perspectives. Furthermore, they had great confidence that everything fits together. What is true is also what is good (has value), right (ethically), and beautiful and is eminently practical for all persons and societies. They were confident that science would lead to a better life for the individual and society.

Modernism followed Descartes in regarding people as autonomous and able to relate to truth as individuals. And as individuals, we can know our inner selves clearly and coherently. We can also describe truth in language that is objectively and unambiguously connected to reality. Using language, we can formulate theories that are universally true and independent of all perspectives and social situations such that they mirror reality itself. Everywhere there was optimism that humanity is steadily discovering truth, solving its problems, and progressing to a bright future.

By the late eighteenth century, however, noticeable cracks were visible in modernism's foundation. By the twentieth century, postmodernism came to reject much of what modernity had stood for.

Disillusionment with Modernism

After dethroning authority as a way of knowing, reason was facing its own demise. David Hume (1711-1776) showed that we cannot conclude even something as basic as that one thing *causes* another by drawing only from objective observation. All we really know is that one thing *follows* another. The idea of causality is added to our experience by our mind.

Immanuel Kant (1724-1804) read Hume and realized something was very wrong with the idea that we must work only by observation (what comes from our senses alone). If talk of causality is anything less than perfectly legitimate, then we cannot know much about the world, and we certainly have no foundation for science. He concluded that knowledge comes not from our minds alone (as many medievals and Descartes thought), nor from our senses alone (as Locke and Hume thought). It comes from both. Our senses give us information, and our minds structure that information.

The point is that after Kant it was widely held that knowledge is irreducibly a matter of interpretation, not just a matter of getting our minds to mirror reality. Furthermore, there is no way to get outside our minds to see what reality is "really" like. Therefore, we know only our experiences, not the way things are in themselves. And that means we cannot know that God exists, although it may be helpful in practical ways to suppose that He does. Kant made it intellectually fashionable both to doubt that we can know reality as it is and to focus on practical things, like ethics. Later that would be echoed in the pragmatism of John Dewey (1859-1952) and the neo-Pragmatism of Richard Rorty (1931-), who both suggest that we cannot know reality in any full and final sense; we must settle for what works.

Whereas in the eighteenth century reason seemed to be the answer to everything, by the early nineteenth century it seemed adequate for only a narrow range of issues. What it missed, people thought, were the depths of the human spirit and the experiences that make us human. Subjectivity was all the rage in what was called *the Romantic Age*, which lasted until the middle of the nineteenth century.

G. F. W. Hegel (1770-1831) challenged the age-old concept that reality is unchanging. Western thought, including Christianity and most Greeks, had long held that behind change is permanence, and the core of that permanence is an immutable God. But Hegel said that reality—including God—is evolving to higher levels. A similar worldview was later held by philosophical mathematician A. N. Whitehead (1861-1947), who inspired Process Theology in recent times. Process thinkers believe that God changes and that evil exists because God can do no more than try to persuade people to do what is right.

Søren Kierkegaard (1813-1855), a Danish Christian, foreshadowed the postmodern critique of modernist society as being destructive of individuality. He thought that modernism's emphasis on such things as analysis, reason, and universal concepts weakened vital aspects of individual human life, such as commitment and "passion"—things at the core of a life with depth and spirituality. Truth and things that really matter in life are not objective—

they are subjective, Kierkegaard claimed. Typical too of postmodernism, he identified the media as a negative influence on culture.

Karl Marx (1818-1883) accepted Hegel's idea that reality is changing on a fundamental level, but he did away with God and made humanity the focus of evolution. Humans are not a product of their sin nature, he said, but of their economic environment. So when workers throw off the yoke of those who control the means of producing wealth, that will usher in an ideal age of common ownership—i.e., communism.

For the most part, Marx's followers did not use reason to show that opposing views are wrong. They simply reinterpreted opponents' views from their own Marxist viewpoint. For example, those who did not agree that the world is divided into the oppressed working class and the oppressive owning class had simply been co-opted by the owning class. This approach contrasted with the modern age, which had sought to make intellectual progress through public discourse using reason and, as much as possible, premises that were common to both sides. Skepticism in the modern age had been rooted in facts or a lack of facts. But the approach used by Marxists has increased in the postmodern age and earned the name *the hermeneutics of suspicion.*

Rather than deal with the truth or falsity of an idea, this approach casts suspicion on the motives of the person holding it and supposes that we are prone to self-deception. It features less epistemological analysis of what is true or false and more psychological and sociological analysis concerning *why* people hold the views they do. Accordingly, skepticism in the postmodern age has more to do with beliefs about the nature of people and consciousness than with objective facts. Sigmund Freud (1856-1939) found cause for suspicion on psychological grounds, proposing that beliefs are products of such things as wish fulfillment and repressed desires. Friedrich Nietzsche (1844-1900), who was as much as anyone a prophet of the postmodern age, supposed that the hidden drive behind all creatures is the desire for power.

The new psychological and sociological approach subverted the modernist idea that the individual has direct access to reality through the knowledge of his own mind. Marx claimed that the individual's thinking is shaped by economic structures, Nietzsche said it was the will to have power, and Freud saw unconscious (sexually oriented) drives. Descartes's autonomous self, which supposedly could build knowledge on clear and distinct ideas, would continue to come under severe attack into the twentieth century. Modernism had made the self the building block of knowledge; postmodernism was making it the stumbling block.

Nietzsche considered morals as well as truth to be relative. There is nothing that is right for every individual to do, he said. Furthermore, he believed that morals have wrongly been built on love and compassion. Darwinian evolution shows that nature's way is for the strong to dominate and exploit the weak, something often mistaken for cruelty. The strong must be freed from the morality of compassion, which was invented by the weak for their own self-protection. Moreover, the strong must be freed from belief in God. He made no secret of what he regarded as the chief culprit in society. He said, "I call Christianity the *one* great curse, the *one* great intrinsic depravity . . . the *one* immortal blemish of mankind. . . ."[3] He rejected the quest of most previous philosophers and theologians for a worldview that provides a unified explanation of things. He thought that constructing such a worldview depends on having self-evident truths, whereas none could be had. Also, such persons wrongly focus on abstractions instead of more practical matters. His skepticism about the possibility of forming an all-encompassing worldview is typical of postmodernism. Also typical of much postmodernism is that it never attempts an all-encompassing systematic analysis or explanation of things.

As philosophy challenged modernism in a number of ways, new discoveries in science were challenging long-held ideas about the very structure of the world. Up to now, modernism had functioned in Newton's universe of rigid causes and natural laws. Since those laws could be discovered by reasoning about observations, there was great optimism that we would know the world and control it. It was even thought that we could discover the natural laws governing things such as human behavior and society, which could also be controlled for the better. Marx thought he had discovered such laws, and Communists came to think they could control individuals and society completely.

Modernism never doubted that more human control was better. That is because they left divine purposes out of explanations of things (since they can't be observed); thus there were no higher purposes than our own. Modernists had no reason to doubt that human purposes are good because they rejected any idea of a sin nature (the Fall couldn't be proved by observation either). History seemed to confirm their overall optimism about human nature because, for example, there was a long productive peace in Europe after the Napoleonic wars.

But by the early twentieth century science seemed to be showing that the world was not that predictable after all. According to the "uncertainty principle" of physicist Werner Heisenberg (1901-1976), we cannot know both the precise location and speed of a subatomic particle. That seemed to show that subatomic particles are unpredictable and—contrary to Newton—events cannot be predicted. Among those who resisted this conclusion was Einstein

(1879-1955), who said this shows nothing more than our present ignorance of causes. The universe is not unpredictable because, he said, God would not "play dice" with it. But Einstein's own theories were wrecking the traditional concept of absolutes, showing that light is affected by gravity, and that mass and even time could change with speed. Like Heisenberg's uncertainty principle, people drew implications that went far beyond physics. It bewildered Einstein that people thought his theories showed that everything, even morals, are relative.

Science itself was being reinterpreted. It was always assumed that a scientist would prove something, and that the next scientist could build on that base. In this way, scientists' knowledge makes steady progress toward objective truth. But Karl Popper (1902-1994) argued that a theory is not proved in any final sense because a new discovery could show it to be wrong. So science is not a matter of proving theories once and for all, but of holding them until they are disproved. Disproof is the key, and theories that cannot be stated rigorously enough to be decisively disproved are not scientific (a problem for the theories of Marx and Freud, he thought).

Then philosopher of science Thomas Kuhn[4] (1922-1996) argued that science does not make steady progress at all. It shifts from one major theory ("paradigm"[5]) to another. Science works under a theory until too many things turn up that can't be explained, and a new theory is then proposed. Some scientists accept it, while others remain loyal to the old view—older scientists who have believed it for a long time, for example. In Kuhn's view, science is not a pure field where people with pure motives find pure truth. Philosopher Michael Polanyi (1891-1976) showed further that science is not uniquely objective but is more like other fields than has been thought; it uses creative imagination, for example.[6]

The view that an individual has direct access to reality by either clear and distinct ideas (Descartes) or sense perceptions (John Locke) was now regarded as simplistic. "Facts" are not outside us to be understood because we bring to any situation such things as assumptions and presuppositions, and they influence what we see and how we interpret it. Facts are already "theory laden," it was said. If so, there is no way to be objective.

A similar revolution was underway regarding language. Ludwig Wittgenstein (1889-1951) started out with the more modernist view that propositions picture reality and are connected to it. As such, they can be formed precisely and are either true or false. Wittgenstein made a remarkable change to the more radical view that the meaning of a proposition is its use. So propositions are not true or false, but useful or not useful. The meaning of propositions, like "God exists," depends on such things as how people use it and how they live. Furthermore, since meaning is a social thing, the individual has no special access to truth, not even when it has to do with his own inner state. So we cannot be more sure that "my foot hurts" than we can that "there are ten chairs in this room." This was yet another attack on Descartes's idea that the individual and his mind is the bedrock of knowledge.

Structuralism continued the attack. The movement continued the earlier work of linguist Ferdinand de Saussure (pronounced so-SYR; 1857-1913), who pointed out that meaning is not a matter of the mental relationship between a word and the thing to which it refers, and therefore a word does not join a concept with a thing in the world. It merely joins a concept with a *sound*. Furthermore, that connection is arbitrary and could have been made by a different sound. In addition, words have meaning only in relation to other words. He thus challenged the traditional view that language is connected to the world. Structuralists looked for meaning not in things but in relationships between things, just as a dollar bill has meaning only in relation to bills of other denominations and the monetary system. And like the constantly changing value of a dollar, structures are dynamic rather than static. It was thought that structures are everywhere in experience and society, and that they can be studied scientifically. Structuralists denied the modernist view that meaning is created by autonomous individuals using their own clear ideas. Instead, they regarded the individual as a product of society and language.[7]

Postmodernism

As fundamentals were being rethought, historical and cultural events were colliding with many cherished assumptions of the modern age. Confidence in the goodness and perfectibility of humanity was crushed by two world wars, a cold war, and ruthless totalitarian states. Perhaps worst of all, after centuries of supposed progress, there was a holocaust in Europe—the very center of modernism. And far from being saviors, science and technology were undermining the quality of life with pollution, were offering governments unprecedented control over individuals, and were threatening humanity's very existence with nuclear weapons.

Tensions in France came to a head in 1968 when strikes and riots by workers and students brought the country to a halt. French President Charles de Gaulle (1890-1970) promised new elections and pleaded for order. Rather than support radical change, the Communist Party denounced the demonstrators and supported the government. Disillusioned, the political left then saw communism as part of the problem and began to look with greater interest on radical French thinkers.

Marxism had already been undergoing change. Even Marxists were beginning to realize that economics and the class struggle could not account for the breadth of history and human experience. As Communist regimes became more impoverished and repressive while capitalism flourished, Marxists modified various core beliefs and embraced democracy. Louis Althusser (1918-1990), motivated by his Kantian interest in the nature of reality, tried to use structuralist insights to make Marxism into a theory of knowledge. By contrast, the so-called Frankfurt school went in a more humanistic direction, critiquing modern culture as dominating and dehumanizing. Mixing Marx and Freud, Herbert Marcuse (1898-1979) said that capitalism represses human instincts. However, they can be liberated and then shaped through labor for a life of beauty, peace, and sensuality. As the father of the New Left, he claimed that revolution had to come from students, minorities, and intellectuals because workers were too stupefied by the products of their labor. Jürgen Habermas (1929-) rejected postmodernism as heading toward relativism and irrationality. He sought to refine the Enlightenment's quest for rationality, science that liberates, free communication, and a unified view of things.

While these Marxists[8] retained some measure of modernism's commitment to a unified worldview, others accepted the postmodern belief in the impossibility of any such worldview. They have dissolved into the left's many disparate and even conflicting social agendas, including gay rights, lesbianism, feminism, multiculturalism, environmentalism, anticolonialism, and anti-nuclear activism.

Michel Foucault (pronounced foo-KO; 1926-1984) broke with the Communist Party in 1951 and developed the view that oppression is multifaceted and pervasive, not just a matter of the owning class oppressing workers. As he saw it, the individual is dominated by society in different ways, especially by what is considered knowledge. He rejected modernism's view that knowledge is neutral and a pathway to liberation. In a view exactly opposite to Francis Bacon's claim that knowledge gives power to its possessor, Foucault regarded knowledge as both a product and a tool of oppression. Those with power decide what will be accepted as "knowledge," and they use it to oppress people. So science is far from neutral, and it is not even clear that it—or the human race for that matter—makes progress.

Rejecting modernism's search for both a single explanation of human problems and an all-encompassing worldview, Foucault as a post-structuralist, along with many postmodernists, have followed Nietzsche's more fragmented approach to reality. According to this perspectivist account, there is no single correct view of the world, but countless views that are correct in their own way. Influenced by this sort of thinking, some in the popular culture have concluded that since there is no single true perspective we should strive to be enriched by as many different views (and behaviors) as possible; all should be included.[9]

In the 1970s, Foucault had a part in developing post-structuralism as he addressed problems within structuralism, a view popular since the 1950s. Post-structuralism took from structuralism the idea that language structures communication and thought itself, and that language is a matter of relationships and differences. It adopted Nietzsche's radical relativism and Foucault's conviction that power underlies knowledge.[10] It challenged structuralism's view that meanings within language and culture are stable and so can be definitively analyzed.

A popular post-structuralist figure, Jacques Derrida (1930-), claimed that meanings are always changing, or "at play." Dictionaries give the false impression that words have stable meanings. However, those meanings depend on such things as our experiences, which constantly change. For this reason he opposed the work of structuralist Claude Levi-Strauss (1908-), who catalogued hundreds of myths because he thought their meanings were stable and could be scientifically analyzed. Not only does the flux of meaning make that sort of project impossible, thought Derrida, but we should welcome future creative meanings and not fixate on some idealized past. On a metaphysical level, he opposed the phenomenology of Edmund Husserl (1859-1938), who thought we can grasp reality intuitively and with certainty, including nonphysical entities. But like others today, Derrida says we have no access to reality apart from language.

What makes this worldview radical is combining belief in the pervasiveness of language—that all thought and access to reality is through language—with a pessimistic view of the complexities and uncertainties of language. If we cannot get hold of language, we cannot get hold of reality, nor can we even communicate in any objective sense. That also means there is no truth in the traditional sense that truth is a matter of correct propositions about reality. The correspondence theory of truth (according to which propositions that correspond to reality are true) that undergirded modernism especially conflicts with postmodernism. We can never gain a neutral perspective outside of language from which to judge whether a proposition corresponds to reality. Even if we could, for Derrida at least, language doesn't stand still long enough to allow us to make statements that would be true forever.

Derrida continued to "deconstruct" assumptions underlying traditional views that language connects us to reality. He pointed out that much of our thought is shaped by opposing pairs of terms ("binaries"). Often the first term is dominant and favored over the second, as is the case with male/female and text/speech. He tries to show that this is overly simplistic. In fact, the very meaning of the first term can be dependent on the second. Such terms do not neatly divide and correspond to reality. Whereas speech is considered primary over writing, distinctions can be made in writing that cannot be made in speech.

Much language is based on distinguishing meanings of words, such as binaries. According to Derrida, we assume that we can grasp differences—and thereby meanings—but it is not so simple. For example, words often interrelate so that differences can never be finally and definitively pinned down. Since in French *difference* and *defer* are the same verb (*différer*), he playfully says that difference is (forever) deferred.

Derrida's use of plays on words and the use by him and others of terms that are not carefully defined or consistently used have earned the suspicion and disrespect of philosophers who work in the more rigorous tradition developed in England and America. In contrast to the daunting style of the Continental tradition, the Anglo-American analytic tradition strives for clarity, consistency, and logical coherence. When Cambridge granted Derrida an honorary doctorate, nineteen professors took the unprecedented step of decrying his work in the London *Times* as incomprehensible gimmickery.[11]

Style and beliefs about language are not the only things that have drawn ire for thinkers like Derrida. His perspectives cast serious doubt on three of the very foundational principles of western thought since Aristotle (384-322 B.C.): the *law of identity* (according to which a thing "is what it is"), the *law of noncontradiction* (a proposition and its denial cannot be true), and the *law of the excluded middle* (a proposition must be either true or false).

A distinction in philosophy that is becoming more significant than that of analytic versus Continental is realism versus anti-realism. Realism is the view that some things exist independent of our minds, concepts, and language. Modernism assumed there is one reality, it is independent of us, and we are coming to know it with increasing accuracy largely through the scientific method. As anti-realists, some postmoderns claim that there are many realities constructed by many languages and cultures; each is equally valid. For the realist, there is one answer to a simple question like, "is the cat on the mat?" For the anti-realist, the answer is, it depends on such things as perspective.

This brings an unwanted consequence for the postmodernist who is a relativist. Is the slave oppressed if the slaveholder doesn't think so and believes his perspective is as valid as the slave's? Judgments about things like abuse, prejudice, and genocide seem to depend on there being a perspective that is correct regardless of what someone thinks—and that points us back to realism. Realists like John Searle (1932-) would say that different languages and cultures only *describe* reality differently, but the reality is the same. He points out that much of our communication presupposes that reality exists independent of our words and thoughts.

Another challenge to realism comes from neo-pragmatists like Richard Rorty (1931-), who considers the idea of truth a myth. Statements are judged by criteria that differ from one culture to another. Since there is no way to get outside ourselves to some objective viewpoint, there is no way to see if the criteria are correct. Of course, we can evaluate the criteria of another culture, but we are only evaluating it from our viewpoint and have no right to say theirs is wrong. So we cannot say something is objectively true or false, just that it meets certain criteria. In the end, "truth" is whatever "survives all objections within one's culture." Similarly, Stanley Fish (1938-) thinks we should give up any talk of truth because "I know x" and "I believe x" amount to the same thing. Fish contends that the meaning of a text depends largely on the community interpreting it. When the community changes, the meaning changes.

The classical view of this issue made meaning a matter of knowing what the author intended to communicate. And that could be understood by looking at his language, background, the issues he was dealing with, and so on. In much postmodern thinking, meaning depends heavily on the person receiving the communication, which makes it a highly subjective matter.

Postmodern sociologist Jean Baudrillard (1929-) deals with the issue of the interpretive community from a different angle. He blames the media culture for removing the proper two-way dimension of communication. In our media-saturated, information-dominated culture, people become mere passive receptors. What is worse, the distinction between reality and imagery is obliterated, and we live in a "hyperreality." We cannot even distinguish between images of ourselves and our real selves. This challenges the modernist assumption that we can interpret symbols accurately and rationally. According to Baudrillard, symbols are linked not to reality but to other symbols; thus we can have no more than partial meaning and understanding. He nihilistically supposes we are at the end of history, doomed to infinite continuation of our postmodern condition.

Jean-Francois Lyotard (1924-) skeptically examines what he calls "metanarratives," which are explanations or mental commitments that people use to give legitimacy to other beliefs or activities (such as, the proper goal of a society is the good of its members). While modernism sought the one true metanarrative, Lyotard rejects such a possibility, professing "incredulity toward metanarratives." Totalizing narratives (i.e., worldviews, roughly) oppress minorities, he claims. They should be rejected in favor of diversity, pragmatic considerations, and micropolitics. He thinks that groups could be so different in their ideas and use of terms that they share no common set of rules to which both could appeal in order to settle disputes. In such cases the best that can be done is not to de-legitimize one side or the other. Lyotard's view undermines the traditional assumption that there are higher principles to which all viewpoints—even very different ones—can appeal. The confidence that *reason* is this type of universal principle was the basis for modernism's optimism that truth and social harmony are attainable.

Scholars debate what all major thinkers have said, and it is no different for postmodernism. Some who study it closely are critical of popular treatments for making it sound more radical than it is. Whatever the case, postmodernism is taking on a life of its own in the popular culture, reminiscent of the way relativity developed cultural dimensions far beyond Einstein. Christianity needs to deal with the whole phenomenon, which could be summarized as opposing realism, foundationalism, the correspondence theory of truth, and all universally binding concepts, distinctions, or descriptions. It also suspects grand narratives and metanarratives (best understood as overarching theories and worldviews).

Christianity and Today's Postmodern World

If understanding postmodernism is challenging, constructing a Christian response is more so. It deserves an in-depth treatment, although here there is room for only a few suggestions. It would be simpler to reject everything to do with what we have broadly called postmodernism. But, like modernism, it occasionally has some valid insights into human knowledge and therefore is helpful in evaluating current worldviews. Modernism accepted the idea that truth is objective and universal—which fits the Christian worldview—but it also gave privileged status to naturalism. Under modernism, supernaturalism of any kind had to be proved. But since drawing conclusions from observations (i.e., science) was the preferred way of knowing, gathering sufficient evidence for religious belief was difficult. Add to that an additional assumption that was sometimes made—that we should believe something only in proportion to our evidence for it—and the result was that religious belief was viewed as, in essence, subjective or even irrational (conclusions Kierkegaard largely accepted).

Postmodernism highlights the limits of the human perspective and difficulties with language; it also questions human intentions. From a Christian perspective, it corrects some of modernism's excessive optimism about mankind's ability to find truth apart from divine revelation, and it has a more realistic view of fallen human nature. On the other hand, postmodernism does not consider the possibility and implications of linguistic revelation from an omniscient being, especially One who has formed the human mind and can illumine it.

The most fundamental problem is that postmodernism has gone farther in the wrong direction. The medieval worldview centered on *God*, modernism centered on *reality* external to the individual, but postmodernism centers on the ever-changing human *perspective*. In postmodern culture, even the line between the world as it is and the world as we create it is disappearing into virtual reality. So in the past few centuries humanity has increasingly departed from the centrality of God in life and thought. There has been a corresponding dimming of the prospect of finding objective truth and of constructing a comprehensive and coherent worldview.

Modernism gave the world science and technology, but at the price of increasing secularity. It built civil society on Locke's idea that if all viewpoints are allowed into the public dialogue the truth will emerge. By contrast, the tendency of elements of postmodern culture—which in some ways goes beyond the theorists we have looked at—is to base tolerance on the metaphysical assumption that there is no single view that is universally true, but that many views are correct in some way. But like other forms of pluralism, a postmodernism that is pluralistic risks crucial contradictions. For example, in what way are the people right who think their view is the only correct one? If the answer is that they may be right about some of their beliefs but wrong to think they alone are correct, then the pluralist himself has the same problem—he thinks pluralism is the only right view! Furthermore, for the pluralist to make the claim that no one view is correct, he has to have the very bird's-eye view of reality that he says no one can have. In practice, this type of postmodernist is assuming he has the very sort of neutral perspective he criticizes others for claiming to have.

There is a further paradox in the way some postmodernism is practiced in the culture (not by theorists we have discussed). Like many forms of relativism, in theory it affirms tolerance; but in practice many who hold it tolerate only those who agree with them, as some victims of political correctness can attest. That may be because their form of postmodernism affirms little or nothing to which different sides can appeal to make a rational case: no shared reasoning process, perspectives, or universal truths. So all that is left to advance one's agenda is power of various kinds, especially legal, political, and social.

More extreme forms of postmodernism have a further problem insofar as they cast doubt on the validity of metanarratives. The problem here is that postmodernism itself is a metanarrative as evidenced by the fact that it has a theory of meaning, truth, justice, political action, and so on. It is akin to the paradox surrounding the statement, "This sentence is untrue." If it is a true statement, it is untrue; if it is a false statement, it is also untrue. What are we to conclude about a metanarrative that challenges the validity of metanarratives?

If we get past that paradox, there is another one insofar as some forms of postmodernism claim that knowledge is not about universal truth but is merely a product and tool of power. We could ask, what desire for power produced postmodernism? And why should we believe it is universal truth about the way things are? Paradoxically, we should suspect that postmodernism is not about the way things are but is itself a manifestation of the desire for power.

Further paradoxes confront those postmodernists who wish to challenge the most basic principles of logic. One postmodernist was explaining how deconstructive logic was better than traditional binary reasoning and wrote, "the clearest distinction between traditionalist and deconstructive logic resides in . . ."[12] But in making her point she was distinguishing neatly between two things, one of which is considered superior. This, of course, is binary thinking. Some postmodern feminists such as Judith Butler and Helene Cixous go farther and argue that the very concept of reasoning is patriarchal and homophobic.[13]

Modernist skeptics said Christianity is untrue as evidenced by its (supposed) lack of support from reason and facts. By contrast, postmodernists may say it is arrogant for anyone to claim their viewpoint is exclusively the correct one.

Christianity developed sophisticated defenses to meet the modernist challenge. Traditional apologists accepted the idea that they could start from a neutral perspective and could reason using facts to the conclusion that Christianity is true. Other Christians rejected that general approach.

Can we arrive at a perspective by examining facts, as modernists suggest, or is there no possibility of a neutral view of facts, as postmodernists suggest? If we cannot reason from facts to a perspective, then it seems we are faced with two possibilities. The first is that we must hold a perspective without the support of any reasons to believe it, accepting it on the basis of our sheer decision to believe it or on some other nonrational basis, such as the feeling that it is true. The second major option is that we can accept our perspective because it best explains or interprets the facts. That is the opposite of reasoning *from* the facts to the perspective (as a modernist approach tries to do). This second approach reasons from the perspective *to* the facts.

But must it be one or the other, either from the facts to the perspective or from the perspective to the facts? It seems to be both since facts and perspective interact.

There is no doubt that our perspective influences how we see the world, including facts. But, too, we can encounter a fact that challenges our perspective. When that happens, we have to choose between maintaining our perspective by reinterpreting the fact or else adjusting our perspective in light of the fact.

A person can, of course, be too stubborn about holding to a perspective, as in the case of prejudice. For instance, a person may believe that all those who are x are lazy (where x is any group—ethnic, religious, etc.). When he meets someone who is x but not lazy, he can adjust his original perspective to the new one that not all x's are lazy. Or he can maintain his (prejudiced) perspective that all x's are lazy and reinterpret the fact by, for example, thinking that this person is not truly an x, or only appears to be hardworking but is not. Paranoia is another example of unwarranted commitment to a perspective.

When Christ's miracles encountered unbelief, there were both reactions. Some changed their perspective from whatever they had believed about Him to the belief that He was from God (e.g., John 4:39; 11:45; 12:11; cf. Acts 9:42). Others stubbornly maintained their original (un)belief, refusing to let the fact of a miracle change it. Taking this approach, some Pharisees reinterpreted the fact of Christ's miracles and concluded that He acted by the power of Satan (Matt 12:24).

There are times when we ought to maintain our original perspective and use it to reinterpret the facts before us. When Job was confronted with what appeared to be evidence of God's unfairness, the right response was for him to maintain his belief that God is fair and conclude that there was another explanation for the facts about what was happening to him.

It seems legitimate, then, to reason both from facts to perspective as well as from perspective to facts. Reasoning from the resurrection to the Christian view of Christ could be one form of reasoning from facts to perspective (e.g., Acts 3:15; Rom 1:4). But there is no reason why we cannot also argue that the Christian perspective (or worldview) best explains the widest array of facts, including such things as why the physical universe is the way we find it, ordered and able to support life; why humans feel guilt and seek meaning in life; why some things in history have happened (such as why, of all ancient peoples, Jews have survived—in spite of persecution).[14]

Christians can confidently enter the arena of thought with a Christian worldview, knowing that they have the author of truth and God's repository of specially revealed truth on their side.[15] In the Christian worldview, truth is absolute, objective, propositional, and eternal—not merely relative, subjective, experiential, and short-lived. And it can critically encounter whatever is the current wisdom of this world, through which the world has not and will never come to know or understand God (1 Cor 1:20-21).

FURTHER READING

Best, Steven and Douglas Kellner. *Postmodern Theory: Critical Interrogations.* New York: Guilford, 1991.

__________. *The Postmodern Turn.* New York: Guilford, 1997.

Erickson, Millard. *Postmodernizing the Faith: Evangelical Responses to the Challenge of Postmodernism.* Grand Rapids, MI: Baker, 1998.

__________. *Truth or Consequences: The Promise and Perils of Postmodernism.* Downers Grove, IL: IVP, 2001.

Lyotard, Jean-Francois. *The Postmodern Condition: Report on Knowledge.* Minneapolis: University of Minnesota Press, 1984.

8

Profiling Christian Masculinity

Stuart W. Scott

A biblical worldview must definitely encompass one's view of men and women. Basic beliefs about who each sex is and what each should be like greatly impacts one's own gender evaluations as well as the shaping of boys and girls, the education of young men and women, the success of marriages, the effectiveness of the church in the world, and even the stability of society. One's view of a man or a woman affects attitudes, character, and interaction with one another.

In some very key ways, men and women *are* the same, but they were not created to be exactly the same: "male and female he created them" (Gen 1:27). There are not only opposing opinions over whether there are any significant differences between the sexes, but also over what those differences really are. Surely, Christians need a clear understanding of what distinguishes a man from a woman *according to their Creator*. Since the issue of true femininity will be addressed in the next chapter, this material will be devoted to understanding what *true masculinity* is and is not. The question of how a man knows whether he is a *real man* or not will be discovered from Scripture.

Imagine this topic being discussed on one of America's most prestigious college campuses. The ideas expressed would be as varied as the many strong opinions found there. One might hear, "A man should be macho and self-reliant," while another may say, "A man should be interdependent and sensitive." Others might insist, "A real man must be romantic," while still others would offer, "All boys should be raised to be good at sports in order to express their masculinity and relate to other men." Perhaps another would say, "A man's man is successful and a leader," while someone else may interject, "A respected man sees himself as an equal—a non-leader, a fifty-fifty partner." Another student could possibly declare, "A man is not a man unless he can rule his family without any questioning from them." How can there be so many opinions among supposedly learned individuals? There are at least two key reasons: the sinfulness of man and the loss of absolutes.

Sinfulness Affects One's Concept of Masculinity

The history of the world's concept of masculinity is a sad commentary of how far man has strayed from God's original intent. It is a confusing and disappointing history. In the beginning, of course, God created the man at his best—Adam. He, being created by the perfect Creator, was the epitome of true masculinity. However, shortly after Adam's creation, his soul and body were gravely affected by his choice to sin (the Fall; Gen 3:1-8). From that point on, left to himself, man's depravity (inherent sinfulness) pushes him to stray in every aspect of life (Jer 17:9). Masculinity is just one of the areas that has been corrupted. One does not have to look far beyond the Fall to see the effects of depravity on the concept of masculinity.

Depraved ideas about what is *manly* have affected men and women negatively through the ages. In the ancient world, there was everything from the mild mistreatment of women to full-scale barbarism. In the early Greek culture, "real men" looked down on their wives as mere child-bearers and housekeepers. They also did not allow them at the dinner table or in any assembly.[1] In the Roman culture, women were no more than a means to legally bear children as well as a temporary fancy that could be discarded on a whim.[2] In contrast, men living in a matriarchal society were absorbed into their wife's family, followed the mother-in-law's or the grandmother's lead, and faded into the background.

Throughout history, some cultures have devised rather extreme ways for young men to prove their masculinity or manhood. While it is not necessarily wrong to have a visible rite-of-passage ceremony for young men, it has historically been a *very* bad idea for a man to have something to prove. In America, the feminist movement came on the scene at least partially in reaction to actual injustices by men against women. With the passing of time, that movement has grown into a far-reaching, immoral catalyst that has further confused and even redefined the lines of gender.

A Loss of Absolutes Affects One's Concept of Masculinity

In more recent western history, the increasing relativism (the belief that there is no ultimate standard) and the resulting individualism ("only I know what is right for me") have had a great impact on gender concepts. This "no absolutes" mentality means that each man is left to his own "wisdom" on the subject of masculinity. That wisdom, of course, is totally subjective and may be based on one's own desires, culture, and/or educational training in the academic fields of psychology, sociology, or anthropology. There are a number of reasons why this kind of wisdom will get a person nowhere close to God's standard. First of all, man's own ideas and desires are very often selfish and self-serving. Second, culture has historically followed man's depravity. Third, American role models today basically consist of pathetic, immoral sports figures, movie stars, and rock musicians. Finally, the higher educational systems of the day are for the most part based on the study of unsaved people by unsaved people. As a result, there is a great reluctance on the part of typical Americans to make any statement about what is *truly masculine*. In fact, the earlier hypothetical college discussion might well be cut short with the postmodern declaration that each man must determine for himself what masculinity is and live within that without imposing his belief on another. This statement could very well be followed by the idea that one really should *not* be thinking in terms of masculinity but rather of genderless individualism.

It is clear from both Scripture and history that the unashamed and unchecked expression of depravity is continually on the increase, and the recognition of God's truth is on the decline (2 Tim 3:1-5). J. I. Packer sees society's decline in this way: "The truth is that because we have lost touch with God and his word we have lost the secret both of community (because sin kills neighbor-love) and of our own identity (because at the deepest level we do not know who or what we are, or what we exist for)."[3]

The first step to regaining a true understanding of masculinity is to acknowledge that man's wisdom is misleading. Here is what the Bible says about personal opinion: "There is a way that seems right to a man, but its end is the way to death" (Prov 14:12).

Men must not follow the way that seems right to them or to society. In reality, following what seems right about masculinity is doing great damage to men's lives. Young men are floundering and grasping at wrong ways to express their manhood. Marriages are also paying the price. Even many Christian women are regularly lamenting that their husbands are either timid or violent. More men seem to be experiencing depression and are abandoning their societal responsibilities during their supposed midlife crises. In the church, there seems to be a growing dearth of exemplary male leadership. Further complicating the problem for God's people is the rise of "Christian" feminism, which clearly departs from Scripture and the will of God. On a larger scale, society as a whole has experienced a great and unfortunate loss of the significance of gender. So much so that it is very acceptable in today's culture to even *deny* one's gender and try to switch to the other.

God's Truth Will Lead the Way

Without an absolute standard, the confusion about masculinity can only get worse. There is no hope of improving people's depraved inclinations or making sense of the confusion. The *Webster's New Collegiate Dictionary* definition of *masculine* is certainly an accurate picture of the ambiguity that surrounds this subject in our culture:

> **Masculine (mas-kyoo-lin)** 1 a: male b: having qualities appropriate to or usually associated with a man.[4]

There is no clear understanding of masculinity in society because it has generally forsaken the only dependable absolute there is—i.e., God's Word. Humans need to know what God has to say about man and his masculinity. God's truth is timeless and transcultural. Furthermore, it is completely sufficient to be the guide for becoming the kind of men God intended (Ps 119:105; John 17:17; 2 Pet 1:3). One must, in submission and obedience, align his thinking and actions with Scripture in order to understand and live out masculinity for the right reason (God's glory).

Basic Characteristics of Masculinity

Understanding masculinity must begin with acknowledging some very basic truths about humans that are found in the Bible. These characteristics are true of both men and women. A man cannot begin to be the man God intended him to be unless he fully acknowledges who *mankind* is. God had a design in mind when He created human beings, and He created just what He intended. Those who are unwilling to acknowledge God as Creator do not have a stable and definitive beginning on which to look back. As a result, they will never be fully able to understand who they are or what they should be like. But those who believe in a perfect, good, and personal God, and who have been given a new heart by the forgiveness of sins through Jesus Christ, can learn greatly from some basic things God has to say about people. There are at least six basic characteristics of humans, as God describes them, that have specific implications as they relate to the subject of masculinity.

1. *Man was created in God's image* (Gen 1:27). This means that he finds his identity in the person of God rather than in the animals. He is rational, creative, and relational. Unlike the animals, he has an eternal soul that needs to find its meaning and rest in God alone. Being creative and relational are part of being made in the image of God. Unfortunately, many men try to escape these aspects of their manhood, claiming they are feminine qualities. Furthermore, if a man sees himself as a mere animal, he can excuse all sorts of behavior and uncontrolled passions.

2. *Man was created a worshiper* (John 4:23; Rom 1:21-25). Because man has been given a soul, he is by nature a *religious* being. He *will* worship something. Though he was given a soul for the purpose of worshiping God alone, the depravity that was discussed earlier pulls him in other directions. Until he bows the knee to Jesus Christ, he might worship himself, another person, money, success and its accompaniments, false gods (idols), or a myriad of other things. Worshiping something or someone other than God is not what man was created to do. This kind of worship is neither manly nor true. Conversely, it *is* manly to seek and passionately love the God of the Bible.

3. *Since the Fall, man has been a sinner by nature* (Rom 3:12). Man was not initially created this way, but he *was* created with the ability to rationally choose. Soon he embraced this basic characteristic with his choice to sin by going against the one and only prohibition that God gave him. Therefore, a man must be aware, contrary to what his pride or his society may tell him, that he can be very wrong. At the core of his very being there is an innate sinfulness and imperfection that will be with him throughout his life. This being true, it is certainly *manly* to admit when he is sinning in his thinking or actions, rather than trying to hide it or deny it. It should also be mentioned at this point that as a result of the Fall a struggle has continued through the ages concerning the God-given roles of men and women. Scripture implies that the woman would "desire" to rule over the man. Put this together with man's sinful inclinations to dominate or shirk responsibility and the outcome is great difficulty, conflict, and a distortion of God's wonderful plan (Gen 3:16). It is only through redemption and an appropriation of God's daily grace that one can overcome these effects of sin.

4. *Man is in need of God's saving grace* (John 3:16; Titus 3:4-7). It stands to reason that when God gave Eve to Adam, making it clear that he was to love and lead her, He would also give him a protective or salvific inclination. Through the ages men have protected and come to the rescue of women, children, societies, and even ideologies. However, man must realize that he also

needs a Savior and protector. Admitting his utter helplessness and need of salvation is a doubly humbling experience for a courageous man. And yet any man who hopes to ever be a *real* man must acknowledge his need to be saved by God. He must be rescued from himself, the evil one (Satan), and the ensuing judgment for his sin by bowing the knee to Jesus Christ as the only Lord and Savior of his life.

5. *Man was not created self-sufficient but needing God and others* (John 15:5; Gal 5:14; Heb 4:16). By virtue of being a created being and a fallen individual, it is obvious that man needs God even more than he needs salvation. He needs God's enduring strength, guidance, and wisdom. It is also obvious that God made him to need others as seen in statements like, "It is not good that the man should be alone" and "I will make him a helper fit for him" (Gen 2:18). John MacArthur writes, "In marriage men cannot be faithful to the Lord unless they are willingly and lovingly dependent on the wife He has given them."[5] The over thirty commands in the Bible pertaining to "one another" reinforce this truism.

6. *Man was created to be different from woman* (Gen 1:27). The fact that God created man unlike woman in appearance is a clear indication that the two are different in other ways as well. In His wisdom, God has fashioned them uniquely inside and out, perfectly corresponding to how they are to *be* different and *function* differently. There was no mistaking God's desire for an outward difference. Adam and Eve's pre-covering existence in the garden reveals that God obviously intended for men and women to look different to themselves and others. There is subsequent Scripture to clearly support this fact (Deut 22:5; 1 Cor 11:14-15). A timeless principle that can be observed from all of this is that God wants individuals to clearly express their own given gender. Today there is less difference in how men and women look, and even act, than ever before in America's history. Though culture is pushing for unisex everything, men and women need to be careful that they are distinguishably different from the opposite sex in appearance, mannerisms, and cultural concepts of appropriate gender behavior. Some men might need help to recognize and change effeminate habits that they have inadvertently developed.

The fact that men and women were created with differences does not mean they are different in every way. Both genders are equal personally and spiritually. No one should argue that women should not be treated with equal appreciation and dignity. Nor should their input or opinions be discounted on either societal or familial levels. Furthermore, the sexes are alike in that they are both able to communicate and even able to cling together as one in marriage. But many want to overlook the existence of the comprehensive difference between a man's and woman's being. By the 1960s and 1970s, the feminist movement took a decidedly new path that has led to a current, full-blown assault on any traditional concept of what constitutes a man or woman.[6] Many proponents go as far as Shulamith Firestone, who pushes for the total obliteration of gender differences.[7] Also, she is not alone in her preference of artificial procreation and the full dismantling of the family, substituting a group setting for the upbringing of children.[8] Werner Neuer accurately writes in his book *Man and Woman*, "The feminist movement tends to confuse a real equality of men and women with their being identical."[9]

Many are not aware (or perhaps want to overlook) that the differences in God's design for the sexes reach far beyond outward appearance. These dissimilarities are amazingly and beautifully consistent with the roles He has set forth in Scripture. Neuer skillfully joins both of these ideas by compiling scientific evidence and research that reveal the extensive physiological and personal differences between men and women. Such differences include bone structure and constitution, muscles, skin, sexual organs and function, blood constitution, bodily liquids, hormones, chromosomal cell structure, cognitive function, abilities, outlooks, and relations. Men and women are distinctly different beings.[10] With this great plan of God in mind John Benton writes, "In particular, gender difference is not fortuitous. It is not a product of chance. It is not something unreasonable and unintelligible. It is not something to be regretted, or to fight against. It is to be gratefully accepted as the good gift of a loving God."[11]

A man cannot ever be a man in the truest sense unless he, in his mind, attests to these basic realities and gives his very life over to them and to the One who created him. Masculinity then is a matter of the mind. A man can go to the gym to work out and even gain the physique of Charles Atlas or Arnold Schwarznegger, but this will not make him any more masculine. It is important to keep in mind A. B. Bruce's statement, "What tells ultimately is, not what is without a man, but what is within."[12]

Characteristics of the Perfect Man—Jesus

Jesus, the God-Man, is portrayed in the Scriptures as the only perfect man (1 Pet 2:21-22). This being so, He is the perfect picture of what one should strive to be as a man. Christ is the pristine example of masculinity in every way (1 John 2:6). Surely, no one would say that any quality He possessed was unmanly. The following is a chart of Christlike character qualities (attitudes and actions) that will help explain authentic manhood more specifically.

Qualities of the Perfect Man as Seen in Christ

ATTITUDES	ACTIONS	REFERENCES
Eternal Mind-set	Did the will and work of the Father Not working toward His own success/desires	Jn 4:34; 5:30; 8:28-29
	Was filled with the Spirit (Word) Not the world's wisdom/ways	Lk 4:1, 14
	Gave the Gospel to others Not temporary pleasures or relief	Mk 1:14-15; Jn 3–4
	Lived a holy, obedient life Not sinful	Phil 2:8; 1 Pet 2:22
Love/ Understanding	Sought to meet needs of others Not uncaring/self-focused	Mt 4:23; Lk 4:18-21
	Sacrificed self and own desires Not self-preserving/selfish	Lk 22:42; Phil 2:6-8
	Was gentle whenever possible Not harsh/demanding	Mt 11:29; Jn 21:15-19
Zeal/Courage/ Confidence (because of God and His promises)	Led the disciples and others Not a follower when He shouldn't be	Jn 6:2
	Showed initiative when He should have Not waiting for someone else	Mk 6:34-44; Lk 6:12-16
	Confronted when necessary Not a compromiser/man-pleaser	Mt 23:1-36; Mk 11:15-18
	Was decisive according to God's revealed will Not wishy-washy or afraid	Mt 4:1-11; Mk 8:31-38
Conscientiousness	Fulfilled responsibilities Not irresponsible	Jn 17:4; 19:30
	Was diligent Not lazy or a quitter	Jn 5:17; Heb 12:2-3
Humility	Served and listened to others in His leadership Not proudly lording it over others	Jn 6:5-10; 13:2-17
	Glorified another (the Father) Not greedy for attention or recognition	Jn 8:50, 54; 17:1, 4

God's will for men is to put on Christlikeness (Rom 13:14). One cannot be a *real man* unless he is increasing in Christ's qualities. Men should pray about these regularly and seek to emulate them in daily living (2 Pet 3:18).

Characteristics Drawn from the Qualifications of Male Leadership in the Church

More insight can be gained into God's expectations about masculinity by examining what God has said concerning male leadership in the church. In the Scriptures we find two very precise lists of positive and negative qualities by which leaders are to be measured: 1 Timothy 3:2-7 and Titus 1:6-9. Although Paul, in these passages, correlates this set of characteristics with church leadership, these qualities (except for "able to teach" and "not . . . a recent convert") are addressed elsewhere in God's Word for the non-elder Christian as well. These instructions were given to ensure that male leaders were habitually the kind of men that God wants *every* man to be. Because a leader is always some sort of example (good or bad), it is very important to God that every male leader reflect Christ (1 Cor 11:1). Therefore, since these two passages were specifically given by God to men, the basic instructions found in them are profitable for understanding what is truly masculine and what is not. It could even be said, from God's perspective, that these commands and prohibitions are prerequisites to genuine *manliness*. A godly man must be:

• "Above reproach": blameless, not able to be accused, having a good reputation.

• "The husband of one wife": a pattern of singular affection for one's wife.

• "Sober-minded": temperate, alert, clearheaded, watchful.

• "Self-controlled": in control of his thinking, emotions, and passions; prudent, thoughtful, decent.

• "Respectable": orderly in time, responsibilities, and behavior; not chaotic.

• "Hospitable": welcoming to others, loves strangers, serves others.

• "Gentle": considerate, gracious, patient, kind in dealing with others.

• "He must manage his own household well": governs, presides over, has authority over; is faithful to lead spiritually, cares for, protects; has children who are not riotous or insubordinate; oversees and/or fulfills affairs of the home.

• "A lover of good": loves virtue and good men.

• "Upright": just; upholds righteousness.

• "Holy": pure, devout.

• "Disciplined": persevering, steadfast, restrained.

• "He must hold firmly to the trustworthy word": learns and upholds sound doctrine; holds to it tightly; able to exhort and convict.

In contrast, a godly man must not be:

• "A drunkard": not addicted to strong drink.

• "Violent": quickly angered, explosively angry.

• "Quarrelsome": contentious, argumentative.

• "A lover of money," "greedy for gain": covetous, greedy for money, materialistic.

• "Arrogant" (self-willed) rather than a steward: pushing his own ideas, desires, goals, or gain.

• "Quick-tempered": inclined to habitual anger; quickly angry.

Examining the qualities for godly spiritual leaders helps us further refine what it means to be a man. When defining masculinity, it is futile to concern oneself with qualities that should be distinctly different from feminine counterparts unless one has first thought about the more foundational traits of manhood. Hopefully it has been made clear that one cannot be truly masculine by centering on only a few distinctive characteristics. Up to this point the basic characteristics of man, the fundamental character of the perfect man (Christ), and some primary qualities that are specifically directed toward men have been discussed. That being accomplished, attention is now directed to those qualities directly related to man's unique, God-given role.

ROLE CHARACTERISTICS IN WHICH A MAN MUST EXCEL

By exploring God's intention concerning gender roles, it becomes clear how a man should differ from a woman. Herein lies the key to distinctive masculine qualities. After understanding from Scripture what God intended for a man to *do*, it is much easier to determine what characteristics must be emphasized. In this process it will become obvious that women may also be expected to possess these qualities to some extent or in certain situations. But a man must excel in them in order to fulfill his major roles. This concept is very similar to spiritual gifts. For example, all Christians are commanded to evangelize and to be hospitable. However, some have been given the gift of evangelism or hospitality and therefore will *excel* in that ability so that they might fulfill their role in the body of Christ. A strong and godly man will be characterized by the qualities that are necessary to fulfill the roles that God has given to him.

Leader

When God placed man in the garden, He gave him specific instructions. Adam was to care for the garden—i.e., to oversee it (Gen 2:15). He was given charge of it, even though God could have done a much better job Himself. Adam also had dominion over and named the animals (Gen 1:28-30; 2:19-20). He was given these tasks before Eve came on the scene. When God placed Eve in the garden, He made it clear that she was to assist Adam in the work he had been given to do. She was to be his helper (Gen 2:18). God did not say, "Eve, you take this half, and, Adam, you take the other." Adam was to lead; Eve was to help and follow.

Later in Scripture, husbands are clearly instructed to be the head in the marriage relationship, and women are commanded to submit to the husband's leadership and to respect his God-given position (Eph 5:22-33). It was to men that God gave leadership positions in the nation of Israel.[13] Furthermore, it is to men that God gave the position of leadership in the church (1 Tim 2:11-12). It is obvious that God has given man the role of ultimate leadership.

This says absolutely nothing (positive or negative) about a woman's capabilities or personal equality. God simply chose to give this role to the man. In any endeavor there must be an ultimate leader. God chose and equipped Adam for this role. If leadership is a God-given role for men, then each man needs to find the way to lead. For some men, who did not develop leadership skills while growing up or who have habitually shied away from leadership, it will be necessary to develop leadership skills over time rather than incompetently try to lead in a full or total capacity. Granted, some men are gifted by God with exceptional leadership abilities to be leaders of leaders. If all Christian men were taught that it is *manly* to initiate and lead, there would not be such a lack of male leadership in the home and the church. In regard to teaching young boys about leadership, Douglas Wilson writes:

> Our boys need to learn humility, and they also need to learn boldness and courage. The only way to accomplish this balance is through a grasp of who God is. Because we have ceased teaching that God is our Father, with the attributes of divine Father, we have lost an understanding of imitative masculinity. Because of this, our boys veer into one of two ditches. Either they embrace humility without boldness which in boys is effeminate, or they embrace boldness without humility which is destructive.[14]

The qualities that one must strongly possess in order to carry out a leadership role are *wisdom* (by a full knowledge of the Word of God, facts, and persons, and then thoughtful application of biblical principles), *initiative*, *decisiveness*, *humility*, *courage*, and *personal involvement*.[15]

Lover (the 1 Corinthians 13 Type)

At creation, Adam and Eve were given to each other as marital companions. This intention for marriage is further made clear later in Scripture (Mal 2:14). Certainly love is involved in this kind of companionship. In the New Testament, husbands are singled out as needing to exemplify the kind of sacrificial love that Christ has for the Church (Eph 5:25). They are also specifically commanded to live with their wives "in an understanding way" (1 Pet 3:7). Clearly, husbands are to excel in this love. Also, Christ commanded the men He left behind to love and serve one another (John 13:15). John Benton writes:

> There is need for repentance. Perhaps single men have used the strength they have to serve themselves rather than other people. Perhaps husbands have

> used their strength to dominate their wives and children. We need to learn to come back to God, back to his Word of Scripture, and learn again to walk with him. To be a loving sacrificial servant of others, as Jesus Christ was, is not to be namby-pamby. It is to be a true man.[16]

A true man, then, will *excel* in qualities that show love, such as *giving*, *gentleness*, *consideration*, *kindness*, *servanthood*, and *self-sacrifice*.

Protector

A natural outworking of the roles of leader and lover produces the role of protector. After the Fall, it certainly became part of Adam's job description to protect his wife. As the supreme leader and lover, God has made a commitment to protect believers (2 Thess 3:3). A man must make the same commitment to protect his wife, his children, and his church. Though God in His love does not always protect people from the consequences of their sin or from every evil in the world, His protection definitely involves both *physical* and *spiritual* aspects, just like a husband's love. However, it must be remembered that only the all-knowing and all-wise God has the right and the wisdom to purposefully allow evil to befall another.

In the Old Testament, men made up the army of Israel to protect cities, women, and children (Num 1:2-3). In 1 Corinthians 16:13 God commanded the brethren of the Corinthian church to protect the faith (the Word of God) with the words "act like men"; i.e., be courageous! Christ certainly protected the disciples He loved and led (John 17:12). He also expected all the church leaders to protect the body of Christ (Acts 20:28). Being manly involves protecting. The qualities a man must clearly possess before he will be a good protector are *courage*, *boldness*, *strength* (both physical and spiritual), and *watchfulness*.

Provider

The roles of leader and lover automatically encompass the idea of *provision*. God, as the one who leads and loves, also provides for every true need (Ps 34:10). Husbands and fathers are specifically given the role of provider in the New Testament (Eph 5:28-29; 1 Tim 5:8). Leaders of God's people are given this role as well (Ezek 34:1-4; John 21:15-17). Men should seek to meet the true needs of those whom God has placed in their care, whether physical or spiritual. In order to fulfill this role, a truly masculine man will abound in the characteristics of *diligence* (hard work), *personal involvement*, and *servanthood*. He will also do all that he can to acquire *a good job* that allows him to care well for those he must love and lead.

A man will be better able to fulfill God's intention as he puts off sin and grows in Christlikeness. Many sins will keep a man from possessing these qualities and fulfilling his God-given roles. These sins include fear of man, self-pity, love of pleasure, pride, laziness, selfishness, idolatry (e.g., work, money, possessions, success, one's wife), and a lack of trust in God and His truth. A real man will, by God's grace, strive to put off these and any other sins that stand in the way of his masculinity. He will seek God's help to implement all of these godly (Christlike) qualities into his daily affairs. John Piper writes, "At the heart of mature masculinity is a sense of benevolent responsibility to lead, provide for and protect women in ways appropriate to a man's differing relationships."[17]

The extent to which these role qualities are present in a man's life determines how well he displays these distinguishing aspects of his masculinity. He should surpass his counterpart in them. Furthermore, he has the freedom to exercise them with both of the genders. Women, on the other hand, may *at times* need to assume these roles with children, other women, and men outside the realm of the church; but she will find true identity and satisfaction if she is *more* characterized by the role of assistant or helper, so far as marriage and spiritual instruction are concerned (Gen 2:18; 1 Tim 2:12).

Furthermore, a woman in leadership in the workplace must be able to deal with a male employee under her in a way that preserves his masculinity and her femininity. Though many women have found a certain prideful satisfaction in leading, they are surely missing a far more pure and holy satisfaction that is found only in fulfilling the roles God has given her.

Similarly, if men were to be more consistent in living out these role qualities, they would not be inclined to strive toward counterfeit expressions of masculinity such as machismo or authoritarianism. Men of this persuasion have fallen into one kind of unbiblical extreme. The other extreme, of course, is that of passive or effeminate men. If a man overly focuses on any one of the characteristics described in this chapter, that will cause him to err toward one extreme or the other—to be unmanly and sin in his duties and relationships. Instead, a man must fully embrace God's superior design for the sexes. About this John MacArthur observes, "They are perfect complements—one the head, leader, and provider; the other the helper, supporter, and companion."[18]

The Bottom Line

So what does it mean to be a *real man*? It means not to trust in one's own judgment about masculinity, but instead to cling to the fact that there *are* absolutes outlined in the Word of God. It means to understand the basic characteristics of mankind and recognize that there should be a difference between the genders. It means possessing saving faith in and a likeness to the person of Christ. It means striving to emulate the qualities that God outlines for godly men in the church. Finally, it means to capitalize on the specific qualities that are needed to fulfill our God-given roles. In short, it means to live out a biblical worldview of masculinity.

Boys need to be taught the characteristics of biblical manhood by parents and other spiritual teachers. Furthermore, these are qualities that should be presented to the male population in all Bible-believing churches and institutions. Christian men need to take personal responsibility to study scriptural teaching in this area, communicating with other godly men about it, reading some of the resources below, and depending on God's grace to change.

Though many of the masculine qualities discussed in this chapter were related to the husband, Scripture also presents them as pertaining to those single men who are God's servants. Therefore, these truths are for each and every man, single or married, young or old. All men should fervently seek to pursue a true and life-changing understanding of the basic characteristics of man and Christ, take to heart specific biblical charges to men, and look for opportunities to lead, love, protect, and provide. Then he will be *a real man.*

> **Masculinity (mas-kyoo-lin-i-ty)**: The possession and pursuit of redeemed perspective and character, enhanced by qualities consistent with the distinguishing male roles of leading, loving, protecting, and providing—all for the glory of God.

FURTHER READING

Benton, John. *Gender Questions*. London: Evangelical Press, 2000.

MacArthur, John. *Different by Design*. Wheaton, IL: Victor Books, 1994.

Piper, John and Wayne Grudem, coeditors. *Recovering Biblical Manhood and Womanhood*. Wheaton, IL: Crossway Books, 1991.

Scott, Stuart W. *The Exemplary Husband*. Bemidji, MN: Focus Publishing, 2000.

Strauch, Alexander. *Equal Yet Different*. Littleton, CO: Lewis and Roth, 1999.

Watson, Thomas. *The Godly Man's Picture*. Edinburgh: Banner of Truth, 1992.

Wilson, Douglas. *Future Men*. Moscow, ID: Canon Press, 2001.

9

Portraying Christian Femininity[1]

Patricia A. Ennis

Holding to a biblical view of femininity is quite unpopular in our contemporary society; it is frequently perceived as demeaning, inferior, and limiting. Regrettably, this attitude has now affected American evangelicalism, so that the issue must be clarified by recovering a biblical worldview of femininity.

Femininity, by dictionary definition, means "having qualities or characteristics traditionally ascribed to women, as sensitivity, delicacy, or prettiness."[2] According to Elisabeth Elliot, "That word 'femininity' is one that we don't hear very often anymore. We've heard the word 'feminist' quite often in the last couple of decades, but we haven't really heard much about the deep mystery that is called femininity. The word has fallen on hard times, partly because of stereotypes as opposed to archetypes."[3]

She then offers several thoughts that place *femininity* in a Christian context:

> To me, a lady is not frilly, flouncy, flippant, frivolous and fluff-brained, but she is gentle. She is gracious. She is godly and she is giving. . . .
>
> You and I, if we are women, have the gift of femininity. Very often it is obscured, just as the image of God is obscured in all of us. . . .
>
> I find myself in the sometimes quite uncomfortable position of having to belabor the obvious, and hold up examples of femininity to women who almost feel apologetic for being feminine or being womanly. I would remind you that *femininity* is not a curse. It is not even a triviality. It is a gift, a divine gift, to be accepted with both hands, and to thank God for. Because remember, it was His idea. . . .

> God's gifts are masculinity and femininity within the human race and there was never meant to be any competition between them. The Russian philosopher Bergiath made this statement: "The idea of woman's emancipation is based upon a profound enmity between the sexes, upon envy and imitation."
>
> The more womanly we are, the more manly men will be, and the more God is glorified. As I say to you women, "Be women. Be only women. Be real women in obedience to God."[4]

Femininity's contemporary downward spiral began in the early 1960s with the advent of Betty Friedan's book, *The Feminine Mystique*.[5] Friedan advocated that strong women pursue power that provides the path toward self-actualization and happiness. Her philosophy drew thousands of women into "the power trap" that eventually resulted in their cynical approach to life and disillusionment in their newfound freedom. Gloria Steinem perpetuated Friedan's teachings in the 1970s and moved the feminist agenda to middle-class suburban mothers. Eventually the trickle-down effect occurred, and the feminist agenda infiltrated evangelicalism. Today many women in mainline evangelical churches have substituted the contemporary, cultural view of femininity for the biblical view. However, it was neither Friedan nor Steinem who authored the philosophy that power provides self-actualization and happiness; rather, it was Satan who first suggested this lie to Eve in the Garden of Eden (Gen 3:1-8) and prompted her to challenge God's command to refrain from eating from the tree of the knowledge of good and evil (Gen 2:16-17).

The woman desiring to embrace *Christian* femininity begins with the presuppositions that God 1) created her in His own image (Gen 1:27) and 2) designed her to fulfill specific roles (Gen 2:18). John Piper and Wayne Grudem write:

> The tendency today is to stress the equality of men and women by minimizing the unique significance of our maleness or femaleness. But this depreciation of male and female personhood is a great loss. It is taking a tremendous toll on generations of young men and women who do not know what it means to be a man or a woman. Confusion over the meaning of sexual personhood today is epidemic. The consequence of this confusion is not a free and happy harmony among gender-free persons relating on the basis of abstract competencies. The consequence rather is more divorce, more homosexuality, more sexual abuse, more promiscuity, more emotional distress and suicide that come with the loss of God-given identity.[6]

Scripture is replete with directives that instruct the Christian woman to portray her femininity by helping (Gen 2:18), exhibiting graciousness (Prov

11:16), living a pure life (1 Pet 3:1-2), dressing modestly (1 Tim 2:9; 1 Pet 3:3), developing "a gentle and quiet spirit" (1 Pet 3:4), submitting to her husband (Eph 5:22), and teaching the younger women (Titus 2:3-5). Of all the Scriptures that teach on this subject, Proverbs 31:10-31 is the only one that presents a thorough literary sketch of the woman who portrays Christian femininity. Thus it demands our attention for this study.

A Biblical Sketch of the Worthy Woman

Virtuous, trustworthy, energetic, physically fit, economical, unselfish, honorable, lovable, prepared, prudent, and God-fearing encompass eleven features highlighting the character of the worthy woman in Proverbs 31:10-31.[7] While many believe that the woman described in this passage is fictional rather than a real woman whose life Christian women are challenged to emulate in principle, the divinely intended truth application cannot be doubted (2 Tim 3:16-17). The immutability (unalterableness) of God demands that Proverbs 31:10-31 is timelessly relevant in principle. If one thinks that God changed His mind about the chief application of one passage of Scripture, how then can one be sure He has not changed His mind about others? J. I. Packer, in *Knowing God*, lists six attributes of God that it would be helpful to remind ourselves of prior to studying the eleven characteristics presented in the Proverbs 31 passage.[8]

1. God's life does not change.
2. God's character does not change.
3. God's truth does not change.
4. God's ways do not change.
5. God's purposes do not change.
6. God's Son does not change.

Since God does not change, then fellowship with Him, trust in His Word, living by faith, and embracing His principles are the same for twenty-first-century believers as they were for those in Old and New Testament times. The description of the godly woman in Proverbs 31:10-31 is not designed to develop an inferiority complex. Rather, it provides a biblical foundation for the development of principles by which Christian femininity can be portrayed. While the outward historical context and practice have changed since King Lemuel wrote that passage in the book of Proverbs, the character principles have not.

Learning from the Wisdom of Others

Biblical wisdom "is both religious and practical. Stemming from the fear of the Lord (Jb 28:28; Ps 111:10; Prv 1:7; 9:10) it branches out to touch all of life, as the extended commentary on wisdom in Proverbs indicates. Wisdom takes insights gleaned from the knowledge of God's way and applies them in the daily walk."[9]

Scripture provides the basis for wise instruction (2 Tim 3:16-17). Paul, in 1 Corinthians 10:6, reminds believers, "Now these things took place as examples for us, that we might not desire evil as they did." Titus 2:4-5 instructs the older women to "train the young women to love their husbands and children, to be self-controlled, pure, working at home, kind, and submissive to their own husbands, that the word of God may not be reviled."

The MacArthur Study Bible introduces the book of Proverbs by stating:

> The proverbs are short, pithy sayings which express timeless truth and wisdom. They arrest one's thoughts, causing the reader to reflect on how one might apply divine principles to life situations. . . . To the Hebrew mind, wisdom was not knowledge alone, but the skill of living a godly life as God intended man to live.[10]

Essential to becoming a worthy woman is the personal appropriation of biblical principles that motivate one's decisions and actions. *Principle* can be described as "an accepted or professed rule of action or conduct."[11] Reflecting upon the question, "What are my specific abilities, heritage, and talents that make me unique and determine my professed rules of action or conduct?" can motivate the manner in which biblical principles are obeyed. Their implementation ultimately determines the character of a woman and whether she is considered wise or foolish; thus the worthy woman possesses a heart that is open to learning from the experience and wisdom of others, including the woman of Proverbs 31, who exhibits at least eleven principles by which to live a godly life.

Being Virtuous

> *An excellent wife who can find?*
> *She is far more precious than jewels.*
> —PROV 31:10

Moral excellence, right actions, and thinking that is true, worthy, just, pure, lovely, of good report, possessing virtue, and praiseworthy (Phil 4:8-9) characterize the principle of being virtuous. Virtue is an effective power and force that should permeate all thoughts, actions, and relationships of the worthy woman. When integrated into her life, the principle generates power and demands respect.

The worthy woman establishes godly guidelines for living according to the Scriptures and purposes, through the strength of the Holy Spirit, to abide by them (Phil 4:13). The Old Testament book of Ruth describes such a woman. Ruth 3:11 is the only scriptural reference to a "virtuous" woman (KJV, NKJV, NIV; ESV "worthy") and explains that Boaz knew about Ruth because of her reputation for excellence. In contrast, Rahab's reputation as a harlot followed her throughout the Scriptures (Josh 2:1; 6:17; Heb 11:31; Jas 2:25). Though God saved Rahab and by His grace allowed her to be included in the Messianic line (Matt 1:5), her reputation as a harlot lingered.

The worthy woman is a crown to her husband. A woman lacking in virtue causes him shame and produces suffering that is like a painful, incurable condition (Prov 12:4). A woman's character prior to marriage will determine her quality as a marital spouse, thus underscoring the importance for every Christian woman to embrace virtue at an early age. To live a life characterized by virtue should be the ambition of every Christian woman (Matt 5:8).

Being Trustworthy

> *The heart of her husband trusts in her,*
> *and he will have no lack of gain.*
> *She does him good, and not harm,*
> *all the days of her life. . . .*
> *Her husband is known in the gates*
> *when he sits among the elders of the land.*
>
> —PROV 31:11-12, 23

The principle of being *trustworthy* is demonstrated by behaviors that lead to confidence in the honesty, integrity, reliability, justice, and loyalty of an individual. Integrity (i.e., the quality or state of being complete [Col 2:10]) is demonstrated through how one handles abundance, because prosperity tends to reveal our value system (1 Cor 10:1-10).

The character of the worthy woman motivates her husband to respond with trust (Prov 31:11). This trustworthy lifestyle includes the nurturing of security, love, service, limits, freedom, enjoyment, faith, and encouragement. Her husband and those under her leadership are challenged to reach their full potential (Prov 18:22; 19:14). She understands that she has the ability to feed or starve their character and thus handles this privilege through the strength of the Holy Spirit (Gal 5:16-26).

The worthy woman can live in today's world with or without a husband. As she 1) implements Psalm 37:3-4, Proverbs 3:5-6, and Jeremiah 29:11-13, 2) trusts in her Heavenly Father, and 3) affirms that He is a sun and shield, He gives her grace and glory. "No good thing does he withhold from those who walk uprightly" (Ps 84:11). If married, her husband's response to her character is trust. If unmarried, trustworthiness is the evaluation of those closest to her.

The fruit of trustworthiness is an understanding, encouraging, sympathetic, and tactful spirit. A trustworthy woman has the ability to retain another's confidence and maintain confidentiality (Prov 10:19) and possesses stability in her life, based upon a growing relationship with the Lord rather than on circumstances (Jas 1:5-6). She also has the ability to resist temptation and exhibits dependability (1 Cor 10:12-13).

Being Energetic

She seeks wool and flax,
and works with willing hands.
She is like the ships of the merchant;
she brings her food from afar.
She rises while it is yet night
and provides food for her household
and portions for her maidens.
She considers a field and buys it;
with the fruit of her hands she plants a vineyard. . . .
She perceives that her merchandise is profitable.
Her lamp does not go out at night. . . .
She makes linen garments and sells them;
she delivers sashes to the merchant. . . .
She looks well to the ways of her household
and does not eat the bread of idleness.

—PROV 31:13-16, 18, 24, 27

Being energetic suggests that strength or power is efficiently exerted. A worthy woman knows her assets and liabilities, develops her talents, exhibits the attributes of being alert and aware, and is a worker, not a shirker. She works willingly with her hands (the word *hands* is used seven times in the twenty-two verses of Prov 31:10-31).

This worthy woman sets an example for her children by her personal and physical involvement in the management of her home. In the context of

Proverbs 31, she trained her servants and then supervised the tasks they performed. She was actively involved in her well-managed household (v. 27), fabric and garment construction (vv. 13-24), trading in the marketplace (v. 24), and ministry to others (vv. 19-20). Application to the twenty-first century would find the worthy woman training her children and then supervising them to efficiently use today's many "electrical servants." Concurrently, she is involved in Christian services that complement those toward her children, rather than neglecting them to perform "her ministries." Her role model is Christ (Phil 2:5-11), who cares much more about those under Him than they care about Him.

Most twenty-first-century women can identify with their lamp not going out at night (v. 18) because of the intense schedules they maintain. However, this verse does not suggest that the worthy woman deprives herself of sleep. Just as exercise contributes to a physically fit body, so sleep is necessary to an energetic woman's mental, spiritual, and physical well-being.

Being Physically Fit

> *She dresses herself with strength*
> *and makes her arms strong.*
> —PROV 31:17

Physical fitness—i.e., being in good physical condition and healthy—is enthusiastically affirmed by many twenty-first-century women. The biblical application is defined by three words—suitable, proper, and fit. They describe the worthy woman's attitude toward the condition of her body. A concern for what is *suitable* guides the worthy woman in the selection of physical toning activities that prepare her to fulfill the demands of her life. A concern for what is *proper* encourages her to select activities that are dictated by good judgment. A concern for what is *fit* expands the definition to challenge her to possess the qualifications necessary to meet the purposes, circumstances, and demands of her life.

First Timothy 4:8 directs wise women to the truth that "while bodily training is of some value, godliness is of value in every way, as it holds promise for the present life and also for the life to come." The worthy woman will be more concerned about the highest priority of her character without neglecting her body tone (1 Pet 3:3-6). The following guidelines addressing her attitude toward her body will help balance the physical and spiritual sides of fitness.

First, she has a realistic attitude toward personal capabilities. God provides health parameters to assist us in being sensible about the responsibilities we assume. Just because a woman *can* perform a skill does not mean that she *should*. Purposely pushing beyond safe health parameters would be like a woman jumping off the Golden Gate Bridge and then praying on the way down that she won't get hurt! This would be sinfully presumptous.

Second, the worthy woman acknowledges that her body is the temple of the Holy Spirit, and that it is her responsibility to make it a fit dwelling-place for Him (1 Cor 6:19-20). It is a sobering thought to acknowledge that the Holy Spirit will not empower a spiritually dirty vessel.

Third, she realizes that she must be healthy to perform her duties efficiently. Cultivating this quality requires freedom from all habits that would injure her physically, mentally, or spiritually (Rom 12:1-2).

Fourth, she understands the importance of recreation to maintain a healthy body. Mark 6:31 and Luke 9:10 describe our Lord's sensitivity to His disciples' need for rest and privacy from their demanding ministry. The worthy woman will adopt our Lord's model.

Fifth, she accepts the fact that sometimes "others can, I cannot." It is an exercise in futility to compare her capabilities with those of others, since each woman is "fearfully and wonderfully made" (Ps 139:14).

Finally, the worthy woman has a clear perspective regarding her body cycling. She wisely accommodates to its ebb and flow. The circumspect physical conditioning of the worthy woman allows her to be involved in the lives of others. She will balance the care of her home with the care of her body to avoid becoming a worried, frazzled, and defensive woman who sacrifices herself on the altar of domesticity or physical fitness.

Being Economical

> *She perceives that her merchandise is profitable.*
>
> —PROV 31:18A

Budget and *diet* are two words that conjure up visions of economic and nutritional deprivation. Each word, however, possesses both a positive and a negative connotation. A budget can be established for either a high or low income. A diet can constitute an unlimited or restrictive daily caloric intake. The principle of being economical challenges the worthy woman to refrain from wasting time, money, fuel, or any other resource. Implementation of this principle ensures that she operates her home on a budget (a plan for spending) and that it balances each month (not too much month at the end of the money).

The worthy woman of Proverbs 31 perceives that money involves stewardship. As an accomplished seamstress and nutritionist, she recognizes quality. With a practiced eye, she seeks out bargains that reflect excellence. Concurrently, her knowledge and skill allow her to make appropriate decisions regarding whether to make the purchase, pay for the service, or personally perform the task.

Being Unselfish

> *She puts her hands to the distaff,*
> *and her hands hold the spindle.*
> *She opens her hand to the poor*
> *and reaches out her hands to the needy.*
> —PROV 31:19-20

Selfishness is a trait that the worthy woman seeks to eliminate from the list of her character qualities. By definition it means having such regard for one's own interests and advantage that the happiness and welfare of others become of less concern than is appropriate. Selfishness stems from pride and is first in the list of sins most detested by God (Prov 6:16-19). Taken to extremes, it can be deadly.

The body of an ancient woman mummified by the volcanic ashes of Mount Vesuvius was unearthed when the Roman City of Pompeii was excavated. Her feet pointed toward the city gate, but her outreached arms and fingers were straining for something that lay behind her. The treasure for which she was grasping was a bag of pearls. Of her it was written, "Though death was hard at her heels, and life was beckoning to her beyond the city gates, she could not shake off their spell . . . but it was not the eruption of Vesuvius that made her love pearls more than life. It only froze her in this attitude of greed."[12] Her position told a tragic story of selfishness.

Anything can fuel the flames of excessive desire and greed. If not checked, they can destroy women (Prov 1:19). The wealthy landowners in Isaiah's day acquired more and more houses and fields until they had a monopoly (Isa 5:8). But God said that they would become desolate and their lands would not produce (vv. 9-10). Wise is the woman who lives by the principle that if she is not satisfied with what she has, she will never be satisfied with what she wants.

Several characteristics describe the worthy woman's attitude toward money and material possessions. All resources are a gift from the Lord to be utilized with discretion (Deut 8:18; Acts 4:32-37; 1 Tim 6:17-19). God does not love the poor and hate the rich. The Bible reports a number of godly individuals who were exceedingly wealthy—Job, Abraham, Joseph, David, Solomon, Josiah, Barnabas, Philemon, and Lydia, to name a few. God does, however, hate false gain (Prov 1:19), wrong motives for acquiring wealth (Prov 13:11), and a lack of compassionate generosity among the wealthy (Prov 14:20-21; 16:19). The wise woman applies the truth of Proverbs 19:17, "Whoever is generous to the poor lends to the LORD, and he will repay him for his deed."

The worthy woman possesses an attitude of contentment that corresponds with the New Testament teaching found in 1 Timothy 6:6-8, which essentially states that *Godliness + Contentment = Great Gain!* Evidence that wealth is not the source of her contentment is found in her attitude of humility patterned after her Lord (Phil 2:8; 1 Pet 5:5). She does not trust in her wealth for security (Ps 20:7; Prov 11:28) and is a gracious (Prov 11:16), generous woman (Prov 31:19-20).

The worthy woman exhibits an absence of selfish attributes. She is not too busy with her own affairs to take time to assist others. The spindle and distaff—two flat, circular objects used to work textile fibers—were tools of the day. The worthy woman used them to provide for her family, herself, and the less fortunate. That "she opens her hand to the poor and reaches out her hands to the needy" indicates her response to calls for help (Prov 31:20). Her actions demonstrate both responsiveness and initiative; she gives when she is asked and is sensitive to offer assistance when she is not asked. Embracing a spiritual attitude toward helping, the worthy woman is like Dorcas, who was "full of good works and acts of charity" (Acts 9:36).

Unselfishness is most graphically demonstrated in the worthy woman's willingness to share her time with others. Time is our most precious commodity, and the highest compliment that can be paid to others is the time we share with them. This woman is not a respecter of persons (Jas 2:1-13) but rather is willing to place before the Lord the requests of all who desire to benefit from her wisdom.

Being Prepared

> *She is not afraid of snow for her household,*
> *for all her household are clothed in scarlet.*
> *She makes bed coverings for herself;*
> *her clothing is fine linen and purple. . . .*
> *She looks well to the ways of her household*
> *and does not eat the bread of idleness.*
> —PROV 31:21-22, 27

Putting events, objects, or people in order, as well as *making suitable and receptive*, are phrases that describe the principle of preparedness in action.

The worthy woman demonstrates planning and foresight that equip her for unforeseen circumstances. She acquires adequate provisions for unknown needs rather than living from crisis to crisis. Concurrent with physical provisions, this worthy woman knows the value of being spiritually prepared. Similar to saving a percentage of each paycheck, she builds a spiritual reserve for challenging times. The prophet Jeremiah refers to the woman who trusts in the Lord as being prepared in that she will be "like a tree planted by water, that sends out its roots by the stream, and does not fear when heat comes, for its leaves remain green, and is not anxious in the year of drought, for it does not cease to bear fruit" (Jer 17:7-8). The heat will come, and the drought is certain; however, there is no fear when one is prepared.

Her firm grip on spiritual priorities allows her to be prepared for the future. Charles Hummel urges his readers to evaluate their priorities daily:

> Sometime ago, Simba bullets killed a young man, Dr. Paul Carlson. In the providence of God his life's work was finished. Most of us will live longer and die more quietly, but when the end comes, what would give us greater joy than being sure that we have finished the work that *God* gave us to do? The grace of the Lord Jesus Christ makes this fulfillment possible. He has promised deliverance from sin and the power to serve God in the tasks of His choice. The way is clear. If we continue in the world of our Lord, we are truly his disciples. And he will free us from the tyranny of the urgent, free us to do the important, which is the will of God.[13]

The worthy woman will refuse to allow the urgent to take the place of the important in her life.

Being Honorable

> *Strength and dignity are her clothing,*
> *and she laughs at the time to come.*
> —PROV 31:25

Being *honorable* is synonymous with *having integrity* and is evidenced by others' high regard or respect for the worthy woman. She possesses a keen sense of right or wrong, and her moral uprightness is apparent to all. Several attributes will emerge as the worthy woman assimilates this principle into her life:

- Her outer adorning complements her inward qualities (1 Pet 3:3-4).
- She abstains from every appearance of evil (1 Thess 5:22).
- She possesses strong convictions of right and wrong (Prov 14:12; 16:25; Matt 7:13-14).

• The convictions she embraces are based upon biblical principles (Ps 119:11, 105) rather than cultural trends.

If married, the worthy woman's high standards of behavior make a significant contribution to her husband's position (Prov 12:4; 18:22; 19:14; 31:23). She functions as a helpmate (Gen 2:18) and purposes to never be an embarrassment or a hindrance to her husband.

The worthy woman acquires a stable, honest reputation. Strength and honor accompany her business acumen (Prov 31:25). Desiring to walk worthy of her calling (Eph 4:1-2), she leads a life that brings glory to God (1 Cor 10:31). Humility, unselfishness, gentleness, mildness, patience, bearing with others, and making allowances for others are characteristic of her godly posture.

The honorable woman has control of her body—it is presented as a living sacrifice to the Lord (Rom 12:1-2). She refuses to yield her body as an instrument to sin (Rom 6:12-13) and acknowledges that her body belongs to Christ (1 Cor 6:15). Realizing that her body is a temple literally inhabited by the Holy Spirit (1 Cor 6:19), she chooses to glorify God in her body (1 Cor 6:20). She becomes a student of her body so that she knows how to control it in honor (1 Thess 4:4); she understands the need for accountability to the body of Christ to maintain her purity (Gal 6:1-2; Jas 5:19-20).

Being Prudent

> *She opens her mouth with wisdom,*
> *and the teaching of kindness is on her tongue.*
> —PROV 31:26

Mothers frequently remind their children, "If you can't say something nice, don't say anything at all!" James 3:2, 6 teaches us that "we all stumble in many ways, and if anyone does not stumble in what he says, he is a perfect man, able also to bridle his whole body. . . . And the tongue is a fire, a world of unrighteousness. The tongue is set among our members, staining the whole body, setting on fire the entire course of life, and set on fire by hell." The principle of prudence—i.e., connoting wisdom and careful consideration of consequences—specifically addresses the use of her tongue. Miriam, Moses' sister, serves as a graphic illustration of the impact of a sharp, complaining tongue (Num 12:1-15). The entire nation of Israel was delayed for seven days because she chose to use her tongue in an inappropriate manner.

The worthy woman's speech exhibits good judgment and discretion (Col 4:6). Rather than being too aggressive or domineering, gentleness (Prov 15:1) and compassion characterize her words (Prov 25:1). She possesses the ability to be kind, yet very firm, as well as the ability to maintain confidences

(Prov 11:13). Truthfulness is evident in her relationships with others (Eph 4:15), and she realizes that what she meditates upon will emerge in her speech (Ps 19:14; Luke 6:45). Within her family relationships, she refuses to defame her husband's character and speaks to her children with firmness balanced with kindness and gentleness. Prior to speaking she asks herself questions that insure that the attitude of Proverbs 31:26 ("she opens her mouth with wisdom, and the teaching of kindness is on her tongue") will characterize her conversations. She inquires:

- Is it kind?
- Is it necessary?
- Is it true?
- Is it gossip?
- Am I defending my own opinion rather than listening to the individual?

Having implemented these criteria for her speech, the worthy woman chooses to make encouragement a part of her lifestyle because it is a spiritual mandate (Heb 10:25). An act of encouragement inspires others with renewed courage, spirit, and hope. It affirms individuals for who they are rather than what they do. Proverbs 25:11 teaches the value of appropriate words. A myriad of actions can provide encouragement to others, including:

- Bestowing notes and small gifts at unexpected times.
- Commenting on desirable character qualities (punctuality, good attitude, tolerance, etc.).
- Calling with specific, encouragement-oriented purposes.
- Affirming a job well done.
- Supporting someone who is hurting.
- Choosing to use confrontation in an appropriate manner (Matt 18:15-19) rather than as a "Christian" way of telling someone off.

The worthy woman cultivates a positive, reassuring attitude, knowing that encouragement does not thrive in a negative atmosphere. She realizes that developing this character quality takes time and does not anticipate repayment (Luke 6:30-31; 1 Tim 6:17-19).

Being Loving

> *Her children rise up and call her blessed;*
> *her husband also, and he praises her:*
> *"Many women have done excellently,*
> *but you surpass them all."*
>
> —PROV 31:28-29

The sense of benevolence that one should possess for another person involves an intense love for others, including one's husband, children, friends, and relations, plus a steadfast commitment to God. The worthy woman demonstrates a strong liking for others and purposes to activate the Titus 2:3-5 principle of the younger women learning from the older women in her life. She is approachable by others and refuses to be a respecter of persons (Jas 2:1-13).

That the worthy woman first concentrates her domestic efforts on those in her own home is demonstrated by their response to her. Her husband and children spontaneously cheer her (Prov 31:28-29). Every day when they open their eyes, they rejoice that she belongs to them. She chooses to live a consistent life as a wife and mother.

Having made her home her priority, the worthy woman works creatively with her husband (Amos 3:3; Eph 5:22-24; Col 3:18; 1 Pet 3:1-6). She knows him well enough to respect and honor him (Eph 5:33b), as well as to be his helpmate and friend (Gen 2:18). Training her children well by implementing child-rearing principles based on the Word of God (Deut 6:6-7; 11:18-21; Ps 78:1-4; Prov 22:6; Eph 6:4; Col 3:21; 2 Tim 3:14-17) is the focus of her life while her children are at home. Finally, she sets an example for the character qualities that she wishes to instill in the lives of her children, realizing that they will assimilate the behaviors she models (1 Cor 11:1; Eph 5:1-2).

Fearing God

> *Charm is deceitful and beauty is vain,*
> *but a woman who fears the* LORD *is to be praised.*
> —PROV 31:30

Fearing God denotes a reverential trust in God, including the hatred of evil. Romans 12:9 challenges the worthy woman to "abhor what is evil; hold fast to what is good." She assimilates a true perspective of values based on the Word of God. The woman embracing the principle of God-fearing will stand in awe and will venerate, worship, and love her Lord with all her heart (Matt 22:37). The practical application of the godly lifestyle will include an individual hunger and thirst after God (Ps 42:1-2a), an attitude of submission to God's will and ways (Jas 4:7), and a consistent evaluation of her spiritual status (1 Cor 11:31-32). She purposes to make spiritual principles a priority in her life (Matt 6:33) and refuses to slump into a tired routine regarding her relationship with her Savior. The joy of the Lord is her strength (Neh 8:10b).

Accepting 1 Corinthians 10 as a warning, the worthy woman acknowledges the traps that the ancient Hebrews fell into regarding their spiritual condition. They craved evil things (v. 6), were idolatrous (v. 7), began practicing immorality (v. 8), became guilty of presumption (v. 9), and were cynical and negative (v. 10). In the midst of God's best blessings, they became cool, distant, and indifferent. Not suddenly, but slowly the keen edge of enthusiasm became dull. Applying the wisdom of 1 Corinthians 10:12-13, she is careful to learn from the example of the disobedient and indolent Jews in Moses' time.

The Reward

> *Give her of the fruit of her hands,*
> *and let her works praise her in the gates.*
> —PROV 31:31

The reward of cultivating these eleven principles is presented in Proverbs 31:31 as the worthy woman receives recognition "in the gates," which refers to the public assembly of people. The worthy woman does not have to brag about herself but rather is praised by those who know her best. The woman who chooses to embrace the principles found in Proverbs 31 is usually rewarded in this life and always in the hereafter. A review of these principles suggests some representative, potential benefits that the worthy woman might anticipate:

Being Virtuous

- An unobstructed relationship with her Heavenly Father (Matt 5:8).
- Blessing from the Lord and righteousness from the God of her salvation (Ps 24:1-5).
- The assurance that her influence will never die (Prov 31:28; 2 Tim 1:3-7).

Being Trustworthy

- That her husband trusts her (Prov 31:11).
- An honorable reputation (Prov 31:25).
- The confidence that as she walks uprightly, her Heavenly Father will provide grace, glory, and all that is good for her (Ps 84:11).

Being Energetic

- The family benefits from her home business (Prov 31:24).
- Enjoying professional and spiritual stimulation (Prov 27:17).
- Exemption from reaping the fruit of slothfulness (Prov 19:15).

Being Physically Fit

• Enjoying the tasks she undertakes to their fullest potential (Col 3:23).

• That her body is an appropriate dwelling-place for the Holy Spirit (1 Cor 6:19-20).

• Avoiding the type of judgment and denouncement God executed on the women of Judah (Isa 3:16-26).

Being Economical

• Embracing a spiritual attitude toward money and material possessions (1 Tim 6:6-10).

• Experiencing the joy of generosity (2 Cor 9:6-8).

• Perceiving that her purchases are sound choices—no guilt (Prov 31:18).

Being Unselfish

• The joy of giving to others with the right attitude (2 Cor 9:7).

• Being pleasing to the Lord (Prov 19:17).

• Enjoying the fruit of giving to others (Acts 9:36-42).

Being Prepared

• Meeting the design of God's plan for her life (Jer 17:7-8).

• Being an authentic role model for others (1 Cor 11:1).

• A lack of frustration and regret (Matt 25:21, 23).

Being Honorable

• That her moral integrity allows her to reflect fulfillment in later life, rather than having lived a wasted life filled with remorse and sin (2 Cor 9:6; Gal 6:7-9).

• Behaving in a way that reflects her position as a daughter in God's royal family (Gen 1:26-27).

• A confidence that her convictions are based upon biblical principles rather than cultural trends (Ps 119:11, 105).

Being Prudent

• That people are willing to confide in her and trust her to retain their confidences (Prov 15:1-2).

• That people will seek and follow her advice (Col 4:6).

• The privilege of encouraging and affirming others (Heb 10:24-25).

Being Loving

• Enjoying a healthy, growing, love relationship with the Lord (Matt 22:37).

• That her closest friends will love, honor, respect, and praise her (Prov 31:28-29).

• Living in such a way that she is an example for the "young women" (Titus 2:3-5).

Fearing God

• Being a positive role model because of her faith (the epistle of James in action).

• Continuing as a faithful servant (Matt 25:21).

• Enjoying the benefits of learning from the experiences of others (1 Cor 10).

Realizing that her motive for cultivating these eleven principles is to glorify God (1 Cor 10:31), to hear her Heavenly Father say, "Well done, good and faithful servant" (Matt 25:21), and to cast her rewards at the feet of her King (Rev 4:10-11), the worthy woman pursues the eternal crown with vigor!

A Final Thought

The conviction of this chapter is that original role differentiations in the home can be biblically traced back to the standards in Eden before sin interrupted marital relationships (Gen 2:7-23). The original, specific roles for male and female were corrupted, not created, by the Fall. Genesis 2:18 reports that God's final act of creation was the woman, to be a "helper fit for him" (literally, a "helper like man"). John MacArthur states:

> When God saw His creation as very good (1:31), He viewed it as being to that point the perfect outcome to His creative plan. However, in observing man's state as not good, He was commenting on his incompleteness before the end of the sixth day because the woman, Adam's counterpart, had not yet been created. The words of this verse emphasize man's need for a companion, a helper, and an equal. He was incomplete without someone to complement him in fulfilling the task of filling, multiplying, and taking dominion over the earth. This points to Adam's inadequacy, not Eve's insufficiency (cf. 1 Cor 11:9). Woman was made by God to meet man's deficiency (cf. 1 Tim. 2:14).[14]

The woman portraying Christian femininity embraces the truth of Genesis 1—2 and Proverbs 31:10-31, behaves in harmony with God's will, and glorifies God with her mind and life. She distinctly possesses a biblical worldview of her femininity.

FURTHER READING

Elliot, Elisabeth. *Let Me Be a Woman.* Wheaton, IL: Tyndale House, 1999.

Ennis, Patricia and Lisa Tatlock. *Becoming a Woman Who Pleases God: A Guide to Developing Your Biblical Potential.* Chicago: Moody Press, 2003.

MacArthur, John. *Different by Design.* Wheaton, IL: Victor, 1994.

Peace, Martha. *The Excellent Wife.* Bemidji, MN: Focus Publishing, 1997.

Piper, John and Wayne Grudem, coeditors. *Recovering Biblical Manhood and Womanhood.* Wheaton, IL: Crossway Books, 1991.

10

Enjoying Spiritual Worship and Music

Paul T. Plew

The date was June 2, 1991; *glasnost* (openness) and *perestroika* (restructuring) were causing upheaval in Russia. We arrived at the First Baptist Church of Moscow two hours before the service. The sanctuary was half occupied, and it was quiet. I sensed an awe and reverence in the room. Within another hour, the room was filled. By the time the service started, it was impossible to tell who was standing and who was sitting because the first floor and balcony were now a mass of faces—faces that longed for one thing: to communicate with God. Yes, they were happy to see each other, but their greater desire was to commune with God.

As the service started, I realized prayer was serious to them. Some stood, heads bowed; many were kneeling together, talking to God. Their attitude was one of humility in recognition of God's greatness as expressed in Genesis 1:16. "And God made the two great lights—the greater light to rule the day and the lesser light to rule the night—and the stars." Those last three words, "and the stars," represent billions of stars that provide a glimpse of the power of God. These believers seemed to recognize that.

As the music began, I looked around and saw everyone standing and singing with an attitude of serious worship. I am sure many could not sing well, but that was unimportant. What was important was that they were releasing their love for God in a song.

The hymns were serious, rather heavy and weighty; they did not reflect much joy. But I was told later that the majority of the congregation had lost close family members to the heavy hand of the Communist Party.

I came back to America and vowed I that would do all within my God-given abilities and opportunities to strive to be a true worshiper myself, and then to encourage others to come together for worship in spirit and in truth.

One of the problems with worship today is that most Christians have not had family or close friends imprisoned or executed because of their faith, thus drawing them closer in dependency upon the Lord. That kind of serious involvement with God, apart from suffering, is hard for people to comprehend and experience. Furthermore, we have been influenced by a pop culture that dictates our actions. Where entertainment and a self-satisfying individualistic attitude prevail, there is a misunderstanding of what worship means, who is involved, who the audience is, what the responsibilities are, and who receives the glory.

What Is True Worship?

The word *worship* is a contraction of an old expression in the English language, *woerth-scipe*, denoting the ascription of reverence to someone or something of superlative worth.[1] "Worship is an act by a redeemed man, the creature, toward God, the Creator, whereby his will, intellect and emotions gratefully respond to the revelation of God's person expressed in the redemptive work of Jesus Christ, as the Holy Spirit illuminates God's written work to his heart."[2] The Hebrew word for worship means "bowing down."[3] Exodus 34:8 states that when Moses was on Mount Sinai and the Lord descended in the cloud, "Moses quickly bowed his head toward the earth and worshiped." Genesis 17:3 tells us that Abram "fell on his face" before God. The Old Testament teaches that humility and servanthood (Ps 95:6-7) accompany true worship.

One Greek word for worship is *latreuō*, "to serve, to give homage."[4] Philippians 3:3 says, "We are the real circumcision, who worship by the Spirit of God and glory in Christ Jesus and put no confidence in the flesh." Worship is spiritual, flowing from the Holy Spirit within the believer. If one is not walking in the Spirit, he/she will not be able to worship.

Proskuneō is a Greek word that means "to make obeisance, do reverence." According to *Vine's Expository Dictionary of New Testament Words*, this is the most frequent New Testament word rendered "to worship."[5] It conveys respect and submission. In John 4:24, Jesus tells the woman in Samaria, "God is Spirit, and those who worship him must worship in spirit and truth." Worshiping in spirit refers to worship being for the obedient, those who have been washed in the blood of the Lamb. Our worship must be from the heart and empowered by God's Spirit.

Worshiping in truth denotes worshiping with sincerity. Not only must we be children of the King, we also must be living spiritually. In other words, we must be authentic and genuine in our obedience to Christ. The phrase "in spirit and truth" relates to the heart of an individual and the outward display of his/her life. When both are in order, true worship is unleashed.

Martin Luther said, "In worship we assemble in order to hear and to discuss God's Word, and then to praise God, to sing and to pray."[6] The worshiper willingly accepts God's truth from the Word and responds in praise and prayer, and in a changed pattern of living.[7]

John Wesley demonstrated in his translation of the hymn "O God, What Offering Shall I Give to Thee?" that worship is given:[8]

> *O God, what offering shall I give to Thee,*
> *The Lord of earth and skies?*
> *My spirit, soul, and flesh receive,*
> *A holy, living sacrifice.*
> *Small as it is, 'tis all my store;*
> *More shouldst Thou have, if I had more.*
> JOACHIM LANGE

Some present-day writers who have defined worship include the following:

> *Donald Hustad*: "The worship service is a rehearsal for the everyday life of worship. All of life should be worship. If the rehearsal is true worship in spirit and truth, life itself should be worship with the whole person—heart, soul, mind, and strength."[9]

> *John MacArthur*: "Worship is the primary essential, and service is a wonderful and necessary corollary to it. Worship is central in the will of God—the great *sine qua non* of all Christian experience. . . . Our definition of worship is enriched when we understand that true worship touches each area of life. We are to honor and adore God in everything."[10]

> *Eugene Peterson*: "Worship is the strategy by which we interrupt our preoccupation with ourselves and attend to the presence of God."[11]

> *John Piper*: "Missions is not the ultimate priority of the church. Worship is. Missions exists because worship doesn't. Worship is ultimate, not missions, because God is ultimate, not man. . . . Missions is a temporary necessity, but worship abides forever."[12]

> *William Temple*: "To worship is to quicken the conscience by the holiness of God, to feed the mind with the truth of God, to purge the imagination

> by the beauty of God, to open the heart to the love of God, to devote the will to the purpose of God."[13]
>
> *Robert Webber:* "Worship is a verb. It is not something done to us, or for us, but by us."[14]

The Theology of Worship

God's Holiness

Isaiah 6:1-8 is a model, in principle, for the believer in worship. Isaiah is near the altar in front of the Temple. The doors open, and the veil hiding the Holy of Holies is withdrawn. At this moment there is a vision of God attended by seraphim. First Kings 22:19 describes a similar scene: "And Micaiah said, 'Therefore hear the Word of the LORD: I saw the LORD sitting on His throne, and all the host of heaven standing beside him on his right hand and on his left.'" God is seen with a host of angels in all His dazzling brightness, the seraphim with Him, as also in Isaiah 6:2. "Each had six wings; with two he covered his face": They were unworthy to look on a holy God. This demonstrated a deep respect and reverence. "With two he covered his feet": This means they covered the entire part of their lower bodies, a posture common when in the presence of monarchs as a continued gesture of homage. "And with two he flew": Two wings were kept ready and available for instant flight for the service of the King.

Of the six wings, four were used for worship and only two were used for service. The principle exemplified by these heavenly creatures is that reverent waiting on God is more important than active service. God designed it this way for us also; worship commands a higher priority than service.

The Psalms overflow with this mandate: Psalm 145:1,"I will extol you, my God and King, and bless your name forever and ever"; Psalm 146:1, "Praise the LORD! Praise the LORD, O my soul! I will praise the LORD as long as I live. I will sing praises to my God while I have my being."

Isaiah 6:3 continues: "And one called to another and said, 'Holy, holy, holy is the LORD of hosts; the whole earth is full of His glory" (the Hebrew is more emphatic: "the fullness of the whole earth is His glory"; cf. Ps 24:1; 72:19). This same picture is seen in Revelation 4:8, as John describes what the angels are doing even now.

Isaiah 6:4 describes God's presence as so immense that the foundation of the Temple shook and trembled at His voice, and the Temple was filled with smoke; the Shekinah cloud was present as in 1 Kings 8:10 and Ezekiel 10:4.

Consider the spiritual, "Were You There When They Crucified My Lord?" The song finishes with, "Sometimes it causes me to tremble, tremble,

tremble." The thought of the Lord and who He is caused a reverential fear. Slave workers knew what fear was. The very presence of the plantation owner caused the workers to fear and tremble—not necessarily out of respect, but out of the ever-present possibility of a whipping if sufficient work was not being accomplished. The trembling (or shaking) in Isaiah 6:4 had to do with awesome respect for the very position of the Most High God. He is holy, perfect, and without sin. This passage reflects on God's holiness.

Besides God's holiness, there are many other scriptural attributes of God that we can emphasize during the Scripture reading and hymn singing portions of our worship. For example:

God's splendorous light: Scriptures could include Isaiah 60:19, 1 John 1:5, accompanied by hymns with texts such as "The whole world was lost in the darkness of sin; the Light of the World is Jesus"[15] and "O Light that knew no dawn, that shines to endless day, all things in earth and heaven are lustred by thy ray; no eye can to thy throne ascend, nor mind thy brightness comprehend."[16]

God's faithfulness, immutability, and compassion: We could read Lamentations 3:22-23 and sing the hymn, "Great is Thy faithfulness, O God my Father; there is no shadow of turning with thee; thou changest not, thy compassions, they fail not; as thou hast been, thou forever wilt be."[17]

God's greatness and power: Scriptural passages such as Psalm 68:34 could be read. Appropriate hymns would include "How Great Thou Art"[18] and "I sing the mighty power of God that made the mountains rise; that spread the flowing seas abroad, and built the lofty skies."[19]

Other attributes of God: A number of attributes are covered by 1 Timothy 1:17 and provide a good companion for the hymn, "Immortal, invisible, God only wise, in light inaccessible hid from our eyes, most blessed, most glorious, the Ancient of Days, almighty, victorious, thy great name we praise."[20]

God's people need to reflect regularly on God's attributes. Our corporate worship services should include hymns that remind us who God is. One approach to achieving this goal would be to focus the worship each time on a different attribute of God to encourage the worshiper to recognize the many facets of His character. He is much more than just a friend. He is the Lord of all the Heavenly Hosts. He is to be worshiped and adored.

Man's Sinfulness

When confronted with God's glory, Isaiah confessed, "Woe is me! For I am lost; for I am a man of unclean lips, and I dwell in the midst of a people of unclean lips" (Isa 6:5). This must be the attitude of the believer. Isaiah saw himself as cursed unto damnation, debauched, dirty, filthy. In himself he was "like a polluted garment" (Isa 64:6). Why was Isaiah so critical of himself? After all, he was the son of Amoz, a contemporary of Jonah, a major prophet who foretold the future 150 years before it happened. His garment was sackcloth (Isa 20:2), which embodied the message of repentance he taught. Why did he see himself as a worm? Verse 5 finishes with, "for my eyes have seen the King, the LORD of Hosts!" If Isaiah had looked at himself next to his contemporaries, he could have said, "I am not evil. In fact, I am better than most." But he did no such thing. His eyes had seen the King, the Shekinah cloud. He measured himself against the ultimate standard and found himself to be unclean and unworthy.

In Zechariah 3:3, Joshua stands in filthy garments before an angel. The Old Testament word rendered "filthy" there is an adjective that comes from a root meaning "excrement," and thus not only vile and dirty but with an offensive odor.[21] Isaiah 64:6 says, "We have all become like one who is unclean, and all our righteous deeds are like a polluted garment." Today we do not appreciate looking at ourselves as unclean. Some hymnals are changing lyrics to accommodate a softening of sin. For example, in Issac Watts's original gospel hymn "At the Cross," the words read:

> *Alas! And did my Savior bleed, and did my sovereign die?*
> *Would he devote that sacred head for such a worm as I?*[22]

In recent hymnals the last line reads ". . . for sinners such as I" or ". . . for someone such as I."

God's view of man's sin is and always has been the same. He has not moved. He has not changed. We are all dust and worms compared to the King of Glory. Yet, some worshipers see themselves as superior to others. The attitude is, "I'm self-sufficient. I am living and serving better than most." This kind of worship could be categorized as mere ritual, dishonest, haughty, and absent of any self-examination (cf. the Pharisee in Luke 18:11-12).

God's Solution

Isaiah 6:6-7 shows the attribute of mercy. "Then one of the seraphim flew to me, having in his hand a burning coal that he had taken with tongs from the altar. And he touched my mouth and said: 'Behold, this has touched your lips; your guilt is taken away, and your sin atoned for.'" It is unknown how long Isaiah was waiting between the two verses of this text. It may have been a very short space in time. But it was an experience he would remember forever. Ronald Allen in *The Wonder of Worship* describes it:

> Then, with a nod from God a pantomime of grace transpired. Isaiah was aware, perhaps in a dreamlike state, of the rustle of angel wings, of a fiery, searing sensation, and then of words that set his heart free of all fear. The words came from the angel, but they had the authority of Heaven's throne. Isaiah had experienced a personal Yom Kippur, his own "day of atonement." He was immediately cleansed of all sin. This was not because he deserved it or earned it; it was all of grace—God's grace.[23]

He was free—free to live for God, free to serve God, free to honor God, and free to worship God.

The model of knowing who we are and who God is must be the reality of every worshiper who truly wants to see God. This picture does not represent a user-friendly paradigm. It takes work. It takes commitment and dedication. It takes a deep love that is understood only when one is moment by moment in communion with God.

Isaiah 6:8 continues, "And I heard the voice of the Lord saying, 'Whom shall I send, and who will go for us?'" There seems to be a sense that few would be willing to hear and accept the self-denial that was needed. This message would not be readily received by the Jewish people (cf. 1 Chron 29:5). However, the response was prompt: "Here am I! Send me." Imagine what could happen in God's congregation if all who attended worship services Sunday after Sunday had the same response as modeled by Isaiah in this passage of Scripture. Not only would worshipers come prepared, having confessed all known sin, ready to serve, but they would also come with the right vision of who God is.

Isaiah 6:1-8 gives the most concise vision of what worship should be:

- Verses 1-4: Adoration
- Verse 5: Confession
- Verses 6-7: Cleansing and forgiveness
- Verse 8: Decision

We are prompted by this picture to burst forth with the hymn:

Holy, holy, holy! Lord God Almighty!
Early in the morning our song shall rise to Thee;
Holy, holy, holy! Merciful and mighty!
God in three persons, Blessed Trinity.

Holy, holy, holy! All the saints adore Thee,
Casting down their golden crowns around the glassy sea;
Cherubim and Seraphim falling down before Thee,
Which wert and art, and evermore shall be.

REGINALD HEBER

In this nineteenth-century hymn, the melody always ascends on the words, "Holy, holy, holy." This illustrates a good marriage between text and music. As the melody rises, the worshiper is made aware musically of the gripping reality of God's holiness. This hymn should always be sung with increasing crescendo as we are being confronted with the vision of a holy God. We should never sing these eternal words, as John Wesley would say, "in a half-asleep manner; but lift your voice with strength."[24]

How Do We Enjoy Worship?

Private Worship

God expects and desires every believer to regularly spend time alone with Him. During this private time we need to *adore* God for who He is (Ps 8), *confess* to God sins and weights (1 John 1:9), *thank* God for what He has done (Ps 69:30; 1 Thess 5:18), and *supplicate*—ask God for strength, help, direction, and guidance (Phil 4:6; 1 Pet 5:7). Some daily worship activities include:

- Scripture reading and study.
- Meditation on a verse or two with the goal of memorization.
- Singing to God.

Yes, sing to God the great hymns and praise songs. Sing from the depths of your heart. Connect what you have studied in Scripture, and find a song that supports that theme.

A series of four hymn story books have been recently published that are valuable aids to our private worship. Written by John MacArthur, Joni Eareckson Tada, and Robert and Bobbie Wolgemuth, each book includes a CD of the music to encourage the individual listener not only to participate and sing along with the album, but also to sing with an understanding of the hymns. Each book has twelve hymn stories that reflect on the devotional, doctrinal, and historical background of the hymns. The CD features the authors' singing supported by The Master's Chorale from The Master's University. The books are entitled *O Worship the King*,[25] *O Come, All Ye Faithful*,[26] *What Wondrous Love Is This*,[27] and *When Morning Gilds the Skies*.[28]

An important ingredient of private worship is consistency—day after day after day. "I will sing to the LORD as long as I live; I will sing praise to my God while I have being. May my meditation be pleasing to him, for I rejoice in the LORD" (Ps 104:33-34). "I will bless the LORD at all times; his praise shall continually be in my mouth" (Ps 34:1). Acts 17:11 exhorts us to "examine the Scriptures daily." In 1 Thessalonians 5:16-17, Paul admonishes us to "rejoice always, pray without ceasing." Hebrews 13:15 says, "Through Him then let us continually offer up a sacrifice of praise to God, that is, the fruit of lips that acknowledge his name."

Corporate Worship

Corporate worship in public should continue what has been done privately all week. If we are "continually offer[ing] up . . . praise to God," corporate worship is a natural response. Conversely, if one does not worship regularly throughout the week, how can one rise to worship with God's people on Sunday? Corporate worship can be defined as *God's people gathered together to give homage to God because of who He is.* Revelation 4:11 says, "Worthy are you, our Lord and God, to receive glory and honor and power, for you created all things, and by your will they existed and were created." Ezra 3:11 urges "praising and giving thanks to our Lord, 'for he is good, for his steadfast love endures forever toward Israel.'" Luke 24:52-53 describes the response to the ascension of Christ: "And they worshiped him and returned to Jerusalem with great joy, and were continually in the temple blessing God." The apostle John gives us a portrayal of created beings around the throne of God in Revelation 4:10-11: "The twenty-four elders fall down before him who is seated on the throne and worship him who lives forever and ever. They cast their crowns before the throne, saying, 'Worthy are you, our Lord and God, to receive glory and honor and power, for you created all things, and by your will they existed and were created.'" A. W. Tozer writes in *Whatever Happened to Worship?*:

> All the examples that we have in the Bible illustrate that glad and devoted and reverent worship is the normal employment of moral beings. Every glimpse that is given us of heaven and of God's created beings is always a glimpse of worship and rejoicing and praise because God is who he is. . . . I can safely say, on the authority of all that is revealed in the Word of God, that any man or woman on this earth who is bored and turned off by worship is not ready for heaven.[29]

Edifying Worship

It cannot be denied that the focus of our worship is God and God alone. He is the only one in the audience. He *is* the audience! So how should we meet Him? We must meet Him with prepared hearts. I usually ask the students before we present a musical offering to God, "Are you confessed up? Is your heart clean before God?" (see Ps 103:12; Prov 28:13; Heb 8:12; 1 John 1:9). Hebrews 10:22 advises, "Let us draw near with a true heart in full assurance of faith, with our hearts sprinkled clean from an evil conscience and our bodies washed with pure water." This verse details how to enter into God's presence. Better said, this verse details how to prepare to enter into corporate worship. The Greek term behind "true" means sincere, genuine, and without ulterior motive (cf. Jer 24:7; Matt 15:8).[30] In regard to the idea of a pure heart, *The MacArthur Study Bible* explains:

> The imagery in this verse is taken from the sacrificial ceremonies of the old covenant, where blood was sprinkled as a sign of cleansing, and the priests were continually washing themselves . . . the washing with pure water does not refer to Christian baptism, but to the Holy Spirit's purifying one's life by means of the Word of God (Eph 5:25-26; Ti 3:5).[31]

When you come to worship, are you spiritually prepared? Do you actually come to worship God? Consider the example of the worship in Herod's Temple. The Outer Court, the Court of the Women, was the farthest that most Israelites were allowed into the Temple. In fact, according to Edersheim, "This was probably the common place for worship."[32] This is where friends were greeted and discussion of daily life took place.

Next was the Court of the Israelites; this was reserved for purified Israelite men to observe the ritual of the Temple Court. At a higher level was the Court of the Priests and the Temple Court where sacrifices were offered on the altar to God.

Then came the Holy Place, which contained the seven-branched lampstand, the table of showbread, and the altar of incense. Behind a veil that separated the Holy Place from the Holy of Holies dwelt God's glorious presence. The High Priest would go in once a year, on the Day of Atonement, and only after special preparation (Lev 16:1-34; Heb 9:7). Here atonement was "made for the people of Israel once in the year because of all their sins" (Lev 16:34).

The second temple had five distinct levels from the Outer Court to the Holy of Holies. It is sad to ponder, but many individuals and many churches never proceed (figuratively speaking) beyond the Outer Court in their worship. They see only each other. Because of the finished work of the cross, we have direct access to the Holy of Holies (Heb 9:11-15). We have the privilege, as the congregation of God, to enter the Throne Room. Yet, the Outer Court, seemingly, is more appealing.

The next time you worship, give yourself a little test. As you enter the church and make final preparations for your own worship, consider to whom you talk more, God's people or God Himself. He wants our worship. He commands us to worship Him:

- "Shout for joy in the LORD, O you righteous!" (Ps 33:1)
- "Because He is your Lord, worship Him." (Ps 45:11, NKJV)
- "Exalt the LORD our God; worship at His footstool." (Ps 99:5)
- "Oh give thanks to the LORD; call upon his name." (Ps 105:1)
- "Oh give thanks to the LORD, for he is good. . . . Let the redeemed of the Lord say so." (Ps 107:1-2)

Worship is much more than an academic exercise. It is a relationship. John 21 contains the familiar passage where Jesus confronts Peter about his love for his Lord. The church today "likes the Lord a lot," but not as Christ loves the church (Eph 5:25). In the same way Jesus was pressing Peter, "do you love me more than these" (v. 15)? Do you love Him more than family, position, status, career, or entertainment? Do you love Him enough to go to bed early Saturday night so you are not tired Sunday morning? Enough to get out of bed early enough to eat breakfast so you aren't distracted by hunger? Enough to arrive at the church with plenty of time before the service starts? Enough to take the time to search your soul for sin that might hinder a wholesome relationship with God? A. W. Tozer, the pastor for thirty-one years of South Side Alliance Church in Chicago, wrote:

> It is my experience that our total lives, our entire attitude as persons, must be toward the worship of God. . . . If you cannot worship the Lord in the midst of your responsibilities on Monday, it is not very likely that you were worshiping on Sunday. . . . My view of worship: No worship is wholly pleasing to God until there is nothing in me displeasing to God.[33]

How do you enjoy worship? Get self out of the way, and focus your eyes upon Him. In the words of a missionary in North Africa:

> *Turn your eyes upon Jesus,*
> *Look full in His wonderful face,*
> *And the things of earth will grow strangely dim,*
> *In the light of his glory and grace.*
>
> HELEN H. LEMMEL

WHAT IS WORSHIP MUSIC?

The first verb in the Bible is "created." It is used five times in Genesis 1. "Made" is also used four times. Everything God made was good. Man was one of those good creations. In Genesis 1:26-27, God said,

> *"Let us make man in our image, after our likeness. And let them have dominion over the fish of the sea and over the birds of the heavens and over*

> *the livestock and over all the earth and over every creeping thing that creeps on the earth."* So *God created man in his own image, in the image of God he created him; male and female he created them.*

Because all humanity is created in the image of God, all humanity has some level of creative ability. However, the redeemed should have the ability and desire to create higher-quality creative works than the unregenerate, because they know the Creator in a personal way. They have the responsibility to represent their Father with the highest form of creativity and excellence.

C. M. Johansson says of music, "There is a necessity to create well because we image Christ through the notes and harmony."[34] The goal of the Christian music creator must be to pattern his music after the Master Creator who is the Master Musician.

Man also has the capability to feel emotions (e.g., love and sorrow). Music brings out these emotions. We feel the emotions, and the composer expresses them for us; the deeper the emotion, the greater the craft required to express that emotion. Music that has substance must be coupled with theology that challenges the intellect. There must be a deeper complexity with our worship music to mirror the depth and vastness of God.

The worship music of the early church was mostly chants and hymns. For 1,500 years the great music was in the church. Luther preached his message of "the just shall live by faith and faith alone" through his own hymn writing. The seventeenth and eighteenth centuries emphasized doctrinal convictions in music, as seen in hymns from the pens and hearts of pastors such as Isaac Watts, John Wesley, and Charles Wesley.[35] Whereas the early nineteenth century was more concerned with improving the literary quality of hymnody, the latter part of the nineteenth century gave way to the gospel song, which had its roots in spirituals and early Sunday school songs. Its impetus was the widespread evangelical crusades of D. L. Moody and Ira Sankey. The music was generally lighter in doctrinal content, used stanzas with refrain plus repetition, and was easier to sing.

In the twentieth century, churches had a lower view of worship and music. Much of the focus of the church continued to be evangelism, not the maturity of the saints. This was reflected in the crusade teams of R. A. Torrey and Charles Alexander, Billy Sunday and Homer Rodeheaver, even Billy Graham and Cliff Barrows. In the mid-twentieth century, church music was influenced by Christian radio, recordings, and traveling musicians. The last quarter of the twentieth century experienced the rise of praise choruses and a stronger emphasis on entertainment and the individual in the pew.

The Theology of Worship Music

The Bible states in 1 Chronicles 23 that 38,000 Levites were assigned to Temple service. Of that number, four thousand were set apart for music ministry. First Chronicles 25 records that these four thousand Levitical musicians were from three large families: Asaph, Heman, Jeduthun. From these families came 288 skilled musicians who constituted the instructional leadership of the remaining 3,712 Levitical musicians.

It is significant to note that the music leadership came from the priestly lines. They knew theology, but they also knew music. In 1 Chronicles 25:7 it is said of these Levites that "[they] were trained in singing to the Lord, all who were skillful." First Chronicles 15:22 indicates that "Chenaniah, leader of the Levites in music, should direct the music, for he understood it."

Martin Luther knew the importance of coupling theology and music. According to Osbeck, "Luther himself said that music was one of the finest and noblest gifts of God in the world, and that young men should not be ordained as preachers unless they had also been trained in music."[36] Where is the training today? It must start with our children in children's choirs. They should be taught to sing correctly when they are young and be exposed to great music.[37]

Frank E. Gaebelein, in *The Christian, the Arts, and Truth*, says that he "seldom wasted his time listening to popular music; he wanted to surround himself with art [music] that would last."[38]

This training should go right through to seminaries. If a pastor has not had some training in music with an underlying biblically-based theology of worship, he will be less prepared to lead worship himself or to model worship for a congregation. If music is foreign to him, he will likely attempt to get somebody else to do it. That is certainly acceptable. However, the pastor has to have a biblically-based theology of worship and music to know how to recruit and supervise an individual who will properly match music and worship. He must have knowledge and training in order to give direction and leadership.

A host of churches today have a low view of worship music. The thought is not to lift the Lord high, but to make Him equal with man, identifying the living God with our popular culture. Worship and music are capitulating to an individualist, narcissistic attitude. There is a deliberate attempt to put the intellect into a passive mode and to work solely on the emotions. We whisper our worship when we ought to be lifting our voices together in joyful sound. Much of the time the reason for this deficiency is the lack of training in music leadership. Leonard Payton has observed,

"So extreme is the case now that anyone who knows half a dozen chords on a guitar and can produce rhymes to Hallmark card specifications is considered qualified to exercise this component of the ministry of the Word [lead a congregation in worship] regardless of theological training and examination."[39]

The rise of praise choruses has proven to be the next generation of the gospel song: a short verse, much repetition, and a single idea or thought expressed. Praise choruses are a wonderful addition to the diet of church worship, but they must be blended with the "psalms and hymns and spiritual songs" spoken of in Colossians 3:16. Calvin Johansson says:

> Exclusive use of choruses tends to produce a people who have the same depth of spirituality as the music they sing. The result is a faith which lacks depth, is simplistic, pleasure-oriented, emotionalistic, intellectually weak, undisciplined, and prone to the changeability of feelings. The end result of nothing but chorus singing is immaturity.[40]

The emphasis seems to be this: Make it easy for the congregation. Do not expect much from them. Treat them like an audience. Perform for their applause. Get the people excited for the moment. This shift to people-centered worship harms true worship in other ways as well.

God's people have lost sight of the contrast between the church and the world. The principle to be learned is that the Christian is different and distinct (1 Cor 8—9; 2 Cor 5:17).

There is a loss of community. Different types of services cultivate a "give me what I want" syndrome. The focus is on the wishes of the people rather than on the people being focused on God.

There is a loss of content in our singing, a loss of good poetry. Good poetry equips the words to mean more than they say. Repetition often makes the phrase seem less significant.

There is also a loss of theology. Songs are often self-centered rather than theologically-centered. The church must be assiduous about sound theological content and foundation.[41] John MacArthur writes:

> Modern songwriters seriously need to take their task more seriously. Churches should also do everything they can to cultivate musicians who are trained in handling the Scriptures and able to discern sound doctrine. Most important, pastors and elders need to begin exercising closer and more careful oversight of the church music ministry, consciously setting a high standard for the doctrinal and biblical content of what we sing.[42]

Enjoying Worship Music

The biblically-focused worshiper is one who is a participant and not a spectator. If you participate, you are to be in fellowship with God in a "without ceasing" manner. Sin breaks fellowship and must be confessed so there will be restoration (1 John 1:9). The heart must have the kind of loving approach that is selfless and not haughty (John 21). Enjoyment of music and worship must come from within (the heart) and not without (the applause of man). God desires to be worshiped by an active, engaged, involved, and anticipating congregation of His children.

John Wesley's *Instructions for Singing Hymns*, dated 1761, still apply:

> Learn the songs first.
> Sing them exactly.
> Sing all.
> Sing lustily.
> Sing modestly.
> Sing in time.
> Above all, sing spiritually.[43]

We have been created to worship God. Even so, our lives on earth are merely the rehearsal; we will worship Him forever in eternity (Rev 4:1-11; 7:9-12; 19:1-7; 21:3, 22).

Further Reading

Best, Harold. *Music Through the Eyes of Faith*. New York: Harper San Francisco, 1993.

Eskew, Harry and Hugh T. McElrath. *Sing with Understanding: An Introduction to Christian Hymnology*. 2nd ed. Nashville: Broadman & Holman, 1995.

Hustad, Donald P. *True Worship: Reclaiming the Wonder and Majesty*. Wheaton, IL: Harold Shaw, 1998.

Lovelace, Austin C. and William C. Rice. *Music and Worship in the Church*, rev. ed. Nashville: Abingdon, 1987.

11

Why Biblical Counseling and Not Psychology?

John D. Street

Biblically-informed Christians ought to be sanctified skeptics. They should direct a justified cynicism toward any discipline or epistemological scheme that seeks obligatory authority as it relates to counseling of personal problems. A natural antagonism has always existed between biblical counselors and therapeutic practitioners because psychotherapeutic theories have aggressively encroached upon the jurisdiction of soul-care.[1] Christians are fully warranted in casting a wary eye in psychology's direction for its Enlightenment-inspired dismissal of the Bible's veracity and its *carte blanche* rejection of the jurisdictional authority that Scripture claims in the matters of the soul.

For the Christian counselor, the Word of God must be more than an interpretative grid for the acceptance or denial of psychological truth-claims; it is the operative domain from which the counselor derives his/her functional and final authority,[2] being accepted as the determinative authority in anthropology. Scripture serves as the only reliable resource for the Christian counselor's diagnostic terminology and remedy. The Word of God possesses the exclusive theoretical framework from which soul-problems can be properly interpreted and resolved.[3] More importantly, it claims exclusive authority in defining the significance of and purpose for the life of man.[4] When placed in juxtaposition with the counsel of man, the comprehensive superiority of the Word is unmistakable. God's purposes in the life of man will prevail. The psalmist states:

The Lord *brings the counsel of the nations to nothing;*
he frustrates the plans of the peoples.
The counsel of the Lord *stands forever,*
the plans of his heart to all generations.

—PS 33:10-11

Theology and Psychology

The historical distrust and innate hostility between psychology and theology exist because each calls into question the legitimacy of the other's *Weltanschauung*.[5] The imperialistic intrusion of the psychotherapeutic into Christianity has attempted to undermine and redefine the supremacy of the Word of God among Christians. Nowhere have its effects been more intrusive and dramatic than in the ministry of the Word in relation to pastoral soul-care.

For over a century graduate schools and seminaries have trained an army of pastoral students in a variety of psychologies under the label *pastoral counseling*. This training often assumed the tenets of some renowned psychologist or psychotherapist, or worse, taught an academic smorgasbord of psychological methods and theories from which the pastor could draw as he saw fit.[6] Some of the most influential, early psychologies in theological graduate schools included the psychoanalysis of Sigmund Freud, the analytical psychology of Carl Jung, the nondirective psychotherapeutic counseling of Carl Rogers, the physiological psychology of the liberal theologian-turned-psychologist G. T. Ladd,[7] and the existential psychology of Søren Kierkegaard. Pastors, trained under these psychologies, influenced an entire generation of parishioners to think and act according to the therapeutic instead of according to the Gospel. Even the authorial intent of Scripture was replaced by a psychological hermeneutic that loaded biblical terminology with psychotherapeutic meaning. Where the Bible was not replaced by a psychology, it was redefined by it.

Few psychologists or psychiatrists today claim to follow these older psychologies exclusively. This underscores the fact that psychology is in constant flux and is far from being a mature science. Psychological theories are frequently replacing other psychological theories. In the spirit of German innovationism, academic psychology relentlessly quests for elusive insight, only to resign itself (eventually) to postmodern relativism. Sigmund Koch expresses his frustration with psychology when he writes:

> The idea that psychology—like the natural sciences on which it is modeled—is cumulative or progressive is simply not borne out by history. Indeed, the hard knowledge gained by one generation typically disenfranchises the the-

> oretical fictions of the last.... Throughout psychology's history as "science" the *hard* knowledge it has deposited has been uniformly negative.[8]

Nevertheless, Christians continue to be taught the essentials of psychology overtly or inadvertently, in sermons, Sunday school lessons, marriage seminars, self-help books, radio programs, missionary training, and Christian universities. The principles of psychology are presented as though they were on the same authoritative level as Scripture and compete for its jurisdiction as the sole authority in determining the well-being of the soul. Mission organizations persist in using psychological assessment tools,[9] built upon secular normality research of unbelievers' attitudes and opinions, to determine the fitness and potential adjustment of prospective candidates. Furthermore, as John MacArthur has observed, "Over the past decade a host of evangelical psychological clinics have sprung up. Though almost all of them claim to offer biblical counsel, most merely dispense secular psychology disguised in spiritual terminology."[10] Many Christian colleges, universities, and seminaries have taken their psychology programs and relabeled them "Biblical Counseling Programs," while maintaining an essentially psychological core of subjects. Because of this, Christians have good reason to be skeptical toward any type of counseling that is not thoroughly biblical.

Psychology in the Bible?

Some believe and even teach that the English term *psychology* is of biblical extraction because of its transliterated Greek original. It is a compound consisting of two Greek words, *psychē* (soul, mind)[11] and *logos* (word, law). The united etymology of this word became *the study or science of the mind or soul.* Actually, this word has closer etymological ties to Classical Greek than to New Testament *koinē* Greek.[12]

The word *psychology* does not occur in the Bible, even though there are endless eisegetical efforts to discover the presence of its earliest meanings. Reading ideas of modern psychology into the biblical term *psychē* is like equating the contemporary idea of dynamite with the New Testament Greek word *dunamis.*[13] D. A. Carson refers to this as a "semantic anachronism."

> Our word *dynamite* is etymologically derived from *δύναμις* (power, or even miracle). I do not know how many times I have heard preachers offer some such rendering of Romans 1:16 as this: "I am not ashamed of the gospel, for it is the dynamite of God unto salvation for everyone who believes"—often with a knowing tilt of the head as if something profound or even esoteric has been uttered. This is not just the old root fallacy revisited. It is

> worse: it is an appeal to a kind of reverse etymology, the root fallacy compounded by anachronism. Did Paul think dynamite when he penned this word? . . . Dynamite blows things up, tears things down, rips out rock, gouges holes, destroys things.[14]

In the first century, Paul was not thinking of the explosive type of dynamite invented by the Swedish industrialist Alfred Nobel (1833-1896) and patented in 1867. He was thinking of the supernatural salvific ability of God the Father. The tendency to assume a contemporary word meaning and impose it upon a biblical word, often in hopes of claiming a dynamic insight or legitimizing a questionable practice, is a common, misleading ploy of interpreters today. In fact, reading various contemporary meanings back into the inspired text, foreign to the authorial intent, is a treacherous postmodern phenomenon.

Therefore, Scripture's usage of the term *psychē* does not biblically validate the supplemental practice of psychoanalysis in Christian counseling.[15] Nor can overtones of psychoanalytic theory—such as the superego, id, and ego—be found latently in this term. Yet it is not uncommon for Christians, psychologists, and others to read neo-Freudian notions of a layered subconscious into the biblical word *psychē*.

Furthermore, the typical bifurcation between the soul and the spirit made by some Christian psychologists cannot be biblically sustained. One Christian psychiatrist offers this explanation: "The soul is the psychological aspect of man, whereas the spirit is spiritual . . . the mind alone lies in the psychological aspect of man and not the spiritual."[16] Such an artificial distinction grows from reading psychological meaning into biblical terms. Both *soul* and *spirit* speak of the same intangible aspect of the inner man, the part of man that only God sees. A concordance study of *psychē* shows that when Scripture uses the term *soul* in relation to man, it refers to that aspect of the inner man *in connection* with his body. When it uses the term *spirit*, it is that aspect of the inner man *out of connection* with his body.[17] No distinction exists in Scripture between the psychologically-oriented and the spiritually-oriented inner man.

The whole of the inner man comes under the dominion of the spiritual. In this arena the Bible reigns not only as a sufficient source for addressing soul-problems, but also as the supreme source. As Agur plainly warns in Proverbs, "Every word of God proves true; he is a shield to those who take refuge in him. Do not add to his words, lest he rebuke you and you be found a liar."[18] Importing late-twentieth-century psychological significance into biblical English (or the original Hebrew, Aramaic, or Greek for that matter) denies the divine intent of its authorship. In fact, anachronistic efforts to legitimize psychotherapeutic practices among Christians by appealing to similar biblical terminology are linguistically fallacious, presumptuous, and misleading.

Using the Bible to justify psychological practices can only be attempted through the broadest of definitions. One author paints his definition with wide strokes before he describes the psychological insights he sees in Matthew 5: "But the study of character, the aspects of its well-being, and the change of character for the better seem to be a sort of psychology and psychotherapy in a broad sense of these words."[19] "Broad sense" implies "simple sense" or something lacking the complexity of contemporary psychological research. Christian psychology views Scripture as the "fountainhead of Christian ideas, including psychological ones."[20] In other words, the Bible is good for introductory thoughts and the germination of new ideas, but it is not sufficiently comprehensive to give substantive assistance to the intricacies of serious soul-problems. Scripture, according to so-called Christian psychology, is a primitive catalog of Christian character development and change; psychology and psychotherapy, however, provide exhaustive ideas for refining character and promoting well-being. So the "fountainhead of Christian ideas" merely moistens the palate but does not quench deep thirst. Supposedly, additional psychological canals must irrigate Scripture's trickle of truth if the counselor is to assuage the thirsty soul-problems of life. According to Christian psychology, the Sermon on the Mount teaches a form of pathology, personality distinctives, and therapeutic involvement, but only in an unsophisticated composition.

While secular psychologists contemptuously dismiss the Bible as an archaic and mistaken psychology, their Christian colleagues desperately labor to prop up its fledgling therapeutic with an apologetic of psychological naiveté. Christian psychologists often act embarrassed, like the illegitimate child of its larger, more sophisticated psychological family—the American Psychological Association (APA) and the International Psychoanalytical Association (IPA). Driven by a deep desire to impress its more affluent parents, it ignominiously acknowledges the dangers of total reliance upon the Bible. Organizations such as the Christian Association of Psychological Studies (CAPS) and to a lesser extent the American Association of Christian Counselors (AACC) have viewed psychology as a supplemental resource to the Bible. As one Christian who functions as a psychologist explains:

> Despite its wealth of information about human beings, their universe, and their God, the Bible is not intended to be a psychology textbook . . . the Bible does not tell us about . . . the developmental stages of infancy, the fine points of conflict resolution, or the ways to treat dyslexia or paranoia. Psychology focuses on issues like these.[21]

In other words, the biblical text is a shallow and imprecise psychology and must be seen only as the starting gate of a more informed therapeutic. The APA sneers at Christians who are "deluded" with religious myths but finds the myths potentially helpful if the Christian psychologist does not take his Bible too seriously when dealing with them. Trying to keep one foot in the Bible and another in the intrusive discipline of psychology presents a precarious balancing challenge. Those who do not slip from the Christian faith are often torn apart. Subjugating Jesus and the disciples to an early, unrefined psychology undermines the Christian's complete confidence in the Bible, and this subjugation is at best a tacit acknowledgment of an alleged biblical insufficiency.

Psychology in the Dictionary

What is psychology? Although a common and often used term, its connotation is misleading. Popular and scholastic definitions cover a wide semantic continuum from scientific research to therapeutic theory and practice, from biological to clinical mental health. Systems include biopsychology, experimental psychology, cognitive psychology, developmental psychology, clinical psychology, social psychology, industrial-organizational psychology, and cross-cultural psychology. In addition, an assortment of psychotherapeutic theories drives many of the psychological systems—psychodynamic, humanistic, existential, family systems, cognitive-behavioral, or postmodern psychotherapy. As mentioned earlier, the brief history of psychology is littered with an untold number of discarded models. In other words, psychology is far from being a unified discipline. It would be better to refer to "psychologies"[22] since a plethora of theories and systems, current and past, abounds.

The more common and basic definition of psychology used by the overwhelming majority of teaching institutions maintains a close connection between psychology and science. According to these institutions, "Psychology is the scientific study of behavior and mental processes."[23] But is this true? Is psychology a scientific discipline? If it is scientific, how can anyone object to its truth-claims? The initial chapters in most freshman-level introductory psychology textbooks draw heavily upon the natural sciences: biology, biochemistry, neurology, the limbic system, the endocrine system, and sensory organs. However, the remaining chapters of the book often move further and further from the hard sciences into personality theory, motivation, emotions, human development, sexual orientation, abnormal psychology, social psychology, and psychotherapies.

Serious questions arise concerning the true scientific nature of psychology as greater reliance is placed upon the so-called "behavioral" sciences. Much of the espoused scientific evidence is no better than opinion research. Psychology's relationship to the natural sciences is like margarine's relationship to real butter. Margarine looks and spreads like the real thing, but anyone who tastes it can tell the difference. Karl Popper detects a major problem in psychology when he writes, "Psychological theories of human behavior, 'though posing as sciences,' had in fact more in common with primitive myths than with science. . . . They contain most interesting psychological suggestions, but not in testable form."[24] A similar note of caution from Scott Lilienfeld concerns the practice of mental health:

> Over the past several decades, the fields of clinical psychology, psychiatry, and social work have borne witness to a widening and deeply troubling gap between science and practice (see Lilienfeld, 1998, for a discussion). Carol Tavris (1998) has written eloquently of the increasing gulf between the academic laboratory and the couch and of the worrisome discrepancy between what we have learned about the psychology of memory; hypnosis; suggestibility; clinical judgment and assessment; and the causes, diagnosis, and treatment of mental disorders, on the one hand, and routine clinical practice, on the other.[25]

Herein lies an epistemological problem at the heart of the *a priori* truth-claims of psycho-science: It is not as scientific as it claims to be. If psychology and psychiatry maintained a strict code of cause-and-effect science instead of research built on causes that appear to be related to effects, they could be credible authorities for biblical pastors and counselors. However, when psychology encroaches upon biblical territory by claiming jurisdictional authority in the counseling arena of what man "ought" to do, it is usurping God's domain. Psychology's illegitimate efforts cannot come to absolute conclusions about life, since at its heart psychology is only one fallible man telling another fallible man what to do. Arrogance abounds in such an environment. Only the divinely inspired Word of God has authority to do that.

Another problem arises with the science of psychology. Even if psychology withdrew from its pseudo-scientific subjectivism and fully relied upon the natural sciences, it would still draw inaccurate conclusions. Why? The *a priori* presupposition of the overwhelming majority of natural sciences is an evolutionary one. Freud (1856-1939) was a Darwin devotee. All the psychological textbooks since Freud's time, graduate and otherwise, espouse that man is an evolved animal. Psychological research studies about the biology of man interacting with his environment are frequently based on animal studies. For example, concrete inferences were made concerning the emotional attachment between a child and his mother through the study of how infant monkeys became attached to soft, warm, terry-cloth "mother-monkeys" instead of to wire "mother-monkeys" who gave milk.[26] The obvious assumption is that human infants, because of their evolutionary heritage, are identical or remarkably similar in development to infant monkeys in their attachment responses. From these foundational studies that garner considerable credibility, psychologists establish sweeping developmental standards that affect governmental and educational child-welfare policies. Even more directly, therapeutic advice given to parents is based upon the same evolutionary research.

Evolutionary biopsychology defines man as nothing more than the sum total of his chemical components. An understanding of the advanced complexity of the highly evolved animal called man illuminates what makes him tick. Most psychology textbooks have an account of the unfortunate mishap of Phineas Gage, the twenty-five-year-old railroad employee who in 1848 had a one-inch-diameter metal spike driven through his skull while blasting rock. Remarkably he lived, but he was a radically changed man. Before the accident, he was a responsible, hard-working, mostly moral, and smart employee. After the accident he transformed into a cussing, carousing, irresponsible man who could not hold down a job or maintain good relationships with others. According to the theories in most psychology texts, the association areas of the cerebral cortex of Mr. Gage's brain were destroyed, an area where higher mental processes such as thinking, language, memory, and speech occur. In other words, the texts make a case that morality is not a spiritual issue after all; it is an organic issue. According to them, man is moral because his brain has evolved over millennia from a central core (the "old brain") to a higher reasoning capacity in the cerebral cortex (the "new brain").

What was destroyed in Mr. Gage's brain was a portion of the highly evolved association areas of the cortex where morality is determined. Then the question must be asked, is morality an issue for biology but not the Bible? Will organic solutions suffice? Could pedophiles be given a pill in the future to stop their molestation of children? Would a prescription end the thievery of a female kleptomaniac? Could drugs be added to the water supply to finally rid society of criminals? Evolutionary biopsychology focuses in this direction.

The cases of traumatically brain-injured people like Phineas Gage and others prove nothing. Again psychology has made associations that appear to be related to causes, but there is no direct cause and effect between injury and immoral behavior. A strong relationship is made because evolutionary psychiatry is committed to a materialistic worldview—the uniformity of natural causes in a closed system. Sudden changes toward wickedness, like that evidenced by Gage, are also evident in cases where no brain damage has been sustained. Conversely, some who have suffered serious brain damage to the associational areas of the brain have not changed morally. Regardless, the sheer trauma of such an accident could sufficiently expose wickedness in the heart of someone like Gage who had suppressed it previously.

Often years of hostility and anger can surface in a counselee who had previously lived a basically moral lifestyle. As Ed Welch explains, an injury can make it harder to think clearly and resist latent wickedness: "When affected by underlying sin, cognitive problems are often translated into childish behavior, unwillingness to be taught, irresponsibility, impulsiveness (especially financial), unusual emotional fluctuations, depression, and irritability."[27] Trauma only magnifies the need to keep the heart pure. Elderly counselees who are suffering from early forms of Alzheimer's or dementia will often have a difficult time restraining ungodly desires, especially if the inner man has not been nurtured over the years. Biblical counselors believe in a uniformity of natural causes in an *open* system. This means that these problems have supernatural/spiritual dimensions. The supernatural work of the Spirit of God through the Word of God can bring about a renewed life of holiness and righteousness in spite of brain damage or disease. Evolutionary materialism ends in nihilism, devoid of such hope.

Is psychology a scientific discipline? The answer to this previously posed question is, at best, debatable. Certainly there are aspects of this discipline that carefully use rigid scientific reasoning. Even then, however, the *a priori* presuppositions necessary to bring about some meaningful significance are patently evolutionary. Psychology is better viewed as a philosophical system of thought disseminated as a materialistic worldview—behaviorism, humanism, determinism, existentialism, epiphenomenalism, and simple pragmatic utilitarianism.

Biblical counseling is not a scientific discipline either. And it does not claim to be, even though it is quick to affirm valid medical science and biological research as applied to genuinely organic problems. Biblical counseling fully acknowledges that its epistemology grows out of a theistic presupposition of a self-revelatory Creator who "has granted to us all things that pertain to life and godliness, through the knowledge of him who called us to his own glory and excellence" (2 Pet 1:3). The Bible is not an encyclopedia of counseling topics that lists every particular counseling problem, but it does contain sufficient revelatory data to establish an effective worldview framework for the diagnosis and remedy of every soul-problem. An extended explanation by David Powlison illustrates this point:

> Biblical counselors who fail to think through carefully the nature of biblical epistemology run the danger of acting as if Scripture were exhaustive, rather than comprehensive; as if Scripture were an encyclopedic catalogue of all significant facts, rather than God's revelation of the crucial facts, richly illustrated, that yield a world view sufficient to interpret whatever other facts we encounter; as if Scripture were the whole bag of marbles rather than the eyeglasses through which we interpret all marbles; as if our current grasp of Scripture and people were triumphant and final. Integrationists view Scripture as a small bag of marbles and psychology as a large bag of marbles. The logic of integrationist epistemology is this: Put the two bags together, weeding out the obviously bad marbles in psychology, and you have more marbles.[28]

Some biblical counselors err in believing that the Bible is the whole bag of marbles. On the other hand, Christian psychologists with an integrationist epistemology do not believe that the Bible has sufficient marbles for soul-care. In fact, they believe that by adding the larger bag of psychological marbles to the mix, they will be able to play a better game of marbles. They increasingly rely, however, upon the psychological marbles that are distorted and misshapen by an errant worldview. Their biblical marbles are eventually marginalized by their integrationist epistemology. With skewed vision, they cannot weed out the bad marbles, much less play an effective game. Powlison asks, "Is the Bible a bag of marbles or the all-sufficient eyeglasses of truth—with lots of illustrative marbles—by which God corrects our sin-tainted vision?[29]

The difference between biblical counseling and Christian psychology is a worldview issue. Biblical counselors believe the counselor needs new glasses. Christian psychologists believe the counselor needs more marbles. When the Bible is the Christian counselor's corrective lens, he has a sufficient worldview perspective, with abundant illustrative material, to biblically reinterpret all human experience for soul-care.

Biblical Counseling in the Bible

Does the Bible justify this counseling worldview? If so, can the biblical counselor trust assertions drawn from research in the natural world? A carefully reasoned justification exists not only for prioritizing the Bible in one's counseling schema, but also for making it the reliable resource for the Christian counselor's etiology of the soul. As such, the Bible provides the diagnostic terminology and remedy, as well as the theoretical framework, from which soul-problems are properly interpreted and resolved. Not only do the noetic (pertaining to the mind) effects of sin cause the counselor to wrongly interpret soul-problems, they also encourage the selection of wrong categories for understanding the significance of these soul-problems, beginning with the counselor's view of God and extending to the counselor's view of man.

The Bible, and not psychology, should set the determinative categories for understanding theology and anthropology. For example, Scripture contains no hint that man struggles with a "poor view of self" or "low self-esteem." Yet this idea has been the rubric of a considerable amount of Christian pop psychology. The theoretical source material came not from the Bible, but from secular psychologists like William James, Erich Fromm, Karen Horney, and Abraham Maslow. In fact, biblical anthropology teaches that man loves himself too much, and if he loved God and others as much as he already loves himself, he would have a better life.[30]

In addition, no justification for personality classification as a major determining factor in interpersonal and marital conflict can be found in Scripture. A psychological etiology of such problems causes Christians to focus on the wrong issues, avoiding the critical matter of the idolatrous heart that needs to change. Classification categories of personality have nothing to do with the Bible; rather they find their inspiration in ancient Greek mythology.[31] Mythology aside, personality in the Bible is fluid and not an intact characteristic. An avid student of the Bible should be able to distinguish psychological claims, both new and ancient, from the authoritative criteria of God's truth. Similarly, the Christian counselor should not only refer *to* scriptural truth in counseling, but should also reason *from* it.

Furthermore, certification organizations have arisen over the last thirty years to return Christians to Bible-based, not-for-profit, church-sponsored, counseling ministries. Notably, the National Association of Nouthetic Counselors (NANC)[32] is the grandfather of such organizations, created to assist the church in developing and maintaining excellence in biblical counseling. The term *nouthetic* is derived from the New Testament word that means to warn, admonish, or counsel. NANC has been extremely influential in helping churches create counseling ministries built upon a biblically-consistent counseling model.

The Psalm 19 Paradigm

The weight that the Bible carries in the counseling process is beautifully illustrated in Psalm 19. It has been called "the Psalm of two books," because the first half presents God revealing Himself in the created domain (general revelation), and the second half presents God revealing Himself through the Word (special revelation). A careful study of the Psalm, however, demonstrates that David did not change topics in the middle of his writing. Psalm 19 is a psalm of one book, not two.

General Revelation

The first half of this psalm theologically describes the scope and extent of general revelation (vv. 1-6). The shepherd/poet introduces the psalm with a riveting display of the glory of God in the heavens by stating, "The heavens declare the glory of God" (v. 1a)! God's glory is painted in brilliant colors across the sky. David asserts that the cosmic design and power of the universe places God's resplendent glory on display like an unfurled banner stretching from horizon to horizon. The Hebrew word for "glory" originally carried the more literal connotation of "weight" or "heaviness." The later, more extended meaning developed into the concept of "importance" or "glory." As his/her eyes scan the glimmering night sky, a person is able to understand the weightiness or importance of Almighty God. General revelation elicits breathless awe for the raw intelligence of the omnipotent Creator.

Next, in synonymous parallelism, there is a restatement of the same idea in the second line using different words. David says, "and the sky above proclaims his handiwork" (v. 1b). Each of the main verbs in the first two lines, "declare" and "proclaims," uses the Hebrew aspect indicating an ongoing action. God's glory is constantly being displayed by the created world around us.

Verse 2 continues to highlight the ongoing duration of nature's work in demonstrating God's glory for man to see. "Day to day pours out speech, and night to night reveals knowledge." "Pours out" is a verb that means "bubbles forth." As a geyser naturally spouts forth steam and water by means of underground pressure, so natural revelation is under pressure to bring to the forefront God's glory.

Without a word being spoken, this is accomplished. The English Standard Version provides a superb translation here: "There is no speech, nor are there words, whose voice is not heard" (v. 3). The King James Version inserts the word *where*—"*where* their voice is not heard"—and thereby confuses the meaning. The emphasis of this verse is not the location of the message; it is the language of the message. God is able to get the essential message across without the use of a single verbal utterance. Through nonverbal communication, people from all cultures and all languages have the capacity to understand that Almighty God exists in all of His weighty importance.

The first part of verse 4 reinforces the message: "Their measuring line goes out through all the earth, and their words to the end of world." No one can escape this powerful nonverbal message because it extends to the horizon. People cannot hide from it, and they cannot run from it. Everyone is visually bombarded with God's might and unrivaled creative design.

Then, in emblematic parallelism, David extends the reader's understanding of the role of general revelation with the use of two vivid images—the bridegroom and the strong runner (vv. 4c-6).

> *In them he has set a tent for the sun,*
> *which comes out like a bridegroom leaving his chamber,*
> *and, like a strong man, runs its course with joy.*
> *Its rising is from the end of the heavens,*
> *and its circuit to the end of them,*
> *and there is nothing hidden from its heat.*

The sun is compared to a determined bridegroom stepping from his tent to claim his bride. It has a predetermined course as it comes forth each morning from the veil of darkness with God's glory promising a fresh day. The sun also runs its course from one end of the heavens to the other like a strong man; it does not stop, and no one can stop it. A good runner keeps focused on the goal of finishing the race, just as the sun is focused on completing the course that the Creator has given it. All of this determination, ordered movement, regularity, and power is abundant evidence of the glory of God.

The description does not end there because a subsequent verse (6c) indicates that no one can escape the influence of God's glory in creation: "there is nothing hidden from its heat." Still using the analogy of the sun, the psalmist emphasizes that everyone can feel the heat of God's glory. Even the limited sensory world of one who is blind, deaf, and mute has the capacity to feel the ebb and flow of warmth from the rhythmic setting and rising of the sun. People with "subaverage intellectual functioning" or those with profound retardation (IQs 39 and below) are significantly impacted with the basic message of the presence of God and His glory. That is the penetration power of this nonverbal message. Clearly, general revelation was intended to put God's power and creative design on display.

At this point a question must be asked: What does the Bible say is God's intended pedagogic role for general revelation? One Christian psychological integrationist has said, "All truth is certainly God's truth. The doctrine of General Revelation provides warrant for going beyond the propositional revelation of Scripture into the secular world of scientific study expecting to find true and useable concepts. . . . Again, let me insist that psychology does offer real help to the Christian endeavoring to understand and solve personal problems."[33] While it is certainly true that "all truth is God's truth," it is also true that "all error is the devil's error."[34] The truism "all truth is God's truth" reduces their argument to *reductio ad absurdum* and begs the question when used simplistically by integrationists. For example, another Christian psychologist holds to a reductionistic view of the Bible by maintaining that "as God's statutes in scriptures are binding upon His people, His 'statutes' or fixed patterns within the framework of heaven and earth are binding upon the whole of the cosmos."[35] Then he suggests that just as the authors of Proverbs appealed to natural phenomena, so the Christian psychologist can do the same in determining psychological "*quasi causal*" laws for life. Not only does this place the psychologist on the same level as the writers of inspired Scripture, but it nullifies the warning of Proverbs 30:5-6 about adding to the unique Word of God.

No one questions the many benefits of natural revelation for mankind, including discoveries made through the natural sciences and medical research. Even then, some of these discoveries may have limited application to the one who believes in the sanctity of life because God created people in His image (e.g., in regard to abortion and fertility technology). But when the metaphysical bridge to the inner being is crossed by an encroaching psychology, what does Scripture identify as the role of general revelation?

According to Psalm 19 the role of general revelation is to alert all men to the supreme glory of God. An ordered Creator with design and might exceeds one's imagination. The apostle Paul understood this role of general revelation and declared, "For his invisible attributes, namely, his eternal power and divine nature, have been clearly perceived, ever since the creation of the world, in the things that have been made. So they are without excuse" (Rom 1:20).

A major limitation hinders general revelation's effect, however, in that it can be totally ignored or even misunderstood by its recipients. This omnipresent, powerful message can be distorted and censored. Paul explains God's anger over this: "For the wrath of God is revealed from heaven against all ungodliness and unrighteousness of men, who by their unrighteousness suppress the truth. For what can be known about God is plain to them, because God has shown it to them" (Rom 1:18-19). Man's heart can never be neutral about the truth. In his unrighteousness, man is opposed to God and any fundamental knowledge of God. Information derived from the natural world can be twisted and obscured by the deceitful cunningness of the sinful heart. While special revelation can be distorted or rejected like general revelation, it is different in one major aspect—it is self-authenticated as true and sufficient, while general revelation is not.

Special Revelation

Now this is the point of Psalm 19: *Far greater than all general revelation is the glory of God revealed in His Word, because the Word transforms the heart of man.* Ronald Barclay Allen comments on this Psalm, "I believe that it is the teaching of this movement of the Psalm that *God reveals His glory more fully in His Word than in all of creation* [author's emphasis]."[36] The general revelation in God's works of creative power fulfills its duty by rendering man without excuse, but it can never yield transforming, authoritative truth for soul-problems because it is too vague for that purpose. The special revelation of Scripture is needed for salvation—divine, authoritative truth that can convert the soul (Rom 1:16-17; 1 Cor 1:18).

The entire psalm pivots on verse 7, which declares, "The law of the LORD is perfect, reviving the soul." "Reviving" is the same word often translated "converting," "restoring," or "turning back."[37] God's Word is "perfect" in the sense that it is ideal or perfectly suited for man; the soul that has been warped and deformed by sin and serious problems can be reshaped by its power. As Hebrews says, "For the word of God is living and active, sharper than any two-edged sword, piercing to the division of soul and of spirit, of joints and of marrow, and discerning the thoughts and intentions of the heart" (Heb 4:12). This text is not saying that God's Word divides soul from spirit, but that it divides man's inner being—so much so that it gets down into the deepest thoughts and intentions (or motivations) of the heart. Information from general revelation can never hope to do that because God never intended that. The occasional helpful insights provided through research on things like sleep disorders, visual perception, and organic brain disorders will never approach the power of the Word of God for change. The Word of God is matchless within the jurisdictional domain of the soul.

Using psychology for soul-care is like treating cancer with aspirin. It may temporarily relieve the pain or even mask the symptoms, but it will never penetrate the issues of the heart like God's Word.

Some may argue that the passage is speaking only about unregenerate men and does not apply to Christians who are being counseled. However, this is not the case. Even though a broader application can be made to the unbeliever, the final eight verses of this psalm (vv. 7-14) describe the sanctifying power of the Word of God in the life of the believer. And if it is true that the Word of God is greater in bringing about the glory of God in man than is general revelation, then why would Christians want to return to the simpler and more fundamental truths of general revelation when they have a far greater life-transforming truth at their disposal?

The effects of the Word in man's life include: "reviving the soul," "making wise the simple," "rejoicing the heart," "enlightening the eyes," "enduring forever"; and it is "righteous altogether." The first five characteristics are participles, meaning the Word of God refreshes life, grants depth of insight, renders joy to the heart, opens the eyes of understanding, and will never be outdated. Where else can a person go to find counsel like that? These phrases express the ongoing ministry and relevance of the Word of God. The sixth characteristic is a summary statement conveying the idea that the Word of God is capable of producing comprehensive righteousness.

The adjectives in reference to the Word of God variously describe Scripture as perfectly suited, reliable, "right," "pure," "clean," and truthful counsel. The synonyms here for the Word of God demonstrate how its counsel should be approached. These synonyms include divine "law" (Torah), a "testimony," directions, commandments, the fear of Yahweh, and the judgments of Yahweh. In other words, God's truth is not optional. It is not a set of His suggestions. If the Word is to have its rightful impact upon the counselee's heart, it must be approached with utmost reverence. When this is done, the counselee will find its aftertaste sweet (v. 10).

Verses 11-14 encompass the final movement of the psalm. The radical impact this Word has had upon the life of David becomes evident. He opens his life to show how he was transformed by the counsel of God, thereby glorifying God. Apart from the written Word, David asks, "Who can discern his errors?" (v. 12). This rhetorical question evokes a strong answer: *No one can!* David prays, "Declare me innocent from hidden faults. Keep back your servant also from presumptuous sins; let them not have dominion over me" (vv. 12-13). Secret sins are the unknown sins of the soul, while "presumptuous sins" are the known sins. Presumptuous sins have an enslaving quality to them; they will assume domination in the counselee's life (e.g., sexual lust, gluttony, drunkenness, or rage). These are the sins done in full knowledge of their sinfulness, and yet they are deliberately committed anyway.

Scripture identifies sin as the chief problem of the human heart in need of counseling (Jer 17:9). Other contributing factors include both organic problems and sins committed by others. These sins by others, against or around the counselee, have a direct impact upon the counselee (e.g., rape, incest, physical abuse, financial irresponsibility, hatred, anger, jealousy). All counseling matters result from the wickedness of a sin-cursed and demon-infested world (Jas 3:14-16). But even in cases of unjust suffering, how does the counselee's heart respond?[38] When the Word of God has its way, the counselee walks free from guilt. David announces boldly, "Then I shall be blameless, and innocent of great transgression."

His final prayer is to be acceptable before God (v. 14). He knows this will be true only if both his actions ("the words of my mouth") and his desires ("the meditation of my heart") are pleasing to God. The Lord is this counselee's Rock and Redeemer.

The Critical Question

Far greater than all of general revelation is the glory of God revealed in His Word, because it *alone* transforms the heart of man. To the critical question, why biblical counseling and not psychology? the answer must necessarily be that the Word of God reigns supreme in the jurisdictional domain of the soul, where psychology trespasses and seeks to usurp spiritual authority. Only the Word of God can effectively instruct believers concerning how to glorify Him.

In keeping with David's sentiments in Psalm 19, Christians have always understood this chief aim of glorifying God and enjoying Him forever. This can only be accomplished through the Word of God. All the psychotherapies and psychologies of man will never sanctify the human heart to such high and noble purposes. In fact, the rudimentary core of all psychologies is *self*—living for the welfare and enjoyment of *self*. Most psychological remedies cater to self with messages of loving self more, esteeming self, and pampering self. All psychologies see this as their "chief end," and tragically, the so-called Christian psychologies have also been dramatically infected with it.

Furthermore, general revelation will never yield absolute, universally authoritative truth on which the counselee can confidently base the welfare of his/her soul. Why? Because that was never its intended purpose. By its very nature, natural revelation cannot express a complete picture of God, much less His will for His creatures. On the deficiencies of general revelation John Calvin comments, "It is therefore clear that God has provided the assistance of the Word for the sake of all those to whom he has been pleased to give useful instruction because he foresaw that his likeness imprinted upon the most beautiful form of the universe would be insufficiently effective."[39] Natural revelation is unqualified when it comes to changing the soul. As David so poignantly describes in Psalm 19, God delivered to man a more powerful revelation that is capable of penetrating the deep recesses of the soul and not only redeeming him but instructing him in righteousness, so that he might glorify and enjoy God forever. Every spiritual counseling problem hangs on these fundamental facts. The Scriptures are the key to what makes life *life!* "Do not my words do good to him who walks uprightly?" (Mic 2:7b).

Further Reading

Almy, Gary L. *How Christian Is Christian Counseling?* (Wheaton, IL: Crossway Books, 2000).

Ganz, Richard. *Psychobabble*. Wheaton, IL: Crossway Books, 1993.

Adams, Jay E. *The Christian Counselor's Manual.* Grand Rapids, MI: Zondervan, 1973.

__________. *Competent to Counsel.* Grand Rapids, MI: Zondervan, 1970.

MacArthur, John and Wayne A. Mack. *Introduction to Biblical Counseling*. Dallas: Word, 1994.

12

Why a Scriptural View of Science?

Taylor B. Jones

It is impossible to overestimate the impact of science in terms of what it produces and its influence on how we think. From the controversial issue of global warming to oral medications, science touches the life of every single person. Moreover, most individuals think that science produces information that is inherently complete, or at the very least highly trustworthy. Some areas of study have been the object of intense scientific scrutiny—e.g., the astronomic study of planetary motion in the solar system. Others, such as the search for extraterrestrial intelligence, rest on very tenuous foundations, described by the vaguest of notions, and are supported by the weakest data.

The goal of any philosophical inquiry should be the development or refinement of a general worldview that is correct; i.e., it must be consistent with an accurate picture of reality. This goal might sound ridiculously self-evident, but few people have even considered that they have a worldview, much less whether it is correct. Although there are many worldviews, not all of them can be correct. A worldview that is correct must be true, an expression of the way things really are. An incorrect worldview is of little value other than being amusing, interesting, or even fascinating. Although such incorrect views might provide a wealth of study for philosophers, they cannot provide much insight into how to live one's life. Since we have to live in a real universe with real people and real situations, a worldview that does not correctly interpret and reflect the way things really are has little practical value. An enormously elaborate and complex map of roads and highways that are incorrectly depicted on a page will never help us navigate successfully from a journey's beginning to its final destination. So it is with aberrant worldviews. They only end up producing lost people.

If we go a step further and consider those aspects of the universe that intersect with the various disciplines of science, the same guidelines for assessing reliability must necessarily apply. The only difference here is that the scope of the investigation has been narrowed to things germane to science. One is still seeking a worldview of science that accurately describes and reliably reflects reality.

Philosophically, a Christian's worldview contains five clusters of belief: beliefs about 1) God (theology); 2) ultimate reality (metaphysics); 3) knowledge (epistemology); 4) ethics (axiology); and 5) human nature (anthropology).[1] Science as a component of epistemology is defined to be:

> 1. the state of knowing: knowledge as distinguished from ignorance or misunderstanding;
>
> 2. a. department of systematized knowledge as an object of study.
>
> b. something that may be studied or learned, like systematized knowledge;
>
> 3. a. knowledge covering general truths or the operation of general laws, esp. as obtained and tested through scientific method.
>
> b. such knowledge concerned with the physical world and its phenomena, e.g., natural science.[2]

The second and third definitions would likely be given by one asked to describe science. The notion that science is an antonym for ignorance is implicitly assumed, but seldom articulated. A more far-reaching implication is the assertion in the third definition, viz., that there is a direct link between science and truth. This critical assumption must be carefully studied and will be addressed in this chapter, both for its impact and its implications.

Before the definition and nature of truth can be addressed, an introduction to the methodology and limitations of science needs to be presented.[3] Even though modern science touches the life of virtually every person on earth, how science functions philosophically to produce the progress from which we all benefit is poorly understood, if at all.[4] For this reason, the methodology of science as embodied in the scientific method will be discussed in some detail, being illustrated through an example to which anyone familiar with an automobile can relate. Then the nature of truth will be discussed, particularly as it relates to science and the ultimate authority, the Truth of God's Word.

It is important to note that some areas of scientific study are inherently more reliable than others. One cannot be nearly as confident in the conclusions one draws in areas like sociology and anthropology compared with those in chemistry or physics. The latter have the advantage of being able to do the same experiment repeatedly to be certain the outcome was due to the experimental conditions and not some incidental circumstance. Therefore, one of the strengths of science as a discipline is rooted in the concept of *reproducibility*.

In such disciplines, factors thought to have a detectable effect can be systematically changed and correlated with changes in the outcome of the study. What is involved in a given process can then be unambiguously clarified. Galileo's (A.D. 1564-1642) study of the effect of gravity on objects[5] proved that the speed of a falling object was not dependent on its weight,[6] disproving the long-held view of Aristotle (384-322 B.C.). Those disciplines that can be studied by systematically changing conditions and noting the effect of such changes are presented as "hard sciences," the word "hard" denoting a quality of reliability. Examples of such disciplines include physics and chemistry.[7]

Disciplines in which reproducibility is difficult or impossible to achieve are termed "soft sciences."[8] The implication is that they are less reliable and justifiably so. One cannot in a sociological study, for example, go back and have a child relive his life with a better education to directly compare the effect of such an influence on the child's life. In such instances, one can only look at a group of subjects and use statistics to indicate possible correlations between education and its impact on a subject's life. One cannot be nearly as certain in such studies that the factor upon which one is focused, enhanced educational opportunity, is necessarily the single factor or even involved in the outcome one is studying. This inherent lack of rigor does not mean that such studies are without merit or that one cannot use the results of such studies; it does mean, however, that one is less certain about the significance of the correlation. Anthropology and psychology are examples of "soft sciences." The lack of consistent reproducibility precludes dogmatism regarding conclusions derived from any study in "soft science."

The study of how science functions, science's logic, and the development of science as a discipline has been the object of consistent scrutiny. The development of the scientific approach is rooted in ancient, primarily western civilization. (The tracing of the development of this approach and of science in general constitutes an area of study in its own right.[9]) This surprising notion is similar to finding studies on how the tools of a mechanic serve to help him in automobile repair. It is difficult to visualize any other area of study in which the *how* of the study is an object of interest in addition to the *what* of the study itself. Consequently, the study of the philosophy of science manifests itself in new book titles on a regular basis.[10] A serious consideration of the development of the philosophy of science is beyond the scope of this chapter. Instead, it would be more helpful to consider how science functions in a general sense.

The Scientific Method

Despite the types of logic involved and the relative reliability of a given scientific discipline, the method employed in any area of science, be it hard or soft, is philosophically the same. The general technique for acquiring, evaluating, and understanding the information from a scientific study is called "the scientific method." Many individuals incorrectly think that understanding science and its practice is beyond their intellect. In reality, the thinking of scientists is not so different from the thinking of non-scientists. Albert Einstein said, "The whole of science is nothing more than a refinement of everyday thinking."[11] To confirm this statement and to define and illustrate the scientific method, consider the following everyday example of events that this author experienced.

Suppose that a chemistry professor walked out of his office building and saw that his brand-new, right front tire was flat. That is an example of the first two components of the scientific method. The chemist recognized the flat tire by observing that the car was lower at one corner and that the tire was horizontal on the bottom and not round. This is called an *observation*. Any piece of scientific data acquired through the senses or with the benefit of some type of scientific equipment is an observation. Observations can be as simple as the number of teaspoons of sugar in a can of cola or as complex as the length of the DNA in every one of the cells of the body.

Observations in and of themselves are the necessary starting point for the scientific method, but to be useful, the observation has to be interpreted. The meaning of this observation, that the tire is flat, is called a *fact,* illustrated schematically below.

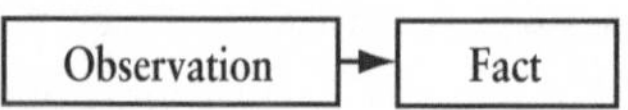

The meaning of the observation in this case is so immediately obvious that no comment is required; but often situations arise in which the meaning of what is observed is not so clear. Consider the results of an experimental, psychological study attempting to measure the reliability of eyewitness testimony.[12] In order to simulate this, a group of subjects were shown an illustration of people on a subway. The picture depicted several individuals, one of whom was a white man holding a razor; another, a black man, is wearing a hat. The likeness of the subway scene was taken away, and some time later the subjects were asked to describe to others in a serial manner what they had seen. The result was a pronounced tendency for the razor to depart from the white man and move to the black man. Regardless of the reason for such a conclusion, the point must be emphasized that the meanings of observations are not always correctly deduced. It is possible to make an observation but to misinterpret its meaning. One would most certainly hope that scientists' susceptibility to such shortcomings would be quite minimal, but that is not necessarily the case. Just as there were both competent and incompetent individuals in the group being tested, so it is with scientists. Wearing a white lab coat and being degreed in a scientific discipline does not somehow mystically confer immunity from error.

How is it that a collection of individuals can look at a picture of a black man wearing a hat and a white man holding a razor and then later communicate that the black man had the razor? The answer lies in the fact that every observer, scientist or layman, brings a perspective to the study that can influence what he/she sees. In this particular case, the perspective that interferes with correctly interpreting what one sees is racial prejudice. Making observations through the lens of bias distorts the understanding of what one perceives. The ultimate source of such distortion is sin that clouds one's ability to rightly interpret what has been seen. The Pharisees saw the miracles of the Lord Jesus Christ and attributed that power to Beelzebul (Matt 12:24). It is this writer's contention that scientists are also susceptible to such bias, just like anyone else.

Other potential sources of errors can occur when observations are being made. A scientist might simply make a mistake during the experimental process. He/she might add twice the amount of reagent, overheat a chemical reaction, or misread the digital output of an instrument. Human error in general can occur. Sometimes shortcomings in experimental design or attributing the effects of a change in the experiment to an uninvolved factor might occur. This is by no means an exhaustive list. Rather, it is used merely to illustrate that numerous things can go wrong in an experiment. Repetition of the experiment, to ensure reproducibility, can reveal many such mistakes.

At this point in the process, an educated guess called a *hypothesis* is made—that is, the initial, untested explanation of why or how the observed and correctly interpreted event happened.

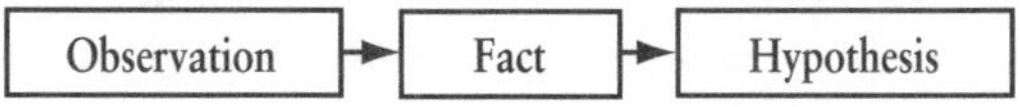

Such a formulation is an explicit acknowledgment of one of the underlying principles of science: *cause and effect*. In the philosophy of science, this is called *antecedent causation*.[13] The cause that gives rise to the effect precedes the effect. Or stated in another, less grammatically correct way, "Nothing ever happens for no reason." For every observed effect there is an underlying cause.

With regard to the flat tire mentioned above, several possible hypotheses come to mind. A vindictive student upset over a grade on a recent examination had let the air out of the tire to express his/her displeasure with the overall or individual low class grade. Alternatively, the tire had picked up a nail. Or perhaps the tire was defective in some way. It remains now to discover which, if any, of the hypotheses is correct.

Removal of the tire and a close examination of both the side walls and the tread prove to be a vain search for a puncture. If someone had let the air out of the tire, one would not be able to locate a puncture. This portion of the scientific method, testing the validity of a hypothesis, is called *experimentation*. This illustrates an important principle about the scientific method. A hypothesis will naturally bring experiments to mind that can be done to test its validity. The outcome of experimentation is to produce more observations and facts that should agree with a correct hypothesis.

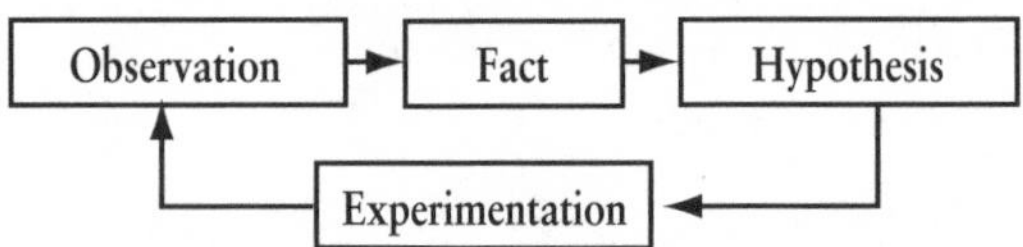

Unable to determine what caused the flat tire and needing to have it repaired, the chemist returned to the shop where the tire was purchased and watched the mechanic repeat the same unsuccessful methodology that had just been performed. The result of the reproducible experiments of the mechanic prompted the elevation of what the chemistry professor dubbed "The Vindictive Student" hypothesis to a higher level of credibility, since neither of them could find any physical evidence for the leak. It was certainly starting to appear that someone had let the air out of the tire, rather than the flat having been the result of some type of puncture or defect.

This higher level of credibility is called a *theory* or, as is more commonly known, a *model*. A theory is a tested hypothesis and must be consistent with all the existing experimental data. The confidence one has in a theory is dependent on the amount and quality of the data. In this case, the theory was tentative at best.

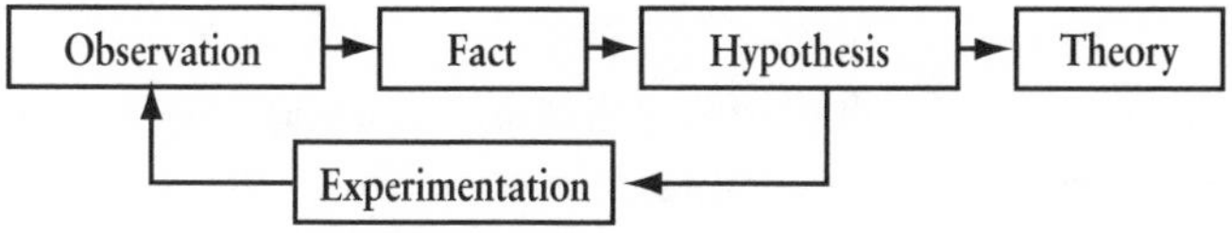

A theory is similar to a hypothesis, because it too will suggest experiments to test its validity. Next the mechanic pressurized the tire and submerged it just below the surface in a tank of water. Immediately a tell-tale stream of bubbles rose to the surface from deep in the recess between the treads. Clearly, a puncture of some sort *had* occurred. The chemist and the mechanic had a far more credible explanation as a result of the last experiment. The "Vindictive Student" hypothesis had to be discarded because it did not fit all the facts. If someone had merely let out the air, no bubbles would have escaped from the inflated, submerged tire.

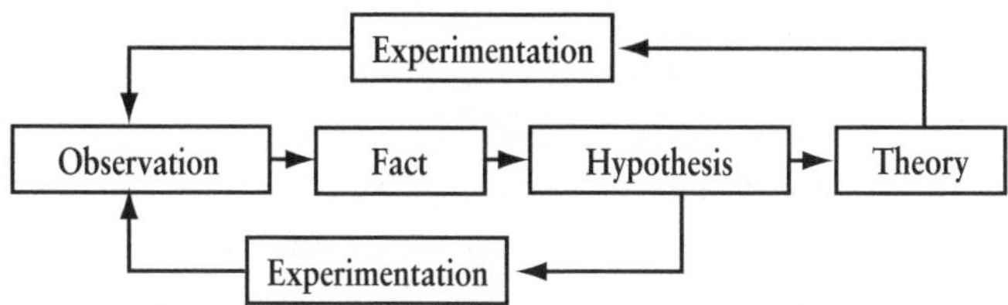

A quick removal of a narrow piece of sheet metal, a patch job by the mechanic, and a settling of the bill ended the saga of the mysterious flat tire. If this same scenario happened over and over again, to the point that every time anyone had a flat tire it proved to be due to a piece of sheet metal, this theory of flat tires could be advanced to the level of a *law*.

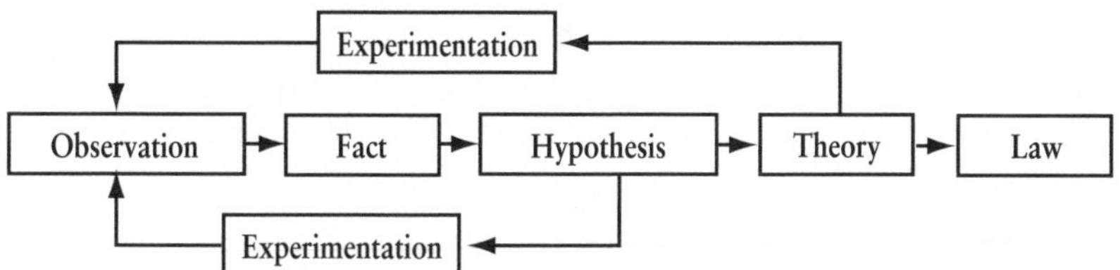

A law is a theory to which there is no known or ever anticipated exception. Very few theories in science ever reach the status of laws. "Every flat tire is caused by a piece of sheet metal" is untrue; this is obvious both from intuition and experience. The laws of thermodynamics, which govern energy and its transformations, and the law of gravity are examples of scientific laws. The explanations for the phenomena in all other "hard" sciences are, and likely always will be, theories. This carries with it the possibility that current theories might one day have to be abandoned if irreconcilable data come to light.

An illustrative example, not widely known outside the scientific community, involves the human immunodeficiency virus, HIV. The sequence of biochemical events that produces protein, a cardinal tenet of biochemistry, was always assumed to be:

DNA → RNA → Protein

It was only while attempting to discover how HIV functioned that enzymes were found that could produce DNA from RNA, thereby contradicting the i.e., dogma. The discovery of reverse transcriptases, i.e., enzymes that could "write" in the reverse direction (RNA —> DNA), mandated a reexamination of this long-held belief. The scientists involved had to be open-minded enough to consider the possibility that one of the great dogmas of biochemistry could be wrong. This is almost as great as clearly explaining how HIV works and what measures could then be employed to retard its reproduction and, hence, the growth of the virus.

Notice, as illustrated in the example just described, that any theory, to be valid, must be consistent with the then existing body of evidence. Whenever new data is discovered that is inconsistent with the current theory, that theory must either be modified to encompass the new data or abandoned altogether if the theory cannot be reconciled with the new data. Sometimes theories become so widely accepted that they are assumed to be "law." Occasionally, new information is discovered that forces scientists to bury a previously trusted theory.

The example above typifies the logic that characterizes the scientific method. It is this self-same approach that is utilized in all of science to clarify the cause-and-effect relationships in the respective disciplines. Contrary to popular opinion, the scientific method and, hence, science in general cannot produce conclusions that are immune to being disproved. What it does produce is logical self-consistency with respect to given data.

The previously cited laws of thermodynamics have been examined frequently enough that scientists are supremely confident that results inconsistent with them will never be found. In a real sense, such laws are truth. However, often scientists will likewise label the results of most experiments as truth. Attaching the same level of certainty to an experiment with a cause-and-effect principle described by a theory as to an experiment described by a law is unjustified and misleading.

Additionally, there is a wide spectrum of certainty associated with different theories. The quantum theory is a great deal more reliable than the theory of global warming. Although the term *truth* may be used to describe the conclusions from both studies, the terms nevertheless do not have the same meaning. What is one left to do? In this writer's judgment, the outcomes from all areas of science, except those described expressly by laws, should be taken logically, self-consistently, and rationally. A reasonable skepticism should be attached to all these results and a willingness to abandon the theory in the face of forthcoming data incompatible with the theory.

This inability to produce truth means that science cannot produce a correct worldview that is completely and totally reliable. It is of questionable utility to have a worldview that might have to be rewritten or discarded in light of future events. How then does one know if a worldview is correct? How does one test a worldview?

Finding the Correct Worldview

Perhaps, in a real sense, it is not immediately obvious how one can evaluate the correctness of a worldview. If one's worldview is to be evaluated in a meaningful way, it must be compared with truth. As has just been demonstrated, one cannot use science or, for that matter, any other body of human knowledge in part or in whole as a standard for evaluating a worldview. One can and most certainly should use the current state of human knowledge as a working model for problem-solving. On the other hand, it cannot be used as a compass for finding one's direction in the world regarding the issues of life.

In the same way that the numerical value associated with any scientific measurement is determined by the measurement of a property in comparison with an arbitrary, external, fixed standard to determine its meaning, so it is analogously true for a worldview. Since our society has implicitly agreed to the definition and hence the meaning of how long a foot is, and further that there are 5,280 feet in a mile, as well as twelve subdivisions of a foot called inches, the distance between any two geographical points can be determined. One merely determines how many times one must traverse the standard distance beginning with the starting point and moving to the final destination. Agreeing on the "truth" of how long a foot or a mile is allows us to determine distance with confidence.

The fact that the lengths of both feet and miles are arbitrary standards of physical measurement creates problems that are perhaps unanticipated. These standards are not in place in Europe and most of the rest of the world, since the SI[14] or metric system, as it is commonly known, is employed. Our system of the measurement of length is not transcendent. It is not always "true" in the sense that it can be successfully applied, utilized, and understood in every country and every culture. This has its origin in the fact that measurement standards are inherently arbitrary and not universally employed. If a standard is not universally agreed upon, the measurements have no meaning for those unfamiliar with the standard or who do not acknowledge that standard. For a standard to be of universal utility, it must be recognized as valid by all countries and cultures.

If a worldview is, likewise, to be of universal utility, it must be in agreement with a standard that depicts the way things really are. Since the way things really are is not a function of geography, culture, or ethnicity, a correct worldview must necessarily coincide with reality. One is immediately led to an obvious question: What is the standard that reflects the way things really are? "What is truth?" The question of Pontius Pilate some two thousand years ago (John 18:38) is just as cogent, just as pressing now as it was then. What is there that is an accurate, unchanging reflection of the way things really are?

The Reliable Standard

The only thing that is completely reliable as truth is the Word of God. This has been a cardinal tenet of orthodox Christianity through the ages.[15] This view is rooted in Scripture's testimony about itself and the fact that the Bible is inerrant.[16] The nature of Scripture (2 Tim 3:16-17; 2 Pet 1:21), being sourced out of the Godhead whose character is truth (Titus 1:2), must necessarily reflect that same character at every juncture (John 17:17). If this criterion is not met, either the veracity of God (Titus 1:2) or His immutability (Mal 3:6) is denied.

There is no doubt that many, if not most people would take more than passive exception to such a position. Today there is almost universal acceptance of the erroneous notion that truth is that which one personally acknowledges to be true. The fallacy of such a perspective should be clear. One could, for example, refuse to acknowledge that Abraham Lincoln (1809-1865) ever existed. Does this mean that the sixteenth President of the United States is a myth? Clearly this question need not be dignified with an answer. That Abraham Lincoln existed is easily demonstrable by countless pieces of irrefutable data. So the fact that one might deny the truth of Abraham Lincoln's existence in no way disproves any of the evidence. Whether one believes it or not has absolutely nothing to do with a statement's veracity. Either a statement is true to reality or it is not.

A person's response to a statement has no impact on the statement per se. However, the number of individuals who think a statement is true or not, based on their assessment, is staggering. Unfortunately, there are many Christians who rightly understand the nature of Scripture and its author, yet whose worldview is similarly impaired. In the 1970s one occasionally saw a bumper sticker on cars driven by Christians. The bumper sticker stated:

God said it.
I believe it.
That settles it.

The implication of such logic was supposed to be a declaration of the authority of Scripture. The fact that some harmony between God's and the car owner's view of Scripture somehow settled the issue of the authority of Scripture is not merely flawed—it is blatantly wrong. The ratification by people has nothing to do with truth. The bumper sticker should have been worded:

God said it.
That settles it.
(And it just so happens that) I believe it.

It is the fact that God said it that confirms it. The issue is the trustworthiness and authority of the author. When it has been established that the author is unimpeachable, then the issue has been decided. Since the fallibility of people is a point that is not debated, the shifting of one's confidence to the supreme authority should logically follow. For the unbeliever, it is his/her unwillingness to come to the light of God's authority, because of one's own sinfulness, that prevents this confession (John 3:19-20). For many scientists, confidence in man's knowledge and pride in human accomplishments are the specific sins that obstruct their path to an acknowledgment of God.

The veracity and complete trustworthiness of Scripture imply that when the Bible speaks to any area, despite the fact that the observation might not be directly a matter of faith and practice, it must be with the level of accuracy intended by God. The view has long been held that the Bible is true only when it deals with issues that are spiritual, but is somehow less reliable in areas outside the spiritual realm. These outside areas have been traditionally called secular. Thus, a *sacred-secular dichotomy* sprang up that, in many ways, continues to this day.

An attempt to bridge the gap between these two areas of understanding was proposed by Arthur F. Holmes.[17] Affirming that "all truth is God's truth," Holmes sought to make the study of creation a valuable and honorable exercise at a time when secular studies, especially the sciences, were deemed to be less lofty than theology. Sadly, this view of considering non-theological disciplines to be less worthy of study continues to be widely held in many Bible-believing churches today. Secular studies are often relegated to corners of intellectual endeavor where "spiritual" Christians should supposedly not traffic.

The result of such a dualistic perspective is that the overall authority and reliability of the Bible is undermined, because some areas of Scripture are not allowed to be brought to bear on scholarship. In practice, the lines of demarcation between the sacred and the secular in the Bible are at best vague. One cannot separate a sacred from a secular point of Scripture, because God cannot be separated from His creation. A consideration of the logical extrapolation of such a view reveals that one is left with a severely weakened Scripture (if one is intellectually honest) that cannot be implicitly trusted in any venue.

When the Bible addresses a matter of science such as physiology, astronomy, or any other area of study, it does so with an intended level of accuracy. However, this is not meant to imply that the Bible should be used as a textbook of science. That is not the purpose of Scripture. The purpose of Scripture is to reveal God to man. Even though it is not a textbook of science, because the Bible is truth, when it addresses any area of science it does so with the truthfulness of the divine author.

At the time when William Harvey (1578-1657) discovered the circulatory system, sick patients were routinely bled to remove "bad humors," which were falsely thought to be sources of illness. These practices undoubtedly resulted in the unnecessary deaths of large numbers of patients; yet the Scripture clearly states, "The life is . . . in the blood" (Lev 17:11). The medical implication, although not the primary intent of the passage, is clear. To take the blood is to take the life. Therefore, in general, bleeding a patient must be poor medicine, since it removes from the patient the very thing he/she needs to survive.

An additional example is found in Greek mythology that placed the earth on the shoulders of Atlas. Ancient Hindus placed the earth on the back of four elephants that, in turn, rested on the back of a turtle swimming in a sea of milk.[18] The biblical book of Job dates from the times of the Patriarchs,[19] many centuries before the first astronomical observations of the Renaissance began to reveal the intricacies of the solar system. Nevertheless, the book of Job correctly describes the position of the earth as suspended in space (26:7). The point cannot be overemphasized that when the Scripture intersects other disciplines, that point of contact is indeed trustworthy.

A source of information that truthfully addresses every issue is certainly true. Furthermore, the extent of the Bible's truthfulness so greatly exceeds that of science that describing it as truth hardly does it justice. In a real sense, the truth of the Bible should be called Truth, with a capital *T*. The deity of Christ, the virgin birth, the resurrection, and the atonement are examples of such Truth. And since the Bible's veracity, reliability, sufficiency, and accuracy extend from Genesis to Revelation, the creation account must be the same Truth.[20]

A worldview that would claim to be biblical must be one that can be harmonized with Scripture at every point of intersection. The worldview of most individuals—i.e., the means they use to function in the world and to understand the created order—has its value determined by a variety of means, with science playing a major role. Sometimes the issue is utilitarian, whether the worldview works in the sense that it explains reality. The search for the correct worldview apart from biblical Christianity can never lead to the one reliable methodology that comprehensively intersects Truth and reality. It is at this juncture that the immovable Word of God resides.

Approaching Scripture

A scientist's view of the Bible will have an enormous impact on how he/she functions as a scientist. Generally, scientists perceive Scripture in one of three ways. Dr. Douglas Bookman has accurately described the three basic approaches in the context of counseling.[21] He categorizes counselors on the basis of the relationship of their recommendations to the Word of God. Those who ignore the Scripture are called "No Book" theorists. "Two Book" theorists use an admixture of the Bible and psychology to counsel. Lastly, "Rule Book" theorists rely completely and totally upon the Bible as the sole resource for counseling.

Although his context is different, the explanation applies directly to science by analogy. In both instances the watershed question is, what is the ultimate authority? Just as counselors can take a "No Book," "Two Book," or "Rule Book"[22] approach to addressing this vital question regarding the role of the Bible in the context of counseling, so can every scientist. The role that Scripture plays in science has enormous influence for every scientist. Every scientist, either knowingly or unknowingly, makes decisions based on his/her worldview.

"No Book" Approach

A scientist who opts for a "No Book" approach completely ignores the contribution that the Bible might make to his/her scientific discipline. Such a scientist chooses to assume that Scripture is either wrong or irrelevant. This is the position that is normally adopted by agnostic or atheistic scientists and is by far the most common view of scientists. Such individuals turn their backs on the potential insights that Scripture offers, preferring to labor in spiritual darkness without benefit from the light of God's Word.

In this writer's judgment, this view can be traced to the Catholic Church's rejection of Galileo's (1564-1642) correct affirmation that the solar system is heliocentric—i.e., that the sun is the center of the solar system, not the earth. At this juncture, initial steps were taken by which a Christian worldview of science was lost. The concession that the Bible had nothing to offer scientists in conjunction with their investigations signaled the beginning of a parting of the ways between science and Christianity. These divergent journeys continue even to this day. What is particularly distressing is that the vast majority of both scientists and Christians have come to accept this as the norm, with each party unwilling to take a step toward the other.

Since the Catholic Church was wrong at this most pivotal point in the history of the development of science, it has since been widely assumed that the Catholic Church and organized religion, in general, are completely inept at understanding science. The consequence of this sad assumption is that the rightful role of a correct understanding of the Word of God and the supernatural were wrongly pushed to the periphery of scientific endeavor. Consequently, the separation naturally led to an antagonistic relationship between science and religion that continues unabated to this day.

The error that the Catholic Church made was not rooted in any inadequacy of Scripture, nor in the inability to understand Scripture. The church chose to adopt Aristotle's (384-322 B.C.) view of the solar system largely due to the teaching of Augustine (A.D. 354-430). The Catholic Church erred in placing man's understanding above Scripture. As a result anyone who has any religious perspective is now painted with the brush of early seventeenth-century Catholicism, a classic case of guilt by association. Such individuals traditionally are not given any credibility whatsoever as scientists by the scientific community at large.

"Two Book" Approach

In recent years a new perspective has enjoyed increasing popularity. This is the "Two Book" approach, which attempts to integrate two supposedly equal disciplines. Those scientists who hold this view are seeking to harmonize their understanding of science with their understanding of the Bible. This, in and of itself, is a laudable exercise that all believing scientists should seek to do at some level. The role of the Bible is necessarily paramount in the life of every believer, since the ultimate source of all that we understand of biblical Christianity, the work of God among men, and the life of Christ is rooted in Scripture. From the perspective of "Two Book" theorists, science and the Bible are two books that are both sources of truth that cannot be mutually contradictory. It is most certainly true that with two correct statements, there must be a way to harmonize them.

What happens when contradictions between science and the Bible arise within this "Two Book" framework? Consider these four possible scenarios: 1) Science is wrong, and the Bible is right. The data of science must be reinterpreted, measured again, or discarded as false, assuming that the interpretation of the pertinent Bible passage is correct. 2) Science is wrong, and the Bible, although inerrant, has been misinterpreted. The result is that both conclusions are wrong. Both areas need to be reexamined. 3) Science is right, and the Bible is right. This is an impossibility. This violates the principle of non-contradiction. The statements "A" and "not A" cannot both be simultaneously true. It cannot be both day and night in the same place at the same time. Both points of view should be reexamined. 4) Science is right, and the Bible is wrong, in that it has been misinterpreted. An infallible document must be misinterpreted to be wrong. The biblical text must be reevaluated.

The "Two Book" theorists err most often in the fourth scenario, assuming that their present understanding of science is right, and the Bible is wrongly interpreted. This is the position of theistic evolutionists who attempt to embrace Darwinism and the Bible equally, despite the obvious conflict. The difficulty in this case is removed by saying that God used evolution to produce the species that actually came into existence by a direct, creative act of God.

The consequence of this approach is that the clear teaching of Scripture has mistakenly been deemed less reliable than science. The sufficiency and authority of science now rests on a supposedly higher level than the Word of God. Fallible, fallen man now stands in judgment of an infallible, glorious, transcendent God. This parallels the elevation of tradition over and above the authority of Scripture in the Catholic Church,[23] much as the Pharisees did in Jesus' day (Mark 7:8-13). Evolution, like embracing a geocentric, Aristotelian view of the solar system, is indicative of a greater trust in man's judgment than in the divine perspective.

This radical and unjustified placement of science above Scripture has great and harmful implications. In this model, science has become the tool used to interpret the Word of God. Science determines the hermeneutic—i.e., the principles used to interpret the meaning of the Bible. The shortcoming of such a methodology lies in using a temporal technique, subject to change at any time and in an unpredictable way, to evaluate the Word of God sourced out of the eternal Sovereign of the Universe.

For example, one could consider the age of the earth. The Bible taken at face value speaks clearly and strongly for a relatively recent creation of the universe. Contrastingly, science currently argues for an age of the earth of about five billion years.[24] The order of magnitude of this proposed age has posed a problem in the interpretation of the Bible for those who favor the perspective of science. To be consistent with the current view of science, one has to insert long ages into the Genesis account of creation, which simply cannot be gleaned from the biblical text at face value.[25]

"One Book" Approach

Lastly, there is the "One Book" theorist. This individual is a scientist who willingly and candidly acknowledges that the Bible is inerrant, infallible, authoritative, and sufficient. He/she perceives Scripture as elevated to a position of authority and reliability that stands in judgment over all other areas of knowledge it intersects. The basis for this is a right view of the loftiness, grandeur, and glory of the divine author. The exalted view is then rightly ascribed to Scripture, since one cannot divorce the words of the author from His character.

The Bible, then, is the only source of tangible, eternal Truth on earth (Isa 40:8). This understanding ensures the total sufficiency of Scripture when applied to every issue addressed therein (Ps 19:7-14). Having embraced this view, a scientist looking at the universe recognizes that the entire creation is the handiwork of a sovereign God (John 1:3). His/her subsequent observations and explanations will be consistent with this perspective. Any observations that appear to be at odds with this declaration of the origin of creation will be reassessed in a way that does not deny the Truth of what God has clearly and unambiguously said He has done.

The "One Book" theorist cheerfully concedes that understanding is not something that God is obligated to provide. Even though the command was given to Adam and Eve to "subdue" the earth (Gen 1:28) and was repeated to Noah after the Flood (Gen 9:1-3), this theorist acknowledges that the understanding and ability required to be obedient to this mandate is likewise given by God.

He/she also grasps that God has promised to help man understand His Word (1 Cor 2:12-16), but God has never made that same guarantee regarding the universe. He/she will never seek to distort the Truth of the clear teaching of Scripture so that it conforms to some current theory of science. In short, a "One Book" theorist will always seek, at those points of intersection, to see that his/her science reflects the Truth of God's Word.

In the End

In becoming a "One Book" theorist, one gains the perspective on science that God intended. Certainly, a crucial part of this view is that science can be of great value to society and can contribute to a wonderful, correct, and *true* understanding of the universe that, in turn, can be used for the benefit of all mankind. To say otherwise is to deny the essence of science. There is also built into this conclusion an appreciation for the fact that *true* does not mean *True*. The distinction between the truth of science that is subject to change and the Truth of Scripture that is a reflection of the immutability of God is also a part of this view.

The adoption of the "One Book" worldview of science retraces the errant steps of contemporary science, begun centuries ago, and begins anew to tread the harmonious and compatible path it enjoys with the Scriptures. Knowledge from the scientific realm has been returned to its proper perspective as valuable, important, a source of logically, self-consistent learning, but in submission to the Word of God. The rightful place of the divine author's authority has been acknowledged. The proper use of the Scripture where it impinges on science has been reestablished. This understanding alone allows science to resume its correct place in epistemology.

The following poem, entitled "The True Scientist," appropriately summarizes this discussion. It was taken from the works of Andre-Marie Ampere (1775-1836), the French physicist who laid the foundations of electrodynamics and after whom the ampere, the unit of electrical current, was named.

> *Happy the one who in his learned watches,*
> *Contemplating the marvels of this vast universe,*
> *Before so much beauty, before so much grandeur,*
> *Bows the knee and acknowledges the divine creator.*
> *I do not share the foolish incoherence*
> *Of the scientist who would contest the existence of God,*
> *Who would close his ears to what the heavens declare,*
> *And refuse to see what shines before his eyes.*
> *To know God, to love him, to render to him a pure homage*
> *That is true knowledge and the study of the wise.*[26]

The final two lines most certainly epitomize the true scientist. His/her response to seeking the majesty of creation is to respond in confession that God alone is worthy of worship (Rom 1:20). The true scientist is not so foolish as to look at creation and deny the One who made it (Ps 14:1). He/she also rightly understands that to close one's eyes to the testimony of creation is not true science (Ps 19:1). To do so is illogical, irrational, and willful unbelief. His/her greatest desire is to know God, which is defined in Scripture to be eternal life (John 17:3). Indeed, this is a fitting description of a Christian view of science.

Further Reading

Lindsell, Harold. *The Battle for the Bible*. Grand Rapids, MI: Zondervan, 1978.

Morris, Henry M. *The Biblical Basis for Modern Science*. Grand Rapids, MI: Baker, 1984.

Ratzsch, Del. *Science and Its Limits*. Downers Grove, IL: IVP, 2000.

13

Why Christian Education and Not Secular Indoctrination?

John A. Hughes

Bobby, the oldest of Robert and Liz Green's four children, felt both excited and apprehensive as he boarded the plane to begin his freshman year at a prestigious eastern university. Bobby had grown up in a stable, loving, actively Christian, suburban family, attending church regularly and coming to know Christ as his Savior during his second grade year at the church's Christian school. Mr. and Mrs. Green were active, mature Christians and caring parents who were willing to make some financial sacrifices in order to enable their children to attend an academically-strong Christian school. Mr. Green was committed to making sure that his children were able to have some of the educational opportunities that he hadn't been able to have. He had begun working as a salesman for a local department store immediately after high school graduation. Through hard work and perseverance, he was now the manager of the store, a business that was both financially successful and a respected, popular shopping location for families throughout the county.

Bobby had excelled at the Christian high school academically, socially, and athletically. Consequently, good grades, high test scores, and a fair level of success as point guard on the school's conference-winning basketball team had landed Bobby several college scholarship offers. It seemed to both Bobby and his parents that the opportunity to attend the college for which he was now bound was too good to pass up, especially since he had received a full-ride scholarship there.

Even during the orientation week, Bobby realized that he was in for an extremely challenging experience. His senses were constantly assaulted by the open, casual attitudes and conversations about sexual topics in the coed dorm, the cafeteria, and the student union. The first week of class added to his anxiety when the professor in his philosophy survey course asked for a show of hands of those who called themselves "Christians." The ensuing foul-mouthed, verbal tirade shocked Bobby. Putting it politely, the professor promised that he would do all that he could to enlighten them to the naiveté and stupidity of their beliefs. Hopefully by the end of the semester, there would be few, if any, such idiots left.

Bobby attempted to find a solid church in which to worship and fellowship. Unfortunately, they were somewhat scarce in this college community. As the fall progressed, his Sunday morning attendance became more sporadic (as also did his personal devotions) with the increasing time demands from study, basketball practice, and travel for road games. He found out early in the semester never to challenge a professor's statements, no matter how outrageous, publicly in class. Just giving the professors what they wanted was the best strategy for avoiding conflict and public humiliation.

By semester break, Bobby was struggling with his faith and his walk with God. His parents saw it when he was home for Christmas (although only briefly because he had to get back to campus for a basketball tournament). By the end of his freshman year, Bobby was a changed man. He wasn't sure he believed in God. He knew for certain that there was no such thing as truth and that the Bible was arrogant to claim that there was. It was also quite clear to him that America, democracy, and capitalism were nothing more than schemes invented and perpetuated by a bunch of old, rich, white men who systematically exploited any and every other ethnic, cultural, and/or economically-underprivileged, underrepresented group that crossed their path. In the end Bobby decided that it was better not to think too hard, believe too much, or care too deeply about anyone else.

Bobby Green's story is intended to be completely fictional. Unfortunately, by changing the name and adjusting some of the story's details, most readers could transform this account into the actual experience of one or more of the promising young people from their own local church. It is a scenario that is repeated with heartbreaking frequency within most evangelical churches across America.

The purpose of this chapter is to explore what the Bible says about education and the educational process. It will hopefully provide readers with some insight about the critical issues that need to be considered when making educational choices for themselves and their children. Issues to be discussed will include the goals of education, educational responsibility, teacher qualifications, and educational curriculum guidelines.

Education Defined

It could be argued that education (the process of teaching and learning) is one of the most central functions within man's existence. Education is a process that is unique to man and is not shared to any significant degree with any other part of God's created world. While there is a measure of learning that takes place in animal young as they mature, inborn instincts provide much of the basis for their learning. While animal handlers using operant conditioning techniques have trained animals to perform a few significant and sometimes entertaining tasks, their work of weeks, months, or even years can never be compared with the learning that occurs in any first grade classroom of children in a week's time.

Further, it may be argued that God has established the educational process as the human mechanism for perpetuating and advancing life on earth. While God has provided every man and woman with the intellectual ability to reason, hypothesize, invent, philosophize, and theorize, it is the educational process that transmits the results of that person's intellectual activity to other individuals and to subsequent generations. And it is the knowledge and discoveries of the previous generations passed along to an individual through the educational process that serve as the input and the basis for his/her intellectual activity. It has accurately been said that each generation stands on the shoulders of the previous generations in developing an understanding of reality and of the universe in which they live. Consider whether it would be possible for civilization to advance without the mechanism of education. Is there any species of animal that has developed a substantially better lifestyle for its kind over the hundreds of generations of existence?

Education of one's self and of others is an ability that God has given uniquely to humans. Since this is the case, could it be considered an aspect of what it means to be made in the image of God? Certainly needing to learn is not a characteristic of God's nature because He is omniscient. However, could the ability and desire to pass along learning to other beings be considered a part of His character stamped on humans since the beginning of creation?

Teaching and learning are separate activities within the educational process. It is possible for an individual to learn without a teacher. Perhaps, in this case, the learner acts as his/her own teacher. On the other hand, it can be questioned whether teaching can be rightly said to occur in the absence of a learner or even in the presence of students who fail to learn. While education must address both teaching and learning, it tends to focus more on the what and how of the teaching side of the process so that effective learning will occur. Teaching can be seen as the cause of the educational process that produces the effect of learning.

Historical Influences That Shape Current Education

As in every aspect of life, the past shapes the present, so it is in the case of current-day educational philosophy and practice. A few of the most significant historical influences that have contributed to current educational thinking will be briefly summarized in the following paragraphs.

The philosophical conception of a "liberal education" began more than 2,500 years ago with the thinking of Socrates, Plato, and Aristotle. In books VII and VIII of *The Politics*, Aristotle describes the characteristics of a "liberal" education that would equip individuals for virtue, leisure, and capable citizenship.[1] The work of these philosophers was expanded and formalized by scholars in the Greek city of Alexandria. "Alexandrian scholarship emphasized an empirical approach to science and to the study of language and literature. . . . Alexandria's advanced studies were built on the current pattern of a broad general education, preparatory to the study of rhetoric and philosophy. This system had developed from the early Greek concern to nurture in youth the aristocratic virtues of their culture, virtues which by the fifth century B.C. had given way to more democratic ideals and which later still gave way to the humanistic values of the Hellenistic age."[2] Over time the Greek educational curriculum broadened to include physical training via gymnastics as well as vocal and instrumental musical instruction. The core of the liberal arts curriculum became formalized to include study in seven areas. The first three, known as the *trivium*, included grammar, rhetoric, and dialectic, while the second group of four, termed the *quadrivium*, included arithmetic, geometry, astronomy, and music.

During the rule of Constantine in the first half of the fourth century A.D., Christianity became first tolerated and then mandated within the Roman Empire. The church came to be understood as responsible for leadership and supervision of educational and scholarly activities. From the fourth to the tenth centuries, cathedral and episcopal schools taught children Christian doctrine as well as the seven liberal arts. "By the ninth century, Christians also had parochial (parish) schools from the cathedral or monastery."[3] The founding of the University of Bologna in A.D. 1158 is generally recognized as the birth of modern university-level education. "From their monastic roots and through the nineteenth century, all universities were founded as Christian institutions, regardless of whether they taught law, theology, or medicine."[4] It was in this intellectual soil that the seeds of the Reformation, the Renaissance, and the Enlightenment germinated and gave birth to modern science.

Christian scholars of the eighteenth-century Enlightenment period sought to develop a deeper understanding of the scope and complexity of the God-created, physical universe through the use of systematic observation and manipulation. They, however, clearly realized that *revealed truth* was authoritative whereas *discovered truth* needed to be held tentatively and never held when in contradiction to revealed truth. Through the next several centuries, rational thinking and scientific exploration became the recognized mechanism for discovering and defining truth. The authoritative role of the Bible was lost, even in many Christian circles. Today many Christian scholars perform amazing intellectual gymnastics to reinterpret clear teaching of Scriptures to fit current-day scientific theory in hope of gaining respectability with the secular, intellectual community. Biblical truth is held tentatively by them, and only when it is not in contradiction to scientific theory.

As rationalism gave birth to evolutionary theory, the goal and study of science shifted from discovery of God's wonderful creation to the development of scientific theories that could completely exclude God's involvement in the natural universe. The principles of the scientific method were extended to study of human behavior, giving birth to the social sciences. A foundational assumption of social science is that man is a natural, not a spiritual or moral, being, the product of evolutionary forces. Consequently, the doctrine of the depravity of man was completely rejected. Man was viewed as being either morally neutral or inherently good. Children's minds are essentially blank slates to be filled in by educators with the content that would shape them to provide the most positive value to society. Wrong behaviors are seen as resulting from a lack of education. Education is seen as the mechanism for equipping individuals with the knowledge, skills, and attitudes that will cause them to not engage in self-destructive, antisocial, or criminal behaviors and will inspire them to place the goals of society over their own personal goals. This foundational vision for the potential of education permeates virtually all of modern western society today.

The purpose, curriculum, and methods of education changed dramatically as a result of the Enlightenment. Rationalism dominated the selection and presentation of content in every subject field. The study of natural and social sciences competed for time and priority within the curriculum. The study of theology became marginalized, compartmentalized, and disassociated from consideration in any academic field outside of itself. Through the twentieth century, the methods of teaching changed as social scientists focused the application of experimentally-derived principles of psychology and sociology to the educational setting. Conditioning techniques developed by classical and behavioral psychologists were adapted for classroom use to enhance student learning and to control behavior.

This section would not be complete without consideration of the effect that the current postmodern worldview (see chapter 7 of this book for a more detailed discussion of postmodernism) has on educational philosophy and practice. The economic hardships and worldwide conflicts of the twentieth century seriously shook the western world's optimism and confidence in science as the key to truth, progress, and prosperity. The more cynical postmodern worldviews began to gain a wider acceptance. A cornerstone principle of these worldviews was the nonexistence of objective truth. In this worldview, "truth" was redefined to be a metanarrative (i.e., an all-encompassing explanatory model) that attempts to organize the flood of sensory inputs an individual receives each day. If truth is defined in this manner, no individual or group can claim to have a metanarrative scheme that is more valid than any other individual or group. Tolerance of all other viewpoints becomes a paramount mandate within a postmodern mind-set. However, tolerance is no longer defined as an individual's gracious response to a person holding erroneous viewpoints. Tolerance is now defined as the expectation that every person must abandon the belief that his/her understanding of truth has any more validity than any other person's viewpoint.

A societal consequence of postmodernism is the rise of tribalism. If truth is conceived to be a person's mental metanarrative to explain the world around him/her, then it would be natural that he/she will have more affinity for those individuals who share similar metanarratives and will have a distrust of those who have a significantly different understanding of reality. The heterogeneity of any large organization would make it automatically suspect. From a postmodern mind-set, history is primarily seen as the record of one dominating group imposing its perception of reality on less powerful groups.

The addition of the postmodern philosophy to the intellectual landscape has resulted in changes to educational philosophy and practice. There is still a strong dominating commitment to enlightenment and rationalism, especially in the sciences. Consideration of non-natural processes for the origin and development of the universe is simply prohibited by custom and, in many cases, by law. In those subject areas of the curriculum that are more inductively and subjectively derived (i.e., the social sciences and the humanities), the effects of postmodern thinking are more pervasive and chaotic. There is no objective basis upon which students or teachers can determine the rightness or significance of historical events, created works, or even individual actions. In this environment, curricular development at the state and federal levels degenerates to a political negotiation process by various interest groups to insure that their voice is heard and their perspectives represented in the curriculum. Similarly, a commonly accepted set of principles for assessing the aesthetic quality and contribution of individual pieces of literature, music, or art no longer exists. Curricula in these subjects is now selected with the primary goal of being representative of the diverse cultural voices within global society today. A postmodern philosophy also makes moral education impossible. At best, schools can only assist students in clarifying their own personal values.

While the preceding whirlwind survey of the historical development of educational philosophy has been extremely brief, hopefully it has given the reader a sense of how thoroughly Enlightenment and postmodern philosophy permeates current-day western educational purposes, curricula, and teaching methodology.

Biblical Principles Relating to Education

Our focus will now shift to consider what direction the Scriptures provide to help Christians define a biblical basis for the purpose and practice of education. A keyword search for the word *education* or *educated* in most translations of the Bible will result in few, if any, references. By this it might be concluded that education is not a particularly important focus of God's instruction to man. However, if education is conceived to be the process of teaching and learning, and a search is made of Scriptures to identify the use of these two terms and their related forms, the picture changes dramatically. These terms are used hundreds of times throughout the Word and provide significant guidance in defining a biblical philosophy of education. It should be recognized that the Bible was not written for the specific purpose of being a teacher preparation textbook, an exhaustive school curriculum outline, or a vocational training manual. However, the Scriptures do provide clear authoritative principles that can form a solid foundation and framework for the development of a God-honoring educational philosophy.

The Purpose and Goal of Education

Education gains purpose and significance to the extent it is consistent with and contributes toward accomplishment of God's highest purpose for man. Succinctly summarizing the teaching in scriptural passages such as Psalm 73:24-26, John 17:22-24, Romans 11:36, and 1 Corinthians 10:31, the Westminster Shorter Catechism states that "man's chief end is to glorify God, and to enjoy Him forever." The highest goal of education must then be to assist individuals in developing the knowledge, skills, and attitudes that will enable them to better glorify and enjoy God. There are a number of specific ways that education can assist people in their responsibility to pursue this highest of all of life's goals.

Jesus declared to the woman at the well that "God is spirit, and those who worship him must worship in spirit and truth" (John 4:24). Worship that honors God involves both the heart and the mind. A God-honoring education will constantly present opportunities and motivation for the student to worship God with broader knowledge of what is true and a deeper awe for God's person. Each academic discipline contains elements and dimensions that can assist the believer to better understand and appreciate the character and work of God. For example, the creation has been designed to testify to God's "eternal power and divine nature" (Rom 1:20). David wrote in Psalm 19:1, "The heavens declare the glory of God, and the sky above proclaims his handiwork." The more a believer learns about the creation through the study of the biological and physical sciences, the greater will be his/her awe for the immensity, variety, complexity, and detail of this universe that the all-powerful, all-knowing God spoke into existence (Gen 1:1) and actively holds together (Col 1:17). The study of human history provides much cause for worship as the student discovers how the King of the ages (1 Tim 1:17) orchestrates the events of history from the individual to the global level to accomplish His purposes and bring Himself glory. The study of the creative works in the fields of art, music, and literature should direct the student's mind to worship God who is full of beauty (Ps 27:4), the One who is the ultimate Creator of beautiful works and who gifts men with creative ability.

Paul challenges believers "to present your bodies as a living sacrifice, holy and acceptable to God, which is your spiritual worship. Do not be conformed to this world, but be transformed by the renewal of your mind, that by testing you may discern what is the will of God, what is good and acceptable and perfect" (Rom 12:1-2). God-honoring education will assist the Christian in this mental renewing process by providing a foundation of worldview assumptions and by cultivating logical thinking processes, habits of analysis, and patterns of evaluation that are distinctively biblical.

Believers are referred to as soldiers in a number of New Testament passages (Phil 2:25; 2 Tim 2:3; Philem 2). Christians are exhorted to recognize that they live in the middle of a war zone and are called to arm themselves for the battle (Eph 6:10-17). Contrary to how some current Christian groups would characterize it, the spiritual warfare described in the Scriptures is waged on the intellectual front. The mighty "weapons" that God has supplied us are to "destroy arguments and every lofty opinion raised against the knowledge of God, and take every thought captive to obey Christ" (2 Cor 10:4b-5). Jude challenged his readers "to contend for the faith that was once for all delivered to the saints" (v. 3b). Without question, believers are called by God to develop their minds for the purpose of intellectual warfare, and the educational process provides a key mechanism to assist the committed Christian toward obeying this mandate.

Properly focused education should also assist individuals to fulfill God's highest purpose through equipping them to live wisely. Throughout the book of Proverbs, Solomon forcefully admonishes the young person to pursue godly knowledge and wisdom. Receptivity to godly instruction produces wisdom. As he states in 9:9-10, "Give instruction to a wise man, and he will be still wiser; teach a righteous man, and he will increase in learning. The fear of the LORD is the beginning of wisdom, and the knowledge of the Holy One is insight." This "wisdom" and "insight" bring both honor to God and success in life (Josh 1:7-8; Prov 3:4).

Responsibility for Education

Having established that education should enable man to better fulfill his/her ultimate God-ordained purpose, and that the pursuit of knowledge and wisdom is commanded by God, the question of who is responsible for leadership in the educational process can next be considered. The Bible provides a number of very clear principles in this regard.

1. Every individual is ultimately accountable to God to be a learner. This principle of educational accountability is so often assumed that it is seldom explicitly stated. However, it needs to be articulated because it is the most foundational and most frequently declared educational accountability relationship in Scripture. God expects every individual in every stage of life to actively and thoughtfully seek to learn from every formal and informal educational opportunity. In Proverbs 2:1-4 phrases such as "receive my words . . . treasure up my commandments . . . making your ear attentive . . . inclining your heart . . . call out for insight . . . raise your voice . . . seek it like silver . . . search for it as for hidden treasures . . ." characterize the passion with which the godly individual is admonished to seek wisdom, understanding, and the knowledge of God. In fact, one of the key characteristics that distinguishes a wise man from a fool is his/her willingness to pursue wisdom or receive instruction (Prov 1:22; 9:7-10; 15:5).

God's most direct instruction to the individual comes explicitly through the Bible and implicitly through the experiences He brings into the individual's life. God expects man to view life's experiences as non-formal educational opportunities and to learn from them. It is obvious from the comprehensive digest of positive and negative character traits presented in

Proverbs that Solomon was a student of human behavior, thoughtfully observing and analyzing people's reactions to life's situations. It is also clear from 1 Kings 4:33-34 and the illustrations presented in Proverbs that Solomon actively devoted himself to study of the natural world around him. Job challenged his comforters to look to nature to learn how God is the sustainer of all life (Job 12:7-10). The kings of Israel were commanded to take responsibility for learning by personally writing out a copy of the law and then reading it repeatedly throughout their lives (Deut 17:18-19). The young Lord Jesus modeled being an active learner during His time with the teachers at the Temple (Luke 2:46-47). He later "learned obedience through what he suffered" (Heb 5:8). Paul learned contentment through material highs and lows (Phil 4:11-12). It seems that many current-day educational settings fail to emphasize this principle for students to take the responsibility for their own learning.

While God holds every individual responsible for being a learner, He also provides the necessary enablement for the task through His own indwelling presence in the person of His Holy Spirit. This is particularly true in regard to understanding spiritual matters, as Paul makes clear in 1 Corinthians 2:1-16. It is the Holy Spirit who reveals the deep things of God (v. 10), and by virtue of His presence we have the mind of Christ (v. 16). John specifically refers to the Holy Spirit as "the Spirit of truth" in John 14:17, 15:26, and 16:13. Paul reminded Timothy that "God gave us a spirit not of fear but of power and love and self-control" (2 Tim 1:7). The Greek term translated "self-control" is sometimes translated "a sound mind" (NKJV). The Holy Spirit assists the believer in clear, disciplined thinking.

2. *Parents, particularly fathers, are responsible for the education of their children.* Beyond the responsibility that God gives to every individual to be a learner, He has given specific responsibility for the formal education of children to parents. God explicitly commanded that Israelite parents teach their children the Mosaic law (Deut 4:9; 6:7-8; 11:19). God commanded memorials to be set up, such as the Israelites built after they had crossed the Jordan River to enter the Promised Land (Josh 4), to provide opportunities for parents to rehearse the history of their nation with their children (Josh 4:6-7). The command to honor one's father and mother (Ex 20:12) implies the attitude of a humble learner toward one's parents. Solomon's admonitions for a young person to hear the instruction of his/her father and mother carries the obvious implication that the parents are responsible to provide that instruction. Our Lord endorsed the educational role of the home by submitting to His parents as He "increased in wisdom and stature and in favor with God and man" (Luke 2:52).

3. *Education is not an explicitly mandated function of government.* Given today's almost complete governmental control of the formal educational process of children, it is appropriate to ask whether this is either mandated or allowed by Scripture. The Bible contains no expectation for or against governmental involvement in education either prior to the establishment of Israel or in the New Testament. But even within the nation of Israel, the home was seen as the primary mechanism for education.

It should be noted that in the Old Testament, education was not explicitly listed as a responsibility of the priesthood. However, there are examples of Levites and priests being involved in educational tasks during the time of King Jehoshaphat (2 Chron 17:7-9) and after Israel's return from captivity (Neh 8:1-9). Ezra, a priest and scribe, took leadership in this teaching role, as indicated in Ezra 7:10: "Ezra had set his heart to study the Law of the Lord, and to do it and to teach his statutes and rules in Israel." By the beginning of the New Testament, the role of teachers (rabbis) and scribes had grown significantly and was intertwined with the Jewish religious and civil functions.

The existence of governmentally controlled educational systems is mentioned in relation to both the lives of Moses and Daniel. It should be noted that neither individual is commended or condemned for having been educated within the context of those secular education systems.

4. *The spiritual leadership within the local church is responsible for the education of its membership.* Our Lord's parting command to the disciples (commonly known as the Great Commission) was to evangelize the nations and to teach believers (Matt 28:19-20). Ten days later the New Testament church was founded as the organizational entity God would use to fulfill this command (Acts 2). The central activities of the church as seen throughout the book of Acts included evangelism, fellowship, teaching, and corporate prayer. The Bereans were specifically commended by Luke for their initiative to verify the accuracy of the teaching they were receiving (Acts 17:11). One of the specific qualifications for elder leadership within the local church is an ability to teach (1 Tim 3:2; Titus 1:9). There is an expectation within every local congregation for experienced, mature believers to teach the younger believers (Titus 2:1-3) and that those who were taught would eventually mature to become teachers for the next generation of learners (2 Tim 2:2; Heb. 5:12).

It could be argued that it is primarily "religious education" that is the mandate and focus of education within the church. If this is so, it is religious education in the broad rather than the narrow sense of the term. The basis of this educational experience was the Scriptures, which are not only able to make one wise to salvation, but also profitable to make the man of

God perfect, thoroughly furnished for every good work (2 Tim 3:15-17). On a philosophical level, it had to be broad enough to transform the believer's mind so it was not conformed to the thinking of the world (Rom 12:2) and to equip the believer for ideological warfare (2 Cor 10:3-5; Eph 6:12; Col 2:8). As is discussed in other chapters of this book, the Scriptures provide a foundation and framework for study in every academic discipline and all areas of life.

It would be appropriate for local church leadership to consider whether their educational vision, structure, and programs "equip the saints for the work of ministry" (Eph 4:12) in this larger context. Some questions that should be asked when considering the broader scope of the church's educational ministry include:

- Is the Sunday school and church curriculum structured in a way that will both enable and encourage students to apply biblical principles to the breadth of those subject areas commonly taught in elementary and secondary schools?
- What is the local church's equipping responsibility toward their children and young people in the congregation who are in formal school settings?
- Are specific steps being taken to equip children who attend secular elementary or secondary schools to identify and refute the false philosophies they encounter on a daily basis?
- As children mature, is there a corresponding advancement in the content and intellectual level of the church's Sunday school and youth curriculum? It seems unfortunate that many Christian teenagers wrestle with serious study of calculus, physics, world history, and literature each Monday through Friday, but are presented a church youth curriculum that is extremely weak in rigor or academic challenge.
- Does the church sense a calling to operate a Christian school that would offer a complete alternative educational experience to their children? While an individual local church may not have the resources to effectively operate a Christian school, are there possibilities to partner with other local-area, theologically like-minded churches in this type of enterprise?
- Is there a supportive structure for those parents who choose to personally complete this educational responsibility of their children through home schooling?
- What is the church's responsibility to its young people at the post-secondary educational level? The educational investment that parents and the church have made to provide a young person a solid biblical foundation can be lost during the transition from youth to adulthood. What

steps can be taken prior to the student's departure to equip him/her for this challenge?

• To what extent should the church promote and support Christian colleges as a post-secondary educational option for their young people?

As the leadership within a local church body considers these issues, a vision will be developed for the broader scope of the educational responsibility that God has given to the church.

Qualifications for Teachers

Having outlined the biblical purpose of and responsibility for the educational process in the development of children and young believers, the qualifications for and characteristics of effective teachers can now be considered. The Bible sets forth high standards for those who would accept the responsibility to be teachers. James 3:1 makes it clear that God will judge teachers' speech even more strictly than that of others. One of the reasons for this higher expectation for teachers is that learners trust their teachers to speak the truth. In fact, the educational process can only function effectively when that trust exists. The whole of James 3 describes the powerful role of spoken communication in every person's life as a tool for good and evil. The teacher is cited as the archetypical example of this principle. A godly teacher, then, must have a supreme commitment to always speak what is true, edifying, and wise.

While a teacher's words are a primary mechanism for instruction to students, his/her actions will inevitably have a significant effect on what the students ultimately learn. The teacher's character and behavior serve as a model for the students. Our Lord made it clear that "A disciple is not above his teacher, but everyone when he is fully trained will be like his teacher" (Luke 6:40). Association will ultimately affect an individual's character, as is made clear in 1 Corinthians 15:33: "Do not be deceived: 'Bad company ruins good morals.'" We are counseled not to have friendship with an angry man (Prov 22:24), in order to avoid the influence of his/her character.

In selecting who to prepare for the teaching ministry in the church at Ephesus, Timothy was commanded to "entrust [what he had been taught] to faithful men who will be able to teach others also" (2 Tim 2:2). A significant portion of the elder qualifications (which included the ability to teach) listed in 1 Timothy 3 focus on character qualities. Paul recognized the need for teachers to have an ability to communicate effectively, a commitment to the truth, and a life that would serve as a model to the students.

While consideration of personal character is a strong factor in selecting teachers for religious educational settings such as Sunday school or youth group, it is rarely given as much weight in selection of teachers in the broader educational context. To what extent do most Christian parents take purposeful steps to get to know the character quality of the teacher in the classroom of their son or daughter? At the elementary educational level, their child will spend more time being influenced by that model figure than by any other adult with the possible exception of the parents themselves.

Educational Methodology

Since the Bible was not written for the primary purpose of being a teacher training manual, it does not provide clearly enumerated lists of various teaching techniques or directions for when and how to effectively use each. However, since God designed the Bible as an instructional book (2 Tim 3:16), it is possible to identify effective teaching methods by examining the techniques and approaches that He embedded in Scripture.

On the larger scope, the educational process is characterized as the process of moving the student from being a dependent learner to being an independent learner to being a teacher (Ezra 7:10; 2 Tim 2:2; Heb 5:12-14). The two primary settings in which a formal educational process occurred in the biblical context were the home and church. Beyond these two educational venues, the Bible alludes to several examples of the use of discipling relationships (similar to apprenticeships) and organized schools to perform educational activities. Samuel was apprenticed to Eli (1 Sam 1—2) to prepare him for the prophetic ministry. Elisha served under Elijah for a time before he assumed Elijah's prophetic mantle (1 Kgs 19:19—2 Kgs 2:18). Paul took personal mentoring responsibility for a number of young men, including Titus and Timothy, to prepare them for later ministry leadership roles. The only explicit biblical reference to a school relates to the "school of Tyrannus" in Corinth (Acts 19:9, NKJV).

The essence of teaching is communication of information, concepts, and skills from the teacher to the learner by use of language and example. The use of verbal instruction as an educational medium began on the sixth day of the world's existence when our Heavenly Father instructed Adam what he should and should not eat in the garden (Gen 2:16-17). It might be reasonably supposed that the walks Adam and Eve had with God in the cool of the evening (Gen 3:8) had, at least in part, an instructional purpose. The Pentateuch could be considered the first biblical use of written materials as an instructional methodology. The Bible contains many examples of the teaching-learning process being conducted through the use of written instructional materials. Virtually all of the New Testament writers seemed to have an instructional goal in mind as they authored their books. Written materials have a benefit over verbal instruction in that there is a permanence to written instruction that will continue to allow for learning in the absence of the teacher.

Scriptures provide us with many examples of teaching being conducted via verbal instruction. When teaching involved a small group of learners, such as Jesus teaching His disciples, it seems that a Socratic, didactic, question-and-answer interaction style was used by the teacher. It is important to note a distinction between this Socratic interaction and what is commonly referred to as a group discussion method. In the Socratic method, the communication is teacher-focused and teacher-controlled. The teacher presents information and asks questions. Students direct their questions and responses back to the teacher. In a discussion the communication begins with the teacher's question but then flows from one student to another. There are few, if any, instances in the Bible of discussions being used as a formal instructional method. The biblical examples of verbal, small-group teaching were teacher-focused. The use of this approach can be seen in Jesus' upper-room discourse with His disciples, particularly the section recorded in John 13:31—14:31. As groups increased in size, the verbal instruction transitioned to more of a lecture-style presentation with less frequent interaction by the students. This can be seen in our Lord's Sermon on the Mount (Matt 5—7) and Peter's message on the day of Pentecost (Acts 2:14-39).

Effective use of language to provide engaging and clear communication is at the heart of every good teaching methodology, whether in verbal or written form. With God as the author of language and the master teacher, the Bible provides an authoritative example for how language can be used to make teaching as effective as possible. Dr. Roy Zuck in *Teaching as Paul Taught* provides an outstanding analysis of how Paul used language in his letters to teach effectively. Some of the linguistic devices cited include:

Simile
Metaphor
Personification
Anthropomorphism
Euphemism
Hyperbole
Litotes
Irony
Sarcasm
Paradox
Oxymoron
Humor
Pun
Alliteration
Assonance
Maxims
Synonyms
Antithesis
Lists
Idioms
Parallelisms[5]

Another important instructional feature that should be noted in the scriptural examples of written and verbal instruction is the effective use of questions to challenge and direct the learner. Dr. Zuck points out that Paul used questions for the following purposes in his letters:

- To petition for information or to recall facts
- To pull persons up short
- To procure assent or agreement
- To promote thinking or reflection
- To prod for an opinion
- To prick the conscience
- To press for application of the truth
- To point out something contrary to fact
- To push for a conclusion
- To pour out an emotion
- To probe for motives[6]

Beyond the use of written and verbal instruction, several other methods for promoting effective learning are found in the Scriptures. God used a "discovery learning exercise" in which He had Adam name every species of animal that He had created in order to show Adam that there was not yet an appropriate helpmate for him (Gen 2:18-21). The importance of distributed practice, repetition, over-learning, and conspicuously-placed visual aids to promote effective learning is clearly seen in God's command to the Israelites:

> *"And these words that I command you today shall be on your heart. You shall teach them diligently to your children, and shall talk of them when you sit in your house, and when you walk by the way, and when you lie down, and when you rise. You shall bind them as a sign on your hand, and they shall be as frontlets between your eyes. You shall write them on the doorposts of your house and on your gates."*
>
> —DEUT 6:6-9

The Scriptures identify the value of using rhymes and songs to assist in the memorization process. God instructed the Israelites: "Now therefore write this song and teach it to the people of Israel. Put it in their mouths, that this song may be a witness for me against the people of Israel" (Deut 31:19). The largest single book in Scripture is a songbook—Psalms.

Educational Curriculum Guidelines

A final question to be considered is: To what extent does the Bible identify subject areas and topics that are either required or prohibited within a biblically-focused educational experience? First, the very term *biblically-focused education* implies that study of the Bible must be a central emphasis in the curriculum. Many scriptural passages can be cited in support of this principle. The importance and personal benefits of knowing God's Word is made abundantly clear in Psalm 119. Second Timothy 3:16 speaks to the comprehensive and authoritative nature of the Scriptures in equipping the man of God for every good work. Paul directly commands Timothy, "Study to show thyself approved unto God, a workman that needeth not to be ashamed, rightly dividing the word of truth" (2 Tim 2:15, KJV).

Within the study of Scripture, theology should have a position of particular importance. Paul, borrowing the words of a Greek poet, declared that in God "we live and move and have our being" (Acts 17:28). John writes that Christ is the Word incarnate (John 1:1-4, 14). Some would argue that in using the term *logos* John meant that Christ is the underlying rationale for existence within the physical universe. He is the Creator of all and the giver of life. He is full of truth (John 1:14) and *is* the truth (John 14:6). In Christ "are hidden all the treasures of wisdom and knowledge" (Col 2:3).

At the other end of the curricular continuum, there are some specific areas that are explicitly prohibited from inclusion in a biblically-focused education. Paul desired that the Roman believers "be wise as to what is good and innocent as to what is evil" (Rom 16:19). While Philippians 4:8 directs Christians to focus their thoughts on what is true, it also sets out additional qualifications that the thought areas should be, including "honorable," "just," "pure," "lovely," "commendable," excellent (or virtuous), and "worthy of praise." The church in Ephesus was to "take no part in the unfruitful works of darkness, but instead expose them. For it is shameful even to speak of the things that they do in secret" (Eph 5:11-12). Biblically-focused teachers should recognize there are topical areas that, while true and historical, are so shameful that they should be avoided.

In his last letter to Timothy, Paul shared a number of guidelines for that pastor's teaching ministry that included exhorting his people "not to quarrel about words, which does no good, but only ruins the hearers" (2 Tim 2:14); he added, "avoid irreverent babble, for it will lead people into more and more ungodliness" (v. 16), and "have nothing to do with foolish, ignorant controversies; you know that they breed quarrels" (v. 23). The Christian teacher needs to be sure to select content to be taught that has substance and inherent weight, rather than focusing on speculative and vaporous topics or arguing over semantics.

To some extent, the principle that Paul gave to the Corinthians is relevant in this regard. He taught that while all things were lawful for him, all things were not helpful (1 Cor 6:12), some things were too powerful and likely to enslave him (1 Cor 6:12), and some things would not build him up (1 Cor 10:23). Teachers need to be very sensitive in the selection of topics to be taught and also in the way selected topics are presented, to avoid inadvertently cultivating any of these possible negative side effects in the lives of their students. In most situations, the student could be considered the weaker brother of Romans 14, and it is the responsibility of the teacher not to put a stumbling block in his/her way. The Lord emphasized this principle in the teaching of children when He said, "Whoever causes one of these little ones who believe in me to sin, it would be better for him if a great millstone were hung around his neck and he were thrown into the sea" (Mark 9:42).

The preceding discussion should not, however, be taken as an excuse for a student to avoid study of subject areas that are personally objectionable and/or with which he/she philosophically disagrees. In their book *Christian Education: Its Mandate and Mission*,[7] the Bob Jones University faculty presents an outstanding discussion of this issue. A chapter in that book identifies the following seven types of objectionable elements: profanity, scatological realism (specific references to excrement), erotic realism, sexual perversion, lurid violence, occultism, and erroneous religious or philosophical assumptions. The chapter describes the strengths and weaknesses of the three major approaches taken by Christians in regard to censorship in these areas (permissivistic, exclusivistic, and pragmatic) and argues that the biblical approach is distinctly different from any of them. It makes the point that the Bible includes all seven types of censorable elements for instructional purposes and recommends that the three biblically-derived criteria of gratuitousness, explicitness, and moral tone must be carefully analyzed in each case of possible censorship when making curricular decisions.

Having briefly described those curricular areas of study that are either explicitly mandated or prohibited by Scripture, there remains a vast middle ground of subjects and topics that the believer is free to explore. There are many subject areas within this category for which Scripture provides implied encouragement for study as a means to enable believers to more effectively glorify and serve God. For example, serious study of God's Word requires an individual to have a well-developed reading ability with a reasonably broad vocabulary as well as strong analytical and critical thinking skills. The command about "always being prepared to make a defense to anyone who asks you for a reason for the hope that is in you" (1 Pet 3:15) implies the need for development of spoken communication and rhetorical skills. It could be reasonably argued that a careful study of history and philosophy is a necessary part of preparation for spiritual warfare to enable believers both to avoid being taken captive "by philosophy and empty deceit, according to human tradition, according to the elemental spirits of the world, and not according to Christ" (Col 2:8) and also to "destroy arguments and every lofty opinion raised against the knowledge of God, and take every thought captive to obey Christ" (2 Cor 10:5). To view one Christian college faculty's perspective about the breadth of subjects and skills that are important areas for study in the context of an undergraduate educational experience, the reader should visit the academic programs section of The Master's University website (www.masters.edu).

The example of biblical figures also provides encouragement for a breadth of study on our part. Job and Solomon demonstrated an in-depth understanding of nature. It is recorded that Daniel and his Hebrew colleagues received extensive training in "the literature and language of the Chaldeans" (Dan 1:4). In fact, God gave them special enablement in this study of secular pagan literature (Dan 1:17) so that "in every matter of wisdom and understanding about which the king inquired of them, he found them ten times better than all the magicians and enchanters that were in all his kingdom" (Dan 1:20). Paul's frequent use of secular Greek literature in his messages make it clear that he had studied this subject area in some depth. The study of art and music are endorsed through the biblical examples of Bezalel (Ex 31:1-5), David, and Asaph.

FOOD FOR THOUGHT

This chapter has highlighted the differences between a secular and biblical focus in regard to the purpose, methods, and content of education. The highest goal of education must be consistent with God's larger purposes—to equip individuals to more effectively glorify God through worship and service. First, priority must be given within the curriculum to the centrality of Scripture. Beyond that, curricular choices should be centered around scriptural principles to equip students in a broader context, avoiding some destructive topic areas and handling other content with sensitivity to the maturity level of the pupils. God holds teachers to a high standard of accountability for their curricular choices, the methods they use, and the personal examples their lives model to the students.

Parents, pastors, and teachers must consider the choices they make for their own continuing education, their children's education, and the educational strategies they recommend for others in their sphere of influence. Current-day, western, public schooling at the elementary, secondary, and collegial levels is, at its best, oblivious to biblical principles of education and more often completely adversarial to them. What steps are pastors and parents taking to counteract the secularizing effects of public schooling in the lives of their children, young people, and collegians? Christian school principals and Christian college academic deans must similarly consider the effect that public school training has had on the perspectives and methods of many of their faculty members and how they can provide effective reeducation in these areas. A thoughtful and definite response must be given to these issues if the church is to provide a biblically-focused education to equip the next generation of Christian leaders and laypeople.

FURTHER READING

Horton, Ronald A., ed. *Christian Education: Its Mandate and Mission.* Greenville, SC: Bob Jones University Press, 1992.

Gaebelein, Frank and Derek J. Keenan. *Christian Education in a Democracy.* Colorado Springs: Association of Christian Schools International, 1995.

Greene, Albert E. *Reclaiming the Future of Christian Education: A Transforming Vision.* Colorado Springs: Association of Christian Schools International, 1998.

Holmes, Arthur F. *The Idea of a Christian College*, rev. ed. Grand Rapids, MI: William B. Eerdmans, 1999.

Moreland, J. P. *Love Your God with All Your Mind: The Role of Reason in the Life of the Soul.* Colorado Springs: NavPress, 1997.

14

Reflecting Honestly on History

Clyde P. Greer, Jr.

God created time and space. A supreme, transcendent, self-sufficient, self-existent, personal God stepped out of eternity to inaugurate history. On the sixth day of history, God created people. "Then God said, 'Let us make man in our image, after our likeness. And let them have dominion . . .'" (Gen 1:26).

God created human beings in His image with the rational faculties necessary for exercising dominion over His creation. Using amazing but fallen minds, men and women now research God's universe of time and space. Astronomers, geographers, and others investigate the solar system and the earth. Historians study events in time.

What Is History?

History is "more than dates and dead people."[1] "Everyone knows, of course, what history was and is: quite simply, the study of the past."[2] "History . . . may be defined as the interpreted literary reconstruction of the socially significant human past, based on data from documents studied by scientific methods."[3] Multitudes of other definitions abound. The etymology of the word *history*, however, illuminates the two basic ways people use the word. The Greek *historia* relates to *knowing* about the past—the written record and interpretation based on deliberate inquiry. The German *geschichte* connotes the *events* of the past. Thus the past itself is history—everything that has ever occurred (*geschichte*). People also classify the written accounts of incidents of the past as history (*historia*).[4] This chapter will employ both of the main meanings of the word *history* (the past itself or the study of the past); the context should clearly indicate which fits best.

How much of the past do historians study? In a classic primer on the discipline, one scholar declared, "History studies everything that man has ever been or tried to be."[5] A recent appraisal begins by stating, "All of human experience falls within the purview of historians."[6] History obviously comprises a vast field of study. In addition, it grows larger every day with the passage of time. Furthermore, Christians often attempt to discern God's superintendence of history.

WHY STUDY HISTORY?

Why do schools routinely require young people to study history? Through the ages, many students who endured tedious, unimaginative, classroom history teaching found the subject only slightly more tolerable than their bland cafeteria lunches. These students have wondered why school officials force them to study history when it appears to have nothing to do with their consuming quest for pleasant weekend social activities. Why study history?

Identity, Citizenship, Wisdom, Pleasure

Individuals need a personal, historical memory to follow the advice of Socrates—"know yourself." The study of history can likewise build group identities. If "history is the memory of mankind,"[7] then widespread historical amnesia—i.e., ignorance or neglect of history—could cause a collective identity crisis, even on a national level. Political leaders and educational administrators, therefore, require students to study history as part of the process of political socialization—identifying with the nation and participating in its public life. Wise people look to history for moral and practical guidance. Individuals, groups, and nation-states can gain insights into present decision-making for the future by studying the past.

Beyond these pragmatic rationales for studying history, many people simply enjoy history. Judging by attendance figures at historical movies, museums, and heritage sites, as well as best selling reading lists, hits on historical websites, and memberships in historical societies, a huge public hunger for history exists. Unfortunately, that appetite frequently gets satisfied with junk food—e.g., docudramas and movies that freely mix fact and fiction.[8] People need to know history to avoid being misled. Professional historians could serve the public well in these confusing situations. They can "point out twistings and falsifications and other mistakes and shortcomings in this or that kind of historical representation . . . [because] the purpose of history is the reduction of untruth."[9]

Edification

Mature Christians, of all people, should greatly appreciate history. Why? "For Christianity . . . is essentially a historical religion: a religion, that is, whose prime dogmas are based on events."[10] Recording real events in time, historical books make up much of the Bible. Biblical characters lived in real time, not as mythical or legendary figures. The Fall, Flood, Exodus, Conquest, Exile, Incarnation, Crucifixion, Resurrection, and Ascension occurred in real history.

In Scripture, God admonished His children to learn from history. "Remember the days of old; consider the years of many generations" (Deut 32:7a). "Give ear, O my people, to my teaching; incline your ears to the words of my mouth! I will open my mouth in a parable; I will utter dark sayings from of old, things that we have heard and known, that our fathers have told us. We will not hide them from their children, but tell to the coming generation . . ." (Ps 78:1-4a). God's Word repeatedly rehearses Israel's history (Deut 1—3; Josh 24:1-13; Ps 105; 106; 136). Even in the New Testament, the apostle Paul reviewed some Old Testament history (1 Cor 10:1-10). He then explained one reason to study such history: "Now these things happened to them as an example, but they were written down for our instruction . . ." (v. 11a). In Acts 7, Stephen delivered a long history lecture before his hearers stoned him to death. (Modern history teachers should be happy that their listeners do not follow this practice.)

Why did God include so many history lessons (conscious reflections about the past) as well as basic history (accounts of what happened) in His inerrant Word? Biblical history helped reinforce the special identity of God's people, but more importantly, it reminded them of His faithfulness. He had worked with a mighty arm in the past. That would reassure them that, despite occasional chastening, He would keep His covenants and fulfill His promises for the present and future. Believers today are blessed by reading this history too.

Of course, God did not retire from involvement in the unfolding of history after biblical times. He did not cease acting in human history after the closing of the canon. Christians should study God's working in His church through the ages, according to Philip Schaff, known as "the founder of the discipline of church history in America."

> How shall we labour with any effect to build up the Church, if we have no thorough knowledge of her history, or fail to apprehend it from the proper point of observation? History is, and must ever continue to be, next to God's word, the richest fountain of wisdom, and the surest guide to all successful practical activity.[11]

Christians certainly have many compelling reasons to study history: faith enhancement, enjoyment, gaining wisdom, citizenship training, and identity development. History, as a field of study, deserves a high status in the church of Jesus Christ.

History of History

History has a history. "Historiography" refers to the "discipline of writing history."[12] People have been writing purposefully about the past for centuries. The ways in which historians approached the past, studied records, and then wrote the stories of past events, however, have all changed over time. "Because of this element of subjectivity in the historical process, any study of meaning in history should include a study of how men have written and interpreted history in other eras."[13] The following sections succinctly summarize the main ideas, works, and worldviews of a few of the western world's most influential historians over the course of time.

Premodern History

The term *premodern* refers to both ancient and medieval eras in western civilization. Traditionally, historians in the West have classified as "ancient" that history from Creation to about A.D. 500, the approximate date for the fall of the Roman Empire and the accompanying end of the cultural synthesis of classical antiquity. The Medieval period, or Middle Ages, encompasses the millennium from roughly A.D. 500 to about A.D. 1500. After the Scientific Revolution and Age of Enlightenment changed medieval mind-sets, western history became *modern*.

Ancient Historians

Like all ancient peoples, the ancient Hebrews and Greeks made history in the German *geschichte* sense of the word—they participated in *events* during past times, but they did much more. They created history in the Greek sense of *historia*—they intentionally wrote meaningful interpretations of past events. In contrast, most non-western civilizations, in ancient times and sometimes continuing onward to the present, have envisioned the past as a series of infinite cycles without intrinsic meaning, unworthy of serious reflection.

Herodotus (ca. 484-420 B.C.), the Greek historian known as the "father of history," chronicled the war between Greece and Persia. Though he loved a good story, "he clearly distinguished in his history between what was based on hearsay and what he had seen and heard personally or had learned by inquiry."[14] Following Herodotus, Thucydides described the Peloponnesian war. The "father of scientific history," Thucydides (ca. 460-395 B.C.) developed rigorous standards for critically checking the accuracy of sources, rejecting supernatural explanations altogether. "The absence of romance in my history will, I fear, detract somewhat from its interest; but if it be judged useful by those inquirers who desire an exact knowledge of the past as an aid to the interpretation of the future . . . I shall be content."[15] He and later Greek historians clearly distinguished their works, which they intended to be true, from poetry and other forms of imaginative literature.

The Greek contention that history establishes practical "exact knowledge" of "particular facts" about the past to guide people in the present and future would provide a bedrock foundation for the writing of history. After the ancient Hebrews and Greeks, "for the next two thousand years . . . there was no profound change in the nature of historical thinking."[16]

> Hebrew historians were the first to have any real philosophy of history. Their development of a linear rather than cyclical concept of time and their consciousness of the unity of the [human] race under one God opened the way for such a philosophy. They also, unlike other ancient people, looked to a future golden age under their Messiah rather than to a past golden age. God as well as man is shaping history, in their view. History is a process that will come to a meaningful climax under the guidance of God. This approach gave a new perspective and wholeness to human history.[17]

"The Jewish messianic and eschatological consciousness was of course handed on to the Christians."[18] That linear and universal perspective dominated premodern Christian historiography and continues to constitute a fundamental component of any biblical view of history today.

The famous Latin Church Father Augustine (A.D. 354-430), bishop of Hippo in North Africa, bequeathed to history an enduring theology of history in *The City of God*. He composed it in response to turbulence in the Roman Empire during its decline. *The City of God* has helped countless Christians reconcile deeply disturbing events in the cities of man with the providence of God. "Divine Providence" involves the idea that God sovereignly guides human affairs. How could a powerful and good Heavenly Father allow disaster to befall His children on earth? Augustine explained that the city of God and the city of man coexist on earth, but Christians must trust God on earth and keep an eschatological outlook.[19] As the apostle Paul reminds God's children, "But our citizenship is in heaven, and from it we await a Savior, the Lord Jesus Christ" (Phil 3:20). The heavenly perspective on earthly history that Augustine articulated exerted a profound impact on medieval history writing—and on Christian worldviews ever since.

Medieval Historians

Writing in Latin, monks and priests in medieval Europe often wrote simple annals or chronicles. Typical among them, the Venerable Bede (ca. A.D. 673-735), described as "the father of English history," conscientiously attempted to distinguish between fact and rumor. His *Ecclesiastical History of the English People*, however, freely identified God's providential hand repeatedly intervening in history, sometimes performing miracles. ". . . what we read in Bede's history is nothing less than the unfolding story of a 'play written by God.'"[20]

Premodern Summary

To summarize moralizing, premodern historiography, ancient Greek historians applied rational faculties to the investigation of all of life, including the past. Greek and premodern history elsewhere tended to be cyclical and pessimistic. In the medieval Christian West, however, historians possessed a linear and providential perspective toward history, which they portrayed as true and morally useful. Accepting the authority of Scripture, they taught that history started with God's invention of time at Creation. Medievalists emphasized His interventions in time as revealed in Scripture and history. They asserted that history would culminate in the future when God fulfills His promise that the Savior will return at the end of time and space in history.

Modern History

Scientific Revolution and Enlightenment Historians

The Scientific Revolution of the seventeenth century and the related eighteenth-century Enlightenment "Age of Reason" caused a most decisive break with premodern worldviews. A monumental worldview paradigm shift occurred as professional historians, like other intellectuals and scholars of that era, tried to harness the scientific method in their techniques. They also perceived progress in the unfolding of history through man's use of reason and science, rather than being a result of the working of Divine Providence.

This Scientific Revolution eventually engendered an intellectual declaration of independence from Scripture. The *philosophes* of the so-called Enlightenment applied, or rather misapplied, the findings of the scientists to create a rational new worldview based on naturalism. Naturalism intentionally excludes spiritual realities and then bases the search for truth only on natural phenomena and empirical explanations. From the standpoint of

Enlightenment naturalism, people simply needed to use reason and the scientific method to reform societies and achieve greatness. "Progress was possible, they insisted, because humans were basically good, not fundamentally evil as Christianity had taught."[21]

Enlightenment conjecture could also omit God from a clockwork universe operating via newly discovered natural laws. Deism, the philosophy that retained God as Creator only as an impersonal historical force, became the religion of many intellectuals. As Voltaire (A.D. 1694-1778), "the father of the Enlightenment," attempted to write history, he said, "Let us leave . . . the *divine* part in the hands of those with whom it is deposited, and confine ourselves solely to that which is *historical*"[22] (emphasis added). Historical accounts written during this era by Voltaire and Edward Gibbon (A.D. 1737-1794)[23] envisioned progress coming through human reason; so they disdained any meaningful role for God in history. In the hands of angry deists, history was no longer considered "His story."

Scientific Historians

German historians purposefully applied scientific methods to history and established the first academic degree in history during the late eighteenth century. The Ph.D. programs in history involved "the insistence on 'primary' sources,[24] the requirements of seminars and of doctoral dissertations, monographs, bibliographies, footnotes, professional journals."[25] The tremendously influential German historian Leopold von Ranke (A.D. 1795-1886) defined the modern historian's job: reconstruct an event from the past "*wie es eigentlich gewesen*"—"as it really was."[26] The method for producing scientific history went something like this:

> . . . data must be approached without prejudices; facts must be clearly differentiated from opinions; evidence must be accepted only from impartial witnesses, and duly subjected to critical analysis; objectivity must be maintained, with any personal prejudices properly suppressed; and the record subsequently written must be scrupulously accurate.[27]

Believing that, like scientists, they derived knowledge through sense data, some considered themselves "empiricists." They accepted John Locke's (A.D. 1632-1704) popularization of Aristotle's (384-322 B.C.) doctrine that "nothing is in the understanding that was not first in the senses."[28]

For some historians, the effort to "make history scientific originated in the Positivism of [French sociologist] Auguste Comte (A.D. 1798-1857). The term Positivism was used to contrast the reliable methods of natural science with the ethereal speculations of metaphysics."[29] As another scholar summarized, "Central to modernism was the belief that the proper use of human reason would guarantee progress. That belief arose in the Enlightenment and culminated with the rise of 19th century positivism."[30] The empirical, positivist, scientific ideal, in modified form, continues to guide many historians when they try to write about the past as accurately as possible.

HISTORICISMS

Instead of studying history strictly from an empirical, positivist position, a few ambitious men wrote speculative history that attempted to formulate historical metanarratives—i.e., all-encompassing explanatory models. Some operated from a philosophical position known as *idealism*. Building on Rene Descartes's (A.D. 1596-1650) view that reason brought certainty, Immanuel Kant (A.D. 1724-1804) "saw history as the record of human progress toward rationality and freedom"[31] guided by a deterministic Nature. Georg W. F. Hegel (A.D. 1770-1831) "is probably the best known of these idealistic philosophers of history, and he has greatly influenced both rightist and leftist twentieth-century totalitarianism."[32]

Like most modernists, Hegel built his historical superstructure on the idea of progress leading "toward the triumph of reason and freedom."[33] Hegel imaginatively employed various terms for the impersonal force directing the advance of history: World-Spirit, Reason, Logos, the Absolute, even God.[34] Hegel's system of dialectics furnished the pattern for the historical progression. A predominate thesis would clash with its opposite, the antithesis. The resolution of the conflict would create a synthesis. This synthesis would become a new thesis, which would generate a new antithesis, and so on.

Karl Marx (A.D. 1818-1883) appropriated Hegel's dialectic in his even more famous philosophy of history. Marx purported that dialectical materialism, based on all-important economic relations,[35] decisively determined human history. According to his famous words in *The Communist Manifesto*, "The history of all hitherto existing society is the history of class struggles."[36] Socioeconomic struggle energized medieval conflict between nobles and serfs, followed by industrial-era strife between capitalists and the proletariat. Ultimately the classless communist utopia envisioned in Marx's scientific socialism would end the dialectic, and the state would wither away. Similar to the liberal vision of continuing progress, Marx portrayed a secularized millennium of indefinite duration.

In Marx's metahistory, economic determinism replaced the historicists'

Nature, Reason, or freedom as the key to finding meaning or direction in the historical process. Though not a historian, Charles Darwin (A.D. 1809-1882) added his earthshaking theory of evolution to the nineteenth-century intellectual stew. He profoundly altered western conceptions of time with a natural selection process that allegedly took millions of years. Moreover, "in providing a solution to the problem of origins that had stymied earlier agnostics and atheists, Darwin made atheism possible."[37] From Enlightenment deists and skeptics to positivists to historicists to naturalists to atheistic Communists, the conclusion became inescapable: Modern historians could ban God from His cosmos.

If modern historians dethroned God, they simultaneously enthroned and dehumanized man as well. Historians accepting Darwin's anthropology failed to see the human species as the crown of creation. Positivists sometimes viewed people as hardly more than social statistics or masses to be manipulated. Speculative historians, including economic and environmental determinists, depicted individuals as hapless, helpless actors swept along by supreme impersonal forces.

Yet most modernists, believing that man is not innately sinful, argue that human reason aided by science will inevitably generate progress, eventually culminating in some form of humanist utopia. The deterministic metanarratives coexisted with this modernist cult of progress. While modern historians undeniably added tremendously to the world's total knowledge base, their philosophies of history strayed from and rejected earlier biblical, God-centered views. This, of course, reflected a gradually growing, widespread rejection of God and Christianity during the entire modern era. Consequently, Christians can celebrate the demise of the modern age. In some ways, however, postmodern perspectives on history are worse than the modern.

Postmodern History

Historians cannot date with precision the beginning of a postmodern era and a corresponding worldview shift.[38] Characteristics of modernity continue—scientific research and development of industrial economies, the growth of democracy, urbanization, and secularization. Of course, traditional traits of premodern periods also continue—agriculture, autocratic polities, and religious activities. In the field of history as well, continuity coexists with change. Historians, Christian and secular alike, still hole up in musty or dusty archives to write history using rigorous old "modern" professional standards (as well as new computerized techniques[39]). How has history changed in a postmodern time?

As an adjective, *postmodern* properly implies a temporal element—*after* premodern and modern history. As a noun, *postmodernism* represents something rather radical, defined in various ways. ". . . in postmodernism we have both a consummation of modernism and a reaction against it. The consummation is evident in postmodernism's secularism and belief in human autonomy. The reaction is a result of disillusionment with modernism."[40] Twentieth-century world wars and depressions undermined the modernist "cult of progress." In breaking with modernism, the postmodernist worldview reflects an intellectual and ideological revolution, comparable to the shift from premodern medieval faith in God to modern faith in human reason, science, and progress.

Central to the postmodernist challenge is its repudiation of both premodern and modern epistemology—the theory of knowledge. Creating an epistemological crisis, postmodernism questions, even rejects, the possibility of truth, historical or otherwise. Since postmodernism, as a worldview, underlies various other related trends in the field of history, popularly (or unpopularly) known as "multiculturalism," "political correctness," and "revisionism," these issues will be addressed along with postmodernism.

Postmodernism's Roots

Of course, postmodernism's philosophical roots lie deep in earlier epochs, especially in modern relativism, existentialism, and philology (linguistics), that developed fully in the twentieth century. For a brief but thorough examination of the development of postmodernism, see chapter 7 ("Understanding Our Postmodern World"). What follows here attempts to address the special challenges postmodernism poses to the discipline of history.[41]

Postmodernism embraces an extreme form of relativism.[42] Relativism holds that standards for judgment vary according to people, times, and situations. To postmodernists, universal absolutes do not exist (except for their dogmatic assertion that universal absolutes do not exist). Some Romantic historical writing during the nineteenth century exhibited relativist assumptions. Moreover, scientific historicists[43] argued that they should study and evaluate all ages and cultures according to their own criteria, rather than according to the historian's contemporary values. If historians could not invoke God's laws, however, who could say what actions in the past were right or wrong? Postmodernists would answer, "No one."

The vaunted scientific objectivity of nineteenth-century scholars came under attack. When choosing topics and sources to study and then writing interpretations based on the facts selected, can a historian completely escape his/her personal perspective based on his/her own past, his/her prejudices, and the prevailing climate of opinion? Postmodernists would again answer in the negative. Personal perspectives determine postmodern realities.

Twentieth-century existentialists, like nineteenth-century Romantics, stressed individuals and individual responsibility to create meaning subjectively. The French existentialist Jean-Paul Sartre (A.D. 1905-1980) asserted that "Man is nothing else but what he makes of himself."[44] To him the realm of objective truth was absurd. "Whereas modern existentialism teaches that meaning is created by the *individual*, postmodern existentialism teaches that meaning is created by *a social group and its language*"[45] (emphasis in original). To postmodernists, an individual's identity derives from and depends on one's culture, transmitted and apprehended entirely via language.

Influential linguistic theorists in the twentieth century "have increasingly come to question the validity of referring to some external reality outside language itself."[46] Post-structuralist thinkers such as Michel Foucault (A.D. 1926-1984) and Jacques Derrida (A.D. 1930-) rejected philosophical realism. Realism contends that an objective reality exists independently of human minds and languages. "Since language is a cultural creation, meaning is ultimately . . . a social construction."[47] Foucault believed that "The traditional devices for constructing a comprehensive view of history and for retracing the past as a patient and continuous development must be systematically dismantled"[48] or deconstructed and ultimately discarded.

A deconstruction or critical analysis of language texts, including historical ones, reveals hidden agendas. These hidden meanings in historical documents, when unmasked by postmodernists, somehow invariably demonstrate that white, capitalist, heterosexual males oppressed and exploited various marginalized social groups, such as blacks, workers, homosexuals, and women. Indeed, Marxist, feminist, and post-colonial historical perspectives challenge the truth-claims of traditional metanarrative histories.[49] "Race-class-gender" categories comprise the grid that guides much postmodernist history writing and threatens to fragment meta-histories into discrete micro-histories.[50]

History and Postmodernist "Truth"

Concerning epistemological issues, postmodernists have redefined history along the following lines:

> . . . history can be redescribed as a discourse that is fundamentally rhetorical, and . . . representing the past takes place through the creation of pow-

> erful, persuasive images which can be best understood as created objects, models, metaphors or proposals about reality.[51]

In the postmodernist view, history differs little, if at all, from poetry or other forms of literature. Current historicity involves a "sliding scale between fact and fiction that defines its place in current 'reality-fictions.'"[52] In the postmodernist worldview, history is no longer telling true stories about the past.[53]

Back to the question, how has history changed in a postmodern time? Postmodernist relativism, skepticism, and deconstructionism undermined earlier philosophical foundations. *Premodern* western belief systems after the ancient Hebrews rested on reasonable fundamental truths about God; *modern* intellectual systems rested on the supposedly unshakably firm foundations of empirical science. With the psalmist, many traditionalists now lament, "if the foundations are destroyed, what can the righteous do?" (Ps. 11:3). What can the righteous Christian historian (or the honest secular historian)[54] do without foundational presuppositions upholding objective reality and universal truth?

Postmodernist Problems

To redress the grievances of oppressed groups, postmodernist scholars write esteem-building histories that also confirm "identity politics." Some radical multiculturalists appropriate history as an ideological weapon, expounding "noble lies" or myths to create an encouraging heritage for oppressed groups.[55]

> The rejection of historical objectivity in favor of advocacy scholarship is currently in vogue throughout the intellectual establishment. "Revisionist scholars" villainize Christopher Columbus and other American heroes, and in doing so argue that the American heritage is not freedom but oppression. They decry the bias of "Euro-centric" scholarship and curricula, only to substitute aggressively "Afro-centric" scholarship and curricula. Histories are rewritten . . . in accordance with feminist or gay agendas. . . . If Eurocentrism is a fault, one would think Afro-centrism would be similarly narrow-minded. If patriarchy is wrong, why would matriarchy be any better? But these quibbles miss the point of postmodernist scholarship. Truth is not the issue. The issue is power.[56]

Moreover, in pleading for tolerance for all social groups, creating their own equally valid, subjective, perspectival "truths" about history, ironically, postmodernists opened the door for people to write anything that promotes a cause, even illiberal ones.[57] Using postmodernist logic, if such exists, no one could condemn bad history written by anyone, no matter how morally or factually wrong. It is all a matter of one's perspective, right? How else can one explain revisionist attempts to deny the factuality of the Holocaust, a phenomenon attested by eyewitnesses, documents, and material artifacts? These powerful means of establishing truth in premodern and modern history get brushed aside as irrelevant in a strange application of the postmodernist mentality.[58] Thinking people should disdain dishonesty in history, regardless of the authors' intended goal or motivation.

Postmodernism's perspective on power presents an alarming problem. Through his discussions on language, morality, and politics, the brilliant German philosopher Friedrich Nietzsche (A.D. 1844-1900) exerted an enormous impact on postmodernism. Christians know him best for the infamous phrase, "God is dead." However, his phrase "will to power" more concisely summarizes his metanarrative explanation of human conduct,[59] similar to Marx's "class struggle" and Sigmund Freud's (A.D. 1856-1939) focus on "the unconscious."[60]

Using Nietzsche's claim that desires for power guide human behavior, many postmodernists condemn white, bourgeois males who have supposedly dominated western power structures and used language to oppress everyone else.[61] Implied or stated in much postmodernist writing is the goal of oppressed groups of overthrowing the oppressors. If no moral absolutes exist to restrain the abuse of power, however, can postmodernist disciples of Nietzsche, when in power, do better than Adolf Hitler in avoiding the totalitarian implications of a philosophy built on a will to power?[62]

Postmodernists have sometimes gained power over certain segments of the American academy. In this setting, their infringements on the free speech of conservatives and traditional scholars who oppose postmodernist versions of "political correctness" serve as a chilling warning of what might happen if they gained total power. Oppression (of old, white, male power-holders) in the name of anti-oppression (empowering formerly powerless peoples) resembles Orwellian doublespeak and cannot advance any sane conception of justice. Furthermore, if truth does not exist, power-wielders can shamelessly lie if it forwards their agenda and then try to use postmodernist language games to cover up. Everything "depends on what your definition of is, is."[63]

History and a Biblical Epistemology

> *Then Pilate said to him, "So you are a king?" Jesus answered, "You say that I am a king. For this purpose I was born and for this purpose I have come into the world—to bear witness to the truth. Everyone who is of the truth listens to my voice." Pilate said to him, "What is truth?"*
>
> —JOHN 18:37-38A

What is truth? A simple dictionary definition says truth is "conformity with fact or reality; verity; genuineness or actual existence." Jesus and the biblical authors repeatedly spoke of truth as if it were real and vitally important. Pilate, however, sounded a bit like a postmodernist in a premodern time. Addressing another man known for doubt, Thomas, "Jesus said to him, 'I am the way, and the truth, and the life. No one comes to the Father except through me'" (John 14:6). Christ not only spoke truth—He embodied it. He also prayed to God the Father, "Sanctify them in the truth; your word is truth" (John 17:17). God's Word is inscripturated truth. Truth exists. Reality is not merely a social construction perceived through a culture's language. Historians can study the past and make true statements about it, even if they cannot reconstruct it perfectly.[64]

Linguistic theorists correctly gauge language to be extraordinarily important. Almighty God spoke the universe into existence and has communicated to His children by His Word. God does not reveal Himself visibly; He usually uses language as a bridge to enable His people to understand Him. Although the Holy Spirit also plays a somewhat inscrutable role in a Christian's life, Christians are primarily "people of the Book." They know by written revelation that God, the physical universe, and spiritual truth all exist. Christians experience them by faith, but reason also confirms their reality. While rejecting naturalism, premodern wholehearted faith in God coupled with a limited faith in modern science[65] can work together to affirm reality—past as well as present.[66] Based upon a rational reaffirmation of aspects of premodern and modern historiography, the discipline of history will survive postmodernism. More importantly, the Lord of history will bring the unfolding of history to an end when His purposes have all been accomplished.

A Biblical Philosophy of History

Earlier this chapter contended that Christians should study history, hold to a linear and providential view of history, and use God-given abilities to understand historical truth, which is real and partially knowable.

Linearity

The Bible contains and elucidates history. The Christian comprehends history not as a cycle, but as a line that began at Creation, climaxed with Christ at the cross, and will consummate at Christ's second coming at the end.[67] Why do Christians consider the crucifixion the pinnacle of history? As one pastor declared, "The cross is the 'core of the gospel.' Its bottom line is sobering; if the account is true, it is history's hinge. Period. If not, it is history's hoax."[68]

Without history's hinge, humanity would still be helplessly and hopelessly dead in trespasses and sins. "But when the fullness of time had come, God sent forth his Son" (Gal 4:4a). Jesus fulfilled prophecies in history through His incarnation, atoning sacrifice for sin, and resurrection from the dead. The line from Creation to final judgment centers on Christ.

A biblical philosophy of history also acknowledges God's sovereignty. "The LORD of hosts has sworn: 'As I have planned, so shall it be, and as I have purposed, so shall it stand'" (Isa 14:24). A philosophy of history is "a systematic interpretation of universal history in accordance with a principle by which historical events and successions are unified and directed toward ultimate meaning."[69] The principle is God's sovereign providential control of history. God is history's unifying and directing force. God's gracious, redemptive plan in history gives it purpose and ultimate meaning. History's highest goal and ultimate outworking is the fulfillment of God's will to His glory.

The apostle Paul's sermon at the Areopagus (Mars Hill) exhibited the essence of a Christian philosophy of history. He started with Creation: "The God who made the world and everything in it . . ." (Acts 17:24a). Paul identified God as the sovereign sustainer of life. ". . . since he himself gives to all mankind life and breath and everything" (v. 25b); "for 'in him we live and move and have our being'" (v. 28a). He is the God of all. "And he made from one man every nation of mankind to live on all the face of the earth" (v. 26a). Paul preached a risen Christ (v. 31) and called on everyone to "seek God" (v. 27) who "commands all people everywhere to repent" (v. 30b) "because he has fixed a day on which he will judge the world in righteousness" (v. 31a). From Creation to Christ to future judgment, Paul described the sovereign God of the whole world working in a linear fashion throughout history.

The author of Acts, Dr. Luke, demonstrated "an excellent summary of the process of historical study in the prologue of his Gospel."[70]

> *Inasmuch as many have undertaken to compile a narrative of the things that have been accomplished among us, just as those who from the beginning were eyewitnesses and ministers of the word have delivered them to us, it seemed good to me also, having followed all things closely for some time past, to write an orderly account for you, most excellent Theophilus, that you may have certainty concerning the things you have been taught.*
>
> —LUKE 1:1-4

Luke drafted a sophisticated, chronological, historical narrative, using reliable primary and secondary sources, with the aim of certainty—telling the truth about Jesus. In short, "the beloved physician" (Col 4:14) practiced the historian's craft quite skillfully. Of course, as with other writers of Scripture,

Luke was also "carried along by the Holy Spirit" (2 Pet 1:21b), an experience historians have not had in exactly the same way since the closing of the biblical canon.

Faith and History

Christians have been writing history since Luke, Eusebius (ca. A.D. 265-339), Augustine, and Bede. Today Christian historians practice their vocation in a variety of institutions and belong to organizations related to their trade. One such organization, the Conference on Faith and History, produces a journal entitled *Fides et Historia* (faith and history). In its pages and at the organization's conferences, as well as via other venues, Christian historians have often discussed and debated how Christian convictions affect the writing of history.[71]

Christians reading and writing history who share a biblical anthropology know that "The heart is deceitful above all things, and desperately sick" (Jer 17:9a). Christians easily discern the sinful nature of humanity in the many appalling historical examples of "man's inhumanity to man." In comprehending the depravity of the human nature from both the Bible and history, Christians must reject godless, humanist schemes, such as the Marxist vision of a classless utopia. If God is truly sovereign, Christians must likewise reject materialist, deterministic metanarratives.

Christian compassion can make Christian historians' portrayals of past peoples, afflicted with the sinful nature, more realistic and empathetic. "We will be greatly helped in our study of the men and women of history if we keep before us this biblical picture of humanity created in the image of God, endowed with the power and responsibility of moral choice, fallen but redeemable."[72] At the same time, all Christians can also evaluate past peoples and policies based on God's immutable standards rather than on relativist human criteria.

Some non-Christians, however, can also display empathy and apply high moral standards when discussing fallible human subjects of historical study. They can also study church history, one area in which Christians claim extra insights. A biblical worldview, however, should truly enable people to develop the antenna for discerning the significance of religious faith in history.[73]

Ironically, multiculturalists have unwittingly given Christian church historians an argument to bolster their claim that, as insiders, they can analyze their topic more efficaciously than outsiders can. Some radical multiculturalists assert that a person cannot write history about a minority group without being a member of that group. Obviously, taking such a position to its logical extreme would preclude people from understanding anyone except people identical to themselves. But if membership in a group furnishes even some special sensitivity to better understand the group, then Christian historians can legitimately contend that they can write insightful church histories. In fact, the successful academic work of talented Christian church historians in recent years has effectively returned religious factors into a historical picture recently broadened by race-class-gender issues.[74]

Providential History

Providential history remains a flash point for sparking the most vigorous debates among Christians examining history. The horrors of the First World War shattered the myth of human progress that provided the underpinning for the modernist historical metanarrative. Oswald Spengler's pessimistic *The Decline of the West*[75] proved an unsatisfactory replacement, with its neo-pagan cyclical view. Then World War II again seemed to demonstrate the veracity of Proverbs 16:18, "Pride goes before destruction, and a haughty spirit before a fall." Prominent historians, such as Reinhold Niebuhr[76] and Herbert Butterfield,[77] in the postwar period, began a reappraisal of the premodern providential view of history. As people grappled with understanding the horrors of modern war and the complexities of cold war, "Niebuhr and Butterfield both believed that the crisis was particularly due to an optimistic view of history which liberalism and Marxism shared."[78]

At Cambridge University, Herbert Butterfield explored the idea of providentialism, though he had made his reputation writing what he called "technical" (i.e., scientifically factual[79]) rather than metaphysical history. What Butterfield called "technical history," some contemporary scholars label "ordinary history," i.e., history limited to "evidence and causes and effects that almost everyone can be convinced might have taken place."[80] Butterfield illustrated a practical biblical philosophy of history with a hypothetical question posed to someone at the end of a journey:

> Why are you here now? You may answer: "Because I wanted to come"; or you may say: "Because a railway-train carried me here"; or you may say: "Because it is the will of God"; and all these things may be true at the same time—true on different levels. So with history . . .[81]

Human free will, laws of nature, and the providence of God all work together simultaneously, albeit mysteriously.[82] The first historical element Butterfield labeled "biographical," the second "scientific," and the third "theological."[83] He "claimed the utter centrality to history of a biblical idea of providence. He affirmed the rationality of the universe as expressed in historical laws, and he believed such laws actually illuminated the ways of God."[84] His explicit identification of precise ways in which God's hand worked in history, however, tended to be somewhat cautious.

"Plenty of historians want to affirm that God is at work in history, but practically nobody wants to say exactly how,"[85] concluded a journalist after interviewing several well-known Christian historians. "In fact, a doctrine of providence teaches that God is at work in everything, both good and not so good. But to determine what God intended by a particular event is another matter altogether."[86] In other words, many historians are reluctant to answer "I do" when reading Paul's rhetorical question, "For who has known the mind of the Lord . . . ?" (Rom 11:34a). Can Christians know with precision why God caused and allowed specific events to occur in history?[87]

Providence in Bible Times

Occasionally God explicitly explained His providential actions during biblical times. These explanations can sometimes provide insights that are useful in understanding His workings after the closing of the canon. Consider the account of Israel's being taken into captivity:

> *In the fourth year of King Hezekiah . . . Shalmaneser king of Assyria came up against Samaria and besieged it, and at the end of three years he took it. . . . The king of Assyria carried the Israelites away to Assyria and put them in Halah, and on the Habor, the river of Gozan, and in the cities of the Medes."*
>
> —2 KGS 18:9, 10A-11

Why did God providentially allow the defeat and deportation of His chosen people? The next verse authoritatively answers. God allowed this "because they did not obey the voice of the Lord their God but transgressed his covenant, even all that Moses the servant of the Lord commanded. They neither listened nor obeyed" (v. 12). While Scripture clearly teaches that sin engenders suffering, is sin the only causal factor involved in specific calamities distressing people in a fallen world?[88]

Do biblical patterns of sowing and reaping always provide direct, simple cause-and-effect explanations for every human debacle in history? Jesus rejected an overuse of this blanket interpretative scheme when people asked Him why God allowed the Romans to kill some Galileans (Luke 13:1-5) and why a man had been born blind (John 9:1-3). Christ preached that human beings face a much more portentous eternal disaster if they fail to repent. He also pointed out that His Father "makes his sun rise on the evil and on the good, and sends rain on the just and on the unjust" (Matt 5:45b).

Must historians receive divine inspiration from the Holy Spirit to write providential history? Alternatively, can circumstantial evidence prove God's actions in history? The apostle Paul accepted reports about the faith demonstrated by the Colossians and Thessalonians without claiming clear divine inspiration for recognizing the work of God in their lives (Col 1:1-9; 1 Thess 2:13; 3:5; 2 Thess 2:13-15). Jesus indicated that people could discern His impact on Christians' lives through their observable actions: "By this all people will know that you are my disciples, if you have love for one another" (John 13:35). In Egypt, Joseph's insight about God's providence seemed to come from understanding circumstantial evidence: "So it was not you who sent me here, but God. . . . As for you, you meant evil against me, but God meant it for good, to bring it about that many people should be kept alive" (Gen 45:8a; 50:20a).[89] Perhaps delineating how God brings ultimate good out of human fiascoes may be one area of focus for credible providential history.

Postmodern Opportunity?

The intimidating impact of the secular academy on history writing poses a problem. The scholarly community has generally praised excellent works of ordinary, technical history produced by a few pioneering Christian historians, such as George Marsden,[90] Nathan Hatch,[91] Mark Noll,[92] and others. Have these Christian intellectuals, like Sir Herbert Butterfield before them, earned the right to be heard now if they want to expound more overt, even outrageous providential history than they normally would? Perhaps the time is ripe for challenging the academy.

In an atmosphere affected by postmodernism, when a variety of opinions are acceptable so long as authors acknowledge their perspectivalism, it seems likely that well-established Christian scholars could get a hearing, even to discuss providentialism. As Butterfield himself said, "the really momentous questions are not eliminated simply by ruling them off limits."[93] Why not admit a Christian perspective and then combine the best modernist scholarship with a modest premodern providentialism, even in areas outside church history?[94] Would this be a "scandal of the evangelical mind," or a bold, sorely needed initiative at a pivotal time in history for influencing a spiritually lost intelligentsia already in a state of flux over postmodernism?

What about lesser-known Christian historians laboring in less prestigious institutions, including Christian colleges? As Paul "had been entrusted with the gospel to the uncircumcised, just as Peter had been entrusted with the gospel to the circumcised" (Gal 2:7b), some historians can serve God in the secular academy and others can minister to the church. People in the world and church need the Gospel, and both the academy and church would benefit from hearing stories of God's power displayed in history. "Evangelical historians have taken a large first step forward, establishing the validity of religious memories. The second step, to tie those memories to everything else, has barely begun."[95]

Christians can fruitfully work on the task of accurately tying Christianity to history. Such a task can certainly edify the church. Forthright humility and tentativeness, however, must characterize all attempts at providential history. As the sovereign Lord declared, "For as the heavens are higher than the earth, so are my ways higher than your ways and my thoughts than your thoughts" (Isa 55:9). Simplistic reductionism and arrogant triumphalism are out of line in the endeavor to write providential history. Christians need to admit that "now we see in a mirror dimly" (1 Cor 13:12a). But with a spirit of modesty and meekness, we should try to see what our finite abilities allow us to see in history.

Revisionism in U.S. History

Partly to avoid political hot potatoes relating to church-state issues,[96] authors for pre-collegiate textbooks in recent years have systematically revised history to downplay the roles of Christianity in U.S. history. In what appears to Christians as a related liberal ideological ploy, textbooks have also incorporated more of the social history of women and minority groups. Their mistreatment and struggles in American history project an embarrassing, generally negative portrayal of what had traditionally been a grand, national epic in earlier textbooks.[97]

The new "politically correct" multicultural revision of U.S. history distresses and angers Americans who continue to believe that patriotism-producing political socialization remains a goal for history in public education. In 1994 former National Endowment for the Humanities chair Lynne V. Cheney's blistering exposé of new multicultural, highly politicized national standards for teaching history ignited a firestorm of debate. Many people agreed with critiques of textbook histories that covered Harriet Tubman much more thoroughly than they covered George Washington.[98] Recently Congress reacted against both the overemphasis on hyphenated American identities (African-American, Native-American, etc.) and on social studies that de-emphasize U.S. history and distinctives in favor of global studies[99] and interdependent perspectives. Congress mandated that public school curricula beef up traditional American political history and civics components. Christians must reflect honestly on these conflicts.

Should history return to the traditional task of nurturing citizenship in young people? During an extended war on terrorism, sane curricula must help young Americans realize that religious toleration, freedom of speech and press, women's suffrage, and other democratic values and practices are worth defending. Honest history programs also need to admit imperfections in American history that included slavery, mistreatment of First Americans, racial and religious bigotry, and other manifestations of the sin nature. Nonetheless, struggles to overcome such defects have produced a nation that many of the world's people admire and envy. History cannot return to depictions that focus solely on potentates, presidents, and popes, all white and male. But a prudently balanced history must likewise avoid an excessively fragmented, negative approach, highlighting racial and gender differences and problems—unless Americans wish to emulate Yugoslavia's disintegration into warring ethnic factions.

The rewriting of history happens for good as well as troublesome reasons. For example, about a century ago secular scholars used the lack of historical data about the ancient Hittites, outside of biblical references, as part of their "higher criticism," questioning the Bible's accuracy and authenticity. Then, between 1906 and 1908, archaeologists unearthed the Hittite capital, complete with abundant written records as well as artifacts. A positive instance of historical revisionism then had to occur to include information on the Hittite civilization in new textbooks.

The philosopher George Santayana somewhat cynically said, "History is always written wrong, and so always needs to be rewritten."[100] Perhaps historical revision, both to include the histories of minority groups and to re-include religious history, is not always so much the righting of wrong history (though that must also occur) as it is giving a fuller, richer picture. Well-written, balanced, scrupulously accurate histories about all kinds of peoples satisfy curiosity, furnish examples, (both positive and negative), and strengthen national identity.

Where Is History Going?

Where is history going? It is going where God wants it to go. While that should not generate debate, genuine Christians in good faith disagree about the future as well as the past. Some have analyzed God's past interactions with His people by emphasizing His covenants—Adamic, Noahic, Abrahamic, Mosaic, Davidic, and New. Other Christians have divided history into dispensations—periods of time in "God's economy for man and the world for the outworking of God's purpose and will."[101] These have sometimes included dispensations of innocence, conscience, human government, promise, law, grace, and kingdom. Whether or not the last dispensation, the millennial kingdom of Revelation 20, will be literal and earthly constitutes a crucial difference in discussing the future direction of history from a theological perspective.

Does knowing the end of the story help in understanding the middle? Knowing that Jesus will return in the future surely encourages all true believers in the present (cf. 1 Thess 4:18). Christians hold to one of three main views on history's end. Using an optimistic, theistic version of the modernist metanarrative of human progress, Christians known as *post*millennialists believe that Jesus will come back *after* Christian revivals and reforms usher in a millennial golden age. Amillennialists, on the other hand, reject the notion of a literal thousand-year reign of Christ on earth. Finally, *pre*millennialists do not envision consistent moral progress before Christ's Second Advent. Their interpretation is pessimistic about sinful human nature and possibilities of earthly utopias, but optimistic about God's power to regenerate sinners and His plans for a glorious future.[102] Premillennialists assert that moral decline will precede Christ's return, which will occur *before* He establishes a literal millennial kingdom on this earth that displays His ultimate triumph and glory. As one scholar concluded about God's working in history:

> . . . each age represents an advance over the preceding age, when looked at from the standpoint of what God is giving and doing for man. It is true that sinful man is always failing; but where sin abounded, grace did much more abound. Thus to the old question, "Is the world getting better or worse?" from one standpoint we might answer, "The age is getting worse, but the course of history by the grace of God is moving forward."[103]

Further Reading

Books

Butterfield, Herbert. *Christianity and History.* London: Collins Books, 1949.

Marsden, George and Frank Roberts, eds. *A Christian View of History?* Grand Rapids, MI: William B. Eerdmans, 1975.

McIntire, C. T., ed. *God, History, and Historians: Modern Christian Views of History.* New York: Oxford University Press, 1977.

McIntire, C. T. and Ronald A. Wells, eds. *History and Historical Understanding.* Grand Rapids, MI: William B. Eerdmans, 1984.

Wells, Ronald A., ed. *History and the Christian Historian.* Grand Rapids, MI: William B. Eerdmans, 1998.

Journals

Fides et Historia, journal of the Conference on Faith and History, often contains articles on the topic of a biblical view of history. In XXXIV, No. 1 (Winter/Spring 2002), the first nine selections are all apropos.

Christian History, XX, 4 (2001) is a particularly fine introduction to church history for someone beginning to study the topic.

15

Developing a Biblical View of Church and State

John P. Stead

Throughout American history there have been numerous American religious movements that have influenced American life and politics. Those with the most impact have included the abolitionist movement, the temperance movement, and the civil rights movement in the twentieth century. While it was the goal of all these movements to change public policy, none of them viewed the government as something to capture and control.

Throughout much of the twentieth century most evangelicals were primarily consumed with fulfilling the Great Commission through evangelism, church planting, and missions. It was not until the increasing secularization of the culture and the cultural elite's hostility toward evangelical Christianity, primarily found in the universities, media, and the arts, that large numbers of evangelicals became seriously exercised about America's moral and social direction. This concern grew to outright anger with the Supreme Court's decision that legalized abortion-on-demand in 1973. Evangelical leaders then began to discuss strategies for taking the government "back" from liberal and secular influences.

Why did they focus on government institutions rather than directly confronting the groups who were supporting "the left" in their attack on Christian values? The reason was quite apparent: The scope of government had radically changed. During the twentieth century, there were four monumental events that had led to the growth of the federal government: two world wars, a great depression, and a cold war that lasted over forty years. Great technological strides, especially in communications, continued to be made. The federal government became increasingly centralized and was viewed by all special interest groups, including evangelical leaders, as the major dispenser of political, social, and economic favors. The two-party system, which for decades served as the moderating vehicle for individuals and interest groups, was and still is in decline, as seen in the ever-increasing numbers of special interest groups along with their fund-raising arms, Political Action Committees (PACs). As a result of the decline of the two-party system, politics came to be characterized as a clash between uncompromising interests. Governmental institutions are now seen as something to be captured and used by a particular interest group for its own ends.

With the rise of such powerful evangelical interests as The Moral Majority, The Christian Coalition, Focus on the Family, The Family Research Council, and Concerned Women for America, among others, evangelicals are seen by those in government, as well as by their vocal opponents, as political interest groups with a policy agenda accompanied by lobbyists who represent them in the halls of Congress and in the bureaucracy. As a result, this has become a life-and-death struggle for political power. Christians are viewed by those who are sympathetic as attempting to control government for good—i.e., morality and traditional family values. Those in opposition see the evangelical church as reactionary, seeking to maintain supposedly repressive moral standards and defending free enterprise, which allegedly exploits the poor and underrepresented groups such as minorities, women, and homosexuals.

There are several problems with attempting to control society through this political approach. Because they are well-organized, interest groups or factions can better achieve their agenda at the expense of the vast unorganized majority. The framers of the Constitution were extremely concerned about the tyranny of irresponsible majority power within a democracy. Their great challenge was to devise a system that would keep the majority responsible. The large geographical size of the United States would allow for the existence of a great number of factions, each attempting to bring to bear its demands on government and to subvert the will of the majority. Each group in and of itself was too small to accomplish this without moderating its most extreme demands in order to coalesce with other groups to form a majority. This process of coalition or compromise would moderate these demands.[1] This can be seen in any number of the above-mentioned Christian groups. Theological and doctrinal issues are set aside so that the "agenda" can be carried forward more forcefully with greater numbers and increased financial backing.

While James Madison (1751-1836) believed that the impetus for the initiation of most factions would be economic, he was concerned with religious factions as well. He saw religious factionalism as a positive force in controlling irresponsible majority power, while he saw monolithic, state-sanctioned religion and its control of governmental institutions as pernicious.

The framers shared the revulsion of the eighteenth century against religious fanaticism and tyranny. The historical record, beginning with the Edict of Milan, A.D. 313 through the sixteenth-century Reformation, was one of extinguished religious liberty and continuous warfare. Madison believed that religious fragmentation would prevent any one religious group from exercising power over the government. No single religious group could by itself achieve a national majority, therefore necessitating the moderating process of coalition. The result would be national protection against oppression by religious majorities. This is the way the framers designed the system to work. A diversity of religious groups would guarantee the freedom of all religious groups with no state-sanctioned national church.

How close was the framers' view of church-state relationships to that of the Bible? Actually, it is much closer than one might initially believe. While the framers for the most part were theistic rationalists,[2] they came to their views on church-state relations historically and pragmatically.

The Historic, Biblical Movement Toward Separation of Church and State

Throughout history, the relationship between the sacred and the state was one of progressiveness, or as Leonard Verduin[3] termed it, a "forward movement"[4] from the birth of the nation of Israel to the calling out of the church until the Edict of Milan in A.D. 313 under Constantine.

Israel, as a nation from its earliest days, was a society based on ritual, from circumcision to the sacrificial system that bound the nation together. One was born an Israelite; one did not normally make a decision to become an Israelite. In this sense, it was much like other nations in the Ancient Near East. There was no obvious sense of mission.[5] There never was any overt desire to go out and make converts from other tribes or nations.

With the crowning of Saul as the first king of Israel, a division between king and priest began to appear. While it is clear from 1 Samuel 8 that God saw Israel's desire for a king as a rejection of His leadership, He nevertheless instructed Samuel to grant the people's desire. This meant that for the first time in Israel's history, there would be a separation of function. The king's function was the provision of what is called *common* or *conserving grace*. That is, the king's role was to preserve order internally and to protect the nation from foreign invasion. The role of the priesthood continued to represent the nation before God.

The seriousness with which God regarded this new relationship is evidenced by His reaction to Saul's usurping the priestly role by offering up a sacrifice prior to going into battle. "When I saw that the people were scattering from me, and that you did not come within the days appointed, and that the Philistines had mustered at Michmash . . . I forced myself and offered the burnt offering" (1 Sam 13:11-12).

If it is recognized that one of the purposes of the sacrificial system was to produce a cultural closeness, then it can easily be understood why Saul would pragmatically resort to taking on the priestly role in offering a sacrifice. Verduin describes the sense of how God would express His new relationship to His people: "Very well, have your king as other nations have, but I must then insist that he confine himself to things that pertain to the *regnum*, that he leave the functions of the priest to a different kind of servant of mine."[6]

God's same displeasure fell on King Uzziah as he also took on the priestly role and died as an outcast (2 Chron 26). The issue here is very clear: There is to be a division of labor; a person cannot be both king and priest. "The problem in question is the problem of an early grace and a later grace: a grace that comes to expression in the Creator-creature relationship in which sin is *curbed*, and a grace that comes to expression in the Redeemer-redeemed relationship in which sin is *vanquished*."[7] This idea came to full fruition in Paul's great treatise on civil government in Romans 13, where he makes it crystal-clear that the purpose of the sword is to suppress evil, not to redeem people or to judge heretics.

Additional insights into the difference in the functions of the church and the state are revealed in the ministries of John the Baptist and the Lord Jesus Christ. John begins his ministry by calling on the people to "repent, for the kingdom of heaven is at hand" (Matt 3:2). He does this in the midst of a renewed, sacral society. He is calling out a group of "repenters" who signify their repentance with an outward sign—i.e., baptism. Remember, those in a sacral society had no choice—they were born into it. John now, for the first time, introduces the element of choice into Jewish culture.

Christ also reinforced the two graces. In His teaching on the Roman coin, Jesus reminded all within the reach of His voice of the government's role and how that role is different from the sacred role (Matt 22:15-22). It is significant that Jesus had no problem living under pagan rulers. It is very clear from the Lord's preaching that there would now be two groups of people in Israel—those who repented and those who did not.

With the creation of the church, this progressive movement continued. The church is by definition the *ecclesia,* or literally "the called-out ones."

They found themselves in the midst of a sacral society. Rome practiced and required emperor worship along with the worship of a whole pantheon of deities. Within this culture, Christians were heretics—they were "choice makers" because they had chosen to worship the one true God. It was not that they worshiped the one true God, but it was the fact that they worshiped Him *alone* that was the heart of the conflict with the Roman authorities. The one thing that a sacral society cannot tolerate is a heretic.

Christians of the first century saw themselves as "the body of Christ." By repenting of their sins and putting their faith in Jesus Christ as Lord and Savior, their status had changed; that is, they were redeemed from sin and death. They also experienced a change of condition—they were new creations in Christ Jesus (Eph 2:1-10). This meant that there were now two types of people in the world—the redeemed and the unredeemed. Culture was no longer sacral or uniform but was now "composite."[8] This is also how Christians viewed themselves. Believer's baptism was an outward testimony of a redeemed individual who had progressed out of a sacral society. It gave testimony to the choice a person had made.

The apostle Paul's view on this is abundantly clear. Christians have the responsibility to judge and discipline those who claim to be believers, but must leave the judging and the disciplining of unbelievers to God (1 Cor 5:9-12). In the area of church-state relations, this was how the church was to function. The apostles believed and taught that society would always be "composite," with Christians facing great persecution and rejection until the reestablishing of the sacral society under the authoritarian reign of Jesus Christ as Prophet, Priest, and King.

The retreat to Christian sacralism began in A.D. 313 with Constantine's (ca. 274-337) Edict of Milan, which made Christianity for the first time *religio licita*, a permitted cult. This was soon followed by the Edict of Toleration, in which Christianity was elevated to the position of being the only legitimate faith. Thus began the fusion of church and state, a retreat from New Testament Christianity. The result was the birth of Christendom. "The Constantinian change put an end to membership by decision: from that time all people were said to be Christians without any foregoing struggle of soul which is impossible."[9]

Corpus Christi, the body of Christ, gave way to *Corpus Christianum*, the body of the christened. The preaching of the Word of God that required decision was replaced by the sacramental passivity of the mass and infant baptism, which did nothing more than take the place of circumcision. Everybody was placed in the Christian community at birth; no individual decision had to be made. "The *regnum* and the *sacretodium* joined hands to make sure no one was skipped; indeed, the regnum made the baptism of every infant born in its domains mandatory."[10]

The early "Father" of Reformed theology, Augustine (354-430), supported the sacral homogeneous society. He had no reluctance about using the sword to keep people from abandoning the faith. This is distinct from the apostolic church that disciplined disobedient Christians by "putting them out of the church fellowship," not by exiling them or putting them to death. By the fourth century, heretics were either exiled or executed. There was no longer room in a mandatory sacral culture for dissidents.

This regressive movement of the church would lead to a number of dissident groups such as the Donatists of Augustine's time, the Albigenses, the Waldensees, the Anabaptists during the Reformation, and, in colonial America, the New England dissenters. While the fringe elements of these groups had aberrant theology, they all shared one belief in common—that true Christians were a called-out minority (*Corpus Christi*) and were called to live in the midst of an unregenerate world. They rejected the retrograde idea of Christendom.

Donatism was a rebellion against the Constantinian change, the reintroduction of sacralism where the roles of church and state were combined. "The Donatist continued to think of the Church of Christ as a 'small body of saved surrounded by the unregenerate mass.'"[11] They insisted that the independence of the church in regard to the emperor and his officials had to be "upheld at all costs."[12] What Donatists attempted to do was to retain the Christian faith and ecclesiology of the first century. They took the claim "Jesus is Lord" seriously. Salvation for the Donatist meant both a change in status (repentance) and a change of condition (sanctification). The fruit of the Spirit and of repentance would be evident in the life of a truly regenerated person. This meant a total rejection of the sacrament of infant baptism, the sacrament that without choice automatically placed a person into Christendom.

The Waldensees were deemed heretical because they dared to preach about the medieval church's fallennness and its corruption from pope to priest. They were also Word-centered. The Word's neglect by the church was evident:[13]

> The priests cause the people to perish of hunger and thirst to hear the Word of God . . . not only do they themselves refuse to hear and receive the Word of God but . . . they, in order that it may not be preached make laws and orders as it pleases them, just so the preaching of the Word is obstructed. The City of Sodom will be pardoned before these.[14]

As the Reformation came into full flower in the sixteenth century with its emphasis on *sola scriptura*, total depravity, and justification by faith alone, one would anticipate a return to the apostolic view of the church consisting of the "called-out ones." This failed to occur. Luther, Zwingli, and Calvin all continued to embrace governmental means to exterminate and banish heretical groups. Infant baptism was also a carryover of medieval sacral society. Civil authorities would be used to imprison or execute those who practiced believer's baptism.

By the time his ministry had matured, Luther was in comfortable cooperation with the German princes. Emil Brunner said that the elder Luther "stopped short of a full reformation. He was content to walk hand in hand with the State, remaining bogged-down half way between Catholicism and New Testament church organization."[15]

In dealing with those who practiced believer's baptism, Luther wrote: "The secular authorities are duty-bound to suppress blasphemy, false doctrine, heresy. They must inflict bodily punishment on those who support such things."[16] In another letter to one of his fellow ministers, Luther wrote: "By the authority of and in the name of, the most serene Prince, we have the custom of frightening and threatening with punishment and exile all who are negligent in things-religious and fail to come to the services."[17] Regarding baptism, Luther said that the water of baptism was "a divine water of God, a godly, heavenly, holy, blessed water, in which faith hangs, a precious sugar water, a perfume, a drug, is what it has become; one with which God has mixed Himself, real Living Water, that drives-away death and hell and makes eternally alive."[18]

It should also be noted that Luther did not attack Jews because of their race but because of their religious practices. They were outside of the sacral society, as were the Anabaptists.

The climate that supported the joining of the cross and the flag was no different in Zurich. Like Luther, Zwingli had his doubts early on about both church and state being involved in religious affairs. He initially had doubts concerning the sacrament of infant baptism. But by the time of the Mantz affair, he had moved in the same direction as Luther. Felix Mantz was tried and convicted of initiating and participating in believer's baptism.

> Because he has, contrary to Christian order and custom, become involved in re-baptism . . . has confessed to having said that he wanted to gather such as want to accept Christ and follow Him, to unite himself with them through baptism . . . so that he and his followers have separated themselves from the Christian church, to raise up a sect of their own . . . such doctrine

> being harmful to the united usage of all Christendom and tending offense, to insurrection and sedition against the government.[19]

This is a classic example of how church and state were viewed in Zurich. There was no recognized difference between loyalty to the state and loyalty to the church. Felix Mantz was then bound hand and foot, taken by rowboat out to the middle of the Limmat River, which flows through Zurich, and drowned. Whereas in the past heretics had been burned (John 15:6),[20] Zwingli thought it appropriate that these dissidents who believed in baptism by immersion should die in that same manner.[21]

What was true in Germany and Zurich was also true in Geneva. Calvin never fully separated from the sacral society of Christendom. The magistrates were to play a major role in ensuring that God was worshiped in their domain, and they were also to exercise their responsibility to put "heretics and blasphemers" to death.[22]

The execution of Servetus plainly reveals Calvin's views on the issue. Few historians question the fact that Servetus was a heretic. The real issue involved what his punishment should be. Should he be banned from Geneva, or should he be executed? He was tried in civil court and was executed by burning at the stake. Luther's aide, Melanchthon, writing to Calvin commended him with these words: "To you the Church owes now and always will owe a debt of gratitude . . . it affirms that your magistrates did the right thing when they put the blasphemer to death."[23]

THE NEW WORLD

To a great extent the first settlers of New England, beginning in 1620, were the children of the Reformation and more specifically Calvin. John Robinson was one of the pastors of the "separatists" known as the Pilgrims. While he was a student and admirer of Calvin, he believed that it was unwise to simply shut oneself off from "further light" that the Scriptures might reveal. He was open to further teaching on church-state relations. The other group that settled in Massachusetts Bay, in 1624, were the "non-conformists" known as the Puritans. They were totally committed to the Reformed view of the magistrate and the church being part of the same structure.

One of the Puritan pastors, Roger Williams (ca. 1604-1684), played a pivotal role in returning church-state relations back to that of the apostolic era in which the magistrate's responsibility was the suppression of evil, both internally and externally, by civil force. Williams found himself immediately in trouble in Massachusetts after writing a booklet titled *Christening Maketh*

Not Christians. His position on infant baptism was in total violation of the civil authority in Massachusetts.

> It is ordered and agreed upon that if any person or persons within the jurisdiction shall either openly condemn or oppose the baptism of infants, or go about secretly to seduce others from the approbation of the use thereof, or shall appear in the court willfully and obstinately to continue therein after due time and means of convictions, every such person, or persons, shall be sentenced to banishment.[24]

Those who disobeyed were not only put out of the church but also banished from the colony. Similar laws were enforced in Virginia, which was Anglican. However, in Virginia parents paid a fine of two thousand pounds of tobacco for not having children baptized. Interestingly, the fact that a couple convicted of fornication was fined five hundred pounds of tobacco provides insight into which violation of the law was considered more serious.

Williams also held and publicly taught that magistrates had no authority over the first table of the Mosaic law. For this belief, he was found guilty and banished along with his wife and son in the middle of winter. Their lives were saved by the kindness of Indians to whom he had ministered, even going so far as attempting to learn their language.

This interaction points to another difference between the Massachusetts authorities and Williams. He saw the Indians in terms of mission, not as heathen outside the borders of Christendom to be exploited and eliminated. The Puritan view was that the church and state, while having different functions, were comprised exclusively of the visible elect. The two, therefore, worked hand in glove. If people were outside the boundaries of the Christian state, they were beyond the concern of Christ.

In his series of debates with John Cotton (1595-1652), Williams pointed out the perniciousness of this sacral theology. In reality, the amalgam of church and state, along with its authoritarian nature, would stifle the free exercise and propagation of the Gospel. "An enforced uniformity of religion throughout a nation or civil state, confounds the civil and religious, denies the principles of Christianity and civility and that Jesus Christ is come in the flesh."[25]

Williams's view of civil government was influenced by the ancient Roman idea of *pax civitatis*—i.e., the peace of the city. Both believing and unbelieving magistrates could carry out this mandate.[26] He likened the visible church to any other group or faction within the city.[27]

> All civil states, with their officers of justice in their respective constitutions and administrations are proved essentially civil, and therefore not judges,

> governors, or defenders of the spiritual, or Christian, state and worship. It is the will and command of the most Paganish, Jewish, Turkish, or anti-Christian consciences and worships be granted to all men in all nations and countries: and they are only to be fought against with that sword which is only, in soul matters, able to conquer: to wit the sword of God's Spirit, the Word of God.[28]

Williams's position concerning the relationship between the magistry and the church is best set forth in what has come to be known as the "shipletter" written from Providence, Rhode Island, to answer the false charge by the Puritan leadership in Massachusetts that there was no civil rule in Rhode Island. It is included here because of its importance.

> There goes many a ship to sea, with many hundred souls in one ship whose weal and wol is common, and is a true picture of a commonwealth, or human combination or society. It hath fallen out sometimes, that both papists and protestants, Jews and Turks, may be embarked in one ship; upon which supposal I affirm, that all liberty of conscience, that ever I pleaded for, turns upon these two hinges—that none of the papists, protestants, Jews or Turks, be forced to come to the ship's prayers or worship, nor compelled from their own particular prayers or worship, if they practice any. I further add, that I never denied, that notwithstanding this liberty, the commander of the ship ought to command the ship's course, yea, and also command that justice, peace and sobriety, be kept and practiced, both among the seamen and all the passengers. If any of the seamen refuse to perform their services, or passengers to pay the freight . . . if any refuse to obey common laws and orders of the ship, concerning their common peace and preservation . . . if any should preach or write that there ought to be no commanders or officers, because all are equal in Christ, therefore no masters nor officers, no laws or orders, nor corrections nor punishments . . . the commander or commanders may judge, resist, compel and punish such transgressors, according to their deserts and merits.[29]

The ideas of Roger Williams clearly resonate with the apostolic era and have made an indelible mark on subsequent history. The United States of America became the first nation out of Europe to reject the sacral society. The first two clauses of the First Amendment put a stake in the heart of Christendom. In America, there is no Christendom; people are free to establish their own modes of worship and are free to worship as they please, as long as other Constitutional conditions are not violated. Biblically speaking, there are only two types of people, neither of which have anything to do with national boundaries or sacramentalism. There are the saved and the unsaved. Those who are saved wait with great expectation and look toward heaven to see that day when Christendom will truly be established on this earth, when the King of kings demands and establishes His rule in the hearts of men as well as over the political kingdoms of this earth. In the meantime, what should be the Christian response in the arena of political activity?

THE CHRISTIAN AS CITIZEN

Today the fear that echoes from our pulpits is the fear that government is increasingly coming under the control of secularists who also are virulently anti-Christian. The recent decision (summer 2002) by the Ninth Circuit Court of Appeals striking down the Pledge of Allegiance as unconstitutional, due to the phrase "under God," would be a prime example.

Too often, however, Christians yearn for a reestablishment of the Christian America of the far distant past.[30] For many, the mechanism to accomplish this is the exercise of political power. The view that God has some kind of covenant relationship with America, a predominant view in the nineteenth century along with postmillennialism, still lingers today.[31] But is this road to political power clearly marked out biblically?

Political activism should be tempered in light of what the Bible has to say about satanic influences in the halls of government. While Satan's domination was broken at the cross and government is given to us for good as well as for the suppression of evildoers (Rom 13:1-7), Satan still remains extremely powerful in the area of governmental affairs. Passages such as Matthew 4:8-9, Ephesians 6:11-12, and portions of Daniel and Ezekiel testify to Satan's power over the institutions of government.

We must never forget that the Christian's fight is against principalities, whose power undergirds political institutions. These principalities will use the weapons of the world system. As in any other area of life, political activism by the Christian demands that he not use the weapons of this world but the spiritual weapons that God has given him (Eph 6:11-20).

> We employ the weapons of "truth", "righteousness", "faith", "salvation", "the gospel of peace", "prayer", "salvation", "the gospel of peace", "prayer", "the Spirit", "perseverance", "intercession", and the "Word of God." In so doing we "find strength" in the Lord, in His "mighty power" and are "to stand firm against the devices of the devil", and to "resist" and "stand our ground" when things are at their worst, to complete every task and still to stand.[32]

The evangelical activist view will be tempered further if we take seriously the New Testament teaching that our citizenship is transpolitical (Phil 3:19-20; 1 Pet 2:9-17). We are citizens of an earthly kingdom (Rom 13:7) with citizenship responsibilities; yet we are still strangers and sojourners in an alien and foreign cosmos. This is not a call for withdrawal, but it is an admonition for the use of wisdom and discernment. Political outcomes, especially in a democracy, are most often transient and are usually a result of compromise. Each election cycle may bring a totally different outcome. Pragmatism rather than idealism usually wins out. Christians are not called to sink their roots down so deep in the political culture that they are consumed by it.

The power of the New Testament is radically different from political power. It is the power of the cross. The world system knows the cross as a place of powerlessness, foolishness, and defeat. Christianity rejects the use of traditional political power to force conformity. It equips Christians to engage the principalities and powers in spiritual warfare (2 Cor 10:3-5). It brings us to our knees, producing a spirit of humility and compassion, thus rejecting the acquisition of political power in Christ's name. Jacques Ellul put it this way: "Every time a church tried to act through the propaganda devices accepted by an epoch, the truth and authenticity of Christianity were abased."[33]

What could be a greater co-option than evangelicals being institutionalized into America's political processes? That is exactly what the framers desired and what Roger Williams feared—that all religious groups would lose their "saltiness"[34] along with their prophetic voice.

Must Christians be caught up in and assimilated by the systems they desire to change? Can the prophetic voice of evangelical Christianity become sharp and clear? The course to be pursued will depend on the Christian community's view of itself, its understanding as to the purpose and function of the church in relation to state and society (i.e., a return to Christendom or the apostolic era), and its view of Christian citizenship.

First, the Christian community needs to view itself in humility, reaffirming the need for confession, repentance, and renewal. Evangelical media leaders today often portray an attitude of arrogance and ignorance on political issues that blunt their prophetic voice and ministry. There can never be much lasting change in our nation until this image changes.

There also needs to be a renewed study of the church; is it *Corpus Christi* or *Corpus Christianum*? There is a need to reaffirm the church's role in "[making] known to the rulers and authorities . . . the manifold wisdom of God . . . realized in Christ Jesus our Lord. . . . This mystery is that the Gentiles are fellow heirs . . . in Christ through the gospel . . . to equip the saints for the work of the ministry, for building up the body of Christ" (Eph 3:6, 10-11; 4:12).

There should be continued study and emphasis about what the Bible has to say concerning Christian citizenship. What about the use of the judicial system? What about disobedience to "unjust" laws? Should Christians ever consider the use of force against governmental authorities?

Christian citizens of this democracy have Constitutional rights, which include political involvement. But what kind of involvement? Christians must reject one of the basic assumptions associated with interest-group politics—i.e., that governmental institutions are prizes waiting to be seized and then to be used to impose on the community at large that group's view of social justice with the force of the law behind it.

There also needs to be an understanding that when a group becomes more accepted and legitimized (i.e., opens offices in Washington, has paid lobbyists, and has members appointed to positions in the political institutions), then a number of things can happen. First, it gains more public control, and its leadership is institutionalized.[35] Second, the group becomes bureaucratized—i.e., subsumed by the institutions it seeks to influence. Influencing governmental institutions is a seductive illusion. The institutions and power centers will end up co-opting the groups that seek to influence them. The cause of Christ has never flourished for any length of time where the church, Catholic or Protestant, has dominated the political institutions of that nation. Third, the church loses its original vision through its misguided quest for greater and greater power as the goal shifts to self-interest and survival rather than redemptive change. With more appeal letters and more headline seeking, the organization is finally reduced to an end in itself. Over the course of his long lifetime, the late Malcolm Muggeridge observed ungodly power being applied by individuals, groups, and governments. The result was corruption. He concluded, "there are in life but two things, love and power, and no man can have both."[36]

Evangelicals should reject becoming involved in a contest for control of political institutions because this is the *modus operandi* of modern authoritarianism and totalitarianism. It is only a short step from the control of governmental institutions to the control of not only people's public lives, but also their private lives. This control would occur even if done in the name of Christ.

Last and most important, Christians should reject the temptation to seek political power for its own sake in view of the pervasiveness of a believer's sin capacity. Will "godly Christians" consistently make biblical decisions concerning morality and social justice? That this has occurred only infrequently through the history of western civilization testifies to the questionable validity of this belief. Christians cannot agree on many moral and social issues, let alone on how governmental institutions should be used. For example, what does the Bill of Rights mean in relation to the establishment and free exercise clauses, and to freedom of speech and of the press?[37] Believers need to be reminded that there can be no healthy or lasting change of social structures without a redemptive change in people, which is why Christ came two thousand years ago.[38]

Christians should consider changing the focus of prophetic action from the national to the local level. James Madison observed that religious faction and feeling was most intense at the local level. The late Speaker of the House Thomas P. "Tip" O'Neill (1912-1994) remarked that "all politics is local." Christians should take a lesson from this observation and focus on social, moral, and political concerns that arise in their own communities, those in close proximity to their local congregations. Practically, it is much easier to focus, build, and maintain intensity at the local level. Because of the growth of the national government and the influence of the national media, Christians often look in the wrong direction and address the wrong audience.[39]

How then might a prophetic voice be articulated locally? First, just as was true in the apostolic age, Christians must be a separated people within the cosmos. There must truly be a demonstrated difference in values and practice. This age is characterized by personal indulgence, materialism, and a search for worldly security (Phil 3:19; 1 John 2:15-17). Too often churches are inward-looking, possessing no vision for their communities, either in evangelism or community involvement.

Second, separation from the world is the beginning of rediscovering Christian community, which is also essential if the church is to speak clearly and act decisively. The issue is not so much the return to the structural forms of the first century, but to the spirit and values of the early church as believers obeyed Scripture. Forms of church community basically mirror the epoch in which they exist, and the church in an agrarian setting will certainly have different forms than the church in an industrial, technological, and suburban setting. To encourage a return to the spirit and values of an earlier time, however, is another matter. Spirit and values transcend epochs and cultures. The warmth, spontaneity, closeness, commitment, and dynamism of the early church should be a part of any church in any epoch. A rediscovering of community could supply at least three things each believer needs.

> From this association he would receive his identity and sense of worth. From this identity he should also receive a large measure of his emotional and some of his material security. If the congregation is truly a community, a genuinely sharing fellowship, it will voluntarily assume a large measure of the responsibility for helpings its numbers in sickness, adversity, and old age. The knowledge that one is part of a sustaining community will give individuals a greater sense of security than the mere confidence that there is a government agency to supply support checks. Finally, the community should help an individual identify and maintain the values by which he will

> conduct his life. The Christian community tells its members that they are creatures of God, made in His image, called to be His children, with privilege, responsibility, and an assured inheritance in heaven.[40]

This kind of spirit and value base would provide a solid foundation for discussion and reexamination of important national values such as rugged individualism, the secular work ethic, self-interest, and self-preservation in light of the biblical imperatives of the Great Commission, the Good Samaritan, and the fruit of the Spirit in the Christian community.

Last, there needs to be an understanding that when a purified Christian community focuses on political and moral issues, there will most likely be intense opposition from the majority in the larger community. To speak and act prophetically means taking the harder way of the Cross; Christians must count the cost, knowing that God's work has always been accomplished by the faithful few.

What America needs, more than anything else, is an evangelizing church exercising the power of the Cross to change people's lives. As people whose primary citizenship is in heaven and as members of Christ's kingdom, we are confronted by a world system concerned with gaining political power. The church must reject the temptation to control political institutions, while seeking locally to alter the lives of those around it. By their speech and lives, Christians must show men and women that there is only one way to have a right relationship with God, the way of the Cross. Believers in Christ need to stand in every way—spiritually, intellectually, morally, and politically—as the vital, separated alternative to a world system that glories in materialism, self-indulgence, and political power.

FURTHER READING

Eberly, Don, ed. *Building a Community of Citizens*. New York: University Press of America, 1994.

Kesler, Charles. *The Federalist Papers*. Clinton Rossiter, ed. New York: Mentor Books, 1999.

Noll, Mark, Nathan Hatch, and George Marsden. *The Search for a Christian America*. Wheaton, IL: Crossway Books, 1983.

Thomas, Cal and Ed Dobson. *Blinded by Might*. Grand Rapids, MI: Zondervan, 1999.

Verduin, Leonard. *The Anatomy of a Hybrid*. Grand Rapids, MI: William B. Eerdmans, 1976. Reprint, Sarasota, FL: The Christian Hymnary Publishers, 1990.

__________. *The First Amendment and the Remnant*. Sarasota, FL: The Christian Hymnary Publishers, 1998.

__________. *The Reformers and Their Stepchildren*. Grand Rapids, MI: William B. Eerdmans, 1964. Reprint, Sarasota, FL: The Christian Hymnary Publishers, 1996.

16

Proposing a Biblical Approach to Economics

R. W. Mackey, II

Although the Bible is not an economics textbook as such, it certainly informs the economic component of a worldview. Over seven hundred passages of Scripture address the concept of wealth, either directly or indirectly. The book of Proverbs is replete with admonitions about prosperity. Christ spoke of wealth management more than He spoke of heaven or hell, causing one to ask, "Why would the Savior place such great emphasis on what seems, at first blush, to be a rather mundane, temporally-focused topic?" The answer to this question centers on the focus of redemption—the human heart! Christ told His followers directly:

> "*Do not lay up for yourselves treasures on earth, where moth and rust destroy and where thieves break in and steal, but lay up for yourselves treasures in heaven, where neither moth nor rust destroys and where thieves do not break in and steal.* For where your treasure is, there your heart will be also.
>
> —MATT 6:19-21, emphasis added

The last sentence of this passage summarizes the concept that the individual's management of wealth is a clear indicator of the heart's allegiance. Taken one step further, the perceived nature of wealth as existing primarily for either immediate use (temporal purposes) or for long-term use (eternal purposes) clearly reveals whether the person is living with an earthbound or heavenly perspective. Since Paul reminds believers that "our citizenship is in heaven" (Phil 3:20), wealth is better reserved for the believer's ultimate destination—an eternity with God.

Many roads in Southern California are lined with job seekers. Some of these day laborers have migrated north into California from Mexico, Central America, or South America to find employment opportunities superior to those in their native economies. When jobs are found, a small portion of the wages earned are applied to the costs of a very modest, albeit temporary U.S. lifestyle, while the lion's share of the earnings are sent to the worker's native home to be saved as a nest egg for future use. Wiring money to other countries is big business in Southern California because wealth follows citizenship! It is little wonder, then, why the Bible gives such an extensive discussion of economic issues when the very nature of the subject so clearly reveals the condition of the human heart.

Foundational Thoughts

Essentially the study of economics is a study of human problems that are rooted in scarcity. Since not enough goods and/or services exist to satisfy all human wants, the need for allocation with its attendant problems arises. How one behaves when solving these allocation problems is a significant theme of God's Word. Although the Bible does not offer formulas for investment strategies or specific rules for accounting practices, the moral guidelines derived from the holy nature of God revealed in Scripture give clear and comprehensive guidelines for economic decisions. In God's Word, one learns about:

- The origin of economics
- The economics of redemption
- The responsibility of stewardship

What better guide in these matters than the one given to us by the Creator and Sustainer of all that is visible and invisible?

The Origin of Economics

When did the concept of *economics* begin? Some say the start of modern economic thought originated with a short book penned by Thomas Robert Malthus (1766-1864), a British clergyman. In his work *An Essay on the Principle of Population as It Affects the Future Improvement of Society* (1798), he predicted human population growth would be approximately 3 percent annually, which would double the earth's inhabitants roughly every twenty-five years.[1] Based on these numbers, he believed that the earth's agricultural resources would be unable to sustain the population growth, eventually resulting in hungry people killing each other for food. The Malthusian scenario was gloomy indeed, causing economics to be dubbed "the dismal science," a nickname that has persisted.

One can't help but ask, did Malthus get it right? The answer is, yes and no. The earth's population *has* doubled roughly every twenty-five years, but Malthus failed to factor human advances into his equation. If he had visited the United States prior to publishing his book, a vast wilderness would have filled his vision. Most of California would have appeared as unarable at best and inhospitable at worst. Now many of the nation's farmers are paid by the government not to plant crops on all of their land in order to keep crop prices up. This is a testament to incredible technological advances that have led to record productivity.

But aside from these issues, Malthus did identify the very foundation of economics: *scarcity*. He knew that food was a scarce commodity. It exists in finite amounts. Furthermore, an item becomes significantly scarce when it exists in less than desired amounts. This explains why diamonds are more expensive than air. Air is certainly more important than diamonds (although some young lady may believe she will "just die" without a diamond); but diamonds are more expensive because they exist in significantly smaller amounts. Air would suddenly garner an exorbitant price if not enough were available for all. No doubt, people would gladly surrender diamonds for air to breathe.

Without the reality of scarcity, economics is not only irrelevant but nonexistent. Economics is simply defined as the explanation of "how scarce resources are allocated among competing ends."[2] In other words, since most goods and/or services are in shorter supply than desired, some method of allocation must be employed. Allocation is the subject of economics, and the occasion for allocation is caused by scarcity. If an item exists in abundance, as air does, then allocation becomes a moot point. If an item exists in relative scarcity, as diamonds do, then guards must be hired and prices set to insure that allocation occurs as intended.

If an economic system performs well, it produces efficiently. This efficiency is the by-product of balancing the factors of production (land, labor, and equipment) in such a way that they complement (or cooperate with) each other and produce little or no waste. In an ideal economy, balance is also realized in the environment as a whole by providing adequate and purposeful work for people within their God-given roles in a constant fashion. A balanced economy produces jobs for all those seeking and able to work.

Questions may arise at this point. When did the human race first experience scarcity, and why does scarcity continue to this day? Does the Bible tell us about the origin and continuation of scarcity? Why do economic systems now need to deal with competition and imbalances? The answers to these questions are found in Genesis 1—3. At least three factors are apparent, and they have great import for economic thinking: abundance, cooperation, and balance.

Abundance

The account of creation is initially an account of *abundance*: An ample amount was made available by God for the earth's human inhabitants. God told Adam:

> *"Behold, I have given you every plant yielding seed that is on the face of all the earth, and every tree with seed in its fruit. You shall have them for food."*
>
> —GEN 1:29

This statement occurred after God made the earth habitable for plant, animal, and human life through introducing life-sustaining ingredients like land, water, atmosphere, light, heat, and seasons. All that Adam and Eve needed to live was available for the gathering. *Plenty* characterized initial creation.

Cooperation

Not only did abundance characterize initial creation, but *cooperation* was present as well. Initially Adam was created to complement his Creator, to subdue, multiply, and cultivate the created realm. The scriptural commentary on the second human's (the woman's) creation is:

> *Then the* LORD *God said, "It is not good that the man should be alone; I will make him a helper fit for him."*
>
> —GEN 2:18

Eve's God-given role was not to compete with Adam, but rather to complement him in the cultivation of the garden. As Adam's complement, Eve accepted his household leadership and worked to help him accomplish the mandates spoken by God. She was designed for this role by God and assumed this role for a time. This complementary activity was true cooperation, not in an egalitarian context, but in fulfillment of God-ordained roles within creation. Competition was not an issue at this point in human history for two reasons:

1. Since the earth's resources were abundant, plenty existed for everyone, and there was no reason to compete.
2. Since Adam's and Eve's motives were pure, they cooperated perfectly. Each performed within the roles that God had designed for him or her and experienced efficient homeostasis.

Balance

Abundance and cooperation existed in an environment of *balance*. The physical conditions of the earth were in balance: darkness and light, land and water, plants and animals, humans and animals, man and woman. This garden, masterfully created by the wonderful Father, was the model of order and, in that sense, capable of infinite existence (Gen 3:22). No mutations were present, and the Second Law of Thermodynamics was not a consideration. Adam and Eve did not need to ever listen to an economics lecture or sit for an examination over the laws of supply and demand. A business cycle with its inherent trade-offs did not exist. Competition for scarce resources and environmental fluctuations were unknown to their world.

However, all of this changed. Economic considerations began with the events recorded in Genesis 3. That chapter describes how sin entered the world and the accompanying results of falling away from God. The conditions of abundance, cooperation, and balance were dramatically marred by the Fall.

Satan approached Eve in the garden and began a process of rationalization with her. His approach culminated in a statement to her that epitomizes the essence of sin—pride. Satan said, "you will be like God" (Gen 3:5). Prior to this encounter, Adam and Eve were not aspiring to be like God but were enjoying the benefits of trusting in the wisdom and goodness of their Creator. God's goodness in creation was theirs to superintend. Now God's way was called into question, and it seemed to Adam and Eve as though a better way had been identified. Since they were not like God, they lacked the foreknowledge to surmise the outcomes of eating the fruit.

One outcome of sin was the advent of scarcity. God said to Adam:

> *"Because you have listened to the voice of your wife and have eaten of the tree of which I commanded you, 'You shall not eat of it,' cursed is the ground because of you; in pain you shall eat of it all the days of your life; thorns and thistles it shall bring forth for you; and you shall eat the plants of the field. By the sweat of your face you shall eat bread, till you return to the ground."*
>
> —GEN 3:17-19

Abundance became *scarcity* due to the introduction of "thorns and thistles." Good things became difficult to cultivate, while potentially productive things, left to themselves, deteriorated. The human enterprise for existence became a struggle with the circumstances that were set in motion by sin. Scarcity partnered with sweat. Getting and keeping enough devolved into an anxious endeavor. As a former professor at Los Angeles Baptist College, Dr. Herbert Hotchkiss, told his students, the fall of man moved mankind from security to insecurity; therefore, mankind would spend the rest of its days looking for food and a home.[3]

Scarcity resulted from and was accompanied by *competition* and *imbalance*. Adam would now compete with the earth's marred conditions—thorns and thistles. These curses did not create equilibrium between crops and weeds, but initiated the domination of harm in the creation without constant, intelligent human effort. Adam would also compete with his wife for household leadership since God had pronounced that her "desire [would be] for her husband" (Gen 3:16). Later the competition became more pronounced between people and devolved into abject corruption, as recorded in Genesis 6. Those who possessed superior attributes dominated less-endowed people for evil purposes—i.e., a raw "survival of the fittest" scenario. The source of this corruption was genetic imbalances—i.e., the lack of parity or balance in innate abilities, coupled with depravity, producing a deplorable culture, so deplorable that God removed it through a worldwide flood.

These conditions of scarcity, competition, and imbalance, set in motion when sin entered the world, made economics a reality. Resources became difficult to acquire and hard to maintain. Competition characterized social interactions. Imbalance began a pendulum swing of extremes in the course of human affairs. How individuals approached the challenges of acquisition and allocation became a huge indicator of the extent to which the effects of the Fall were being reversed through the redemptive process.

Interestingly enough, when redemption is finally culminated in the believer's eternal habitation with the Father, economics will no longer be an issue. The apostle John wrote:

> *No longer will there be anything accursed, but the throne of God and of the Lamb will be in it, and his servants will worship him. They will see his face, and his name will be on their foreheads. And night will be no more. They will need no light of lamp or sun, for the Lord God will be their light, and they will reign forever and ever.*
>
> —REV 22:3-5

The eternal existence in the new heaven and earth will restore the abundance, cooperation, and balance found only in humanity's proper relationship to God. Christians would expect this to be so since the Father is totally sufficient, and life with Him, therefore, will be free from want. It is little wonder that, historically, believers who have undergone great persecution thought often of heaven and saw death as a joyous release, while affluent believers focused more on this life and saw death as a much more dreaded event. One's view of future life with God is a barometer of one's love or lack thereof for the world.

THE ECONOMICS OF REDEMPTION

Scarcity

The people of God, whether in the nation of Israel or in the church, have found themselves living in a fallen world and subject to challenging economic conditions. First of all, the believer must overcome scarcity through ongoing, intelligent effort. The often-cited passage that extols work makes the point:

> *Go to the ant, O sluggard;*
> *consider her ways, and be wise.*
> *Without having any chief,*
> *officer, or ruler,*
> *she prepares her bread in summer*
> *and gathers her food in harvest.*
> —PROV 6:6-8

The ant is the example of industry (work). This industry is simple, thoughtful, planned, consistent, and self-motivated. The passage says that without this initiative, poverty will take over (cf. Prov 6:10-11; 10:4-5).

The apostle Paul exhorted the Ephesians to work by writing:

> *Let the thief no longer steal, but rather let him labor, doing honest work with his own hands, so that he may have something to share with anyone in need.*
>
> —EPH 4:28

To the believers in Thessalonica, Paul wrote:

> *. . . aspire to live quietly, and to mind your own affairs, and to work with your hands, as we instructed you, so that you may live properly before outsiders and be dependent on no one.*
>
> —1 THESS 4:11-12

WORKING

The biblical norm for overcoming scarcity in order to survive and to give is honest, consistent labor. Biblical principles are also given to outline the care of those unable to work. This scriptural mandate for work is so strong that those who do not engage in work are called *sluggards* in the book of

Proverbs. These sluggards are glued to their beds (26:14), make poor excuses for laziness (26:13), fail to begin tasks (6:9), fail to complete tasks (19:24), and are useless to those who employ them (10:26; 18:9).[4] Ultimately, these lazy individuals find that their lives are irretrievably wasted (24:30-31). Paul is so opposed to laziness that he tells the Thessalonian believers how to deal with those who are able to work but will not work: *no work—no food!*

> *For even when we were with you, we would give you this command: If anyone is not willing to work, let him not eat. For we hear that some among you walk in idleness, not busy at work, but busybodies. Now such persons we command and encourage in the Lord Jesus Christ to do their work quietly and to earn their own living.*
>
> —2 THESS 3:10-12

Lazy men with families are especially castigated by Paul. He instructs Timothy that men who do not provide for their families have denied the faith and are worse than unbelievers (1 Tim 5:8).

Under normal conditions, scarcity is the problem and honest work is the solution. Many social activists believe that the solution to most cultural ills is wealth; they believe that a sizable group of people are problem people because they lack wealth. Such individuals often promote programs that give away resources only to find that the resources have been squandered or abused in time. The Scripture teaches, however, that problem people often lack resources because they are foolish, failing to work hard and to manage properly (Prov 24:30-34).

Saving

Scripture also teaches that a portion of what is earned should be saved. Another visit with the ant in Proverbs 6:6-9 and 30:25 demonstrates this principle. The key words for this lesson are *summer* and *winter*. These words demonstrate the ant's foresight in laying aside provisions when they are available (summer) against the time when provisions are scarce or nonexistent (winter). This sort of activity parallels in principle Joseph's planning and provision in Genesis 41. Saving is simply preparing for future scarcity that may be brought on through predictable circumstances (e.g., old age) or somewhat unpredictable circumstances. The word *somewhat* is used because in a fallen world difficult circumstances are to be expected; only the time of the circumstance is unknown (everything is in a state of decay). This seems to be the thrust of Proverbs 21:20 where Solomon wrote, "Precious treasure and oil are in a wise man's dwelling, but a foolish man devours it." The "treasure and oil" have been stored for future need, but foolish people live hand-to-mouth, as if undesired events will never occur, often relying on borrowed funds to handle emergencies.

Saving is mentioned by the apostle Paul in 2 Corinthians 12:14. In reminding the Corinthians of his relationship to them, Paul uses a tender parent-child metaphor. He tells them that he will not be a burden to them because it is the responsibility of parents to save up for their children. Although Paul does not mention the purpose of parental savings, he extols the disciplined activity of setting aside resources for the future needs of offspring.

Giving

The third antidote for scarcity is giving. Giving relieves the scarcity experienced by others. Jesus encouraged giving when he said, "give, and it will be given to you. Good measure, pressed down, shaken together, running over, will be put into your lap. For with the measure you use it will be measured back to you" (Luke 6:38). The early church set a pattern for weekly giving as a part of its Sunday gathering (1 Cor 16:1-4). Giving was directed to the advancement of the Lord's work (2 Cor 9), to those generally in need (Gal. 6:10; Eph 4:28), to the poor (Prov 14:21; 1 John 3:17), to qualified widows (1 Tim 5:3-16), and to those who have devoted themselves to spiritual leadership (Gal 6:6; 1 Tim 5:17-18).

Early Christians, who serve as godly examples, gave generously (2 Cor 8:2), sacrificially (2 Cor 8:2-3), joyously (2 Cor 9:7), lovingly (2 Cor 8:7), and worshipfully (2 Cor 8:5). Some of these contributions resulted from saving. This giving was voluntary (2 Cor 8:4), with no obligation to Old Testament law being mentioned. The New Testament is silent regarding Old Testament laws pertaining to giving. If a person were to adopt the tithe expected from the Israelites, the total tithe would be approximately 25 percent.[5] One thing, however, remains consistent between the two testaments—giving to God has always been a matter of the heart (Ex 25:1-2; 2 Cor 9:7)!

Competition

But how does the second economic problem, *competition*, find its redemptive solution? Or, more specifically asked, how does the believer cooperate with God's created order? The focus of this question is not initially upon competition among people for scarce resources, which is a worthy topic, but rather upon the believer's willing cooperation with God's design. This design contextualizes individuals within creation and therefore allows them to utilize their God-given abilities best, thereby aligning themselves with the blessing of God (Jas 1:25).

Initially Adam found himself under God's authority, and Eve was placed under Adam's leadership. The remainder of creation was subjugated to humanity (Gen 1:26). As creation continued in the established order, abundance persisted. When the order was broken, scarcity began. Economic well-being was ultimately dependent upon following God's order. God reminded the nation of Israel that following His way would result in prosperity (Deut 6). Medieval theologians spoke of a plentitude inherent in gradation. When each stratum of God's creation was willingly obedient to its role, plentitude was seen as the by-product.

Insightfully, Hamish McCrae has observed that the primary threat to prosperity in North America is the demise of the family unit,[6] which many Christians believe has resulted from a movement away from cooperation with God-ordained structures. Since the home is the primary vehicle for value transmission within society, this familial meltdown affects every sector of the economy, including:

- Effectiveness of the legal system
- Proliferation of laws
- Need for more police officers and prisons
- Ethics of the workforce
- Costs of insurance
- Taxpayers' burdens for social programs
- Adequate preparation of the workforce
- Attitudes toward debt and saving

Following the patterns established by God for the home (Deut 6; Prov 2; 31; Eph 5; Titus 2) positions a family and consequently a society for prosperity. Is it possible that poverty eventually accompanies a failure to cooperate with God's order? Is the study of the sweep of successful endeavor in human history in reality a mapping of God's sovereign movement geographically and culturally because His Spirit quickened hearts to obedience?

Imbalance

The restoration of balance to creation will also occur when redemption affects economics. The current human condition seems to be characterized by extremes. These extremes are promoted when individuals argue for the man-made systems of socialism exclusively or capitalism exclusively.

Socialism

The proponents of socialism assume that people will put others before themselves and will work for the common good. Goods and services will be corporately owned and allocated on the basis of need, with some form of central planning to assess needs in advance. Socialists argue:

• Socialism is more noble than capitalism because socialism presupposes that people are capable of selflessness (i.e., goodness).

• The "haves" will take unfair advantage of the "have-nots" if capitalism is allowed to evolve freely (capitalism is no more than "survival of the fittest").

• Eventually the "have-nots" (i.e., the poor working class) will overthrow the "haves" to restore equality.

• Capitalism simply panders to the base instinct of greed.

• Socialism prizes compassion for the less fortunate.

• Socialism emphasizes community over autonomous freedom.

Some Christians have cited Acts 2:44-45 as a defense for a "sanctified socialism" to be practiced by the church. The use of this Scripture for this defense, however, doesn't work for a number of reasons. The church in Jerusalem practiced this communal approach to giving on a one-time, voluntary basis, with no biblical or apostolic command preceding it. No mention of this practice as normative for the churches appears in the remainder of Acts or in any other New Testament book.[7]

Capitalism

Capitalism, in a pure form, relies solely on market forces (buyers and sellers) to establish and regulate an equilibrium price as dictated by surpluses and shortages. Supply and demand govern free exchange, with the participants privately owning whatever they are able to garner through that exchange. The proponents of capitalism argue that it:

• Works because it best accounts for the depravity of man (self-interest).

• Allows market equilibrium to coordinate buyers and sellers, while outside interventions (externalities) tend only to cause problems.

• Solves the subjective nature of pricing.

• Is truly egalitarian as proposed by Adam Smith and is not predicated on a "zero sum gain" (both parties in an exchange benefit).[8]

• Allows its participants to amass great wealth.

• Motivates (provides incentive to) workers because they may keep or give the fruits of their labors as they see fit.

• Has spawned a poor class of people who are relatively better off as compared to the poor in other parts of the world ("a rising tide raises all boats").

• Self-corrects market imperfections when predicated on free exchange (mistakes cause losses, while correct actions produce profits).

• Has an antithesis, socialism, that has failed (as demonstrated by the collapse of the Soviet Union).

Balance

But again balance is needed. God's economy, as portrayed in the theocracy of Israel, possessed both systems of allocation. Laws protecting property ownership were established and enforced (Ex 20:15; 22:1-5). Giving was expected from the one who loved the Lord, which implied ownership (one may give only what one owns). Yet, the year of jubilee returned property back to its original owners—an egalitarian/socialistic norm (Lev 25:10-16). Welfare was commanded in the Law as evidenced in the practice of gleaning (Lev 19:9-10), but laziness was allowed to run its course without a safety net. Because giving was a personal endeavor, the lazy could be differentiated from the truly needy, which is an impossibility under one-size-fits-all government welfare programs. God's approach to managing a national economy was balanced.

One would think that an economic system from God would solve the problems of wealth acquisition and distribution, but Israel slipped time and again into imbalance. The problem was not with the system, but with the hearts of those in the system. In some respects John Kenneth Galbraith got it right in his famous aphorism, "Under capitalism, man exploits man; under communism, it's just the opposite."[9] Economic principles are only as viable as the moral character of the participants. No system works unless it is adhered to by the majority of its participants, and even then it must be reinforced by an adequate legal system.

It behooves the individual believer to restore a redemptive balance as well. This balance may never be restored on a macroeconomic level, since the chances of the church's affecting the business cycle seem rather remote. But it is certainly possible to live in such a way that believers demonstrate a balanced walk. In Ephesians 4:1, Paul exhorts the believer to walk "worthy," using a word that originally meant "balanced" in classical Greek. Christlikeness will result in balance, since He was perfectly balanced in His approach to all things.[10]

This balance will demonstrate itself in a proper approach to working, saving, and giving. *Work* will not be an end in itself, robbing the believer of time in the church and the home. *Saving* will not be an end in itself, resulting in hoarding and its attendant false sense of security. *Giving* will not be an end in itself, with household neglect and religious pride. God's child will learn to balance the enjoyment of the Father's creation with a sense of self-sacrifice. The mature believer is growing "in the grace and knowledge of our Lord and Savior Jesus Christ" (2 Pet 3:18) who was perfectly balanced in all facets of life. The believer should be balanced because each of the three activities is ordained by God, and to neglect any of the three is an affront to His order.

The Responsibility of Stewardship

The oft-used word describing the believer's relationship to wealth is *stewardship*, and it is not a bad choice. A steward is "one who acts as a supervisor or administrator, as of finances and property, for another or others."[11] The underlying issue in this concept is ownership. The steward does not own property; the steward manages property for the rightful owner. This lack of ownership limits the steward's freedom. The museum curator does not own the impressionistic painting on display. The painting cannot be taken from the museum and placed in the curator's home simply because the masterpiece matches his/her interior decor. The point is, the steward is responsible to use the property in the manner and the time designated by the owner. To do otherwise would be a violation of property rights.

The psalmist declares, "The earth is the Lord's and the fullness thereof, the world and those who dwell therein" (Ps 24:1). Paul, when addressing an Athenian audience, said that "God made the world and everything in it," and that "he himself [God] gives to all mankind life and breath and everything" (Acts 17:24-25). Actually the earth has always belonged to God by right of creation, and stewardship (dominion) has been the role of mankind since the beginning (Gen 1:28). Stewardship was marred by the Fall, however, and mankind began to see the material world as existing for human purposes rather than viewing creation as from God, for God, and to God.

A person may counter, "I made this money with my own time, energy, and expertise!" The question remains: What is the source of one's time, energy, and expertise? How do individuals find themselves in the right place at the right time, allowing market forces to produce wealth? Moses told the nation of Israel, "You shall remember the Lord your God, for it is he who gives you power to get wealth" (Deut 8:18a). Ultimately, all wealth comes from God.

Redemption—i.e., reversing the effects of the Fall—is temporally expressed by the believer in subduing the created world in all of its facets (time, energy, expertise, wealth) to the sole purpose of God's glory (1 Cor

10:31). The problem lies in the preoccupation with the temporal (mankind's ambitions) to the neglect of the eternal (God's purposes). Jesus said:

> *"If anyone would come after me, let him deny himself and take up his cross and follow me. For whoever would save his life will lose it, but whoever loses his life for my sake will find it. For what will it profit a man if he gains the whole world and forfeits his life? Or what shall a man give in return for his life?"*
>
> —MATT 16:24-26

The cross was an instrument of death. The life of discipleship is a life of death—death to self with its ambitions, but life to God through the Lord Jesus Christ. Dead people are not concerned with their own affairs. Does this mean, however, that believers are not at all concerned with the cares of this world? No, but it does mean that believers should first seek God's kingdom and His righteousness; it is a matter of priority (Matt 6:33).

One morning, as this author prepared to face the day and looked at the bathroom mirror, he noticed a card taped there by his oldest daughter. On the card were these words from 2 Corinthians 4:16-18:

> *So we do not lose heart. Though our outer nature is wasting away, our inner nature is being renewed day by day. For this slight momentary affliction is preparing for us an eternal weight of glory beyond all comparison,* as we look not to the things that are seen but to the things that are unseen. For the things that are seen are transient, but the things that are unseen are eternal. *(emphasis added)*

The author's first thought was, *I guess she noticed the outward wasting away too!* The second thought, however, was by far the better thought: *Am I preoccupied with the transient?* This preoccupation with the material will produce sadness because the material either departs from the person because of "moths . . . rust . . . thieves" or the person leaves the material behind by physical death. A focus on the eternal—the person and purposes of God—produces great joy in anticipation that the best is yet to come!

The believer's attitude toward wealth (acquiring and using the temporal) is paramount in assessing whether one's walk is by faith or by sight (2 Cor 5:7). Paul reminds believers to "set your minds on things that are above, not on the things that are on earth. *For you have died,* and your life is hidden with Christ in God. When Christ who is your life appears, then you also will appear with him in glory" (Col 3:2-4, emphasis added).

One divine by-product of having a heart focused on the eternal is a spirit of contentment. When the believer is concentrating on the eternal purposes of God, the hand of God is not only seen as paramount in circumstances, but "slight momentary affliction" pales in light of "an eternal weight of glory beyond all comparison" (2 Cor 4:17). The apostle Paul testified:

> *I have learned in whatever situation I am to be content. I know how to be brought low, and I know how to abound. In any and every circumstance, I have learned the secret of facing plenty and hunger, abundance and need. I can do all things through him who strengthens me.*
>
> —PHIL 4:11-13

Paul also wrote about wealth to Timothy, who was serving as a pastor to the church in Ephesus. Ephesus was a city known to prize wealth, sports, and entertainment, sort of a miniature precursor to the current American culture. Apparently some Ephesians were embracing Christianity because they believed it to be the path to riches (a miniature precursor to the "health and wealth gospel"). Paul said that these people imagined that "godliness is a means of gain" (1 Tim 6:5). Paul employs an intriguing thought process when he counters this false idea in verse 6: "Now there is great gain in godliness with contentment." This frequently cited statement summarizes the sentiment well:

> Many Christians believe that: God + wealth = contentment.
> The Bible teaches that: God + contentment = wealth!

Sometimes individual Christians and churches will fail to live within their incomes. In many instances the debt is merely a symptom, the root cause being a lack of contentment. Contentment comes when the believer is resting in the sovereignty of God (allowing Him to lead through circumstances) and is being controlled by His Spirit (one virtuous element in the fruit of the Spirit is "patience"). A spirit of discontent dictates the unending need for more, which is satisfied with more borrowing. When believers are content, they accept God's hand in their standard of living. When believers are content, they patiently save (allowing compound interest to work for them) rather than rushing to borrow (causing compound interest to work against them).

One role of advertising in the world is to keep the population in a perpetual state of discontent. The world, living for the present, will desire the newer, shinier, bigger, better, more convenient, faster, more enjoyable, more luxurious, and tastier. God offers His children the opportunity to step off the treadmill and rest in Him. "Do not be conformed to this world, but be transformed by the renewal of your mind, that by testing you may discern what is the will of God, what is good and acceptable and perfect" (Rom 12:2).

Contentment's primary source is found in having God's perspective on wealth. Knowing what God prizes, as expressed in His word, is a tremendous encouragement to His children as they find themselves in the world, but not of the world. According to the Bible, a number of things are of greater value than gold, i.e., material riches. These treasures include:

- The souls of people (Matt 16:26)
- Righteousness (Prov 16:8)
- Wisdom and understanding (Prov 16:16)
- A good name (Prov 22:1)
- The law of the Lord (Ps 19:9-10)
- Integrity (Prov 19:1)
- An excellent wife (Prov 31:10)
- Children (Ps 127:3, 5)
- Knowing Christ (Phil 3:7-9)
- Knowing God (Jer 9:23-24)

The world sees material wealth as a source of happiness, an end in itself. It is little wonder that so many people are driven to accumulate wealth since they perceive it to be the primary source of happiness in a finite existence. God sees material wealth as a means of advancing His purposes, and on many occasions a lack of material wealth may give rise to and even deepen the qualities that matter most. Some of God's people may possess wealth, while others may not. In either case, a spirit of contentment delivers God's people from a preoccupation with wealth. The believer, then, accepts those amounts given by a loving and wise Father as a sign of His leading. This attitude is wonderfully reflected in the prayer of Agur (Prov 30:7-9):

> *Two things I ask of you;*
> *deny them not to me before I die:*
> *Remove far from me falsehood and lying;*
> *give me neither poverty nor riches;*
> *feed me with the food that is needful for me,*
> *lest I be full and deny you*
> *and say, "Who is the LORD?"*
> *or lest I be poor and steal*
> *and profane the name of my God.*

Having an Attitude

When the world fell into sin, abundance was supplanted by scarcity, cooperation was replaced by competition, and balance was taken over by imbalance. God has revealed His remedy for this part of sin's material results: overcoming scarcity through working, saving, and giving; cooperating with God-ordained structures; and balancing otherwise extreme positions. Between the historical bookends of God's perfect environments (i.e., the garden [Gen 2] and the new earth [Rev 21—22]), believers have a powerful indicator of the heart's affection—their attitudes toward wealth.

FURTHER READING

Blue, Ron. *Master Your Money*. Nashville: Thomas Nelson, 1986. Rev. ed. 1997.

Burkett, Larry. *What The Bible Says About Money*. Brentwood, TN: Wolgemuth and Hyatt, 1989.

Clouse, Robert G. *Wealth and Poverty: Four Christian Views of Economics*. Downers Grove, IL: IVP, 1984.

Getz, Gene A. *A Biblical Theology of Material Possessions*. Chicago: Moody Press, 1990.

Gilder, George. *Wealth & Poverty*. San Francisco: Institute for Contemporary Studies, 1993.

MacArthur, John F. *Whose Money Is It Anyway?* Nashville: Word, 2000.

Novak, Michael. *The Spirit of Democratic Capitalism*. New York: Madison Books, 1982.

Stapleford, John E. *Bulls, Bears & Golden Calves: Applying Christian Ethics in Economics*. Downers Grove, IL: IVP, 2002.

17

Glorifying God in Literary and Artistic Culture

Grant Horner

We live in a fallen world. Oftentimes it looks as if it's fall*ing* as well as fall*en*. Human culture seems to get worse and worse. Whole armies of commentators, both political conservatives and Judeo-Christian culture supporters, flood the bookracks, magazine pages, and airwaves with messages of amoral cultural doom and proclaim that if we do not fight back to preserve the moral center of western culture, we will be overrun by the evils of the "isms." You may supply the "ism" of your choice: Marxism, postmodernism, feminism, etc.

Ironically, it is both easy and common for Christians to look at the area of life called *the humanities*—art, culture, literature, philosophy, and so forth—and identify these human achievements as the *source* of much of the evil in the world. But perhaps we should consider the possibility that these cultural achievements—as well as all the "isms" from both the left and the right—are not simply or merely sources but are rather reflections of the basic nature of humans. These reflections should be interpreted by a standard that is biblically based and not culturally determined. If Christians attempt to approach *culture*—literature, film, the arts and philosophies of humanity—from a human, cultural standpoint, they will be acting in disobedience to God. Culture's reference point is relative and ever-changing, while God's standard is absolute and immutable.

The Example of Calvin

While it may seem an unusual starting place, this essay will begin with a passage from one of the most important and influential thinkers in Christian history, John Calvin (1509-1564). His most famous work, *The Institutes of the Christian Religion*, was repeatedly revised between 1536 and 1559 and is surprisingly readable. It was so widely read that no less than thirty-nine separate editions, including versions in Latin, French, Spanish, Dutch, German, and Italian, were produced from 1557 to 1599.[1] Calvin's work, whether or not one agrees with his theological position, is a compelling example of biblical discernment[2] regarding culture. It is fascinating to observe his treatment of various human ideas about this basic issue.

> It would be foolish to seek a definition of "soul" from the philosophers. Of them hardly one, except Plato, has rightly affirmed its immortal substance. Indeed, other Socratics also touch upon it, but in a way that shows how nobody teaches clearly a thing of which he has not been persuaded. Hence Plato's opinion is more correct, because he considers the image of God in the soul.[3]

When Calvin discusses the nature of the human soul, he first begins by examining the thinking of the great philosophers, whom he has studied extensively[4] in his typical sixteenth-century, classical, Christian, humanist education. He observes that Plato (ca. 429-347 B.C.), though a pagan philosopher, has a somewhat accurate view—he is "more correct." This implies that there is a final standard of judgment that it is possible to be closer to or further from. One may ask, "More correct than whom?" The other philosophers who are in *deeper* error. How does Calvin know this? Quite simply, by reading and analyzing their works and comparing them to Scripture—the ultimate standard for truth. Calvin then continues:

> We are forced to part somewhat from this way of teaching because the philosophers, ignorant of the corruption of nature that originated from the penalty for man's defection, mistakenly confuse two very diverse states of man.[5]

Calvin observes that the philosophers' basic error is their presupposition that mankind is *not* in a state of depravity. One cannot understand man's *nature* apart from understanding his/her *fallen nature*—and recognizing one's own fallen nature as well. He then explains the biblical view of the human soul:

> . . . the human soul consists of two faculties, understanding and will. Let the office, moreover, of understanding be to distinguish between objects, as each seems worthy of approval or disapproval; while that of the will, to choose and follow what the understanding pronounces good, but to reject and flee

> what it disapproves. Let not those minutiae of Aristotle delay us here, that the mind has no motion in itself, but is moved by choice. . . . Not to entangle ourselves in useless questions, let it be enough for us that the understanding is, as it were, the leader and governor of the soul; and that the will is always mindful of the bidding of the understanding, and in its own desires awaits the judgment of the understanding.[6]

He also mentions Aristotle (384-322 B.C.), who was a student of Plato and held many different ideas about the nature of the universe. He partially critiques Aristotle's conception of how the mind works; he even calls these ideas "minutiae" (insignificant) and "useless."

The point is the relationship between the *understanding* and the *will*. The *understanding* makes distinctions or judgments about what is perceived. The *will* follows the understanding and involves the capacity to follow judgments with action. Step 1: I see a slice of cake and decide it will be delicious—understanding the nature of German chocolate. Step 2: moving the cake from the plate to my mouth—the will to eat.

The purpose for examining this writing from one of the church's greatest theologians is twofold: First, it shows that studying and interacting with culture does not necessarily corrupt a person. In fact, it should make him/her stronger, as it did Calvin. Second, according to the Bible, believers have the facilities of understanding and will that Calvin affirms in his writing. It is in this critical relationship between *understanding* and *will* that is found the mandate and necessity for exercising discernment.

Discernment: Exploration, Discovery, and Choice

Good and evil are located in the realm of choice. Sculpture, music, poetry, painting, film—these are abstract entities without an inherent moral nature. In the abstract, they have no more or less moral nature than a V-8 engine block or a pair of swim fins. Moral nature is what we create when we invest content. All human creations demonstrate the fallenness of mankind and reflect, whether they mean to or not, what God has said about man—that although he/she is utterly fallen, yet he/she still possesses the *imago dei*, the image of God. Furthermore, by the Lord's sovereign design, fallen humans will make some essentially accurate observations and then create cultural artifacts (e.g., Shakespeare's *Hamlet*, Plato's *Ion*, or Billy Wilder's *Sunset Boulevard*) that to an extent correctly represent aspects of the universe. Due to our fallen natures, these observations and representations will, nonetheless, always also contain error. As fallen observers, our difficult task is to discern truth from error.

Many will say, "What is the point of all this? It's only entertainment or educational material or simply irrelevant pop culture." But these responses are oversimplified, and none of them is biblical. In fact, in the life of a Christian, *nothing is irrelevant*. If believers have been purchased, not with corruptible, earthly things, but with the incalculably precious blood of Christ (1 Pet 1:18-19), then every action and thought must come under His Lordship (2 Cor 10:5). A scriptural response to literary and artistic culture is not only pragmatically valuable, it honors God and is, in reality, an act of direct obedience. Ignoring or minimizing it is, in fact, disobedience. Isolationism and permissiveness are equal and opposite errors.

Consider the current craze among evangelicals for "Christian" fiction and movies. Without considering the aesthetic merits of these commodities, we may observe that many Christians are getting a large dose of their theology (especially eschatology) from such sources, rather than going directly to Scripture. There is potentially a great danger in this trend. The very best Christian film or fictional work never has the powerful effect of "mere" Scripture. Only the Word can discern the thoughts and heart intents—of authors as well as readers (Heb 4:12), and it alone is perfect, converting the soul (Ps. 19:7).

It is crucial to understand that this chapter is not a critique of certain authors, genres, styles, or even content. It provides, rather, a set of skills and strategies for negotiating a world filled with decisions. Some of these decisions involve one's response to cultural artifacts—books of various kinds, movies, music, and so on. It is an approach that is not only applicable to this author's area of study in literature and film, but also useful to apply to other forms of artistic and cultural expression, from television commercials to Italian opera, from Steinbeck to Camus, from *Seinfeld* to *Doonesbury*. Every day we encounter radio talk shows, magazine advertisements, "edutainment" programs on cable television, and an almost numbing onslaught of cultural material. Further, we are constantly exposed to a wide variety of information that comes to us with the label "Christian": sermons, tapes, books, magazines, music, conferences, Internet discussion forums. How can we possibly process, sort, and evaluate all of this material? With biblical *discernment*:

> *. . . for everyone who lives on milk is unskilled in the word of righteousness, since he is a child. But solid food is for the mature, for those who have their powers of discernment trained by constant practice to distinguish good from evil.*
>
> —HEB 5:13-14

Having an "expert" merely deliver a lecture about the "do's and don'ts" of aesthetic involvement for the believer will not likely result in true spiritual growth. Teaching the process of discernment, however, plants a garden that will bear much fruit. Consider that the "expert" must also use discernment to reach conclusions. Merely handing over a defined list of acceptable material to a group of listeners is hardly teaching discernment. But examining the various cultural elements that inevitably surround us, and then teaching the students how to discern biblically between good and evil, bad and worse, and better and best is the way strategies for living as strangers and pilgrims in this fallen world are passed from one generation of believers to the next. The first element in this process is correct discernment of the human condition. If this critical issue is not properly understood, then no accurate discernment of anything else can take place.

The crucial starting point in the Christian's engagement with any aspect of culture must always be a biblical anthropology. One must have a scriptural understanding of humanness, derived from the explicit doctrine and implicit principles of Scripture. Therefore, the most important question is, what does God say about our fallen nature and our relationship to fallen human culture? Unfortunately, the issue of artistic culture does not resolve itself with simple biblical passages like "Thou shalt not watch films" or "Thou shalt read Montaigne and Lyotard, but none of Shakespeare's late romances or the comedies before 1596." It is necessary to look at larger principles, always keeping at the discussion's forefront the foundational doctrine of the depravity of man.

Some Useful Questions

There are several core areas that must be considered when attempting to approach cultural artifacts from a biblical perspective:

• *What is the apparent moral stance of the work in question?* Is good represented as good, and evil as evil? Are these categories blurred or even reversed? Is there a sense of justice involved at any level? Is man represented as good, evil, or neither?

• *What is the apparent worldview of the author?* Is there a God in the universe whom the work represents, and what kind of God is He (or he/she/it)? Is the universe a place of free will or fatalistic determinism? Does good or evil win in the end? Is life meaningful or meaningless, random or purposeful? Is the universe a place that makes sense and is going somewhere, or not?

• *What can be accepted—i.e., what is true*? What parts of this representation agree with the biblical revelation, and to what degree?

• *What must be rejected as untrue?* What is against biblical revelation, and to what degree?

• *Should one retreat from or participate in culture, and to what extent?* How can a person glorify God throughout his/her experience with this cultural artifact?

The rest of the questions are more directly personal and practical:

• *Can participation in this cultural artifact be used for God's glory?* Is it possible and likely that participation (watching the movie, reading the book) will glorify God through obedience? Is it edifying?

• *Will participation be detrimental to one's spiritual life?* Will this lead to a person's becoming desensitized to sin and the desperate plight of lost people? Will one buy into the worldly philosophies that may be presented positively or negatively?

• *Is this a personal problem area?* Has the person had past struggles in any of these areas (e.g., the negative portrayal of an affair in a novel like *Madame Bovary*, or the positive depiction of materialistic atheism in a contemporary movie)? Could one find any of the material presented alluring or enticing in a sinful way? If so, should the person risk his/her mental purity, using his/her freedom in Christ as a rationalization? Is the person's conscience uncomfortable about participating in the activity?

• *Has the person's obedience been compromised to a point that he/she doesn't recognize this as a problem area?* What is the person's motivation? Is there a wholehearted desire to glorify God by discerning obedience, or is the person being fooled into thinking that sin is not sin or that temptation is not temptation? Is there an understanding of a truly biblical anthropology?

Christianity and the Arts Through History

Many Christians have used Old Testament narratives as biblical justification for total separation from culture. For example, in Exodus 34:11-16 the Lord commands the Israelites to destroy the idolatrous altars of the local pagans to avoid infection by their wickedness. However, using this passage to justify a simple, anti-culture attitude universally applicable to all Christians is without biblical warrant for several reasons. First, the church and Israel are *not* the same (Rom 11). Second, Christians are not commanded to fight (in the physical sense) for the kingdom of God (John 18:36). Third, the issue with Israel and the pagans was primarily idolatry (Ex 34:17), not culture per se. Although idolatry is the contaminated root that eventually corrupts a culture, the problem is essentially with *sin*, not *culture*, which merely bears the marks of sin. The existence of prophets who live in but reject and decry the sin of their society is evidence of this. God neither judges nor redeems the cultures that are corrupted due to the individuals who create the cultures. Rather, He judges individuals in their individual sinful natures.[7]

Early Middle Ages

Augustine (354-430), a distinguished church thinker and leader, was trained in rhetoric, which, in the ancient world, was a mixture of philosophy and literature designed to make one a powerful communicator. Augustine seems to have been led, via his study of philosophy, to seek wisdom in Scripture,[8] and he saw both the vanity and potential usefulness of the arts. In his book *On Christian Doctrine*,[9] Augustine distinguishes between "using" and "enjoying." We are surrounded by things we may "enjoy," but the most important thing that we must do is to "use" everything to bring us closer to God, the true object of "enjoyment." Our fallen tendency is to miss true enjoyment (found only in God) by distracting ourselves with mere earthly enjoyment. We must learn to make right choices.

On the other hand, the church father Tertullian (ca. 160-220), a strict separatist, blasted philosophy and entertainment. However, his remarks show that he was educated in the classical teachings, at least in his younger years. He devotes a brief but vehement chapter denouncing philosophers and philosophy from one end of the spectrum to the other in his *Apologeticus*.[10]

These two early thinkers represent the typical range of views of Christians throughout the ages. We can either make some discerning use of the cultural elements around us, or we can separate radically from all culture. The first approach is risky; the second is essentially impossible.

The Reformation

Most Christians are surprised to learn that the vast majority of the Protestant Reformers were thoroughly educated in the pagan classics. The period of the Reformation coincided with the Renaissance, a rebirth of interest in classical pagan *and* early Christian culture that occurred in Italy in the fifteenth and sixteenth centuries and moved north through Europe, culminating in the English Renaissance of the sixteenth and seventeenth centuries. Many evangelicals consider the Renaissance an "evil period" because it signaled the rise of what later became secular humanism. However, it also paved the way for the Reformation. Martin Luther (1483-1546) remarked on the parallel growth of the Renaissance and the Reformation by saying that God always prepares the way for a great move of His hand by raising up a generation of language scholars, like so many

John the Baptists, making the road straight and clear.[11] Indeed, the Reformation would not have taken place without the rise of printing, the study of Greek, and the critical examination of texts, all of which were hallmarks of the Renaissance.

Humanism

Humanism began as a cultural and educational theory or system, focused on the recovery of classical learning by examining ancient Latin and Greek texts. While Latin was widely used among scholars throughout the Middle Ages (500-1500), Greek was virtually unknown. This, however, began to change slowly in Italy during the latter part of the Medieval period.

All that remained of the Greek and Roman past were ruins and books. Ruins don't speak, but books do. The new scholars came to be known as *umanistas*—i.e., "teachers" of classical learning. From this Italian word we derived our English word *humanism*. Humanism, then, did not originally refer to a human or man-centered philosophy, but rather to the process of learning and teaching languages in the Renaissance that paved the way for the Reformation. Most humanists were in fact classical Christian theists, and humanism was strongly linked to Protestantism. The greatest of the humanists, Desiderius Erasmus (1466-1536), produced the first critical Greek edition of the New Testament in 1516. This meant that scholars could study the *original text of the New Testament*, no longer bound to Jerome's (ca. 345-419) official Catholic Latin translation, the *Sacra Vulgata*. Luther and the Reformers used this new Greek scholarship to launch their attacks on the medieval Catholic church.

Humanism literally paved the way for the Reformation because the ideals it promoted became the standard for the education of men like Luther and Calvin. Early English Protestants such as John Colet (ca. 1467-1519—the first Englishman to preach from the New Testament Greek text) were almost all classical humanists, whose training enabled them to read carefully and critically in the ancient languages. The New Testament, written in *koinē* or common Greek, is a comparably short document (the Author was very good at coming straight to the point!). To facilitate the study of Greek, and also to learn about the past, the humanists studied every ancient text they could get their hands on, whether it was philosophical, theological, or literary, and whether it was Christian or pagan. Their skills necessarily included more than just linguistics—the obedient and effective Christian reader needed to develop the skill of discernment as well.

Luther

Luther received an essentially classical, liberal-arts, humanistic, Renaissance education. Glancing at his work, we find this showing through. He was, however, highly critical of the pagan thinkers in which he had been steeped. His famous work *De Servo Arbitrio* (*The Bondage of the Will*, 1525) was written in response to his friend Erasmus's book *De Servo Libero* (*On the Freedom of the Will*). Erasmus held that man had the moral capacity to reach out and choose obedience to God. Luther argued back vehemently that man was utterly corrupt, that his/her will was in bondage to a sin nature inherited from Adam. Both men had rich humanistic educational experience, but Luther marvelously turned Erasmus's less discerning humanism on its head and used a litany of references to pagan as well as biblical texts to show his friend the unscriptural compromises he was making regarding human nature. In just a dozen pages, Luther makes allusions to classical authors, philosophers, and rhetoricians like Horace, Lucian, Epicurus, Virgil, Quintilian, Boethius, Pliny, Aristotle, Demosthenes, and Cicero. These are intermixed with a flood of references to biblical texts.

Luther, in reference to Erasmus's handling of Scripture (and by extension his pagan sources also), chides the humanist by remarking, "you see, then, how sleepily you examined those passages."[12] Despite his excellence as a textual scholar, Erasmus did not read and study *discerningly enough*. He simply mixed pagan and biblical thinking instead of judging human learning based solely upon the standard of the Divine Word. Luther's scholarship stands out as a prime example of biblical-critical discernment.

Calvin

Calvin is a similar case. Classically trained in the humanities, especially law and theology, but also literature and philosophy, he shows the crucial role that discernment must play in all intellectual activities. Calvin's first topic in *The Institutes of the Christian Religion* relates to Paul's address to some Athenian philosophers, a group of Epicureans and Stoics on the Areopagus (i.e., Mars Hill). In his discussion of human knowledge of God, Calvin quotes Paul's words, "in whom he lives and moves" (Acts 17:28).[13] What is fascinating to note here, as Calvin is not so subtly hinting, is that this quotation is itself a quotation. The apostle is citing two classical, pagan Greek poets (probably Epimenedes and Aratus) in this passage.[14] Paul's point was to show the Greeks that even their own poets, separated from the one true God by their sin, recognized a few basic things about His existence. What should be noticed about Paul's quotation—and Calvin's quotation of Paul's quotation—

is that Paul had to some extent read the pagan poets and was willing to use their own words. Furthermore, Calvin had read Paul's handling of the pagan authors and considered this such an important text regarding theology in general and cultural knowledge in particular that he opened his greatest work with it and referred to it later several times.[15]

What characteristics did Paul, Luther, and Calvin share? *The desire and ability to read and think discerningly*. Did they agree with everything they read or heard? Of course not, and they reached agreement or disagreement by careful exposure and biblically informed critical thinking. Did they recognize truth and error, and did they use that recognition, that discernment, to make right decisions and to serve God and His people? Absolutely. It is an easy matter to see this process at work in Calvin. Nearly every page of his *Institutes* and much in his other works is crammed with pagan allusions and quotations. These are inevitably compared with Scripture. Most of the pagans get it wrong most of the time, but some of them make correct observations some of the time. This principle, known as Calvin's doctrine of *common grace*, finds its ultimate scriptural source in Romans 1:19-20. Certain basic qualities about God and therefore about man are built into every human mind. This information will then infrequently lead to some correct, and many incorrect, conclusions. God gives this knowledge to us, knowing that we will reject it unless His grace calls us to repent. But those who do not repent are without excuse.

Puritanism

The current-day, popular image of sixteenth- and seventeenth-century Puritans from England and America is little more than a caricature of dour-faced, unhappy, anti-sex, black-garbed merchants obsessed with being "the elect of God." In actual fact, Puritans were often criticized by high-church Anglicans for being too merry! The Puritans were certainly very serious about their faith, but their focus was on the holiness, majesty, and sovereignty of God, which leads to a joyful life, and not to legalistic religion.[16]

Of course, Puritans were not a monolithic group, and so there was a variety of opinion about art, education, and human culture. The Puritans were split on the arts, with a few arguing against all art, reacting strongly against Catholic sensuality. Most held that literary works and the arts in general were an opportunity to exercise biblical-critical discernment and obedience. Literary art always depends on conflict, conflict based on an opposition between some force of "good" and another of "evil." Literature represents the way the fallen world works. One of the greatest examples of this is the stunning work of the Puritan John Milton, particularly his great epic poem *Paradise Lost* (1674). Milton is the ultimate example of the classical Christian humanist. *Paradise Lost* is a 10,576-line poem retelling the story of the falls of Satan and mankind that is modeled after the classic epics of Homer, Virgil, and Dante. Milton alludes to no less than 1,500 authors, pagan and Christian, across every conceivable subject. What is truly amazing is the fact that Milton *dictated the poem*—he was blind and recalled from memory an immense lifetime of learning. His discerning utilization of the full spectrum of human learning for the glory of God is a humbling example.

In *The Sinfulness of Sin*[17] the Puritan Ralph Venning quotes from the mythological epic *Metamorphoses*, the central work by the most important classical Latin poet, Ovid, who was also notorious for authoring some of the most vivid, erotic poetry ever written, the *Amores* and the *Ars Amatoria*. Venning's text overflows with Scripture, yet also demonstrates his study of the pagans. Does this mean Christians should steep themselves in pagan material? Not at all! What Venning did was to biblically critique everything that he had encountered in his life. In this case, he had read and made fertile use of *some* Ovidian material in an appropriate way.

Contemporary Christianity

Some twentieth-century fundamentalists were strongly anti-art. However, as a general rule their real concern was not with art itself but with *positive portrayal* of evil and immorality. The central issue is how evil is portrayed—negatively or positively? Film was the primary target, due to the rapid growth of this media form during the same period as the rise of fundamentalism. Legalistic branches of Christianity decried all film, literature, and artistic culture as inherently evil and to be shunned, whereas those of a more liberal persuasion tended to swing excessively in the direction of wide permissiveness. Neither position is biblical. Mindless, uncritical exposure to everything available for consumption is foolishness; but extreme isolationism is neither biblical nor possible.[18]

What Does Scripture Say?

Since the issue simply does not always resolve itself with clear biblical passages, it is necessary to look at principles. Because the Word is utterly sufficient and entirely perfect for all matters of faith and practice and is inerrant and infallible, these principles provide all that is needed to effectively interact with culture. The Spirit does not hold a believer's hand and provide a simple yes or no to every possible option, but He does provide wisdom for making right choices, and an uncomfortable conscience when making wrong choices (Rom 2:15).

Certainly creativity itself is not inherently evil. God is the Creator of everything, including creativity. Human creative ability is a direct reflection of the image of God in man (Gen 1:26-27). Creativity is never forbidden in Scripture, but the idolization of the objects created is clearly sinful (Ex 20:4-6). Due to the Fall, mankind is now utterly corrupt; he can do no good, though he knows what good is (Rom 1; 3:10-12), and he cannot help but do evil (Eph 2:3). Men sometimes appear to be doing good, but even this is evidence of human depravity. When a fallen, unredeemed person does a "good deed," there is often at least some underlying selfish motivation, and even if (theoretically speaking) there isn't, the mere fact that the person performing the deed is inherently sinful makes the deed corrupt in God's eyes (Prov 21:4). Dirty hands handling good deeds make the good deeds dirty. Holiness is utter purity, not general cleanliness.

Perhaps the most familiar and useful passage when considering a Christian's response to artistic culture is Philippians 4:8. This is a positive list of qualities that characterize the things believers should think about, the things to set their minds on, the things to fill themselves with. Verse 8 is enclosed within two references to the peace of God (vv. 7, 9); God's peace leads the Christian to meditate on the things that are good in verse 8, and that meditation fills him/her even more with the peace of God. It should also be noted that this passage contains a general presupposition: If believers are to think on the things that Paul explicitly lists, then they must *discover* these things.

This, then, is a process of discernment, of seeing what is out there, and then deliberately, obediently choosing the good over the evil and making it the object of our meditation. This exhortation must not be used as an excuse to expose oneself to things that will inflame sensual desires, dishonor God, and pollute the mind. Discernment may result in immediate outright rejection and refusal to explore the object or idea, or it may communicate a sense of freedom of conscience to pursue study in that area. Philippians 4:8 should always be used in harmony with 1 Thessalonians 5:21: "test everything; hold fast what is good." Unfortunately, the flesh wants to read that as *carte blanche* permission to try out everything that comes along, instilling a false confidence that it will be easy to keep a safe distance from any damaging sinful material. In order to cut off this line of thinking, the apostle immediately follows this admonition with a terse command in verse 22: "Abstain from every form of evil." The KJV is perhaps even more vivid: "Abstain from all appearance of evil."

The principle is clear. When in doubt, the question must be asked, does participation in this activity even *look* evil? Evil often masquerades as good, but only rarely and briefly can a discerning Christian be fooled into thinking that something good is actually evil. Goodness is essentially open and clear; it has nothing to hide. Evil works by misdirection, disguise, and deception. Again the key is discernment: Good and evil are often intermixed in this world and difficult to discern, due to fallen and therefore limited perceptual abilities. A poem, for instance, will never have all of the positive qualities of Philippians 4:8. It may be "true," but not "commendable"; it may be "lovely" in an aesthetic sense, but not "just." Many a "beautiful" poem is radically opposed to God and His justice.

Another crucial passage is 2 Corinthians 10:2-7. One often hears the central part of this passage, verses 4 and 5, but the context is extremely enlightening. Paul contrasts walking *in* the flesh with walking *according to* the flesh.[19] He says that although he has a normal fleshly body and lives in a fleshly world filled with flesh-feeding opportunities for disobedience, he will not walk under the power or control of the flesh. Further, believers should never expect to fight against the flesh with fleshly weapons. It is only because of the power that God provides that weapons of spiritual warfare are mighty through God to pull down strongholds.

The meaning of the "strongholds" metaphor is contested, but in context it refers to the fleshly thoughts that characterize a world of ideas—a human culture at enmity toward a holy God. This enmity is ultimately idolatry, and Paul sees it in the form of reasonings, imaginations (KJV), and ideas exalting themselves against *the knowledge of God*. The believer's task is to bring *all* these reasonings, thoughts, theories, philosophies, literary works, artistic creations—everything, the sum total of human thought and creativity—into a place of submission before the knowledge of God. The knowledge of God is located in a single place: Scripture. Paul is urging us to gauge everything, to measure everything, to *discern everything* with the standard of Scripture.

One may ask, how is it possible to look up a Bible verse while watching a movie or reading a magazine or a poem? It isn't. But as James 1:21 explains, the believer is to "receive with meekness the *implanted* word, which is able to save your souls" (emphasis added). The KJV translation is "engrafted," and the Greek figure of speech means "rooted word." Scripture commands the Christian to let Scripture take root in one's being through constant reading, meditation, memorization, and obedience. The implanted, engrafted, rooted-in-us Word remakes, rebuilds, and renews the mind, conforming it to the mind of Christ. Then issues and events can be judged properly. This does not provide license to expose oneself to everything in equal measure. A person doesn't have to get close either to pornography or a salivating Bengal tiger to know they're dangerous. But even judging from a distance is judging; it is discernment, and it honors God.

The more biblical-critical discernment is practiced, the better the skill will be developed. With the mind thus armed and renewed (Rom 12:2; 2 Cor 4:16; Eph 4:23; Col 3:10; 1 Pet 2:2), a believer can encounter *anything* and make a right judgment. Hebrews 5:11-14 urges that the mind be saturated with *Scripture*, which enables proper discernment during the daily, unavoidable interaction within the culture. Christians are *not* being called to saturate their minds with culture, which they then try to understand by whipping out *Strong's Concordance*. Overconfidence in one's abilities of discernment and self-control (Prov 25:28) is itself very poor discernment. Proverbs 21:12 states that the wise man *wisely considers* the house of the wicked. It *is* possible to learn by negative example. However, it is important to beware of the human tendency (Prov 23:17) to linger too long over such examples and to become envious of the apparent pleasures of evil.

The Three Crucial Questions

At some point a discerning Christian must make a series of choices. Consider the following three central issues.

1. Can humans make right choices as well as observations and representations?

Humans are entirely depraved in every aspect of their being and can make no right choices outside of the assisting grace of God. Though we are responsible to God for our lives, He still rules sovereignly over us (Prov 16:9). This includes our decisions, both right and wrong. No humans can be right with God or make right decisions without His grace (Rom 3:10), whether that grace is saving grace or the non-saving common grace given to all men (Matt 5:45). Therefore, we should not trust our own wisdom but rather fear God and avoid evil (Prov 3:7). Christians are enabled by the indwelling Spirit of Christ to live lives filled with decisions that please God (Gal 2:20). But even believers still struggle against sin, self-deception, and self-absorbed arrogance (Col 3:5-9). The single most important decision a human can make, that of submitting entirely to God's plan of salvation in Christ through repentance, is not something we can do but something He does (John 15:16; Eph 2:8-9).

2. Is there such a thing as wisdom or truth outside the sphere of God and His Word?

Here the definition of truth is crucial. Accurate (i.e., true to reality) observation and representation is obviously possible.[20] A man may see a photograph of the woman who gave birth to him and raised him and refer to her as his mother. This is a true and accurate statement. He may write an essentially accurate biographical story about her, or a poem, or a song, or make a sculpture or drawing. These could all, more or less, be referred to as true or accurate. However, if he begins to produce a philosophical (or fictive) text that deals with her essential nature, and that text departs from basic biblical principles—for instance, suggesting that she is by nature "good"—at that point a problem arises. It is no longer true.

Here's the difficulty: Part of the representation *is* "true" (she is the woman who bore and raised him), and part is *not* (she is by nature good). The phrase "all truth is God's truth" is the cliché most often heard in this kind of situation. Again, definition of terms is central. If "truth" is the sum total of everything that accords with the reality of the world God has made and rules over, from the simple meaning of Scripture in John 3:16 to the way cells divide, then of course all truth is God's truth. But because of man's utterly fallen nature before salvation and the still active fallen human nature after salvation, our tendency is to see something for which there is (or appears to be) evidence and then hastily judge it to be part of "God's truth." But nothing is proven to be true just because it is hard to argue against. Every day people whom the Bible says are totally depraved do things that appear "good."

How can bad people do good things? Part of the answer lies in a proper biblical understanding of fallen human nature and perception. If a person's presuppositional authority is Charles Darwin's naturalistic, mechanistic view of the universe, then he/she will likely find evidence for evolution in the study of nature. If one chooses to follow the dictates of psychological theory, then he/she will see the evidence for it. A person relying on the authority of the tabloids will believe that aliens are receiving pre-invasion advice from Elvis Presley and John F. Kennedy, who were abducted and replaced with look-alike dead bodies. Similarly, a Christian's belief in the Bible both creates and affirms his/her worldview. A person's chosen attitudes and presuppositions about the world are a major influence in forming one's conceptions of the world. *Some* kind of faith precedes *every* kind of knowledge; it's just that Christians are willing to admit this, while most others are not.

So the question is not, is there wisdom or truth outside God's Word? That is an absurd question. The only important question is, are my beliefs and perceptions attuned to God or to something else?

3. Is there any value to the study of human culture—particularly artistic culture?

All must be done for the glory of God (1 Cor 10:31),[21] and certainly studying or participating in human culture must be done in carefully weighed proportion. Only Scripture enlightens, convicts, and changes men and women. Shakespeare makes some very sharp observations on human experience, but his works have never once converted a sinner. It is not beyond the realm of possibility, however, for God sovereignly to use a Christian's educational experience occasionally, including the study of Shakespeare, to bring about genuine spiritual growth. What is crucial to understand, however, is that a careful reading of *Hamlet* will not in and of itself lead to true spiritual insight. It will be the prayerful, thoughtful, discerning comparison of what Shakespeare says with what Scripture says that brings about the change. Scripture is the ultimate judge of everything on earth. By reading a novel, listening to a song, or studying a philosophical argument *in the light of Scripture*, we do several things: First, we obey God (if we will judge angels, shouldn't we be able to judge books? [1 Cor 6:3]), and, second, we are enabled to *deliberately and knowledgeably* shield ourselves from worldliness, which will surround us whether we engage with "culture" intentionally or not.

The same Christians who condemn a believer for studying "that pagan Shakespeare" or "that demonically inspired philosopher Plato" will unknowingly absorb large doses of Platonism and secular humanism each day as they listen to radio programs and music or watch television and movies. The important thoughts of the most influential thinkers and artists eventually filter down out of the books, universities, and classrooms into the minds of those who never pursue formal studies. Virtually every television commercial communicates either Platonism or Aristotelianism. Ads in *Vogue* for Italian shoes are as filled with philosophy as the works of Marcus Aurelius or Descartes—it's just a different kind of philosophical delivery system. It would be difficult to find a single person in the western hemisphere who doesn't have some idea about "the unconscious mind" and the "formation of the psychē in childhood." It's not necessary to take a college psychology course to learn about Freud. Psychological theories have literally created our culture and have even penetrated the church deeply. Several years ago, during a conversation with the famous Yale historian and leading Freud biographer Peter Gay, I asked whether Freud was "prescriptive or descriptive"—whether he had properly described the human mind, or simply produced a new way to explain ourselves to ourselves. He answered very frankly: "both." Freud, Jung, and Piaget are in the yogurt commercials and the op/ed pieces; Louis Althusser and the French Marxist theorists have given truck drivers from Alabama "their" view of how society "really" works. There is no real difference between low culture and high culture, except that the basic ideas may be expressed in more sophisticated form. Or is it the case that the most sophisticated ideas (2 Cor 2:11) are those that are able to penetrate the heart without being detected?

The Greatest Aesthetic Pleasure of All

So, Christians are enjoined to be biblical-critical discerners of culture. But how can one judge when one is wrapped up in an aesthetic experiential moment? Having aesthetic experiences is clearly a gift from God, as all godly pleasures are. In one's fallenness, however, he/she perverts God's good gifts and turn them into idols. Instead of thanking God for His gracious provision of everything—including pleasure—he/she turns from Him to *anything and everything else* so as to evacuate all thoughts of Him from his/her mind (Rom 1:21-23). Anything can become an idol, and aesthetic pleasure is no different.

Believers are given the privilege of worshiping Almighty God in the *beauty* of holiness (Ps 96:9). God is, therefore, the ultimate object of beauty, the ultimate object of aesthetic pleasure. Loving, serving, and worshiping God is *pleasurable.*[22] He is more lovely than any painting, more satisfying than the tastiest gourmet meal, and richer than the finest concerto. Christians should be absolutely enraptured by His incomprehensible beauty. He is the Creator of beauty and the finest example of it. One's reason for existence and the most beautiful thing he/she can experience is "to gaze upon the beauty of the Lord" (Ps 27:4).

One must of course be aware that earthly beauty can blind him/her to ugly realities. An appealing exterior can mask a deadly core. Christians often find themselves wrapped up in the appreciation of beauty, only to let their guard down and allow the entrance of evil thoughts. Yet, all of life is an aesthetic experience. Every tree one lies under, every warm breeze one feels, every laugh between mother and daughter is an aesthetic experience. Aesthetic objects that are deliberately created for enjoyment—sonatas, lyric poetry, dramatic works, novels—are very similar, though they require, like everything else in life, an attitude of discernment. A mother's laugh may not exactly contain a worldview as such—but one can be sure that Shakespeare's *King Lear* does. The difficulty is learning how to enjoy aesthetic experiences in a way that pleases and glorifies God without turning them into idols. Believers must learn to experience all of life as "*coram Deo*"—i.e., "before God," in His presence. Every moment of life is an opportunity for obedience. One must hold to what is good, and cling to it, and resist and reject what is evil, what is against God, His Word, and His will. Christians may "enjoy," as Augustine says, but the proper object of enjoyment is God. It is only proper to "enjoy" the other things in the universe when one "uses" that enjoyment to enjoy God and obey Him.

But how is it possible to enjoy something while concurrently passing judgment on it? As I type this essay on a Friday afternoon in my study, with a mild California summer breeze drifting through the window, I am listening to Mozart's *Serenade No. 10 in B Flat*. It's perhaps the sweetest musical work I've ever heard. I'm not even really thinking about it though—I'm thinking about my deadline! I don't really need to analyze it for a complex worldview. If I turn around and pull a book from my shelves, it's a different story. Even if the author is a Christian whom I know personally, I have to really think hard and compare the message with Scripture. This is difficult work, but it can also be pleasurable—especially if Mozart is playing. But how can biblical-critical discernment—i.e., carefully considered criticism from a scriptural perspective—be *pleasurable*? It sounds like sitting through a lecture on *Beowulf*!

Before the Fall, *free enjoyment* of everything in God was central for Adam and Eve. There was a single command to obey, and all else was left for their pleasure in God and His creation. After the Fall, *discerning obedience* in a world of ambiguity and potential temptation became the central activity. But twenty-first-century America is a leisure culture, a simulated garden of earthly delights. People work hard, but they play harder. Americans' clothes, homes, and even vehicles are designed for "recreation." Most Americans and, unfortunately, most Christians sit like zombies before their television, movie, and computer screens numbed into a state of leisure narcosis, unwilling (and perhaps unable) to ever actually formulate a genuine *thought* about what they are encountering. And participation without critique is mere absorption. When exposed to something potentially destructive, it is possible to discern one's way through the cultural artifact and emerge safely on the other side a better man for it. On the other hand, one may also be exposed to something with only marginal error or temptation and be seriously affected because of spiritual numbness. One of the reasons there is so much error in evangelical churches today is because Christians don't have time to read Scripture *and* also keep up with their favorite entertainments. So their Bible—the one tool that will help them be discerning in regard to culture—becomes a leather coaster for their soft drink and satellite remote.

Again the question is raised, "Well, how can I *enjoy* when I'm busy analyzing, critiquing, and theologizing?" Several critical points must be understood. First, believers are *not* here to enjoy the world or to love the world's system of culture. Second, Christians *are* called, commanded even, to judge the world by biblical standards. Third, if one does the first without the second, one will become more and more like the world and less and less like Christ. However, if Christians do the second, they will be participating *biblically* in their culture, learning how to enjoy some of the pleasures of being a human while enjoying the greatest pleasure of all—obedience to God (Ps 119:35, 103). The first (participating in culture, including aesthetic pleasures) is a mere by-product of obedience to God and must never become an idol. It is simply a subsidiary form of God's grace, which He showers down upon all. Similarly, I can enjoy the pleasure of my wife's marvelous beauty; and because she is a gift from God to me, it is only appropriate *that I love God more than her*. The result of this is true, God-honoring marital joy.

What believers need to recognize is that, like the world, they too often look in the wrong place for pleasure. All godly pleasure is in God, in obedience to His commands, which are not burdensome. *I strongly believe that the highest aesthetic pleasure is the pleasure of biblical-critical discernment.* This is not due simply to interaction with beautiful objects or stimulating ideas; it is because obedience is lovely and precious and pleasurable. Believers should be able to critique, judge, and enjoy human culture better than anyone else. Christians should not walk away from a cultural experience—reading a book, listening to a song, considering a painting—having merely had a temporal, brief, and now concluded existential moment. *Obedient Christians exercising discernment have made a mark on earth by exercising godliness founded on the Word. Every moment every choice in our lives has a spiritual impact.* God is glorified in one's obedience as well as in His gracious forbearance when one sins.

Judgment, discernment, is a privilege and a pleasure that God has given to His children. Believers are to test and prove all things—some by outright rejection, some by simple exploration, and some by deep analysis. This skill is developed over time by careful practice, preferably under the wise guidance of discerning, older Christians, and always conducted in light of the biblical standards for holiness. Christians get stronger by practicing biblical discernment in practical ways, knowing that while they cannot avoid all temptation, they don't need to seek it out either. It will come.

Aesthetic pleasure is a creation of God, part of our faculty of judgment. We must not separate the two. If we deny our natural sense of the aesthetic and view it as wicked, *then we have in fact exercised a judgment*—a wrong one—*in which we will inevitably take pleasure*. Judgment can be a wicked pleasure or a righteous pleasure, depending upon our attitude. We must not make aesthetic pleasure an idol (aestheteism); but a more subtle danger is making the process of discernment an idol (judgmentalism), either by holding unbiblical, anti-art/anti-intellectual views or by a dangerously permissive attitude (aestheteism again). A believer's discernment must be humble and scriptural, recognizing the tendency to err, to justify sin, and to engage in self-sufficiency—but also holding forth the precious hope of God's dazzling beauty and glorious goodness as the ultimate standard.

We live in a fallen world, one that looks as if it's fall*ing* as well as fall*en*. We cannot change the course of culture; it's not redeemable, because it's not lost—people are. What Christians *can* do is live in the now for the then, always holding before their minds the eternal glory of the Living God.

> *"Hear me, all of you, and understand: There is nothing outside a person that by going into him can defile him, but the things that come out of a person are what defile him."*
>
> MARK 7:14-15

FURTHER READING

Schaeffer, Francis A. *The God Who is There: Speaking Historic Christianity into the Twentieth Century*. Chicago: IVP, 1968; also available in *The Complete Works of Francis A. Schaeffer*, Vol. 1 (Wheaton, IL: Crossway Books, 1982).

Sire, James W. *How to Read Slowly: A Christian Guide to Reading with the Mind*. Downers Grove, IL: IVP, 1978.

__________. *The Universe Next Door: A Basic World View Catalog*. 2nd ed. Downers Grove, IL: IVP, 1988.

Notes

Preface

1. For additional information on this dimension of worldview studies see Norman L. Geisler and William D. Watkins, *Worlds Apart: A Handbook on World Views*, 2nd ed. (Grand Rapids, MI: Baker, 1989); W. Andrew Hoffecker and Gary Scott Smith, eds., *Building a Christian Worldview*, Vol. 1 (Phillipsburg, NJ: Presbyterian and Reformed, 1986); Ronald H. Nash, *Worldviews in Conflict: Choosing Christianity in a World of Ideas* (Grand Rapids, MI: Zondervan, 1992); David A. Noebel, *Understanding the Times* (Manitou Springs, CO: Summit Press, 1991); James W. Sire, *The Universe Next Door*, 2nd ed. (Downers Grove, IL: IVP, 1988); and R. C. Sproul, *Lifeviews: Understanding the Ideas That Shape Society Today* (Old Tappan, NJ: Fleming H. Revell, 1986).
2. For further help see Gordon H. Clark, *A Christian View of Men and Things* (Grand Rapids, MI: William B. Eerdmans, 1952; reprint, Grand Rapids, MI: Baker 1981); Arthur F. Holmes, *Contours of a World View* (Grand Rapids, MI: William B. Eerdmans, 1983); Gary North, ed, *Foundations of Christian Scholarship* (Vallecito, CA: Ross House Books, 1979); W. Gary Phillips and William E. Brown, *Making Sense of Your World from a Biblical Viewpoint* (Chicago: Moody Press, 1991); Francis A. Schaeffer, *How Should We Then Live?* (Old Tappan, NJ: Fleming H. Revell, 1976); and Herbert Schlossberg and Marvin Olasky, *Turning Point: A Christian Worldview Declaration* (Wheaton, IL: Crossway Books, 1987).

Introduction

1. The German word translated "worldview."
2. Ronald H. Nash, *Faith and Reason* (Grand Rapids, MI: Zondervan, 1988), 24.
3. W. Gary Phillips and William E. Brown, *Making Sense of Your World from a Biblical Viewpoint* (Chicago: Moody Press, 1991), 29.
4. Carl F. H. Henry, *God, Revelation and Authority*, Vol. 1, *God Who Speaks and Shows* (Waco, TX: Word, 1976), 212.
5. Carl F. H. Henry, "Fortunes of the Christian World View," *Trinity Journal* 19 (1998): 168.
6. Ibid., 166.
7. Nash, *Faith and Reason*, 47. He gives the same answer in *Worldviews in Conflict* (Grand Rapids, MI: Zondervan, 1992), 52.
8. For a brief history of the Christian worldview in general and the recent spiritual climate in America, see Henry, "Fortunes," 163-176 and Carl F. H. Henry, "The Vagrancy of the American Spirit" *Faculty Dialogue* 22 (Fall 1994): 5-18. Historically speaking, James Orr is generally credited as the first modern theologian to organize Christian thought around the core idea of "worldview," in *The Christian View of God and the World* (Edinburgh: A. Elliot, 1893; reprint, Grand Rapids, MI: William B. Eerdmans, 1948).
9. This suggestive list has been adapted from James Sire, *Discipleship of the Mind* (Downers Grove, IL: IVP, 1990), 30-31 and *The Universe Next Door*, 2nd ed. (Downers Grove, IL: IVP, 1988), 18.
10. The exclusivistic Christian worldview does not allow for pluralistic convictions. See John MacArthur, *Why One Way? Defending an Exclusive Claim in an Inclusive World* (Nashville: W Publishing Group, 2002).
11. Arthur F. Holmes, *All Truth Is God's Truth* (Grand Rapids, MI: William B. Eerdmans, 1977), 37.
12. Henry, "Fortunes," 175.
13. Additional Christian worldview resources are listed on The Wilberforce Forum website (www.wilberforce.org).

Chapter 1

1. 1.6.
2. H. C. Leupold, *Exposition of the Psalms* (Grand Rapids, MI: Baker, 1969), 182.

Chapter 2

1. The registered trademark of the United Negro College Fund.
2. One of the great spiritual/intellectual tragedies of our time involves the majority view of Christian scholars that God created the heavens and earth through some other means than *ex nihilo*, by divine fiat. See John MacArthur, *The Battle for the Beginning* (Nashville: Word, 2001) for a stellar defense of a literal, six-day creation.
3. Both the Hebrew (Ps 19:14) and Greek (Heb 4:12) idea behind "heart" frequently emphasize the intellectual capacity and function of a human mind as in this text from Proverbs.
4. Most scientists simply dismiss the idea that humans use less than 10 percent of the mind as a myth that originated in the latter nineteenth or early twentieth century. This may be true. But while it cannot be measured, certainly the mental capacity of the post-Fall human race has been severely diminished from that of Adam and Eve before they sinned. This is particularly true in the spiritual realm of understanding God, His created world, and His will for the human race.
5. The Greek noun employed here is *methodeia*, which connotes a scheming tactic to mentally deceive one's opponent.
6. Note the phrase "we know" (*oidamen*) that begins each verse in 1 John 5:18-20. Also observe the use of *ginōskōmen* ("we may know") in 5:20.
7. "Mind," "thinking," and "knowledge" are major subjects in the NT. Over forty different words are used to describe/discuss one's intellectual life.
8. This assessment will be made abundantly clear in Chapter 7 ("Understanding Our Postmodern World") and Chapter 14 ("Reflecting Honestly on History"), where many schools of human philosophy and various secular approaches to understanding past events are discussed in detail.
9. Harry Blamires. *The Christian Mind* (London: SPCK, 1963; reprint, Ann Arbor, MI: Servant Books, 1978), 110-111.
10. Charles Colson. *Against the Night* (Ann Arbor, MI: Servant Books, 1989), 26-27.
11. The original illustration is from John Owen, "The Grace and Duty of Being Spiritually Minded," in *The Works of John Owen*, ed. William H. Goold, Vol. 7 (Edinburgh: Johnstone & Hunter, 1850-1853; reprint, Edinburgh: Banner of Truth, 1965), 297-298. The far more readable paraphrased version used here is from John Owen, *Thinking Spiritually*, ed. John Appleby (London: Grace Publication Trust, 1989), 21-22.
12. Ronald H. Nash, *The Word of God and the Mind of Man* (Grand Rapids, MI: Zondervan, 1982), 14.
13. Richard Mayhue, *Unmasking Satan* (Grand Rapids, MI: Kregel, 2001), 21.
14. *Methodeia* and *noēma*.
15. Cf. 119:16, 24, 35, 70, 77, 92, 97, 113, 127, 140, 143, 159, 163, 165, 167, 174.
16. The psalmist prayerfully invites God to be his teacher (119:12, 26, 33, 64, 66, 68, 108, 124, 135) and cries out for divinely bestowed understanding (119:27, 34, 73, 125, 144, 169).
17. Note the psalmist's promise to obey in 119:57, 106, 129, 167-168.
18. Insightfully did Increase Mather observe, ". . . for ignorance is the mother (not of devotion but) of Heresy." *A Discourse Concerning the Danger of Apostasy* (Boston: n.p., 1679), 92. He specifically had in mind ignorance of Scripture, not of general education.
19. For further elaboration on the nature of Scripture, see Don Kistler, ed., *Sola Scriptura!: The Protestant Position on the Bible* (Morgan, PA: Soli Deo Gloria, 1995), which discusses the authority and sufficiency of the Bible. See Norman L. Geisler, ed., *Inerrancy* (Grand Rapids, MI: Zondervan, 1980) for the finest single volume ever published on the inerrancy of Scripture, written as a result of the 1978 International Council on Biblical Inerrancy (ICBI) meetings, overseen by the late James Montgomery Boice.
20. Mark A. Noll, *The Scandal of the Evangelical Mind* (Grand Rapids, MI: William B. Eerdmans, 1994), 6.
21. Ibid., 7.
22. Ibid., ix.

23. J. Gresham Machen, *The New Testament*, ed. W. John Cook (Edinburgh: Banner of Truth, 1976), 374.
24. Blamires, *The Christian Mind*, 110.
25. Arthur F. Holmes, *All Truth Is God's Truth* (Grand Rapids, MI: William B. Eerdmans, 1977), 130-131.
26. Ibid., 125.
27. Kate B. Wilkinson, "May the Mind of Christ, My Savior," Stanza 1.

Chapter 3

1. This essay appears in *The Battle for the Beginning: The Bible on Creation and the Fall of Adam* (Nashville: W Publishing Group, 2001), 11-45 and is used with the publisher's permission.
2. Michael Ruse is an evolutionist who testified in the 1980s at the infamous Arkansas creationism trial (*McLean v. Arkansas*). During the trial, he claimed that creationism is a religion because it is grounded in unproven philosophical assumptions. But Darwinism is a science, he said, because it requires no philosophical or religious presuppositions. Ruse has since admitted that he was wrong, and he now acknowledges that evolution "is metaphysically based"—grounded in unproven beliefs that are no more "scientific" than the set of beliefs on which creationism is based. See Tom Woodward, "Ruse Gives Away the Store: Admits Evolution Is a Philosophy." Found at http://www.origins.org/real/ri9404/ruse/html.
3. Carl Sagan, *ABC News Nightline*, December 4, 1996.
4. Carl Sagan, *Pale Blue Dot* (New York: Random House, 1994), 9.
5. Thomas Huxley, "Evolution and Ethics," The Romanes Lecture, 1893. Huxley nonetheless went on to try to justify ethics as a positive result of humanity's higher rational functions, and he called upon his audience neither to imitate "the cosmic process" nor to run away from it, but rather to combat it—ostensibly by maintaining some semblance of morality and ethics. But what he could not do—what he and other philosophers of his era did not even bother attempting to do—was offer any justification for assuming the validity of morality and ethics per se on purely naturalistic principles. Huxley and his fellow naturalists could offer no moral compass other than their own personal preferences, and predictably their philosophies all opened the door wide for complete moral subjectivity and ultimately amorality.
6. Stephen Jay Gould, *Ever Since Darwin* (New York: Norton, 1977), 26.
7. Meredith G. Kline, "Because It Had Not Rained," *Westminster Theological Journal* 20:2 (May 1958): 146-157. Also "Space and Time in the Genesis Cosmogony," *Perspectives on Science and Christian Faith* 48:1 (March 1996): 2-15.
8. Edward J. Young, *Studies in Genesis One* (Phillipsburg, NJ: Presbyterian & Reformed, n.d.), 99.
9. Ibid.
10. Marvin L. Lubenow, *Bones of Contention: A Creationist Assessment of Human Fossils* (Grand Rapids, MI: Baker, 1992), 188-189.
11. Douglas F. Kelly, *Creation and Change* (Fearn, Ross-shire, U.K.: Christian Focus, 1997).
12. John Ankerberg and John Weldon, *Darwin's Leap of Faith* (Eugene, OR: Harvest House, 1998).
13. Phillip Johnson, *Reason in the Balance: The Case against Naturalism in Science, Law, and Education* (Downers Grove, IL: IVP, 1995).
14. Henry Morris, *The Genesis Record* (Grand Rapids, MI: Baker, 1976).
15. Ken Ham, *Creation Evangelism for the New Millennium* (Green Forest, AR: Master Books, 1999).
16. Ingrid Newkirk, cited in Katie McCabe, "Who Will Live and Who Will Die?" *The Washingtonian* (August 1986), 114.
17. Ingrid Newkirk, cited in Chip Brown, "She's a Portrait of Zealotry in Plastic Shoes," *Washington Post*, November 13, 1983, B-10.
18. Ibid.
19. Les U. Knight (pseudonym), "Voluntary Human Extinction," *Wild Earth* 1:2 (Summer 1991), 72.
20. They "advocate" cannibalism, for example, with the slogan, "Eat people, not animals"—to make the point that in their view the act of eating any animal is the moral equivalent of cannibalism.

21. The fact that we can carry on this rational dialogue and animals can't is itself reason to believe man is far above animals, possessing sensibility and personhood, which are totally absent in the animal realm.
22. Jacques Monod, *Chance and Necessity* (New York: A.A. Knopf, 1971), 112-113, cited in Ankerberg and Weldon, *Darwin's Leap of Faith*, 21.
23. Scripture teaches that such "random" events are actually governed by God's sovereign providence (Prov 16:33). God Himself ultimately controls all the factors that determine the flip of the coin. Nothing whatsoever happens by "chance."
24. George Wald, "The Origin of Life," *Scientific American* (May 1954): 46.
25. Ibid., 48.
26. Herbert Spencer, *First Principles* (London: Williams and Norgate, 1862), chapter 3.
27. Spencer maintained that human consciousness is a manifestation of an infinite and eternal cosmic energy; hence, even consciousness is ultimately a material, rather than a spiritual, reality. Many modern evolutionists still hold such a view.
28. Spencer's "solution" to this dilemma was to regard force as eternal.
29. Interestingly, Spencer spoke of force as "the ultimate of ultimates" (ibid., paragraph 50).
30. Morris, *The Genesis Record*, 18.
31. Ankerberg and Weldon include a long section documenting evolutionists' attempts to silence and marginalize their colleagues who do not toe the naturalist line. See *Darwin's Leap*, chapter 6, "Professional Objectivity and the Politics of Prejudice," 93-111.
32. Kelly, *Creation and Change*, 15-16.
33. Ibid., 17.

Chapter 4

1. This essay appears in *The Battle for the Beginning: The Bible on Creation and the Fall of Adam* (Nashville: W Publishing Group, 2001), 195-212 and is used with the publisher's permission.
2. G. K. Chesterton, *Orthodoxy* (London: Lane, 1909), 22.
3. Edward J. Young, *Genesis 3* (Edinburgh: Banner of Truth, 1966), 34-35.

Chapter 5

1. Charles Spurgeon, "A Defense of Calvinism," eds. Susannah Spurgeon and Joseph Harrald, *The Autobiography of Charles H. Spurgeon*, Vol. 1 (4 volumes in series) (Philadelphia: American Baptist Publication Society, 1895), 177.

Chapter 6

1. Bob Goundward, *Globalization and the Kingdom of God* (Grand Rapids, MI: Baker, 2001), 19-20.
2. Roger E. Hedlund, *The Mission of the Church in the World: A Biblical Theology* (Grand Rapids, MI: Baker, 1991), 22.
3. Ibid., 29.
4. George W. Peters, *A Biblical Theology of Missions* (Chicago: Moody Press, 1972), 85.
5. Bryant W. Hicks, "Old Testament Foundations for Missions," in *Missiology: An Introduction to the Foundations, History, and Strategies of World Missions*, eds. John Mark Terry, Ebbie C. Smith, and Justice Anderson (Nashville: Broadman and Holman, 1998), 61.
6. John Piper, *Let the Nations be Glad: The Supremacy of God in Missions* (Grand Rapids, MI: Baker, 1993), 183.
7. Michael A. Grisanti, "The Missing Mandate: Missions in the Old Testament," in *Missions in a New Millennium*, eds. W. Edward Glenny and William H. Smallman (Grand Rapids, MI: Kregel, 2000), 49.
8. Walter C. Kaiser, Jr., *Mission in the Old Testament: Israel as a Light to the Nations* (Grand Rapids, MI: Baker, 2000), 63.
9. Ibid., 19.
10. Ron Blue, *Evangelism and Missions: Strategies for Outreach in the 21st Century* (Nashville: Word, 2001), 5.
11. Hedlund, *The Mission of the Church in the World*, 205.
12. Blue, *Evangelism and Missions*, 70.
13. Peters, *A Biblical Theology of Missions*, 133.

14. Ibid., 18.
15. W. Edward Glenny, "The Great Commission: A Multidimensional Perspective," in *Missions in a New Millennium*, 107.
16. Kaiser, Jr., *Mission in the Old Testament*, 7.

Chapter 7

1. In a narrower, more technical sense, Lyotard and Baudrillard are among the few postmoderns. Lacan, Levi-Strauss, Althusser, and Chomsky are Structuralists. Deleuze, Derrida, and Foucault are post-Structuralists. Saussure, Barthes, and Eco are semioticians. Adorno and Habermas are post-Marxists. Rorty is a neo-Pragmatist.
2. In Descartes' philosophy, it is God who guarantees that our clear and distinct ideas are linked to truth.
3. *The Anti-Christ*, section 7; in Friedrich Nietzsche, *Twilight of the Idols and the Anti-Christ*, trans. R. J. Hollingdale (reprint; London: Penguin, 1990), 196-197. Emphasis original. He subtitled the work, "Curse on Christianity."
4. Thomas Kuhn, *The Structure of Scientific Revolutions* (Chicago: University of Chicago Press, 1962). His later thoughts are in *The Road Since Structure* (Chicago: University of Chicago Press, 2000). For an in-depth analysis, see Paul Hoyningen-Huene, *Reconstructing Scientific Revolutions: Thomas S. Kuhn's Philosophy of Science* (Chicago: University of Chicago Press, 1993).
5. Kuhn was interested in units larger than single theories. Hoyningen-Huene said Kuhn later regarded paradigms in the broadest sense as "everything subject to professional consensus in a given scientific community" (*Reconstructing Scientific Revolutions*, 142, and chap. 4, "The Paradigm Concept"). For clarity's sake, I am using "theory" and "paradigm" as synonymous.
6. Michael Polanyi, *Personal Knowledge* (Chicago: University of Chicago Press, 1958).
7. Steven Best and Douglas Kellner, *Postmodern Theory: Critical Interrogations* (New York: Guilford, 1991), 19.
8. As a second-generation member of the Frankfurt school, Habermas greatly modified Marx's views and is often regarded as only remotely Marxist.
9. Among theorists, Lyotard accepts a more radical subjectivity, whereas Habermas and Rorty advocate a more limited subjectivity.
10. "[P]ost-structuralism," Christopher Norris, *The Oxford Companion to Philosophy*, ed. Ted Honderich (Oxford: Oxford University Press, 1995), 708.
11. Brooke Noel Moore and Kenneth Bruder, *Philosophy: The Power of Ideas*, 5th ed. (Boston: McGraw Hill, 2002), 445.
12. Jerry Aline Flieger, "The Art of Being Taken by Surprise," *SCE Reports* 8, Fall 1980; quoted in Millard J. Erickson, *Truth or Consequences: The Promises and Perils of Postmodernism* (Downers Grove, IL: IVP, 2001), 250.
13. "Postmodern," Bernd Magnus, *Cambridge Dictionary of Philosophy*, 2nd ed. (Cambridge, England: Cambridge University Press, 1999), 726.
14. Though a case has been made involving each of these, I am not suggesting that each case would be equally strong.
15. For a much more detailed treatment of postmodernism and a Christian's response to it, see Brian Morley, *Pathways to God: Comparing Apologetic Methods* (Downers Grove, IL: IVP, expected 2004). Also, the author would like to thank colleagues Joe Suzuki and Grant Horner for their insights.

Chapter 8

1. Demosthenes, "Speeches 51-61," http://www.perseus.tufts.edu/cgi-bin/ptext?doc=Perseus:text:1000.01.0080&query=section53.
2. Jo-Ann Shelton, *As the Romans Did* (New York: Oxford University Press, 1998), 37-55.
3. J. I. Packer, *Knowing Man* (Wheaton, IL: Crossway Books, 1979), 43.
4. *Webster's New Collegiate Dictionary* (1980), s.v. "masculine."
5. John MacArthur, *Different by Design* (Wheaton, IL: Victor, 1994), 44.
6. Werner Neuer, *Man and Woman* (Wheaton, IL: Crossway Books, 1991), 15-16.
7. Shulamith Firestone, *The Dialectic of Sex: The Case for Feminist Revolution* (New York: Bantam, 1971), 1-13.
8. Ibid., 223, 261-262.

9. Neuer, *Man & Woman*, 25, referencing Werner P. Lersch, *Vom Wesen der Geschlecter* (München-Basel: n.p., 1968), 126.
10. Ibid., 26-51.
11. John Benton, *Gender Questions* (London: Evangelical Press, 2000), 18.
12. A. B. Bruce, *The Training of the Twelve* (Grand Rapids, MI: Kregel, 1971), 38.
13. John M. Frame, *The Doctrine of God* (Phillipsburg, NJ: Presbyterian and Reformed, 2002), 384-385.
14. Douglas Wilson, *Future Men* (Moscow, ID: Canon Press, 2001), 49.
15. Stuart W. Scott, *The Exemplary Husband* (Bemidji, MN: Focus Publishing, 2000), 117-142.
16. Benton, *Gender Questions*, 43.
17. John Piper, *What's the Difference?* (Wheaton, IL: Crossway Books, 1990), 22.
18. MacArthur, *Different by Design*, 44.

Chapter 9

1. Portions of this chapter have been adapted from Patricia Ennis and Lisa Tatlock, *Becoming a Woman Who Pleases God: A Guide to Developing Your Biblical Potential* (Chicago: Moody Press, 2003), with the publisher's permission.
2. *Random House Webster's College Dictionary,* s.v. "femininity."
3. Elisabeth Elliot, "The Gift of Femininity," http://www.backtothebible.org/gateway/today/18731 (October 6, 1998).
4. Ibid.
5. Betty Friedan, *The Feminine Mystique* (New York: Dell, 1963).
6. Piper and Wayne Grudem, *Recovering Biblical Manhood and Womanhood* (Wheaton, IL: Crossway Books, 1991), 33.
7. See Ennis and Tatlock, *Becoming a Woman Who Pleases God* for further elaboration.
8. J. I. Packer, *Knowing God* (Downers Grove, IL: IVP, 1973), 68-72.
9. *The New Bible Dictionary*, eds. I. Howard Marshall, A. R. Millard, J. I. Packer, and Donald J. Wiseman (Downers Grove, IL: IVP, 1962), s.v. "wisdom."
10. John MacArthur, *The MacArthur Study Bible* (Nashville: Word, 1997), 877.
11. *Random House Webster's College Dictionary* (1995), s.v. "principle."
12. Clovis Chappell, *Feminine Faces: Sermons on Women of the Bible* (Grand Rapids, MI: Baker, 1974), 21.
13. Charles Hummel, *Tyranny of the Urgent* (Downers Grove, IL: IVP, 1967), 12-15.
14. MacArthur, *The MacArthur Study Bible,* 19.

Chapter 10

1. *Oxford English Dictionary Online*, 2nd ed., 1989, s.v. "worship."
2. Kenneth W. Osbeck, *The Ministry of Music* (Grand Rapids, MI: Zondervan, 1971), 177.
3. Edwin Yamauchi, "חָוָה (*hawa*)," *Theological Wordbook of the Old Testament* (*TWOT*), eds. R. Laird Harris, Gleason L. Archer Jr., and Bruce K. Waltke, Vol. 1 (Chicago: Moody Press, 1980), 619, 267-269. Cf. Edwin Yamauchi, "שָׁחָה (*shaha*)," *TWOT*, Vol. 2, 2360, 914-915.
4. W. E. Vine, *Vine's Expository Dictionary of New Testament Words* (Old Tappan, NJ: Fleming H. Revell, 1966), 236.
5. Ibid., 235.
6. Quoted in Donald P. Hustad, *True Worship: Reclaiming the Wonder and Majesty* (Wheaton, IL: Harold Shaw, 1998), 272.
7. Ibid.
8. "O God, What Offering Shall I Give to Thee?," *Hymns and Psalms* (London: Methodist Publishing House, 1983), 801.
9. Donald Hustad, *Jubilate II* (Carol Stream, IL: Hope, 1993), 124.
10. John MacArthur, *The Ultimate Priority* (Chicago: Moody Press, 1983), 16, 20.
11. Quoted in Philip Yancey, *The Bible Jesus Read* (Grand Rapids, MI: Zondervan, 1999), 127.
12. John Piper, *Let the Nations Be Glad! The Supremacy of God in Missions* (Grand Rapids, MI: Baker, 1993), 11.
13. William Temple, "The Hope of a New World," in Vernon M. Whaley, *Understanding*

Music and Worship in the Local Church (Wheaton, IL: Evangelical Training Association, 1995), 10.

14. Robert Webber, *Worship Is a Verb* (Waco, TX: Word, 1985), 10.
15. Philip P. Bliss, "The Light of the World Is Jesus," stanza 1.
16. Gregory Nazianzen, "O Light That Knew No Dawn," trans. John Brownlie, stanza 1.
17. Thomas O. Chisholm, "Great Is Thy Faithfulness," stanza 1.
18. Stuart K. Hine, "How Great Thou Art," stanza 1.
19. Isaac Watts, "I Sing the Mighty Power of God," stanza 1.
20. Walter Chalmers Smith, "Immortal, Invisible," stanza 1.
21. Merrill F. Unger, *Unger's Bible Handbook* (Chicago: Moody Press, 1966), 438.
22. Isaac Watts, "At the Cross," stanza 1.
23. Ronald B. Allen, *The Wonder of Worship* (Nashville: Word, 2001), 45.
24. Ken Bible, *Wesley Hymns* (Kansas City, KS: Lillenas, 1982), Foreword.
25. John MacArthur, Joni Eareckson Tada, and Robert and Bobbie Wolgemuth, *O Worship the King* (Wheaton, IL: Crossway Books, 2000).
26. John MacArthur, Joni Eareckson Tada, and Robert and Bobbie Wolgemuth, *O Come, All Ye Faithful* (Wheaton, IL: Crossway Books, 2001).
27. John MacArthur, Joni Eareckson Tada, and Robert and Bobbie Wolgemuth, *What Wondrous Love Is This* (Wheaton, IL: Crossway Books, 2002).
28. John MacArthur, Joni Eareckson Tada, and Robert and Bobbie Wolgemuth, *When Morning Gilds the Skies* (Wheaton, IL: Crossway Books, 2002).
29. A. W. Tozer, *Whatever Happened to Worship?* (Camp Hill, PA: Christian Publications, 1985), 13.
30. John MacArthur, *The MacArthur Study Bible* (Nashville: Word, 1997), 1997.
31. Ibid.
32. Quoted in Leen and Kathleen Ritmeyer, *Worship and Ritual in Herod's Temple,* Ritmeyer Archaeological Design, Slide Set 5 (Harrogate, England: Ritmeyer Archaeological Design, 1999), 6.
33. Tozer, *Whatever Happened to Worship?*, 23, 122, 125.
34. C. [Calvin] M. Johansson, unpublished lecture notes on "Church Music and Theology: Some Philosophical Bases for Church Music" (July 1994), 5.
35. Osbeck, *The Ministry of Music*, 24, 26.
36. Ibid., 22.
37. Piano is often considered a good instrument on which to start a child. It represents both treble and bass clefs and good hand, eye, and ear coordination and is basic to many other instruments.
38. Frank E. Gaebelein, *The Christian, the Arts, and Truth* (Portland: Multnomah, 1985), 34.
39. Leonard R. Payton, "Congregational Singing and the Ministry of the Word," *The Highway* (July 1998), quoted in John MacArthur, "With Hearts and Minds and Voices," *CRI Journal* (Winter 2000), 12.
40. Calvin M. Johansson, *Discipling Music Ministry* (Peabody, MA: Hendrickson, 1992), 136.
41. Douglas Bookman, unpublished lecture notes, The Master's College, April 10, 2002.
42. MacArthur, "With Hearts and Minds and Voices," 14-15.
43. *The Works of John Wesley* (Grand Rapids, MI: Zondervan, n.d.), 346, quoted in Osbeck, *The Ministry of Music*, 61.

Chapter 11

1. For a historical discussion of this jurisdictional dispute of who is qualified to give counsel, the psychiatrist or the pastor, see Andrew Abbott, *The System of Professions: An Essay on the Division of Expert Labor* (Chicago: University of Chicago Press, 1988) and David A. Powlison, *Competent to Counsel? The History of a Conservative Protestant Anti-psychiatry Movement*, Ph.D. dissertation, University of Pennsylvania, 1996.
2. Cf. Ps 1:1-2; 119:50, 92; 2 Tim 3:15-17; 2 Pet 1:3, 19-21.
3. Cf. Luke 2:35; Heb 4:12-13.
4. Cf. Ps 73:25-28; Rom 11:36; 1 Cor 10:31; 1 John 1:3-4.
5. German for a comprehensive worldview.
6. One universal axiom taught to pastoral students regardless of the psychological tradition of

the seminary illustrates the jurisdictional encroachment of the therapeutic agenda: "Pastoral counseling is only for the most basic problems of life (e.g. interpersonal struggles, pre-marital counseling). The pastor should never assume the counseling of the weightier issues of 'mental diseases' (e.g. manic depression, the suicidal, panic attacks, schizophrenia, sadomasochism, multiple personalities, attention deficient, etc.) for which only a trained psychotherapist is qualified." This reasoning is based upon the fundamental presupposition that the Word of God does not speak to the substance of these problems and referral needs to be made to a trained "professional" in the matters of the psychē (i.e., humanistic psychology).

7. Few realize Ladd was appointed the second president of the American Psychological Association before the more well-known William James.
8. Sigmund Koch, "Psychology Cannot be a Coherent Science," *Psychology Today*, September 1969, 66.
9. The more common are the Minnesota Multiphasic Personality Inventory (MMPI/MMPI-2) and the Taylor-Johnson Temperament Analysis (T-JTA).
10. John F. MacArthur and Wayne A. Mack, *Introduction to Biblical Counseling* (Dallas: Word, 1994), 7.
11. This word occurs 101 times in the New Testament and over 900 in the Septuagint, most often translating the Hebrew *nepeš* (soul, breath), but occasionally *lēb* (heart, inner man, 25 times), *hayyâh* (life, 5 times), *rûah* (spirit, 2 times), and *'îš* (man, 1 time, Leviticus 17:4).
12. Biblical usage of the term *logos* meant "word" or "law" while the Classical stressed the human discipline or study—*ology*. Also see an early distinction of *psychē* (unconscious soul) and *thymos* (conscious soul) in Homer, *Iliad*, 11, 334.
13. Matthew 25:15; Mark 5:30; Rom 1:16; 1 Cor 4:19-20; Phil 3:10.
14. D.A. Carson, *Exegetical Fallacies* (Grand Rapids, MI: Baker, 1984), 32-33.
15. In practice, it is the Bible that ends up supplementing psychotherapeutic theory in Christian psychology, not vice versa.
16. Frank B. Minirth, *Christian Psychiatry* (Old Tappan, NJ: Fleming H. Revell, 1977), 64-65.
17. Jay E. Adams, *A Theology of Christian Counseling* (Grand Rapids, MI: Zondervan, 1979), 116.
18. Prov 30:5-6; cf. Deut 4:2; 12:32; Matt 5:18-20; Rev 22:18-19.
19. Robert C. Roberts, "A Christian Psychology View," *Psychology & Christianity: Four Views*, eds. Eric L. Johnson and Stanton L. Jones (Downers Grove, IL: IVP, 2000), 159.
20. Ibid.
21. Ibid, 110. The Bible does not claim to be a textbook on biology, chemistry, physics, astronomy, or business administration either; but when it speaks in these areas, it speaks infallibly and authoritatively. However, the Bible does claim to be the counsel of God for man.
22. This is Dr. David Powlison's term (instructor at the Christian Counseling and Education Foundation and professor at Westminster Theological Seminary in Philadelphia).
23. Robert S. Feldman, *Essentials of Understanding Psychology*, 4th ed. (Boston: McGraw Hill, 2000), 4.
24. Karl Popper, "Science Theory and Falsifiability," *Perspectives in Philosophy*, ed. Robert N. Beck (New York: Holt, Richart, Winston, 1975), 343.
25. Scott O. Lilienfeld, "The Scientific Review of Mental Health Practice: Our Raison d' tre," *The Scientific Review of Mental Health Practice*, Spring-Summer 2002, 5.
26. See psychologist Harry Harlow's classic study: H. F. Harlow and R. R. Zimmerman, "Affectional Responses in the Infant Monkey," *Science* (1959), 130, 421-432.
27. Edward T. Welch, *Blame it on the Brain?* (Phillipsburg, NJ: Presbyterian & Reformed, 1998), 91.
28. David Powlison, "Critiquing Modern Integrationists," *The Journal of Biblical Counseling*, XI (Spring 1993), 32.
29. Ibid., 33.
30. 1 Sam 18:1; Matt 22:37-40; Mark 12:30-31; Eph 5:28-29; see also Jay E. Adams, *The Biblical View of Self-Esteem, Self-Love, Self-Image* (Eugene, OR: Harvest House, 1986) and Paul Brownback, *The Danger of Self Love: Re-examining a Popular Myth* (Chicago: Moody Press, 1982).
31. *Sanguine*, *phlegmatic*, *melancholy*, and *choleric* have Latin roots that refer to the four bodily humors respectively—blood, phlegm, black bile, and yellow bile. It was believed by the

ancient Greeks that an abundance of any of these humors in the body determined personality characteristics.

32. National Association of Nouthetic Counselors, 3600 W. 96th St., Indianapolis, IN 46268-2905, www.nanc.org.
33. Lawrence J. Crabb, Jr., *Effective Biblical Counseling* (Grand Rapids, MI: Zondervan, 1977), 36-37.
34. A phrase coined by Jay Adams and heard personally by this author.
35. John H. Coe, "Why Biblical Counseling Is Unbiblical," CAPS 1991 position paper presentation, 7, www-students.biola.edu~jay/bcresponse.html.
36. Ronald Barclay Allen, *Praise! A Matter of Life and Breath* (Nashville: Thomas Nelson, 1980), 140.
37. Ernst Jenni, Claus Westermann, *Theological Lexicon of the Old Testament*, Vol. 3, trans. Mark E. Biddle (Peabody, MA: Hendrickson Publishers, 1997), 1312-1317.
38. An excellent treatise for instructing counselees enduring unjust suffering is 1 Peter 2:13—4:19.
39. John Calvin, *Institutes of the Christian Religion*, Vol. 1, ed. John T. McNeill, trans. Ford Lewis Battles (Philadelphia: The Westminster Press, 1960), 72.

Chapter 12

1. Ronald H. Nash, *Life's Ultimate Questions* (Grand Rapids, MI: Zondervan, 1999), 14-17.
2. *The American Heritage Dictionary*, s.v. "science."
3. Del Ratzch, *Science and Its Limitations* (Downers Grove, IL: IVP, 2000).
4. Henry H. Bauer, *Scientific Literacy and the Myth of the Scientific Method* (Urbana, IL: University of Illinois Press, 1992).
5. Isaac Asimov, *Asimov's Biographical Encyclopedia of Science and Technology*, 2nd ed. (Garden City, NY: Doubleday, 1982), 100.
6. Although mass and weight are not synonyms, they are related. Mass is a measure of the amount of substance present. Weight is a measure of the gravitational attraction of the earth for an object. In science, the terms are used interchangeably, even though in the laboratory mass is always measured.
7. For a list of hard sciences see http://www.hardsciences.info/.
8. For an indication that this is a widely held perspective see http://www.columbia.edu/cu21stC/issue-1.1/soft.htm.
9. An Internet search using google.com produced 223,000 hits for "Scientific Method."
10. See Thomas S. Kuhn, *The Structure of Scientific Revolutions*, 3rd ed. (Chicago: University of Chicago Press, 1996); John Losee, *A Historical Introduction to the Philosophy of Science*, 4th ed. (New York: Oxford University Press, 2001); Jeffery C. Leon, *Science and Philosophy in the West* (Upper Saddle River, NJ: Prentice-Hall, 1999).
11. John Bartlett, *Familiar Quotations* (Boston: Little, Brown and Company, 1968), 950a.
12. Elizabeth Loftus, *Memory* (Reading, PA: Addison Wesley, 1980), 39.
13. Leon, *Science and Philosophy in the West*, 13.
14. SI is an abbreviation for Le Système International d'Unités, French for the International System of Units, http://physics.nist.gov/cuu/Units/introduction.html.
15. For example, the *Westminster Confession of Faith* (A.D. 1647) regarding all sixty-six books of the Bible: "All [of] which are given by inspiration of God to be the rule of faith and life" (I,I).
16. See Chapter One, "Embracing the Authority and Sufficiency of Scripture" for an elaboration of this theme.
17. Arthur F. Holmes, *All Truth Is God's Truth* (Downers Grove, IL: IVP, 1977).
18. See http://www.acesonline.org/Columnists/Jacobyarticle 21 dj.htm.
19. John MacArthur, *The MacArthur Study Bible* (Nashville: Word, 1997), 693.
20. For an excellent treatment of this topic see John MacArthur, *The Battle for the Beginning* (Nashville: Word, 2001).
21. In John F. MacArthur and Wayne A. Mack, *Introduction to Biblical Counseling* (Dallas: Word, 1994), 63-97.
22. The writer has taken the liberty of labeling Dr. Bookman's "Rule Book" view as the "One Book" view to place this perspective in sharper relief with the "Two Book" view.
23. James G. McCarthy, *The Gospel According to Rome* (Eugene, OR: Harvest House, 1995), 11.

24. See, for example, http://www.talkorigins.org/faqs/faq-age-of-earth.html.
25. MacArthur, *Battle for the Beginning*, 53-54.
26. *Les Moments Poetiques d'Andre Marie Ampere*, trans. Frederick N. Skiff (Paris: Sodel, 1986).

Chapter 13

1. Aristotle, *The Politics*, trans. T. A. Sinclaire (Baltimore: Penguin Books, 1972), 295-316.
2. Arthur F. Holmes, *Building the Christian Academy* (Grand Rapids, MI: William B. Eerdmans, 2001), 9.
3. Alvin J. Schmidt, *Under The Influence: How Christianity Transformed Civilization* (Grand Rapids, MI: Zondervan, 2001), 173.
4. Ibid., 187.
5. Roy B. Zuck, *Teaching as Paul Taught* (Grand Rapids, MI: Baker, 1998), 198-240.
6. Ibid., 172.
7. A. Horton, ed., "A Biblical Approach to Objectionable Elements," *Christian Education: Its Mandate and Mission* (Greenville, SC: Bob Jones University Press, 1992), 47-70. This article is also available on the Bob Jones University Press website (www.bjup.com/resources/articles).

Chapter 14

1. Stephen L. Mansfield, *More Than Dates and Dead People: Recovering a Christian View of History* (Nashville: Cumberland House, 2000). A brief, breezy, humorous book to help Christian students appreciate history. Many subsequent footnotes will concisely comment on sources. Some footnotes will also contain significant, substantive information not entirely essential to the narrative of the chapter. "If historians could not quote, they would deem it a disastrous impediment to the communication of knowledge about the past." J. H. Hexter, "Historiography: The Rhetoric of History," *International Encyclopedia of the Social Sciences*, Vol. 6 (New York: Macmillan and Free Press, 1968), 385, quoted in David L. Sills and Robert K. Merton, eds., *Social Science Quotations: Who said What, When, and Where* (New Brunswick, NJ: Transaction Publishers, 2000), 89.
2. Beverley Southgate, *History: What and Why? Ancient, Modern, and Postmodern Perspectives,* 2nd ed. (New York: Routledge, 2001), 13. A sophisticated primer on history from a postmodern perspective.
3. Earle E. Cairns, *God and Man in Time: A Christian Approach to Historiography* (Grand Rapids, MI: Baker Book House, 1979), 15. A truly outstanding work that ought to be updated and republished.
4. Earle E. Cairns, *Christianity Through the Centuries: A History of the Christian Church*, 3rd ed. revised and expanded (Grand Rapids, MI: Zondervan, 1996), 17. A great one-volume church history that every Christian should read.
5. Bernard Norling, *Towards a Better Understanding of History* (Notre Dame, IN: University of Notre Dame Press, 1960), 10. This book is so good there have been numerous printings without being revised.
6. Elizabeth Fox-Genovese and Elisabeth Lasch-Quinn, eds., *Reconstructing History: The Emergence of a New Historical Society* (New York: Routledge, 1999), xiii. Superb anthology published mainly to explain the formation of The Historical Society, whose members reject postmodernist political correctness.
7. John Lukacs, *A Student's Guide to the Study of History* (Wilmington, DE: ISI Books, 2000), 1. A fine, very brief primer.
8. Southgate, *History*, 2; Lukacs, *A Student's Guide to the Study of History*, 34.
9. John Lukacs, "Popular and Professional History," *Historically Speaking* III, 4 (2002), 5. See also John Wilson, "The Decline of Popular History?" and Allan Megill, "Are We Asking Too Much of History?" in the same issue.
10. Marc Bloch, *The Historian's Craft,* trans. Peter Putnam (New York: Vintage Books, 1953), 31. A classic work by a heroic French author who was not an evangelical Christian.
11. Philip Schaff, *What Is Church History? A Vindication of the Idea of Historical Development* (Philadelphia: J.B. Lippincott and Co., 1846), 5, quoted in Michael Bauman and Martin I. Klauber, *Historians of the Christian Tradition: Their Methodology and Influence on Western Thought* (Nashville: Broadman & Holman, 1995), 273, 279 (quotation). Strangely, my paperback edition of Bauman and Klauber's book does not contain a table of contents, a very unhelpful feature of an otherwise good book.
12. Cairns, *God & Man in Time*, 11.

13. Ibid., 59.
14. Ibid., 64.
15. *The Peloponnesian War*: Book 1, chap. 1, 14-15. In *The Complete Writings of Thucydides: The Peloponnesian War* (New York: Modern Library, 1951). Quoted in Sills and Merton, *Social Science Quotations*, 230.
16. Lukacs, *A Student's Guide*, 12.
17. Cairns, *God & Man in Time*, 62.
18. Paul K. Conkin and Roland N. Stromberg, *The Heritage and Challenge of History* (New York: Dodd, Mead & Company, 1972), 6-7.
19. "The fact that Rome may have had its purpose to play in the purposes of God does not mean that Rome is sacred as a result, or that her fall has any negative implications for the Christian understanding of the providence or power of God . . . there is room for a radical reversal of fortunes [on earth], without the need to give up hope . . . the Christian's [ultimate] home is not of this world." Alister McGrath, "Augustine of Hippo," in Bauman and Klauber, *Historians of the Christian Tradition,* 90 (the quotation is McGrath's wording of Augustine's ideas).
20. Southgate, *History*, 44. The phrase "a play written by God" is attributed to R. G. Collingwood, author of classic works of historiography: *The Idea of History* (Oxford: Clarendon Press, 1946) and *Essays in the Philosophy of History* (New York: McGraw-Hill, 1965).
21. Joyce Appleby, Lynn Hunt, and Margaret Jacob, *Telling the Truth About History* (New York: W.W. Norton & Company, 1994), 62. A powerful, well-written book by prominent historians that "confronts head-on the uncertainty about values and truth-seeking" raised by postmodernism.
22. Quoted in Southgate, *History*, 48.
23. Edward Gibbon, *The History of the Decline and Fall of the Roman Empire* (New York: AMS Press, 1974 reprint). Gibbon's anticlerical prejudices made him negatively conclude that Christianity was a major force in Rome's demise.
24. "In historiography, a primary source is distinguished from a secondary by the fact that the former gives the words of the witnesses or first recorders of an event." Jacques Barzun and Henry F. Graff, *The Modern Researcher*, 4th ed. (San Diego: Harcourt Brace Jovanovich, 1985), 124. An unparalleled guide for research and writing, particularly in history.
25. Lukacs, *A Student's Guide*, 19-20.
26. Ibid., 20.
27. Southgate, *History*, 13. Although Professor Southgate rejects the possibility of historians deriving truth from the method, he summarizes it well.
28. Frederika Oosterhoff, *Ideas Have a History: Perspectives on the Western Search for Truth* (Lanham, MD: University Press of America, Inc., 2001), 101. An erudite treatment from a Christian perspective.
29. Gordon H. Clark, *Historiography: Secular and Religious* (Nutley, NJ: The Craig Press, 1971), 110.
30. Oosterhoff, *Ideas Have a History*, 193.
31. Ibid., 166.
32. Cairns, *God & Man in Time*, 120.
33. Oosterhoff, *Ideas Have a History*, 168.
34. Ibid.
35. In a speech at the graveside of Karl Marx in 1883, his coworker Frederick Engels summarized this essential Marxist idea: "Just as Darwin discovered the law of development of organic nature, so Marx discovered the law of development of human history: the simple fact, hitherto concealed by an overgrowth of ideology, that mankind must first of all eat, drink, have shelter and clothing, before it can pursue politics, science, art, [and] religion." *Karl Marx and Frederick Engels: Selected Works*, Vol. 2 (London: Lawrence and Wishart, 1950), 153. Quoted in Sills and Merton, *Social Science Quotations*, 59.
36. Karl Marx and Frederick Engels, *The Communist Manifesto* (1848) (New York: Modern Reader, 1964), 37. Quoted in Sills and Merton, *Social Science Quotations*, 155.
37. Ibid., 195.
38. Though it may be too early to tell, the period of the turbulent 1960s seems as a good candidate as any for a turning point. As one articulate defender of traditional modern history

pointed out, "the movers and shakers of this [postmodernist] movement are the old New Left crowd from the 1960s . . . just as addicted to the latest fashions as they were back in the days of hippy beads and flared trousers." Keith Windschuttle, *The Killing of History: How Literary Critics and Social Theorists Are Murdering Our Past* (San Francisco: Encounter Books, 1996), xiv.

39. Geoffrey Rudolph Elton: "The new 'scientific' or 'cliometric' history—born of the marriage contracted between historical problems and advanced statistical analysis, with economic theory as bridesmaid and the computer as best man—has made tremendous advances in the last generation." *Which Road to the Past? Two Views of History* (New Haven, CT: Yale University Press, 1983), 3. Quoted in Sills and Merton, *Social Science Quotations*, 64. For discussions and examples of quantitative history from a Christian perspective, see the writings of Robert P. Swierenga.
40. Oosterhoff, *Ideas Have a History*, 261.
41. The title of an excellent refutation of postmodernist threats to history summarizes the scene well—Keith Windschuttle, *The Killing of History: How Literary Critics and Social Theorists Are Murdering Our Past.*
42. Gene Edward Veith, *Postmodern Times: A Christian Guide to Contemporary Thought and Culture* (Wheaton, IL: Crossway Books, 1994), 19. An extraordinarily trenchant and readable explanation of postmodernism from the Turning Point Christian Worldview Series by Crossway Books.
43. "The term 'historicism' originated in the nineteenth century to describe an approach to history writing and literary criticism that emphasized that each era of the past should be interpreted in terms of its own values, perspectives and context, rather than by those of the present." Windschuttle, *The Killing of History*, 12. Karl Popper and others have also used the term *historicism* to describe meta-histories such as those of Hegel and Marx. Literary critics resurrected the original meaning in the 1980s.
44. Quoted in Oosterhoff, *Ideas Have a History*, 245.
45. Veith, *Postmodern Times*, 48.
46. Southgate, *History*, 76.
47. Veith, *Postmodern Times*, 51.
48. Michel Foucault, "Nietzsche, Genealogy, History," in *Language, Counter-Memory, Practice: Selected Essays and Interviews (1971)* (Ithaca, NY: Cornell University Press, 1977), 153-154. Quoted in Sills and Merton, *Social Science Quotations*, 65.
49. Southgate, *History*, chap. 5.
50. Lynn Hunt, American Historical Association president as of this writing, added a postscript chapter to a book entitled *Encounters: Philosophy of History After Postmodernism*. She perceptively commented on the book's reflections on postmodern history and then concluded, "it is difficult to find examples of history written in the postmodern spirit." In Ewa Komanska, ed., *Encounters: Philosophy of History After Postmodernism* (Charlottesville: University of Virginia Press, 1998), 273. How can postmodern scholars who reject narratives take historical research and writing seriously, if it is all untrue anyway? It becomes "a tale told by an idiot, full of sound and fury, signifying nothing." In the final analysis, postmodernism has actually done much more harm than good in the field of history—and other fields. (In the quotation from *Macbeth*, Act 5, Scene 4, lines 26-28, the topic was life, but it fits a postmodernist view of history.)
51. Hans Kellner, "Introduction," in *A New Philosophy of History,* eds. Frank Ankersmit and Hans Kellner (Chicago: University of Chicago Press, 1995), 2.
52. Ibid., 3.
53. Open-minded historians want to learn from criticism. They acknowledge that postmodernists made a valid point in criticizing the historian's inability to attain perfectly neutral objectivity. In doing so, however, they constructed a straw man to deconstruct. That is, by the early twentieth century, professional historians had given up on purely positivist history. They were already honestly admitting that their personal perspectives affected their narratives and that they had to guard against excessive subjectivity. Next, linguistic theorists correctly demonstrated the power and slipperiness of language. Of course, historians had long recognized that their "science" displayed elements of a literary "art" as well, and they became more careful about their writing, especially avoiding blatantly sexist and racist wording. Young historians began writing about women, common people, and minority groups in new social histories and culture studies, rather than just the Great Men, before

postmodernist extremists raised an outcry over such groups' lack of proportional representation in older historical accounts. Postmodernists have prodded historians to give up claims of total impartiality, to watch their language, and to write inclusively, things that could have occurred without an epistemological crisis. Postmodernists have contributed little else.

54. The community of professionals contributes to the quest for historical truth. ". . . knowledge-seeking involves a lively, contentious struggle among diverse groups of truth-seekers . . . a community of practitioners acts as a check on the historian." Appleby, Hunt, Jacobs, *Telling the Truth About History*, 254, 261. Especially when reflecting honestly about their backgrounds, historians can help one another avoid the pitfalls of excessive subjectivism or careless use of evidence. ". . . there is enough clarity about our situation to continue doing our work." Shirley A. Mullen, "Between 'Romance' and 'True History': Historical Narrative and Truth Telling in a Postmodern Age," in *History and the Christian Historian*, ed. Ronald A. Wells (Grand Rapids, MI: William B. Eerdmans, 1998), 40. In its successful recruiting efforts, The Historical Society articulated sound principles for historians today. "All we ask of members is that they lay down plausible premises; reason logically; appeal to evidence; and respect the integrity of all those who do the same." Eugene D. Genovese, "A New Departure," in *Reconstructing History: The Emergence of a New Historical Society*, eds. Elizabeth Fox-Genovese and Elisabeth Lasch-Quinn, 8.
55. Arthur M. Schlesinger, Jr., *The Disuniting of America: Reflections on a Multicultural Society* (New York: W.W. Norton & Company, 1992) still provides one of the best exposés of shoddy history writing in the name of multiculturalism, all the more incisive because of the author's well-known liberal sympathies.
56. Veith, *Postmodern Times*, 50, 57.
57. "They [postmodernists] are happy to legitimize a multiplicity of voices as long as they all belong to leftist groups of which they approve. However, by abandoning truth and endorsing the interpretation of the past 'any way we like,' they unwittingly provide legitimacy to political positions they might find less congenial, such as those of neo-Nazis, neo-Stalinists, white and black supremacists, holocaust deniers, ethnic cleansers or any other variety of political depravity." Windschuttle, *The Killing of History*, 320-321.
58. Postmodernism's effects extend beyond a few crackpots in academia. In 1994 one writer reported, "22 percent of all Americans believe it's possible that the Holocaust never happened. Another 12 percent say they don't know." Cited in Southgate, *History*, 155.
59. ". . . postmodernism continues modernism's rejection of God. The result of the denial of both reason and faith is intellectual and moral nihilism and led Nietzsche to proclaim the will to power as the force that energizes man and the world. It is also the force that energizes mankind's use of language." Oosterhoff, *Ideas Have a History*, 262.
60. Rousas J. Rushdoony, *The Biblical Philosophy of History* (Nutley, NJ: Presbyterian & Reformed, 1977), 14. "For the Darwinist, history is the product of impersonal biological forces, for the Marxist, the forces are economic, for the Freudian, psychological and unconscious. Not only is meaning in history de-personalized, but man is de-personalized as well."
61. How can a nihilistic postmodernist who rejects all moral values make moral judgments in condemning oppression? Who says oppression is wrong? The God of the Bible does, but the god of postmodernism cannot consistently make such absolute moral claims.
62. Veith, *Postmodern Times*, 159.
63. Famous words of then-President Bill Clinton trying to evade self-incrimination.
64. Richard J. Evans's masterful treatise aptly entitled *In Defense of History* concludes with the following:

    "I remain optimistic that objective historical knowledge is both desirable and attainable. So when . . . [postmodernist] Roland Barthes announces that all the world's a text, and Frank Ankersmit swears that we can never know anything at all about the past . . . and Keith Jenkins proclaims that all history is just naked ideology . . . I will look humbly at the past and say, despite them all: It really happened, and we really can, if we are very scrupulous and careful and self-critical, find out how it did and reach some tenable conclusions about what it all meant." Evans, *In Defense of History* (New York: W.W. Norton & Company, 1997), 220.
65. In an intriguing article published back in 1984, George Marsden described a philosophical arena shared by Christian and non-Christian historians as well as by most people outside academia: common sense. An eighteenth-century Scotsman, Thomas Reid, even elaborated a Common Sense school of philosophy. Instead of relying on the speculations of philosophers, "Human knowledge, Reid argued, actually stands on a firm foundation: the common

sense of mankind . . . virtually everyone is forced to believe in the existence of the external world, in the continuity of one's self from one day to the next, in the connection between past and present, in the existence of other persons, in the connections between causes and effects, and (given the right conditions) in the reliability of their senses and of their reasoning." Normal people use such common-sense insights daily. Even postmodernists and Hindu mystics move aside when a truck rushes in their direction. When Thomas Kuhn and others questioned the omniscience and omnipotence of modern science, people questioned common sense as well. They should not. Christians realize that God designed His rational image-bearers to comprehend His creation through their senses and with their minds. Historians of all kinds should use common sense as well as their thorough professional training. George Marsden, "Common Sense and the Spiritual Vision of History," in *History and Historical Understanding*, eds. C. T. McIntire and Ronald A. Wells (Grand Rapids, MI: William B. Eerdmans, 1984), 57 (quotation), 56-60 other ideas.

66. Appleby, Hunt, Jacobs, *Telling the Truth About History*, 247-251. Many historians who do not share the theological premises above nonetheless argue that historians can discern some truths about the past. In *Telling the Truth about History*, three distinguished UCLA professors advise the adoption of a pragmatic "practical realism." They reject extreme nineteenth-century positivist claims to complete truth, and they acknowledge problems of language. They assert, however, that an objective reality outside the self and language actually exists. Lastly, they admit that a gap exists between the events of the past and the historical account interpreting those events, while simultaneously contending that some partial correspondence is possible and necessary.
67. John Warwick Montgomery, *Where Is History Going?* (Grand Rapids, MI: Zondervan, 1969); chapter 1 provides a fine elaboration of the linear view of history.
68. Max Lucado, *No Wonder They Call Him the Savior* (Portland: Multnomah, 1986), 13.
69. Karl Lowith, *Meaning in History: The Theological Implications of the Philosophy of History* (Chicago: University of Chicago Press, 1950), 1.
70. Cairns, *God & Man in Time*, 10.
71. For a helpful summary and analysis of the journal's articles over the years, see D. G. Hart, "History in Search of Meaning: The Conference on Faith and History," in *History and the Christian Historian*, ed. Ronald A. Wells (Grand Rapids, MI: William B. Eerdmans, 1998), 68-87.
72. Roy Swanstrom, *History in the Making: An Introduction to the Study of the Past* (Downers Grove, IL: IVP, 1978), 77. A fine primer from a Christian perspective. See also George Marsden's article in *History & Historical Understanding*, already cited, 64-65.
73. "There's a tendency of reductionism in history, to reduce something to some essential cause, [an] economic or social factor. I think it's worth giving religious factors their due. You don't have to be a religious person to do that, but certainly it helps. Most American historians just don't have any antenna for recognizing that." George Marsden, quoted by Tim Stafford, "Whatever Happened to Christian History?" *Christianity Today*, April 2, 2001, 48.
74. Ibid., 43-49.
75. Oswald Spengler, *The Decline of the West* (New York: A.A. Knopf, 1939).
76. Reinhold Niebuhr, *Faith and History: A Comparison of Christian and Modern Views of History* (New York: Scribner's, 1949).
77. Herbert Butterfield, *Christianity and History* (London: Collins, 1949), *History and Human Relations* (London: Collins, 1951), *Christianity in European History* (London: Collins, 1952).
78. C. T. McIntire, "Introduction: The Renewal of Christian Views of History in an Age of Catastrophe," in C. T. McIntire, ed., *God, History, and Historians: An Anthology of Modern Christian Views of History* (New York: Oxford University Press, 1977), 12.
79. C. T. McIntire, ed., *Herbert Butterfield: Writings on Christianity and History* (New York: Oxford University Press, 1979), 134. Butterfield stated, "Now I, personally, would never regard a thing as 'historically established'—that is to say, as genuinely demonstrated by historical evidence—unless the case for it could be made out in a coercive and inescapable manner to any student of the past—Protestant or Catholic, Christian or non-Christian, Frenchman or Englishman, and Whig or Tory."
80. *Christianity Today*, April 2, 2001, 45. The statement is attributed to Mark Noll. In an introduction to a generally excellent book on a fascinating subject, another scholar explains the approach: "While written from a Christian perspective about the nature and destiny of

humans and their history, this work is an exercise in ordinary history. . . . I write history with the assumption that these spiritual forces are at work in human events, albeit in ways not easily discerned. Not claiming to be an inspired prophet, however, I am largely content to focus on ordinary historical causation." Joel Carpenter, *Revive Us Again: The Reawakening of American Fundamentalism* (New York: Oxford University Press, 1997), xiii.

81. McIntire, *Butterfield*, 195.
82. "Ultimately, the relationship between God's providence and human freedom is a mystery. In theology, the term 'concurrence' is used to express the idea that God is working in the universe, and at the same time man is also working. God brings His providential government to pass through real human agency." R. C. Sproul, *Tabletalk*, August 1989, see 33, 34, 38.
83. McIntire, *Butterfield*, 199-200.
84. C. T. McIntire, "Herbert Butterfield: Scientific and Christian," *Christian History*, XX, No. 4 (2001), 48.
85. Stafford, "Whatever Happened to Christian History?" *Christianity Today*, 46.
86. Ibid. D. G. Hart is being quoted here.
87. Fairly recently, a professing Christian historian at Yale University published a biography of George Whitefield without incorporating a providential analysis of any supernatural agency involved in the Great Awakening. Harry S. Stout, *The Divine Dramatist: George Whitefield and the Rise of Modern Evangelism* (Grand Rapids, MI: William B. Eerdmans, 1991). Another Christian historian who had written well and extensively on the history of revivals took umbrage at this absence of providential perspectives. Iain H. Murray, *Jonathan Edwards: A New Biography* (Edinburgh: Banner of Truth, 1987) and *Revivals and Revivalism: The Making and Marring of American Evangelicalism, 1750-1858* (Edinburgh: Banner of Truth, 1994). D. G. Hart, in *History and the Christian Historian*, provides a short summary of this clash, 68-71, 85. In 2001, the magazine *Christian History* set up an interesting point-counterpoint contrast of the positions on providentialism, interviewing George Marsden, highly respected proponent of the muted "background faith commitment" approach, and John Woodbridge, advocating an openly providential approach. Marsden elaborates his non-providential view in *The Soul of the American University: From Protestant Establishment to Established Nonbelief* (New York: Oxford University Press, 1994) and *The Outrageous Idea of Christian Scholarship* (New York: Oxford University Press, 1997). The Winter/Spring issue of *Fides et Historia* similarly juxtaposes provocative papers and erudite responses on the topic of Christian scholarship, also the theme of the October 2002 national meeting of the Conference on Faith and History. While lively discussions stimulate much honest reflection, a consensus seems impossible.
88. Butterfield, *Christianity and History*, chap. 2, "Cataclysm and Tragic Conflict" provides a splendid analysis.
89. The ideas in this paragraph come from an unpublished manuscript by Professor Jim Owen, whose overall wise counsel, encouragement, and bibliographical aid in the composition of this chapter has been quite considerable and very much appreciated. Professor Emeritus Edmund Gruss in years past was also a great mentor relating to understanding a biblical philosophy of history.
90. George M. Marsden, *Fundamentalism and American Culture: The Shaping of Twentieth-Century Evangelicalism 1870-1925* (New York: Oxford University Press, 1980). *Reforming Fundamentalism: Fuller Seminary and the New Evangelicalism* (Grand Rapids: William B. Eerdmans, 1987). *Religion and American Culture* (San Diego: Harcourt Brace Jovanovich, 1990). *Understanding Fundamentalism and Evangelicalism* (Grand Rapids, MI: William B. Eerdmans, 1991).
91. Nathan O. Hatch, *The Democratization of American Christianity* (New Haven, CT: Yale University Press, 1989).
92. Mark A. Noll, Nathan O. Hatch, George M. Marsden, *The Search for Christian America* (Wheaton, IL: Crossway Books, 1983). Mark A. Noll, *Christians in the American Revolution* (Grand Rapids, MI: Christian University Press, 1977). *One Nation Under God? Christian Faith & Political Action* (San Francisco: Harper & Row, 1988). *The Scandal of the Evangelical Mind* (Grand Rapids, MI: William B. Eerdmans, 1994).
93. Quoted in Donald A. Yerxa, "A Meaningful Past and the Limits of History: Some Reflections Informed by the Science-and-Religion Dialogue," *Fides et Historia*, 34:1 (2002), 21.
94. This modest proposal was influenced by the ideas in the following from the *Fides et Historia*

issue just cited: Christopher Shannon, "Between Outrage and Respectability: Taking Christian History Beyond the Logic of Modernization," 6, and Ronald A. Wells, "Beyond 'Religious History': The Calling of the Christian Historian," 46.

95. Stafford, "Whatever Happened to Christian History?" *Christianity Today*, 49.
96. Many supposed church-state battles emerge from a misunderstanding of the First Amendment. See David Barton, *The Myth of Separation: What Is the Correct Relationship Between Church and State? A Revealing Look at What the Founders and Early Courts Really Said* (Aledo, TX: Wallbuilder Press, 1992).
97. Appleby, Hunt, Jacobs, *Telling the Truth About History,* 299.
98. Fox-Genovese and Lasch-Quinn include a superb, four-article section summarizing and commenting on the controversy over these national standards for teaching history commissioned by the NEH and U.S. Department of Education and prepared by the National Center for History in the Schools at UCLA; *Reconstructing History*, 237-298.
99. Kay S. Hymowitz, "Anti-Social Studies," *The Weekly Standard*, May 6, 2002, identifies and critiques some of the problems inherent in the ways the National Council for Social Studies overemphasizes global perspectives at the expense of U.S. national perspectives.
100. George Santayana, quoted in Sills and Merton, *Social Science Quotations*, 204.
101. Richard P. Belcher, *A Comparison of Dispensationalism and Covenant Theology* (Southbridge, MA: Crowne Publications, 1986), 8. A good, balanced, very short treatment. See also Renald Showers, *There Really Is a Difference: A Comparison of Covenant and Dispensational Theology* (Bellmawr, NJ: The Friends of Israel Gospel Ministry, 1990).
102. Cairns, *God & Man in Time*, chap. 7.
103. Alva J. McClain, *The Greatness of the Kingdom: An Inductive Study of the Kingdom of God* (Winona Lake, IN: BMH Books, 1959), 529-530.

Chapter 15

1. Charles Kesler, *The Federalist Papers*, ed. Clinton Rossiter (New York: Mentor Books, 1999), nos. 10, 51.
2. Gregg Frazer, "Nature's God: The Political Theology of the American Founding Fathers" (Ph.D. dissertation, Claremont Graduate University, 2002).
3. In this chapter I have relied extensively on the writings of Leonard Verduin in the areas dealing with biblical and church history. It is unfortunate that his works have not received greater circulation. He reads all the languages of the Reformation fluently, thereby allowing him access to the actual writings and documents. In my estimation, his historiography is of the highest quality. What Paul Johnson did for historiography in exposing the utopian schemes of the twentieth century, Verduin does in bringing forward the great contributions of the dissenters from A.D. 313 to the founding of this nation.
4. Leonard Verduin, *The Anatomy of a Hybrid* (Sarasota, FL: The Christian Hymnary Publishers, 1990), 29.
5. Ibid., 26.
6. Ibid., 30.
7. Ibid., 33.
8. Ibid., 85.
9. Ibid., 112.
10. Ibid., 118.
11. Leonard Verduin, *The Reformers and Their Stepchildren* (Sarasota, FL: The Christian Hymnary Publishers, 1991), 33.
12. Ibid.
13. Ibid., 143.
14. Ibid., 153.
15. Leonard Verduin, *The First Amendment and the Remnant* (Sarasota, FL: The Christian Hymnary Publishers, 1998), 195.
16. Ibid., 199.
17. Ibid.
18. Ibid., 208.
19. Verduin, *The Anatomy of a Hybrid*, 170.
20. This is the verse that the Inquisition used to justify burning heretics at the stake. Unfortunately, so did the Reformers.

21. Verduin, *The Anatomy of a Hybrid*, 169.
22. Verduin, *The First Amendment and the Remnant*, 257.
23. Verduin, *The Anatomy of a Hybrid*, 208.
24. Verduin, *The First Amendment and the Remnant*, 327.
25. Alpheus T. Mason, *Free Government in the Making*, 3rd ed. (New York: Oxford University Press, 1965), 68.
26. Ibid., 66.
27. Ibid., 55.
28. Ibid., 66.
29. Roger Williams, *The Complete Works of Roger Williams,* Vol. II (New York: Russell & Russell, reprint 1963), 278.
30. Mark Noll, Nathan Hatch, and George Marsden, *The Search for a Christian America* (Wheaton, IL: Crossway Books, 1983), 128.
31. *Time Magazine*, October 1, 1979, C.
32. James Wallis, *Agenda for Biblical People* (New York: Harper & Row, 1976), 105-106.
33. D. G. Kehl, "Peddling the Power and the Premises," *Christianity Today*, March 21, 1980, 20.
34. Ibid.
35. Theodore J. Lowi, *The End of Liberalism*, 2nd ed. (New York: Norton, 1979), 60.
36. Ian Hunter, *Malcolm Muggeridge, A Life* (Nashville: Thomas Nelson, 1980).
37. Daniel J. B. Hofrenning. "Religious Lobbying and American Politics," *In God We Trust?*, ed. Corwin Smidt (Grand Rapids, MI: Baker, 2001), 122.
38. Klaus Buhmuhl, "The Socialist Ideal, Some Soulsearching Constraints," *Christianity Today*, May 23, 1980, 56.
39. Jeff M. Sellers, "NAE goes to Washington," *Christianity Today*, June 10, 2002, 17.
40. Harold O. J. Brown, *The Reconstruction of the Republic* (New York: Arlington House, 1976), 7, 177.

Chapter 16

1. Thomas Malthus, *An Essay on the Principle of Population* (London: J. Johnson, 1798).
2. Roy J. Ruffin and Paul R. Gregory, *Principles of Macroeconomics* (New York: Addison Wesley, 2000), 32.
3. John Hotchkiss, Literature Professor, The Master's College, July 25, 2002. Interview by author, Santa Clarita, CA.
4. Derek Kidner, *Proverbs: An Introduction and Commentary* (Downers Grove, IL: IVP, 1964), 42.
5. John MacArthur, *Whose Money Is It Anyway?* (Nashville: Word, 2000), 113.
6. Hamish McRae, *The World in 2020: Power, Culture and Prosperity* (Boston: Harvard Business School Press, 1994), 43.
7. It is even possible that the liquidation of the assets of those in the church was a mistake, causing the church in Jerusalem to be in constant need of future support by other churches (Acts 11:29; Rom 15:26; 1 Cor 16:1-4; 2 Cor 8:1-4). In other words, having given up the means to generate future income, the Jerusalem church was forced to rely upon the larger community of believers.
8. Adam Smith, *An Inquiry into The Nature and Causes of the Wealth of Nations*, Vol. I (Indianapolis: Liberty Classics, 1981), 26.
9. "Capitalism," *Quote Project*, http://www.quoteproject.com/subject.asp?=subject=44, accessed August 15, 2002.
10. Earl E. Cairns, *Christianity Through the Centuries* (Grand Rapids, Mi: Zondervan, 1954), 50.
11. *New World Dictionary* (New York: William Collins & World Publishing, 1976), s.v. "steward," 1397.

Chapter 17

1. This is approximately one new edition (not simply a reprint) *per year* for forty years. This does not even include the first dozen editions from 1536 to 1559. This kind of popularity is equivalent to the bestselling fiction authors on today's popular secular market. Alister McGrath, *A Life of John Calvin* (Oxford: Blackwell Publishers Ltd., 1990), 141-142.
2. Discernment is one of the most crucial skills for Christians to develop, and probably the one most lacking in contemporary evangelicalism. The term in question (*diakrino*) occurs in sev-

eral different forms in Matt. 16:3, 1 Cor. 11:29 and 12:10, and Heb 5:14. In these passages, the original Greek carries the meaning of separating, distinguishing, judging, discerning, or making a judicial estimation (i.e., weighing the facts and reaching a proper conclusion).

3. John Calvin, *Institutes of the Christian Religion* (*ICR*), 1.15.8
4. Many evangelicals and fundamentalists who might call themselves Calvinists and also hold the view that Christians should never involve themselves in "contaminating" cultural activities like philosophy or literature are surprised whenever they actually read any of Calvin's original writings. Contrary to popular belief, his works are quite simple, straightforward, and very accessible; but what really startles those who encounter his work for the first time is his constant and knowledgeable reference to pagan as well as Christian sources. Not that Calvin cites pagans with agreement on a regular basis; rather he sets the standard for Christians in his discerning, critical study and in his use of the culture that surrounded him.
5. Calvin, *ICR*, 1.15.7.
6. Ibid.
7. God, of course, has judged cultures, people groups, and nations; the root, however, is always individual sin that makes the larger cultural group anti-God. I can go into a museum of Egyptology and view a statue of Anubis (an idol for the Egyptians, though not for me, 1 Cor. 8:4) and learn about ancient mythology and culture without actually falling into idolatry. The idolatrous cultural object itself (a statue of a guy with a jackal's head) is not the problem—it is the result of the problem, which is sin. The cultural object can be discerned and judged by the careful, Scripture-saturated Christian. This does *not* mean that all cultural artifacts can be safely discerned at the same level of exposure. I can look at a work by the Italian Renaissance artist Giorgione with little worry about being corrupted while experiencing the mysterious beauty of a painting like *The Tempest*. Reading a work by the existentialist theologian Søren Kierkegaard requires considerably more care and discernment, though it is of some value to me as someone interested in historical theology. Viewing pornography, however, holds no value and would lead only to sin on my part. I know it's out there; I know what the content is like; I know it dishonors God, degrades humans, violates the beauty of marriage, and wrecks real relationships. I don't need to know more.
8. In *Confessions* 3.4, Augustine relates how he was drawn to the practice of wisdom by reading Cicero's *Hortensius*. He describes how he began to alter his desires for glory to seek after the *immortalitatem sapientiae*—the immortality of wisdom. Augustine seems to recognize, however, that he was not converted by pagan philosophy—he cites Colossians 2:8 to remind himself not to be ruined by vain human philosophy; but he acknowledges that God sovereignly used his experience with Cicero to draw the sinner Augustine to Himself. He concludes the chapter by remarking that he has learned the importance of discernment: No matter how "learned, politely and truly penned" a book may be, if it does not center on the name of Christ, he will never be able to entirely approve it. So he will read widely, but carefully. Ironically enough, the next chapter should serve for us as a warning about becoming confident in our ability to detect and resist error: Augustine recounts how he was easily ensnared by the error of the Manichean cult.
9. Augustine, *On Christian Doctrine*, Book I, chapters 4—5.
10. Tertullian, *Apologeticus*, chapter 46.
11. Luther recognized that education, especially language education, was an absolutely necessary component for a successful Reformation. See Philip Schaff, *History of the Christian Church*, Vol. 7 (Grand Rapids, MI: William B. Eerdmans, 1910), 512-515.
12. *Martin Luther: Selections from His Writings*, ed. John Dillenberger (New York: Anchor Books, 1961), 174.
13. Calvin, *ICR*, 1.1.1.
14. This is amazing evidence of the absolute sovereignty of God. The *very words* of pagan philosopher-poets end up incorporated into Holy Scripture—which is inspired by God and perfect, eternally settled in heaven (Ps 119:89)!
15. Calvin later discusses this passage again in *ICR*, 1.5.3, acknowledging Aratus as the probable source of Paul's quotation in Acts 17.
16. One of the most balanced treatments is Leland Ryken's very accessible *Worldly Saints* (Grand Rapids, MI: Zondervan, 1986).
17. Ralph Venning, *The Sinfulness of Sin* (Edinburgh: Banner of Truth, 1997), 61.
18. See John MacArthur's *Successful Christian Parenting* for a succinct and practical treatment

of why engaged discernment (and in the case of parenting, training in discernment) is preferable to isolationism (Dallas: Word, 1998), 35-40. John Milton (and other Puritans) made the same point repeatedly:

> . . . to the pure all things are pure, not only meats and drinks, but all kinds of knowledge whether of good or evil; the knowledge cannot defile, nor consequently the books, if the will and conscience be not defil'd. . . . Good and evil we know in the field of this world grow up together almost inseparably; and the knowledge of good is so involv'd and interwoven with the knowledge of evil, and in so many resemblances hardly to be discerned . . . he that can apprehend and consider vice, with all her baits and seeming pleasures, and yet abstain, and yet distinguish, and yet prefer that which is truly better, he is the true warfaring Christian. I cannot praise a fugitive and cloister'd virtue, unexercis'd and unbreath'd, that never sallies out and sees her adversary, but slinks out of the race, where that immortal garland is to be run for, not without dust and heat . . . (*Areopagitica,* 1644, in *John Milton: Selected Prose and Poetry*, ed. C. A. Patrides [Columbia, MO: University of Missouri Press, 1965], 211-213).

19. "Flesh" (*sarx*) here means the "natural attainments of men," which are of course limited and tainted by sin (*Vine's Expository Dictionary of New Testament Words,* Vol. 1 [London: Oliphants Ltd., 1940), 108.
20. If literary texts, movies, or other artworks present true (i.e., accurate) representations of the world, then they will accord with a biblical worldview (such as a story that features evil characters who have evil motivations and are justly punished or will be at some point; i.e., they deserve it—though at the same time the "good guys" have their own flaws, weaknesses, etc.). No such artifact will ever be entirely "true," of course. But if a text presents man as basically good with good motivations, then that text *also* accords with the biblical worldview—because the *text itself*, as a human cultural artifact, shows man's depraved tendency to represent himself as *good*! A discerning believer will judge all things through Scripture. A mind saturated with Scripture can be edified by either experience. The difficulty comes with the question, what about immature believers with weak discernment?—and this is precisely why stronger, mature Christians *absolutely must teach discernment* by example and practice to younger believers. This is a supreme need in the church today. If such believers can't spot incorrect worldviews in movies and books, how will they fight it in the church?
21. As always, when speaking of the liberty we have in Christ as in this passage, the Spirit warns the reader not to turn liberty into license: The next verse warns us to give no offense in what we do.
22. See, for example, any of John Piper's books, especially *The Pleasures of God* (Sisters, OR: Multnomah, 2000).

Index of Scriptures

INDEX OF PERSONS

Index of Subjects